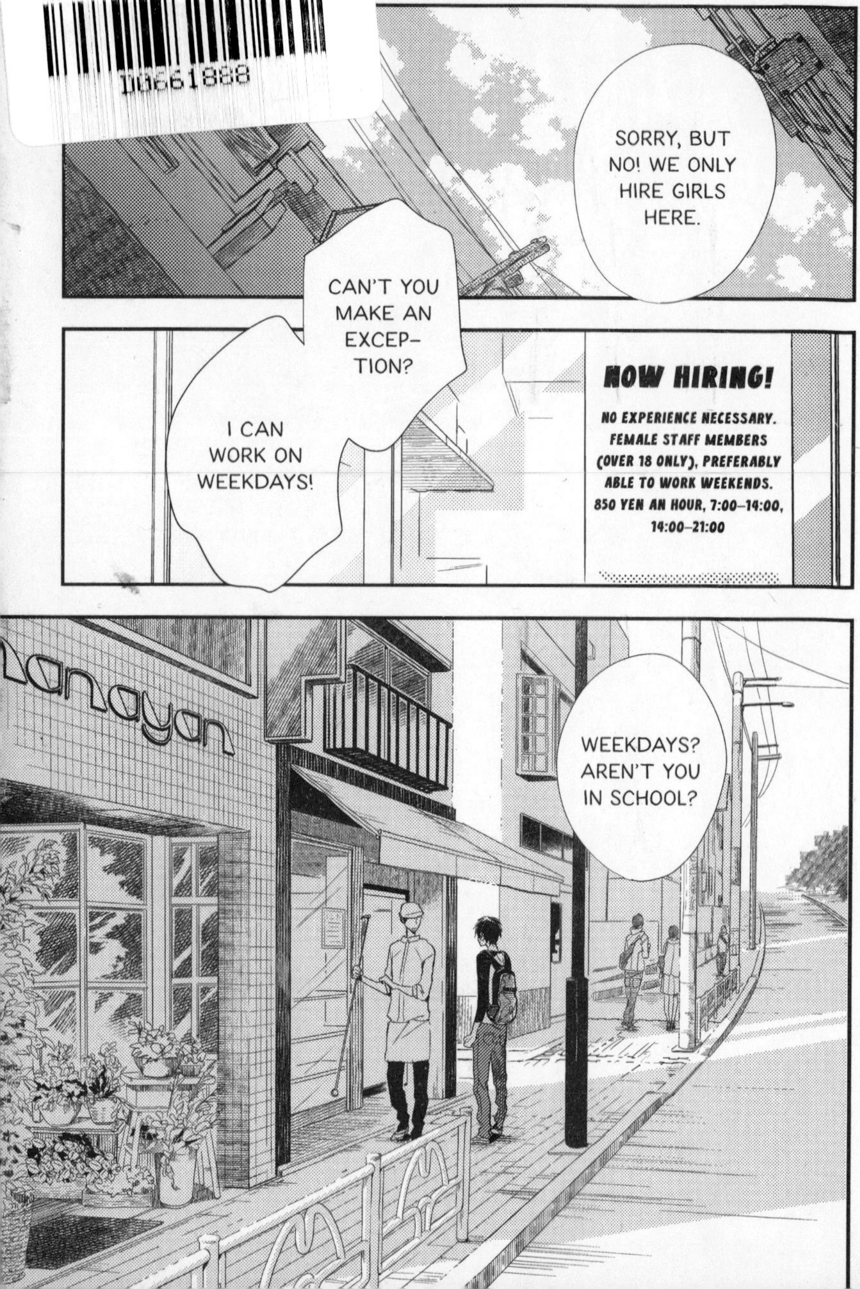
SORRY, BUT NO! WE ONLY HIRE GIRLS HERE.
CAN'T YOU MAKE AN EXCEP- TION?
NOW HIRING!
NO EXPERIENCE NECESSARY. FEMALE STAFF MEMBERS (OVER 18 ONLY), PREFERABLY ABLE TO WORK WEEKENDS. 850 YEN AN HOUR, 7:00–14:00, 14:00–21:00
I CAN WORK ON WEEKDAYS!
WEEKDAYS? AREN'T YOU IN SCHOOL?

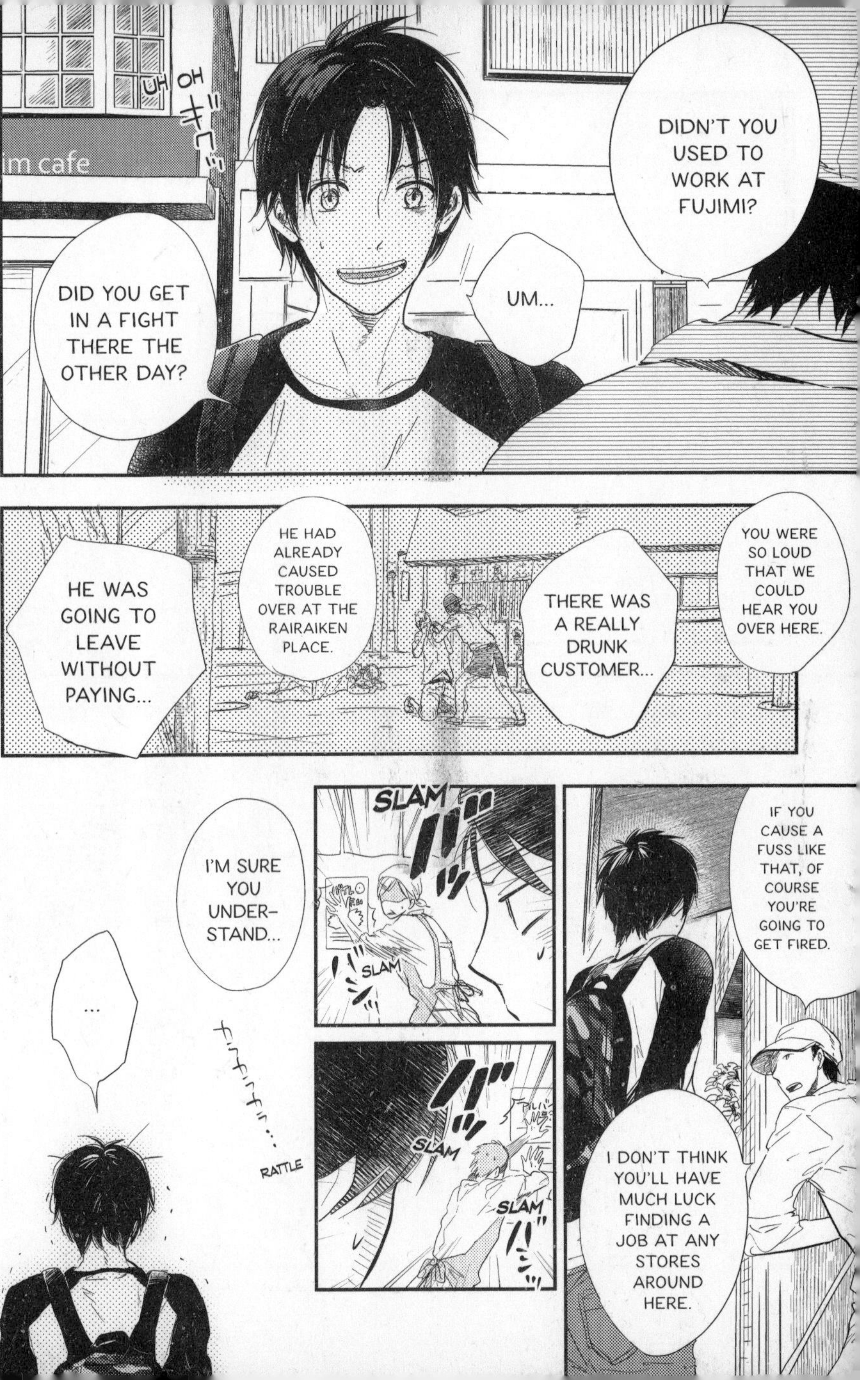
DIDN'T YOU USED TO WORK AT FUJIMI?
im cafe
UH OH
UM...
DID YOU GET IN A FIGHT THERE THE OTHER DAY?
YOU WERE SO LOUD THAT WE COULD HEAR YOU OVER HERE.
THERE WAS A REALLY DRUNK CUSTOMER...
HE HAD ALREADY CAUSED TROUBLE OVER AT THE RAIRAIKEN PLACE.
HE WAS GOING TO LEAVE WITHOUT PAYING...
IF YOU CAUSE A FUSS LIKE THAT, OF COURSE YOU'RE GOING TO GET FIRED.
I DON'T THINK YOU'LL HAVE MUCH LUCK FINDING A JOB AT ANY STORES AROUND HERE.
SLAM
SLAM
SLAM
SLAM
RATTLE
I'M SURE YOU UNDER-STAND...
...

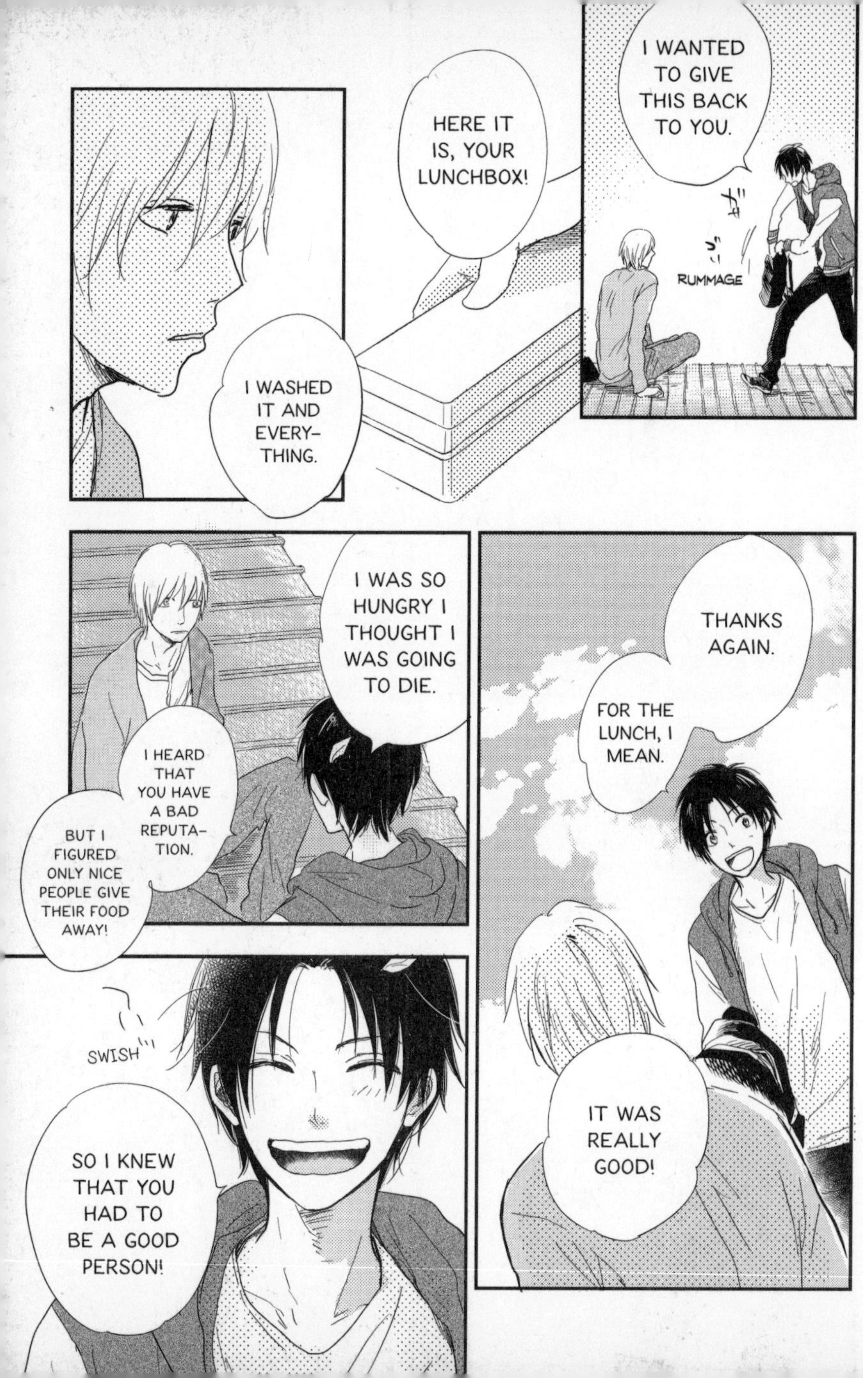
I WANTED TO GIVE THIS BACK TO YOU.
RUMMAGE
HERE IT IS, YOUR LUNCHBOX!
I WASHED IT AND EVERY-THING.
THANKS AGAIN.
FOR THE LUNCH, I MEAN.
IT WAS REALLY GOOD!
I WAS SO HUNGRY I THOUGHT I WAS GOING TO DIE.
I HEARD THAT YOU HAVE A BAD REPUTA-TION.
BUT I FIGURED ONLY NICE PEOPLE GIVE THEIR FOOD AWAY!
SWISH
SO I KNEW THAT YOU HAD TO BE A GOOD PERSON!

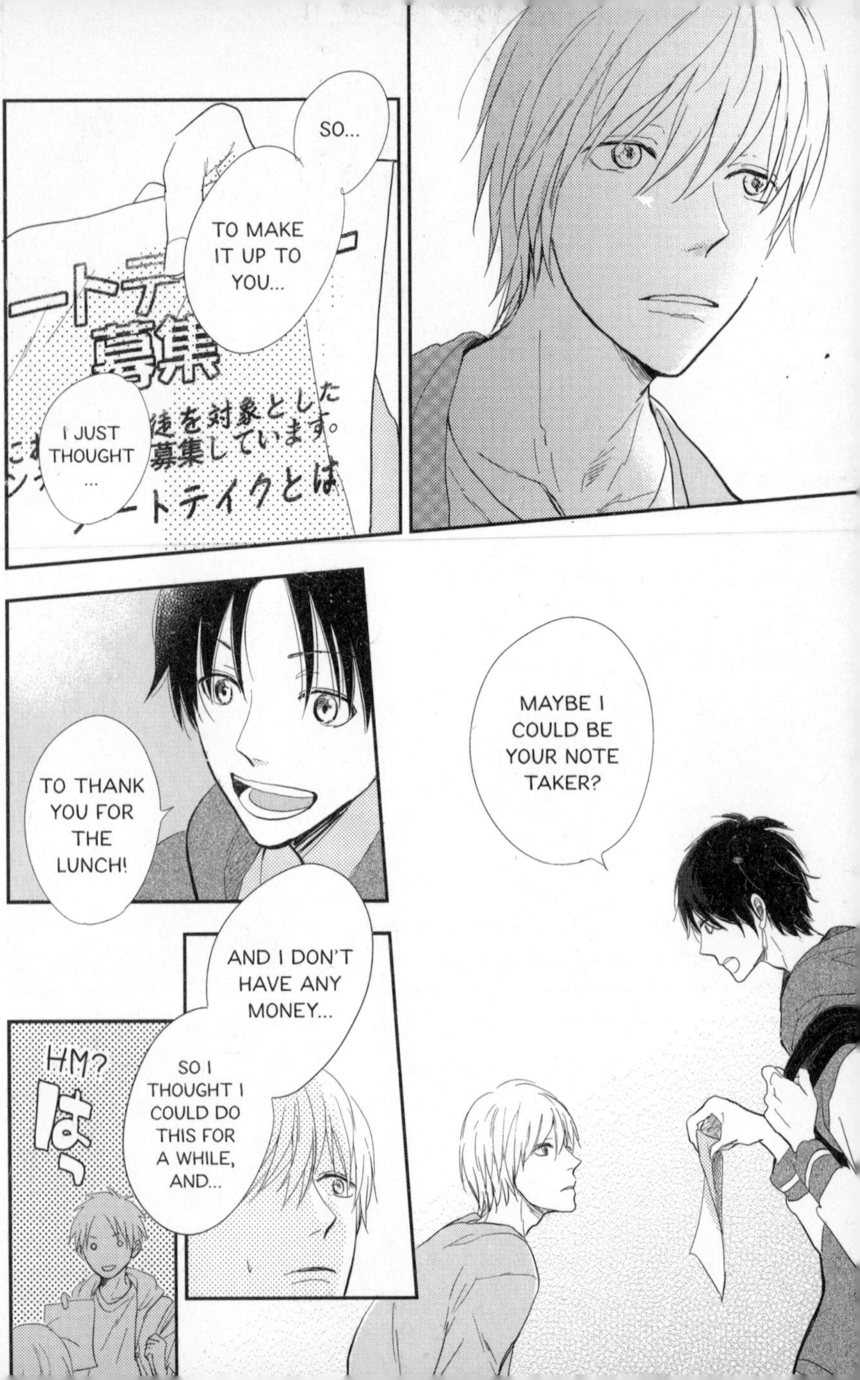
SO...
TO MAKE IT UP TO YOU...
募集
I JUST THOUGHT ...
MAYBE I COULD BE YOUR NOTE TAKER?
TO THANK YOU FOR THE LUNCH!
AND I DON'T HAVE ANY MONEY...
SO I THOUGHT I COULD DO THIS FOR A WHILE, AND...
HM?
は

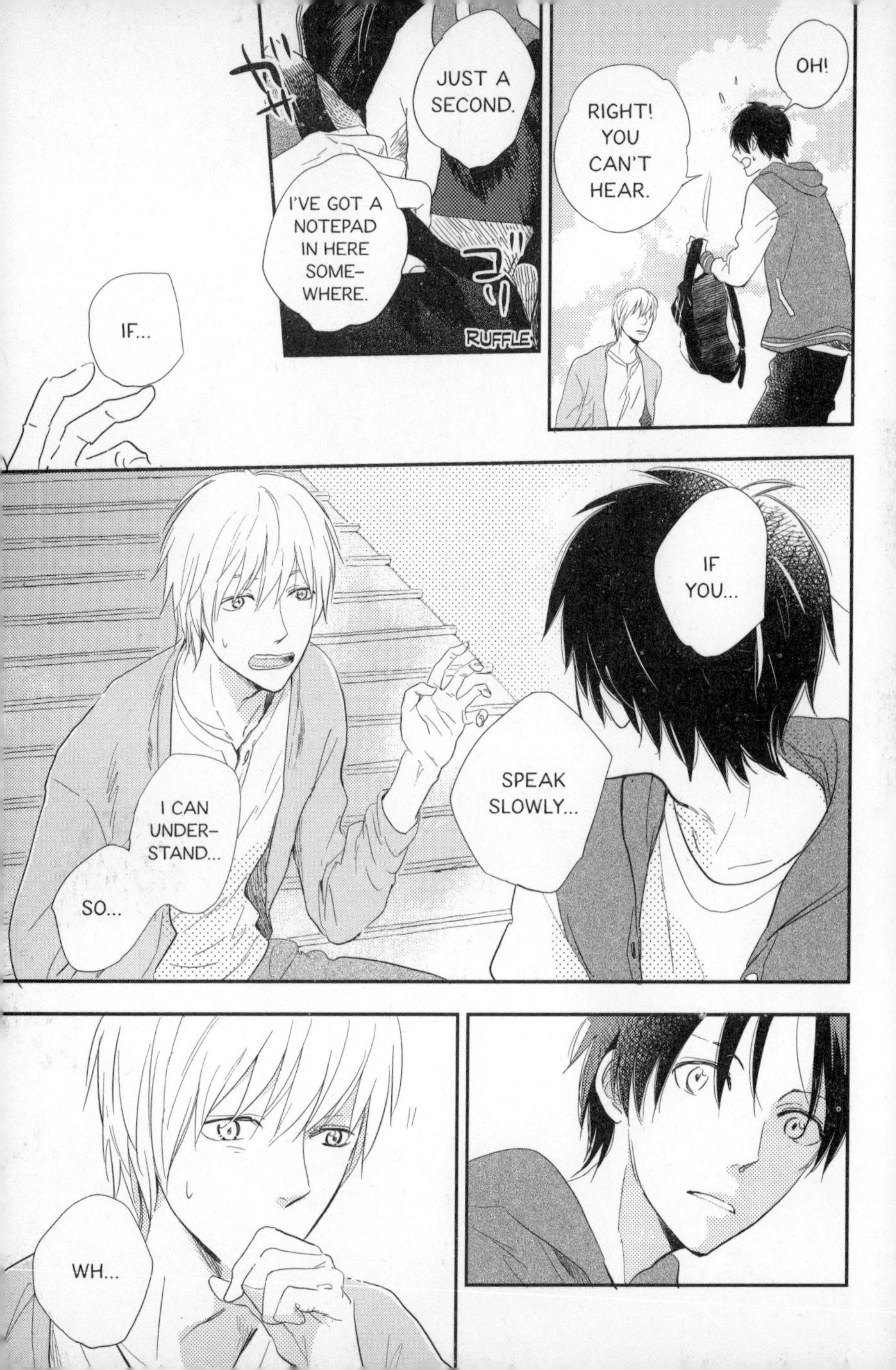
OH!
RIGHT! YOU CAN'T HEAR.
JUST A SECOND.
I'VE GOT A NOTEPAD IN HERE SOME-WHERE.
RUFFLE
IF...
IF YOU...
SPEAK SLOWLY...
I CAN UNDER-STAND...
SO...
WH...

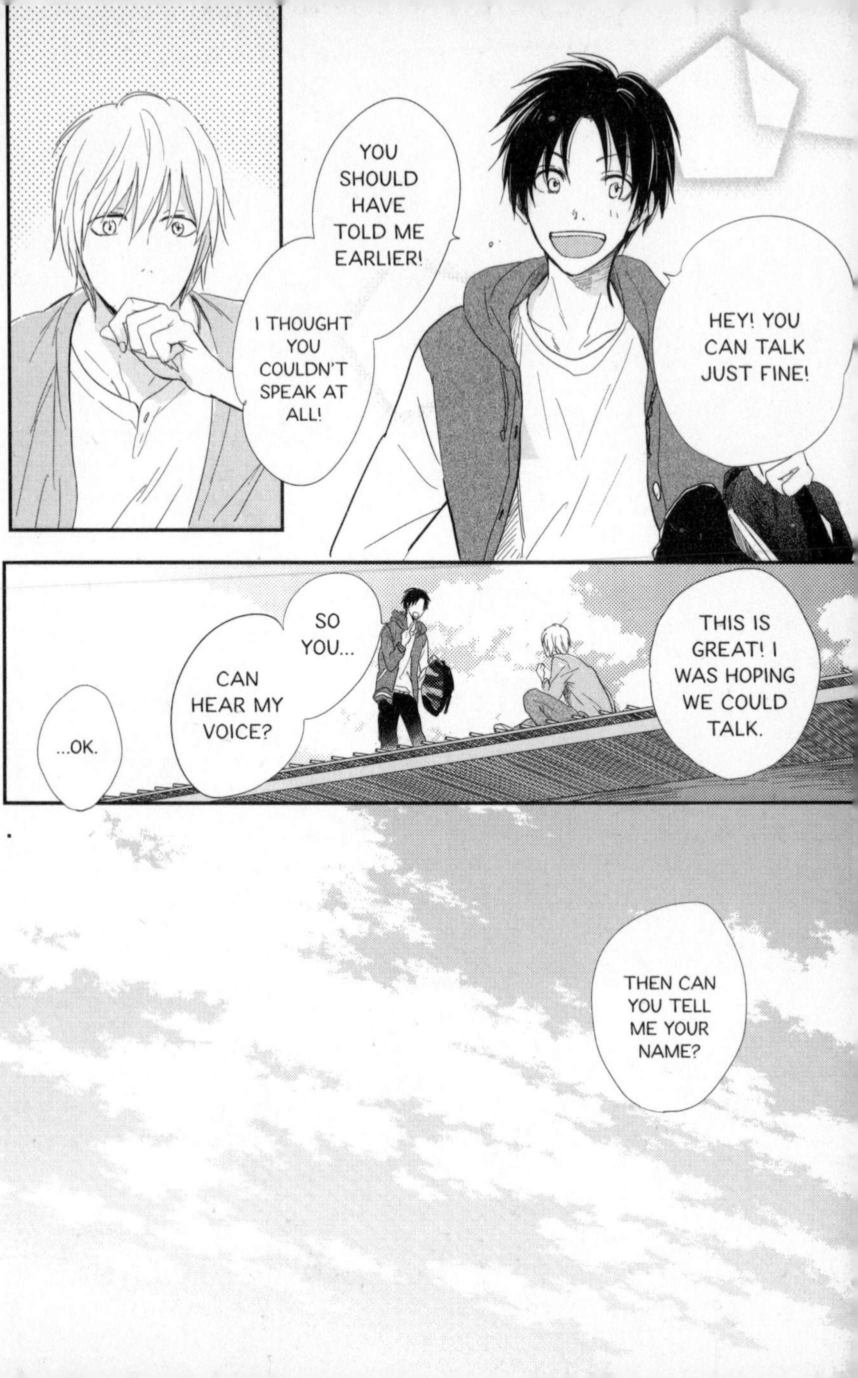
HEY! YOU CAN TALK JUST FINE!
YOU SHOULD HAVE TOLD ME EARLIER!
I THOUGHT YOU COULDN'T SPEAK AT ALL!
THIS IS GREAT! I WAS HOPING WE COULD TALK.
SO YOU...
CAN HEAR MY VOICE?
...OK.
THEN CAN YOU TELL ME YOUR NAME?

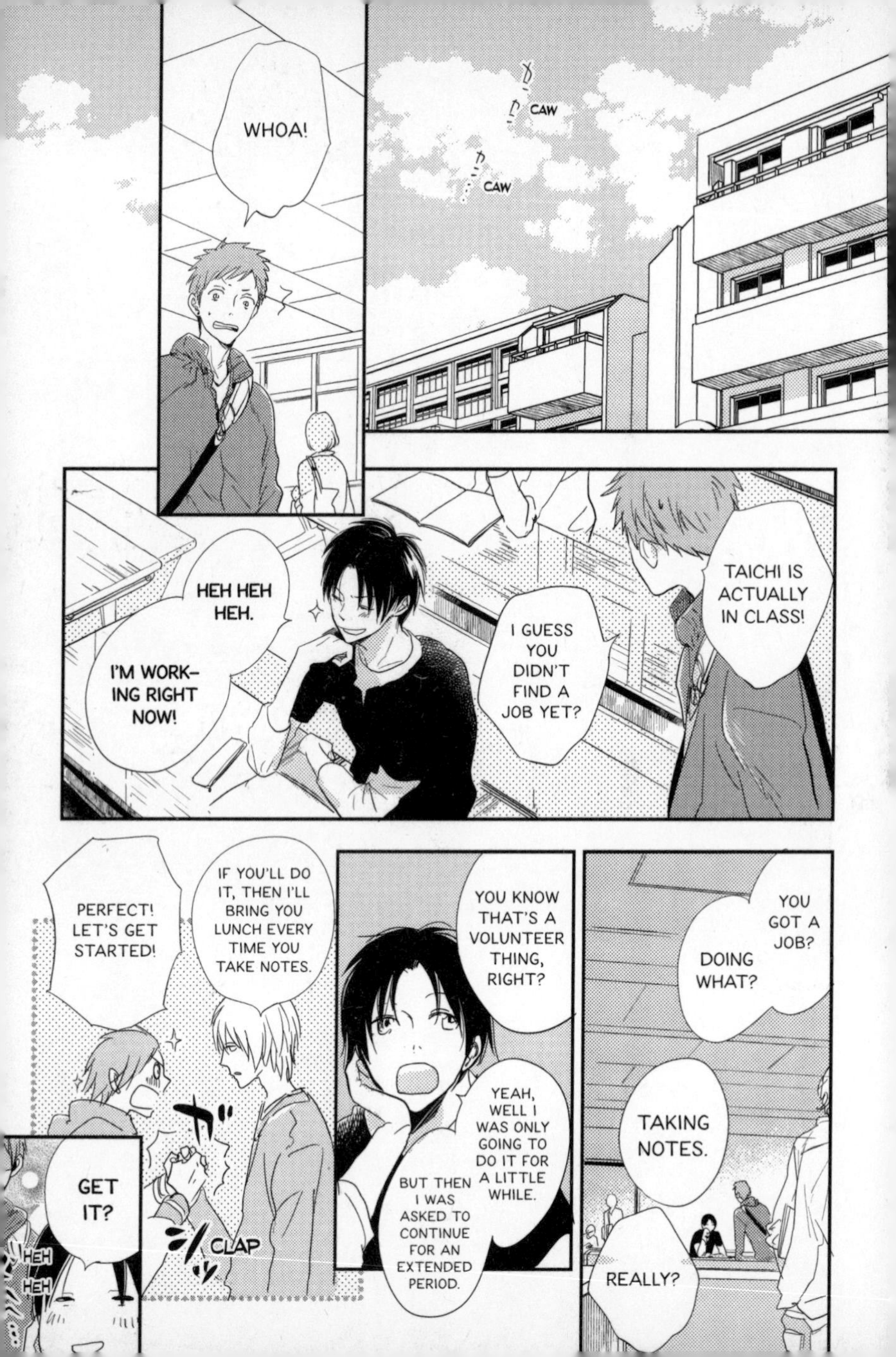
CAW
CAW
WHOA!
TAICHI IS ACTUALLY IN CLASS!
I GUESS YOU DIDN'T FIND A JOB YET?
HEH HEH HEH.
I'M WORK-ING RIGHT NOW!
YOU GOT A JOB?
DOING WHAT?
TAKING NOTES.
REALLY?
YOU KNOW THAT'S A VOLUNTEER THING, RIGHT?
YEAH, WELL I WAS ONLY GOING TO DO IT FOR A LITTLE WHILE.
BUT THEN I WAS ASKED TO CONTINUE FOR AN EXTENDED PERIOD.
IF YOU'LL DO IT, THEN I'LL BRING YOU LUNCH EVERY TIME YOU TAKE NOTES.
PERFECT! LET'S GET STARTED!
CLAP
GET IT?
HEH HEH

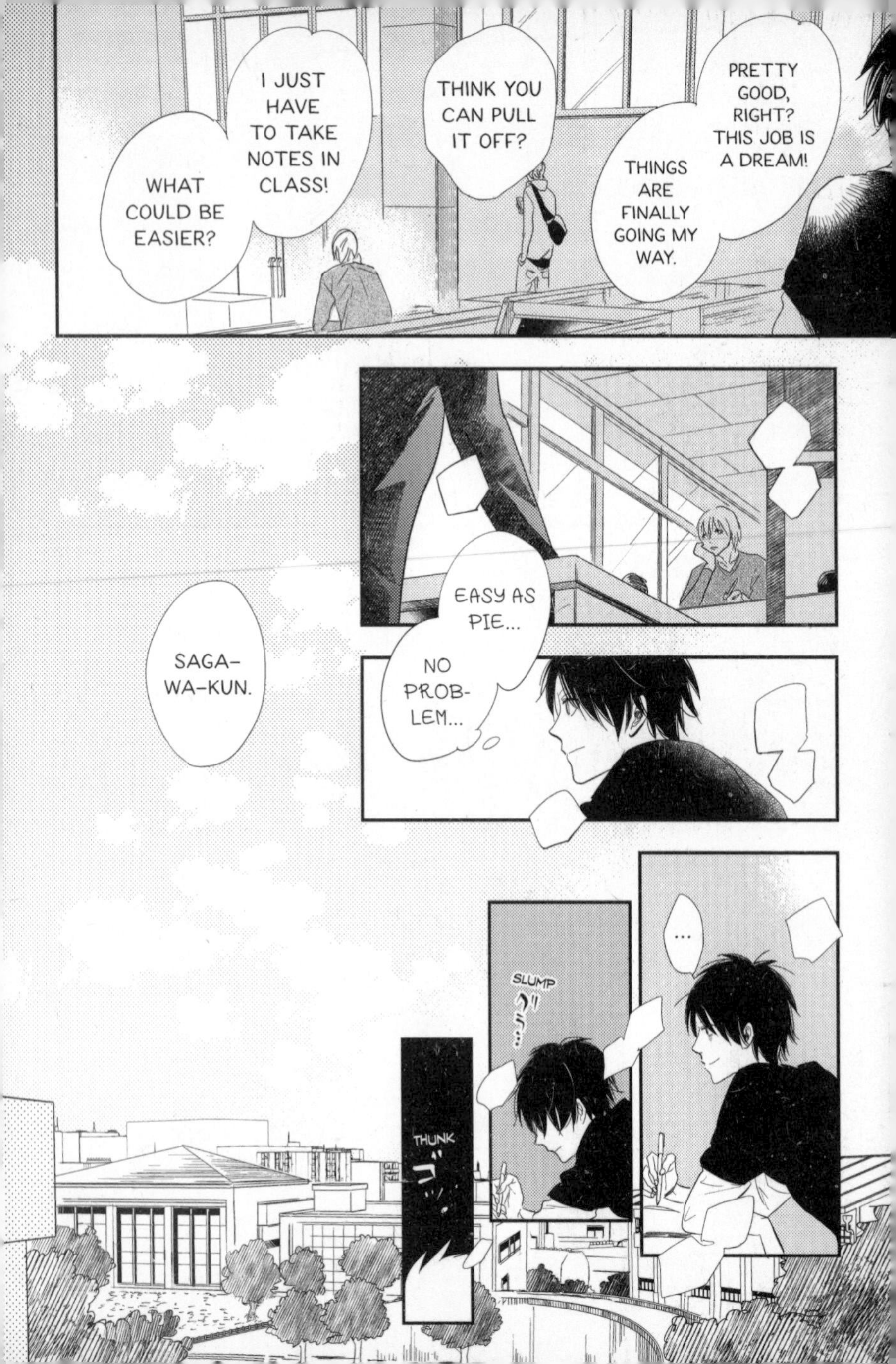
PRETTY GOOD, RIGHT? THIS JOB IS A DREAM!
THINGS ARE FINALLY GOING MY WAY.
THINK YOU CAN PULL IT OFF?
I JUST HAVE TO TAKE NOTES IN CLASS!
WHAT COULD BE EASIER?
EASY AS PIE...
NO PROB-LEM...
SAGA-WA-KUN.
...
SLUMP
THUNK

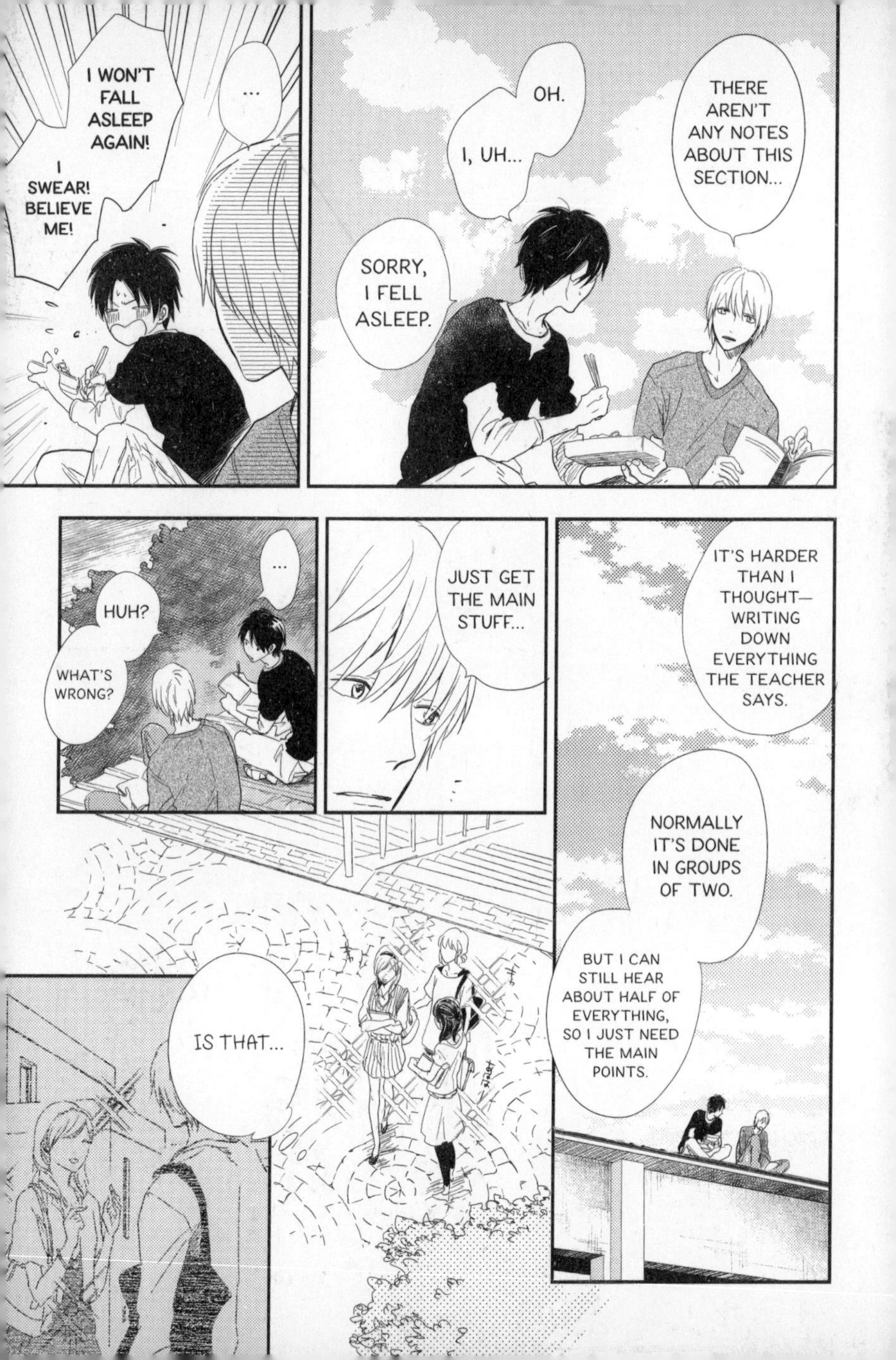
THERE AREN'T ANY NOTES ABOUT THIS SECTION...
OH.
I, UH...
SORRY, I FELL ASLEEP.
...
I WON'T FALL ASLEEP AGAIN!
I SWEAR! BELIEVE ME!
IT'S HARDER THAN I THOUGHT—WRITING DOWN EVERYTHING THE TEACHER SAYS.
NORMALLY IT'S DONE IN GROUPS OF TWO.
BUT I CAN STILL HEAR ABOUT HALF OF EVERYTHING, SO I JUST NEED THE MAIN POINTS.
JUST GET THE MAIN STUFF...
...
HUH?
WHAT'S WRONG?
IS THAT...

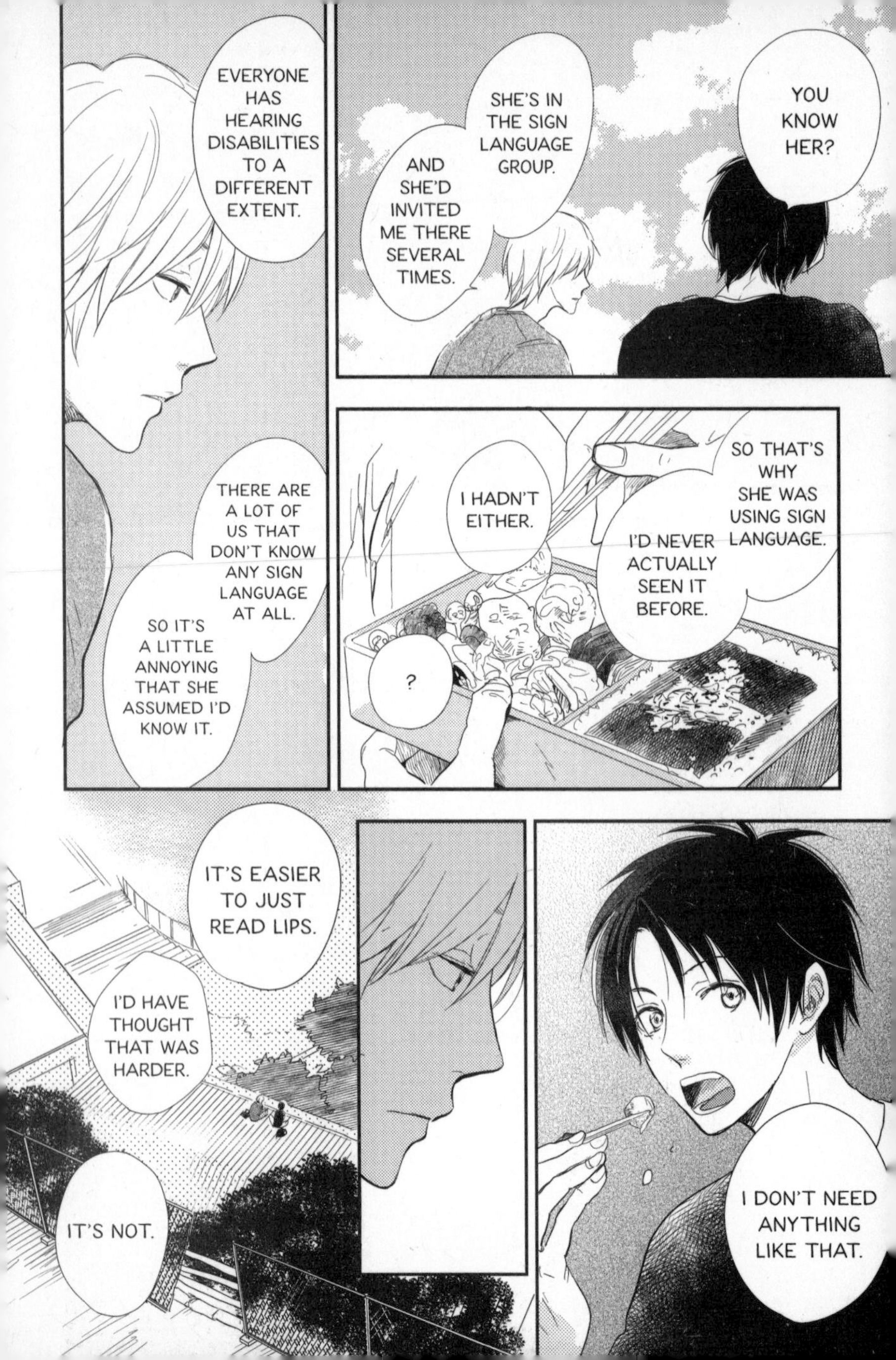
YOU KNOW HER?
SHE'S IN THE SIGN LANGUAGE GROUP.
AND SHE'D INVITED ME THERE SEVERAL TIMES.
SO THAT'S WHY SHE WAS USING SIGN LANGUAGE.
I'D NEVER ACTUALLY SEEN IT BEFORE.
I HADN'T EITHER.
?
EVERYONE HAS HEARING DISABILITIES TO A DIFFERENT EXTENT.
THERE ARE A LOT OF US THAT DON'T KNOW ANY SIGN LANGUAGE AT ALL.
SO IT'S A LITTLE ANNOYING THAT SHE ASSUMED I'D KNOW IT.
I DON'T NEED ANYTHING LIKE THAT.
IT'S EASIER TO JUST READ LIPS.
I'D HAVE THOUGHT THAT WAS HARDER.
IT'S NOT.

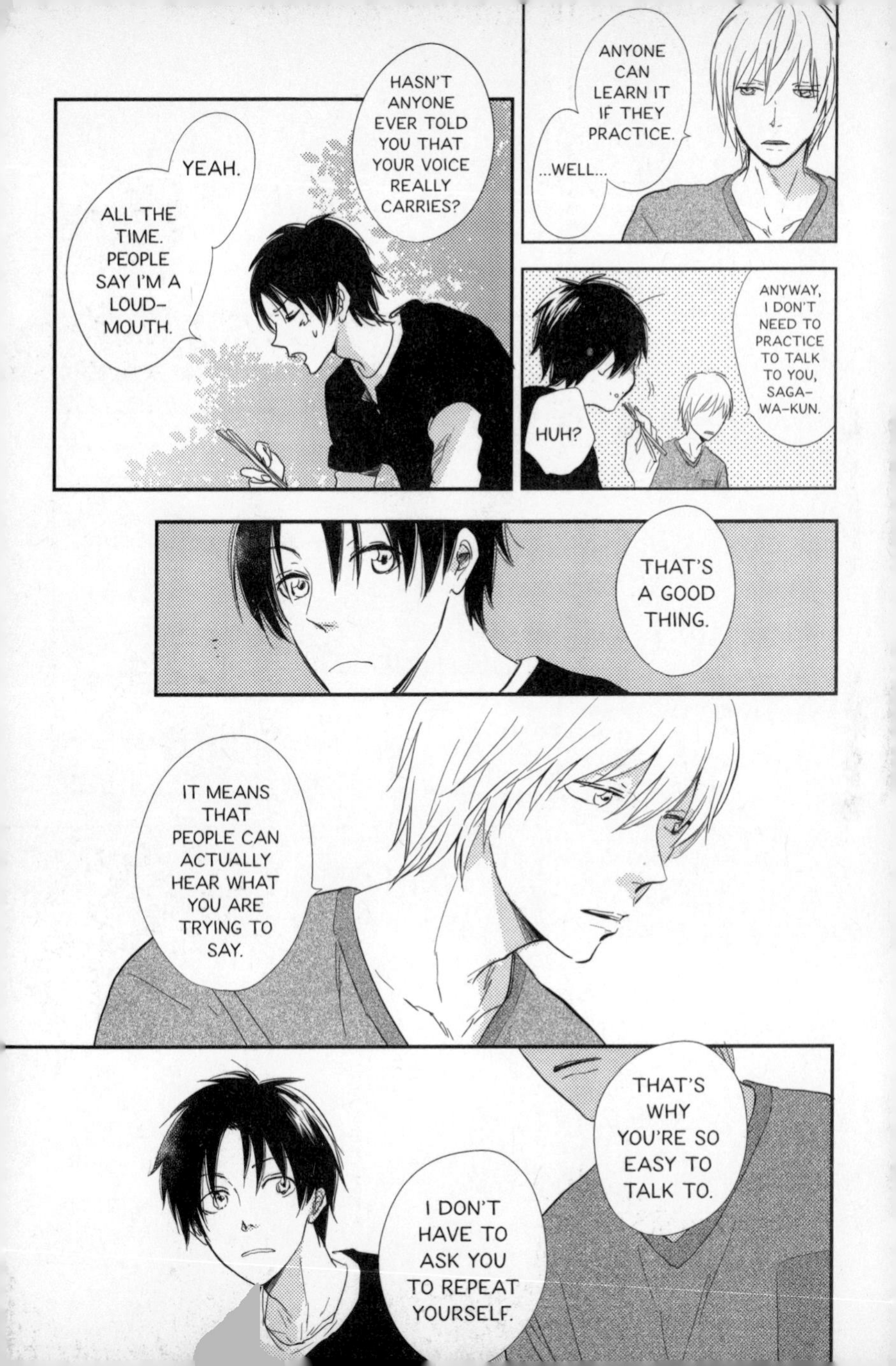
ANYONE CAN LEARN IT IF THEY PRACTICE.
...WELL...
ANYWAY, I DON'T NEED TO PRACTICE TO TALK TO YOU, SAGA-WA-KUN.
HUH?
HASN'T ANYONE EVER TOLD YOU THAT YOUR VOICE REALLY CARRIES?
YEAH.
ALL THE TIME. PEOPLE SAY I'M A LOUD-MOUTH.
THAT'S A GOOD THING.
IT MEANS THAT PEOPLE CAN ACTUALLY HEAR WHAT YOU ARE TRYING TO SAY.
THAT'S WHY YOU'RE SO EASY TO TALK TO.
I DON'T HAVE TO ASK YOU TO REPEAT YOURSELF.

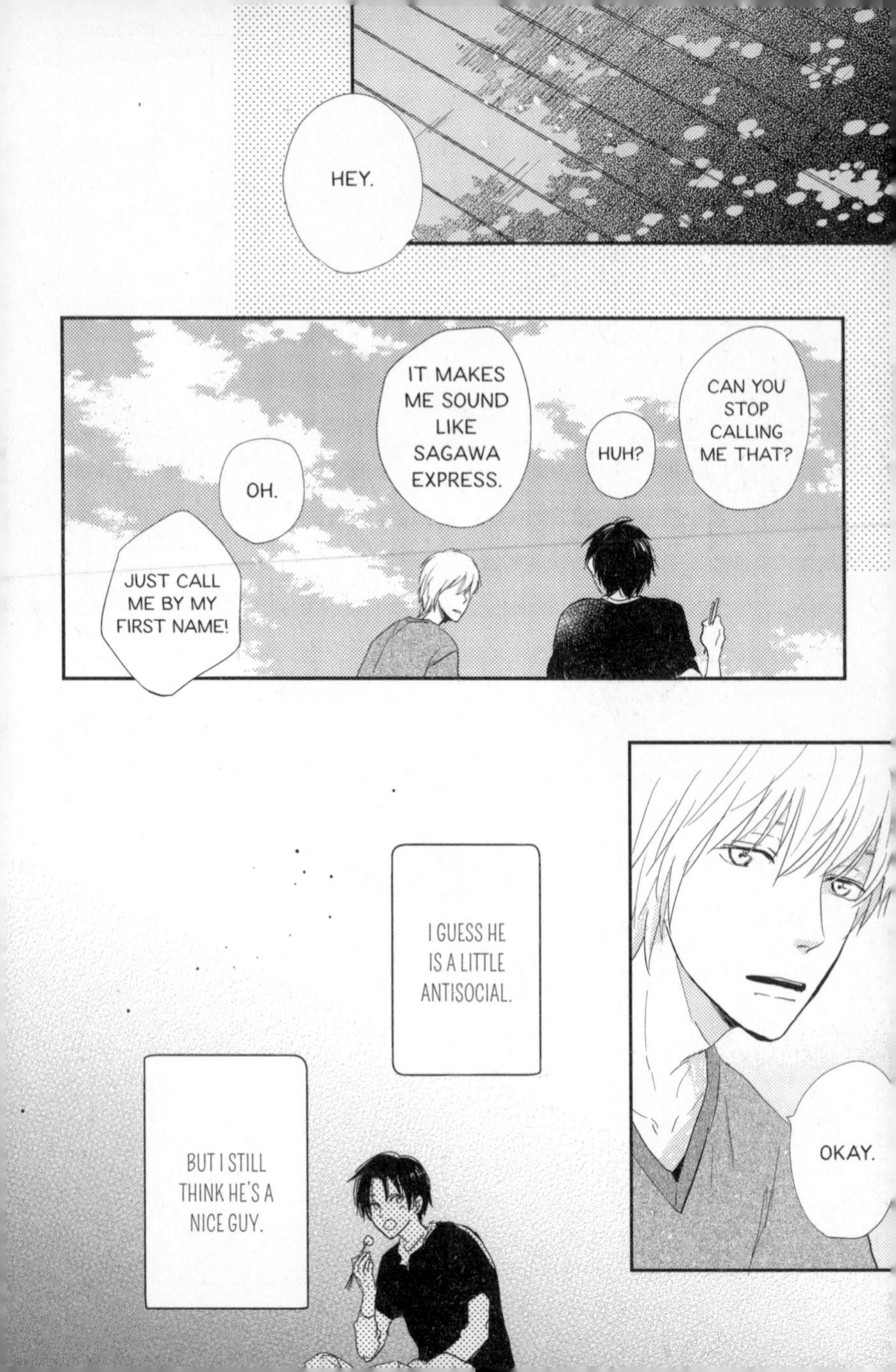
HEY.
CAN YOU STOP CALLING ME THAT?
HUH?
IT MAKES ME SOUND LIKE SAGAWA EXPRESS.
OH.
JUST CALL ME BY MY FIRST NAME!
OKAY.
I GUESS HE IS A LITTLE ANTISOCIAL.
BUT I STILL THINK HE'S A NICE GUY.

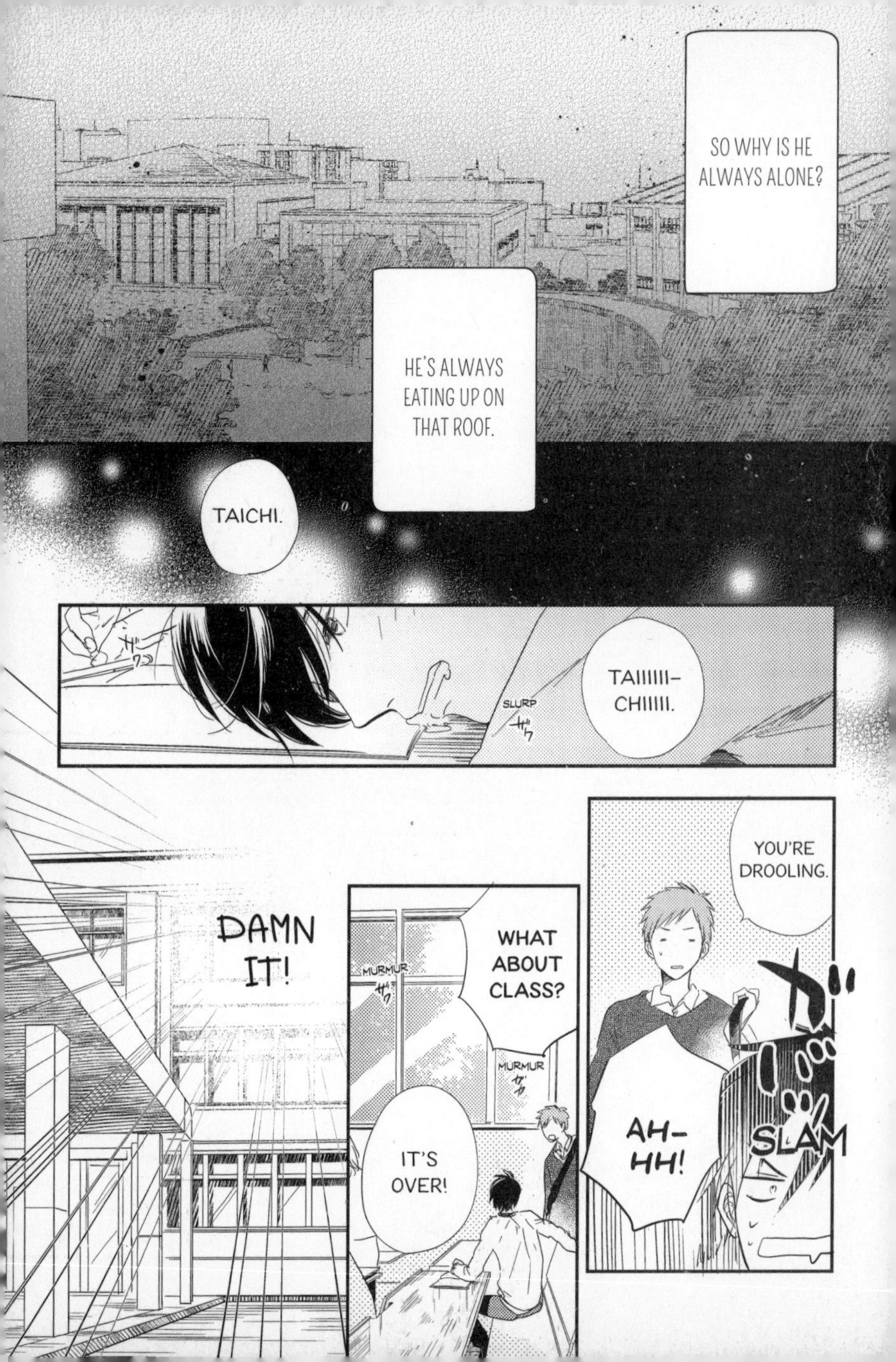
SO WHY IS HE ALWAYS ALONE?
HE'S ALWAYS EATING UP ON THAT ROOF.
TAICHI.
TAIIIIII- CHIIIIII.
SLURP
YOU'RE DROOLING.
SLAM
AH-HH!
WHAT ABOUT CLASS?
MURMUR
MURMUR
IT'S OVER!
DAMN IT!

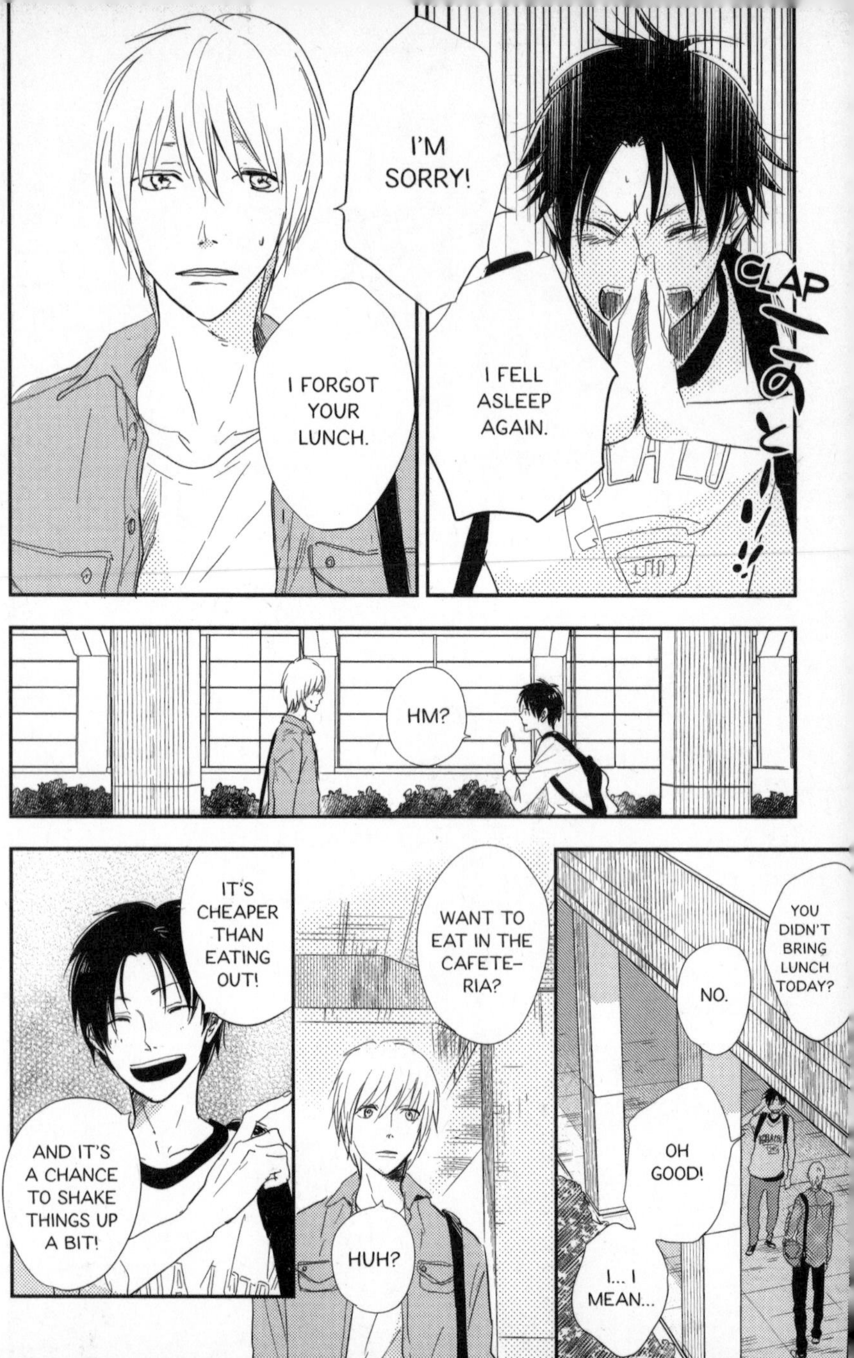
I'M SORRY!
I FELL ASLEEP AGAIN.
CLAP
I FORGOT YOUR LUNCH.
HM?
YOU DIDN'T BRING LUNCH TODAY?
NO.
OH GOOD!
I... I MEAN...
WANT TO EAT IN THE CAFETE-RIA?
HUH?
IT'S CHEAPER THAN EATING OUT!
AND IT'S A CHANCE TO SHAKE THINGS UP A BIT!

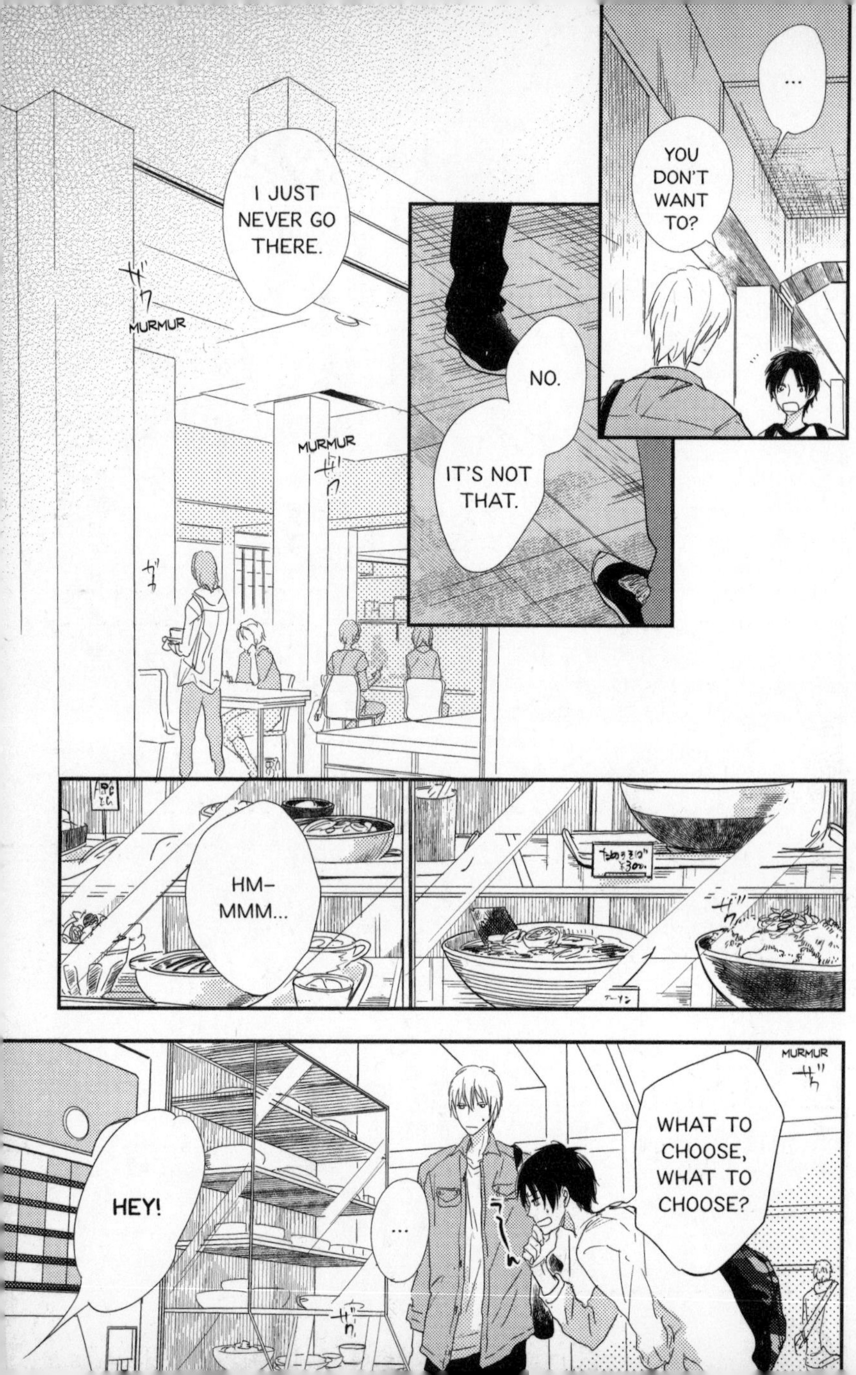
...
YOU DON'T WANT TO?
NO.
IT'S NOT THAT.
I JUST NEVER GO THERE.
MURMUR
MURMUR
HM-MMM...
MURMUR
WHAT TO CHOOSE, WHAT TO CHOOSE?
...
HEY!

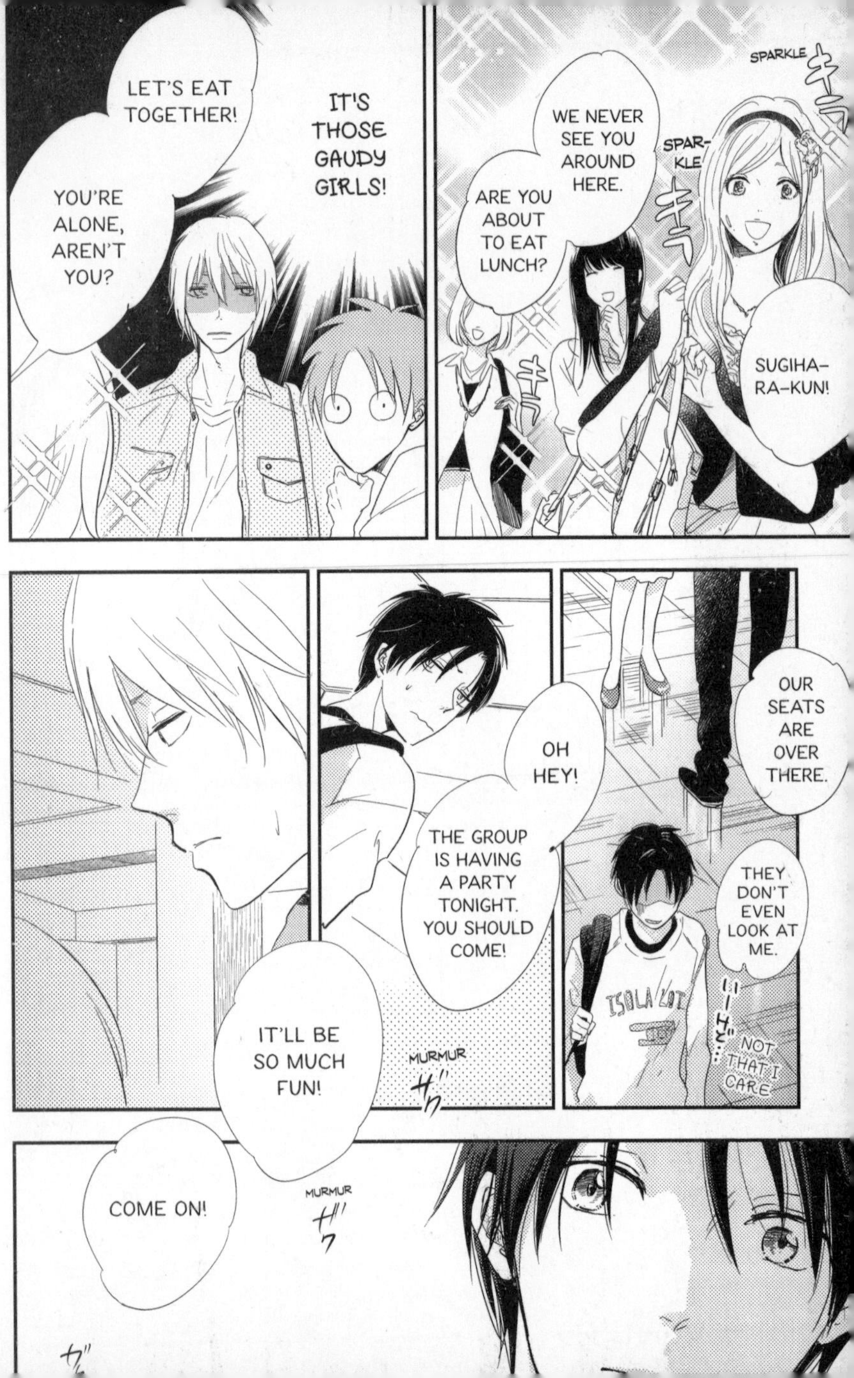

SPARKLE
SPAR-KLE
SUGIHA-RA-KUN!
WE NEVER SEE YOU AROUND HERE.
ARE YOU ABOUT TO EAT LUNCH?
IT'S THOSE GAUDY GIRLS!
LET'S EAT TOGETHER!
YOU'RE ALONE, AREN'T YOU?
OUR SEATS ARE OVER THERE.
THEY DON'T EVEN LOOK AT ME.
NOT THAT I CARE
ISOLA LOT
OH HEY!
THE GROUP IS HAVING A PARTY TONIGHT. YOU SHOULD COME!
MURMUR
IT'LL BE SO MUCH FUN!
COME ON!
MURMUR

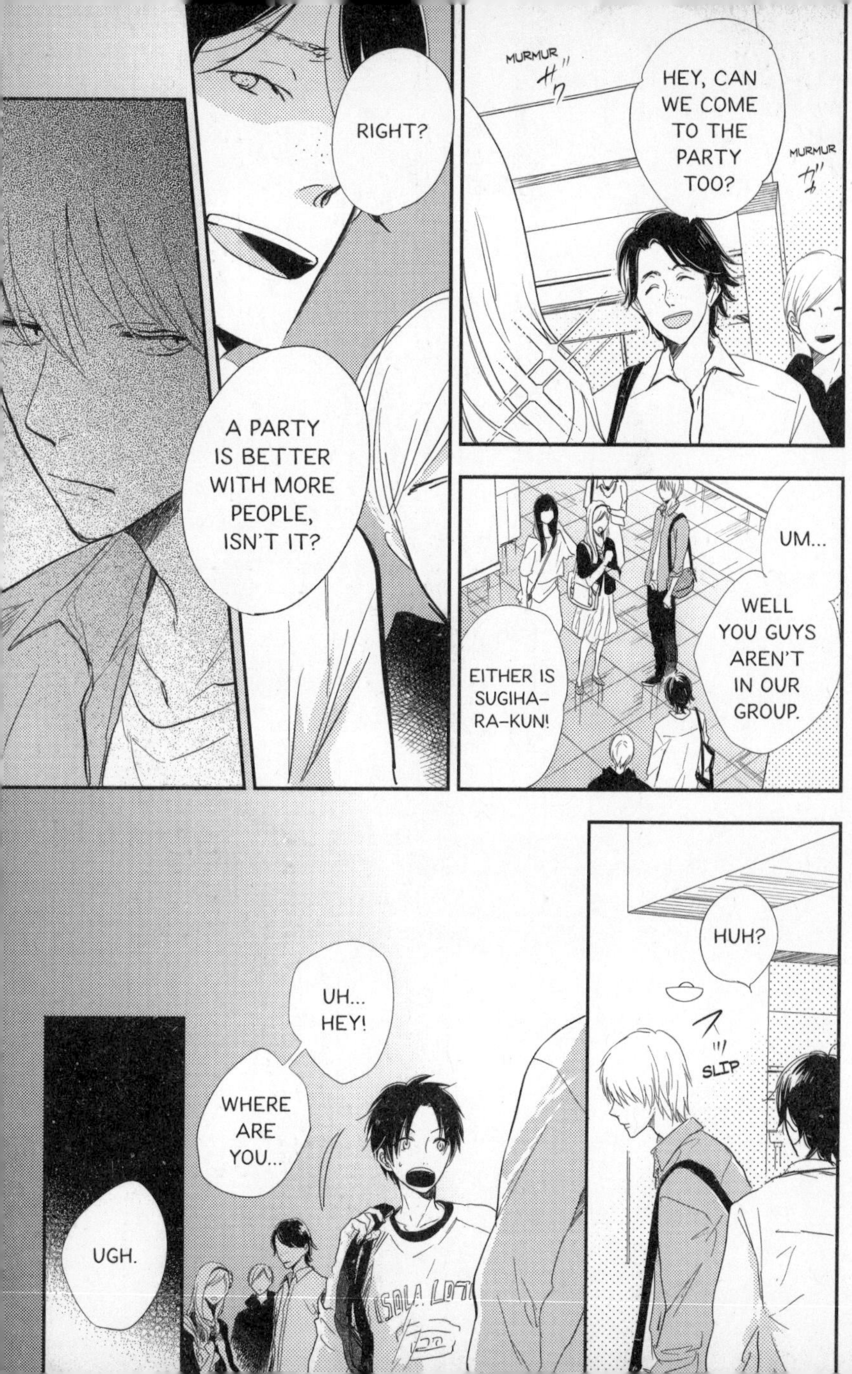
MURMUR
HEY, CAN WE COME TO THE PARTY TOO?
MURMUR
UM...
WELL YOU GUYS AREN'T IN OUR GROUP.
EITHER IS SUGIHA-RA-KUN!
RIGHT?
A PARTY IS BETTER WITH MORE PEOPLE, ISN'T IT?
HUH?
SLIP
UH... HEY!
WHERE ARE YOU...
UGH.

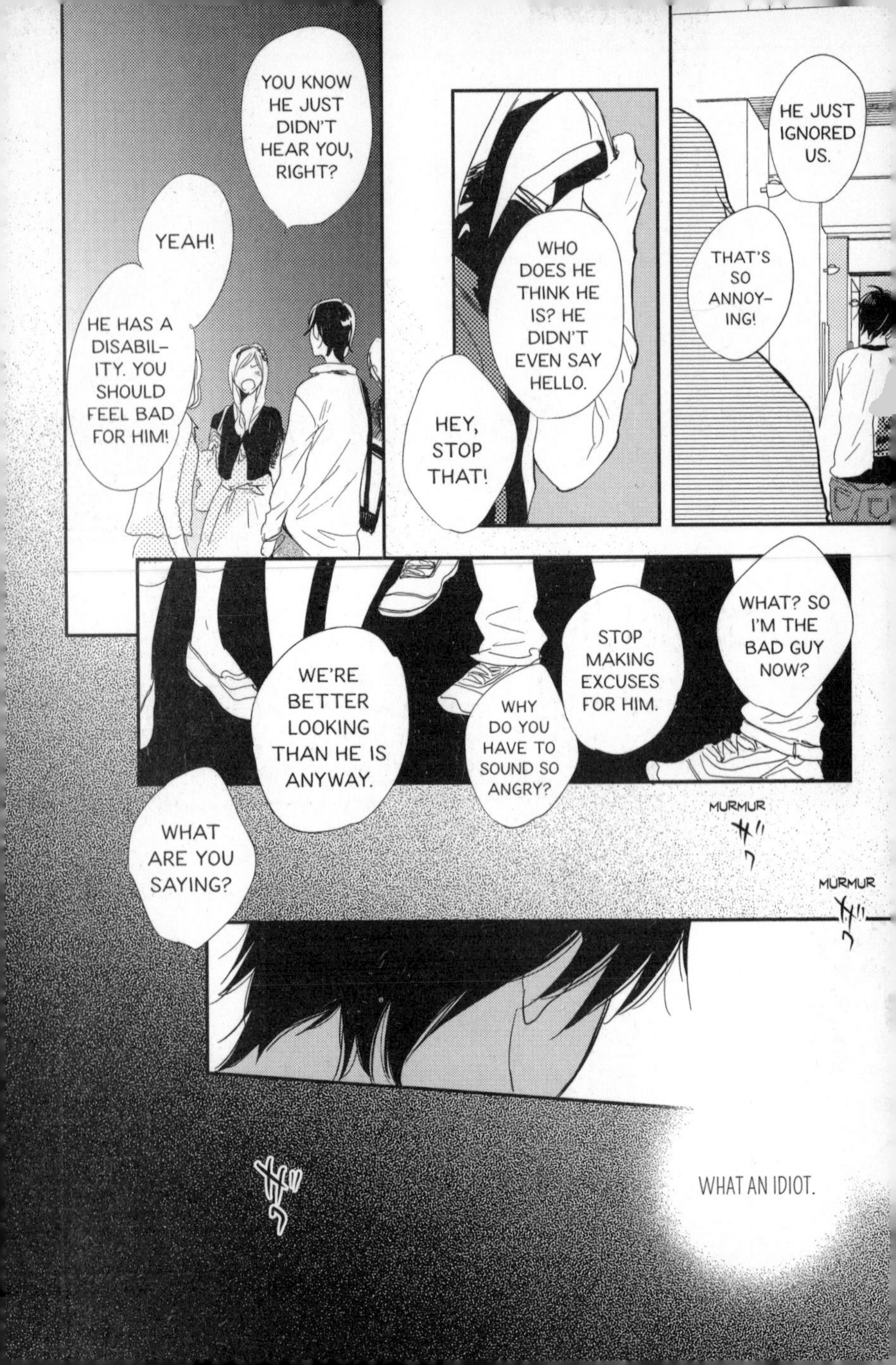
HE JUST IGNORED US.
THAT'S SO ANNOY-ING!
WHO DOES HE THINK HE IS? HE DIDN'T EVEN SAY HELLO.
HEY, STOP THAT!
YOU KNOW HE JUST DIDN'T HEAR YOU, RIGHT?
YEAH!
HE HAS A DISABIL-ITY. YOU SHOULD FEEL BAD FOR HIM!
WHAT? SO I'M THE BAD GUY NOW?
STOP MAKING EXCUSES FOR HIM.
WHY DO YOU HAVE TO SOUND SO ANGRY?
WE'RE BETTER LOOKING THAN HE IS ANYWAY.
WHAT ARE YOU SAYING?
MURMUR
MURMUR
WHAT AN IDIOT.

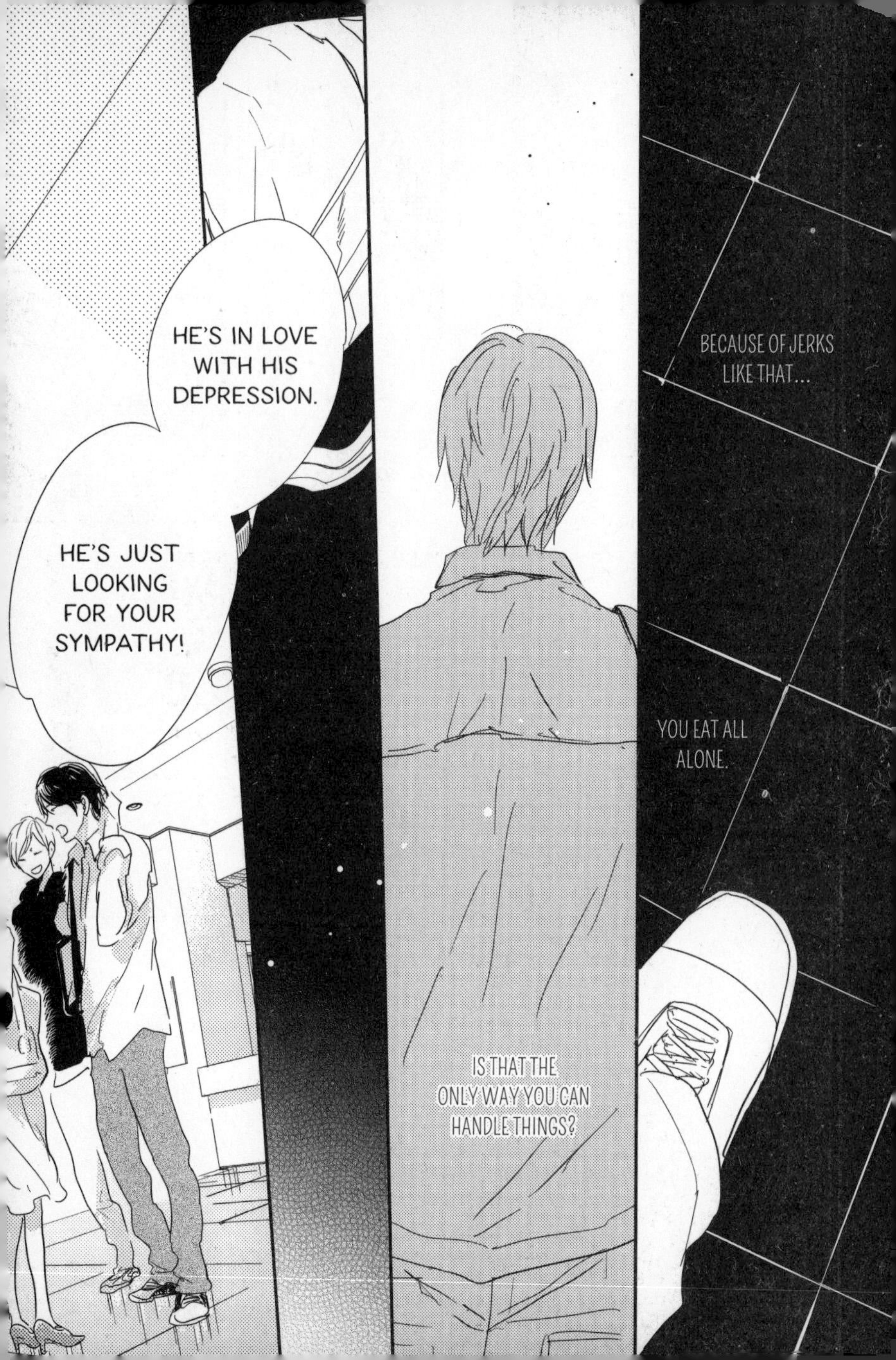
BECAUSE OF JERKS LIKE THAT...
YOU EAT ALL ALONE.
IS THAT THE ONLY WAY YOU CAN HANDLE THINGS?
HE'S IN LOVE WITH HIS DEPRESSION.
HE'S JUST LOOKING FOR YOUR SYMPATHY!

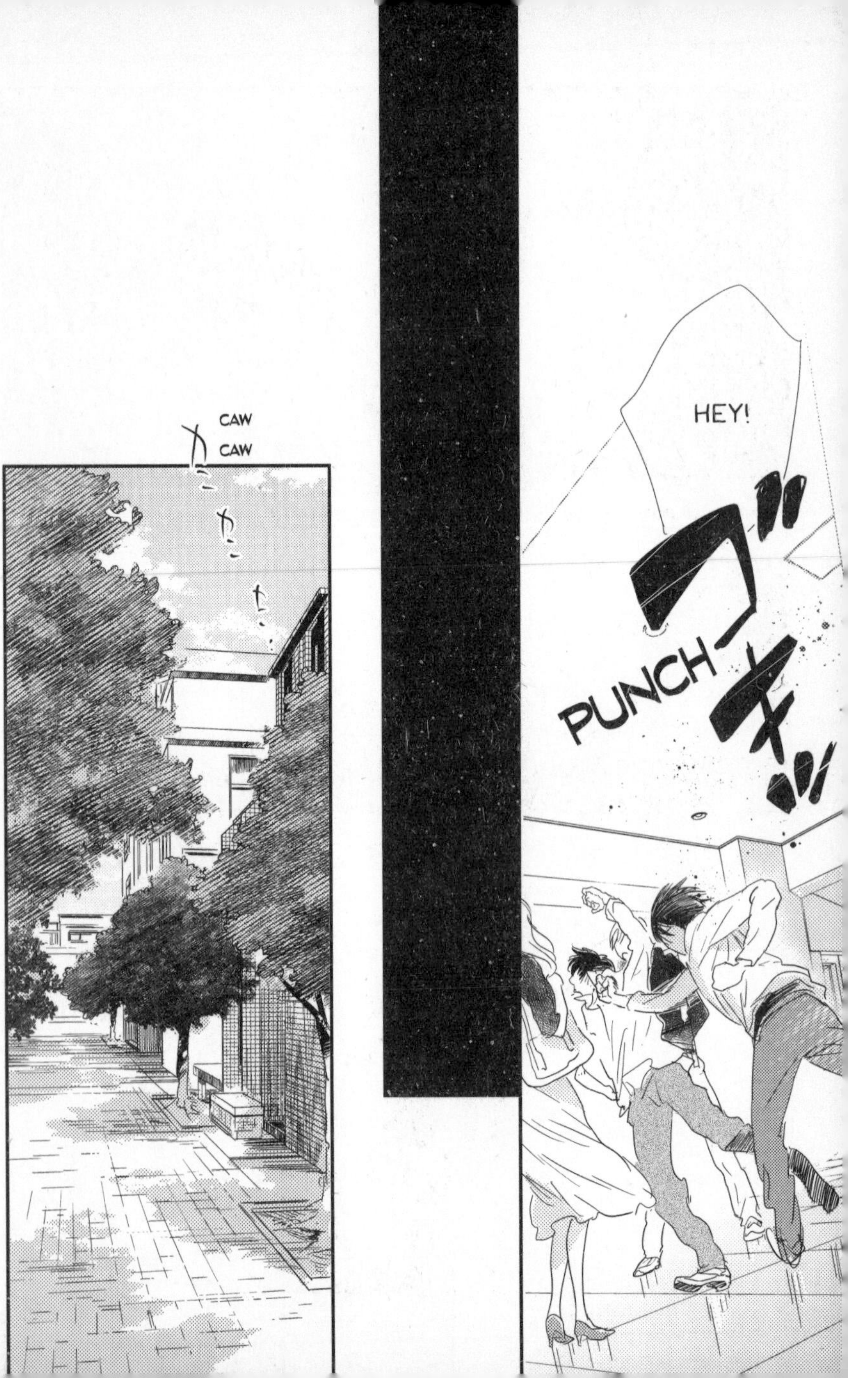
HEY!
PUNCH
CAW
CAW

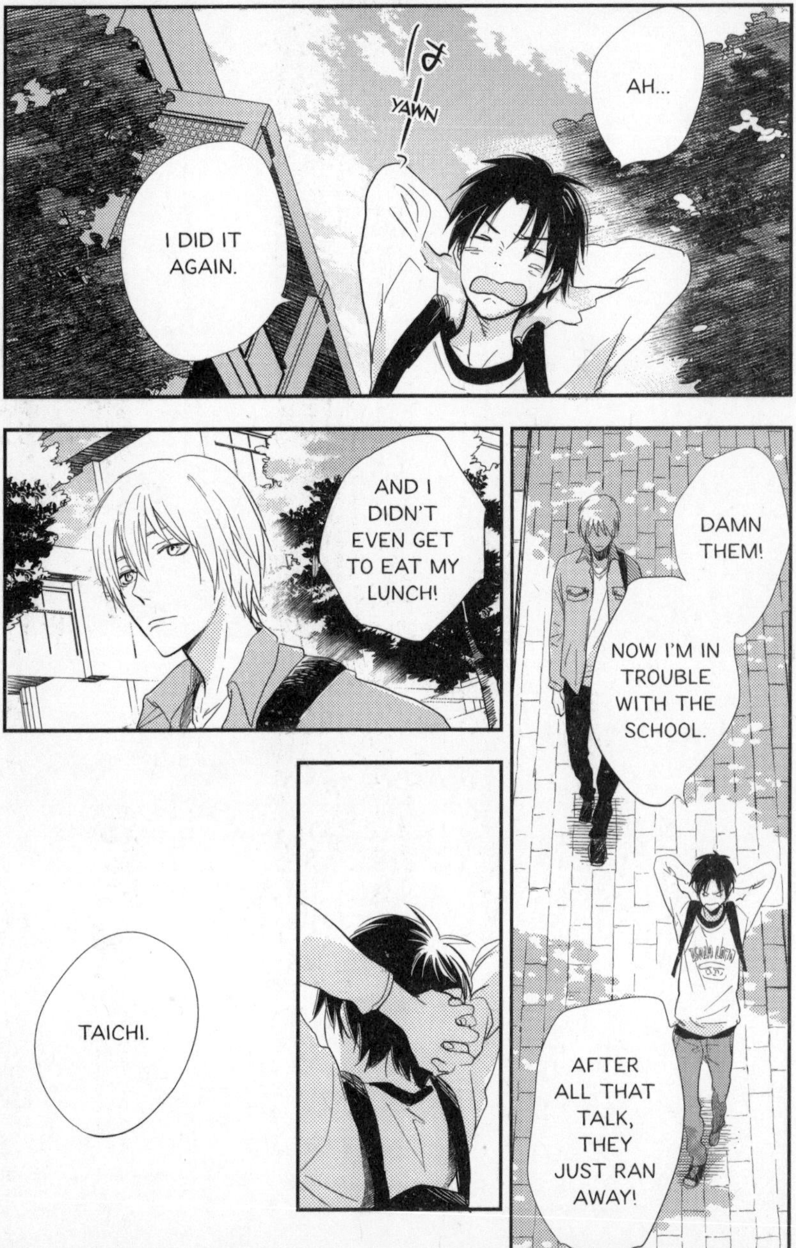

AH...
YAWN
I DID IT AGAIN.
DAMN THEM!
NOW I'M IN TROUBLE WITH THE SCHOOL.
AFTER ALL THAT TALK, THEY JUST RAN AWAY!
AND I DIDN'T EVEN GET TO EAT MY LUNCH!
TAICHI.

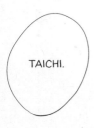

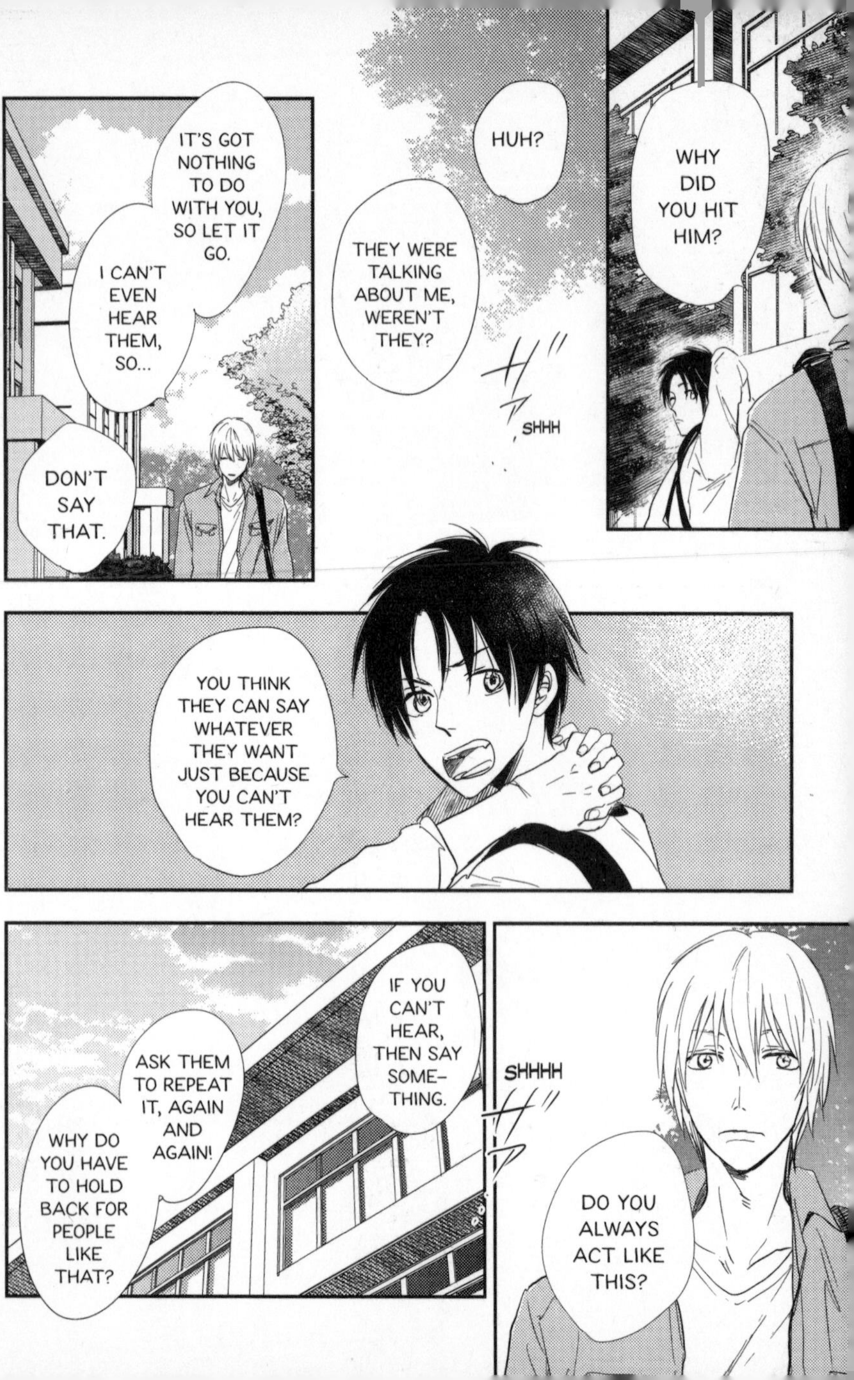
WHY DID YOU HIT HIM?
HUH?
THEY WERE TALKING ABOUT ME, WEREN'T THEY?
SHHH
IT'S GOT NOTHING TO DO WITH YOU, SO LET IT GO.
I CAN'T EVEN HEAR THEM, SO...
DON'T SAY THAT.
YOU THINK THEY CAN SAY WHATEVER THEY WANT JUST BECAUSE YOU CAN'T HEAR THEM?
SHHHH
DO YOU ALWAYS ACT LIKE THIS?
IF YOU CAN'T HEAR, THEN SAY SOME-THING.
ASK THEM TO REPEAT IT, AGAIN AND AGAIN!
WHY DO YOU HAVE TO HOLD BACK FOR PEOPLE LIKE THAT?

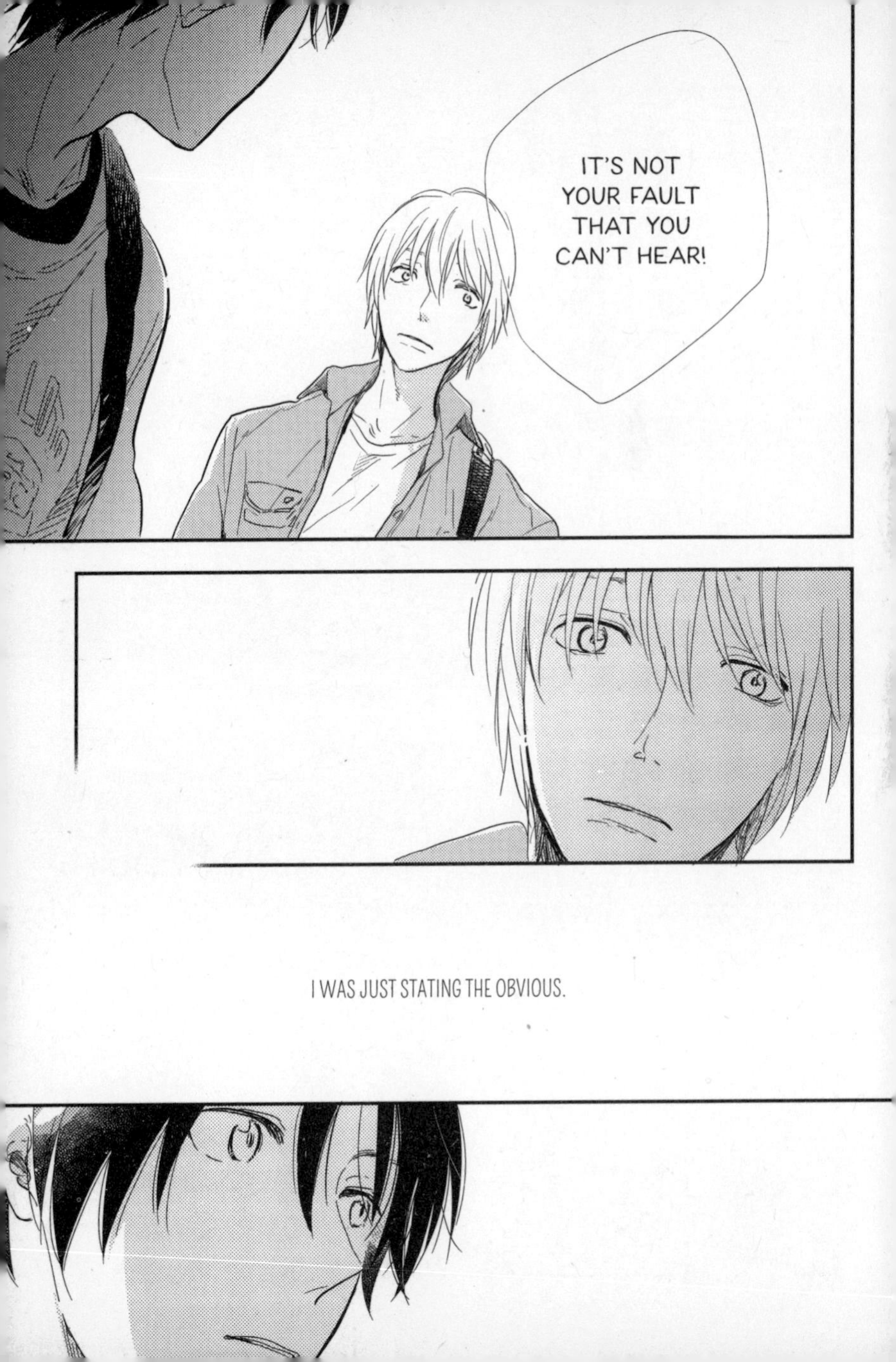
IT'S NOT YOUR FAULT THAT YOU CAN'T HEAR!
I WAS JUST STATING THE OBVIOUS.

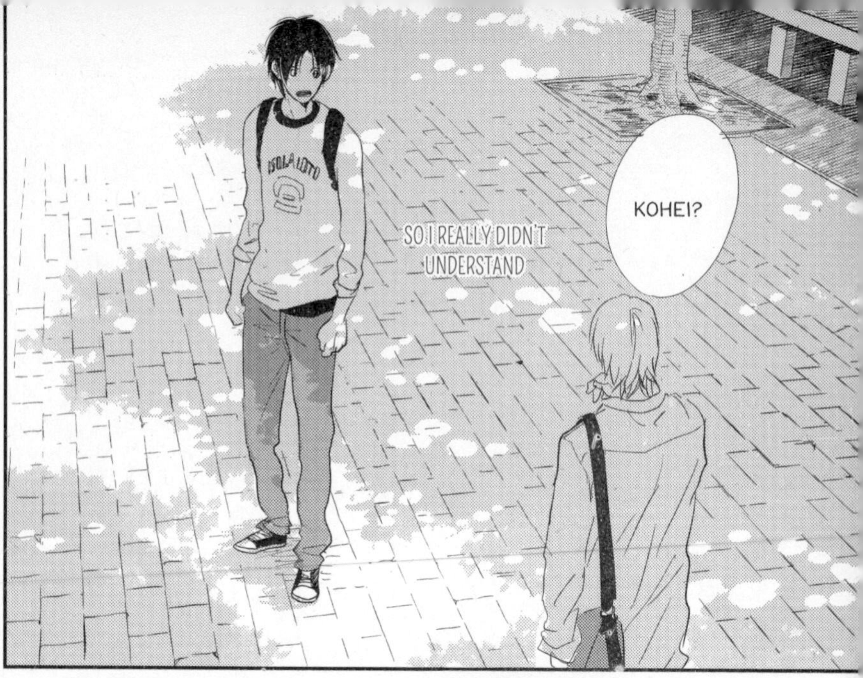
KOHEI?
SO I REALLY DIDN'T UNDERSTAND

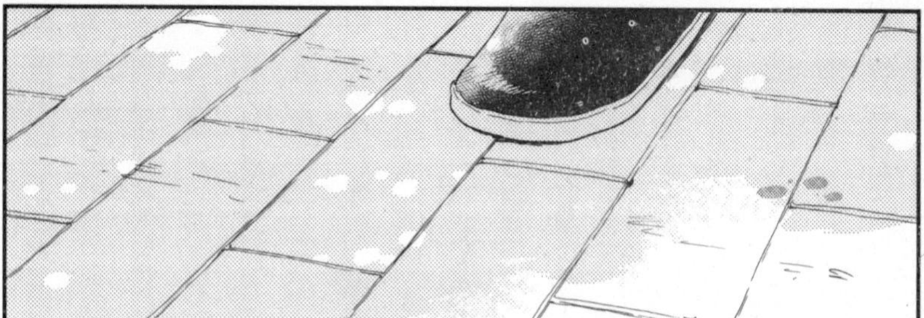

WHY YOU CRIED THAT DAY.

i hear
the
sunspot

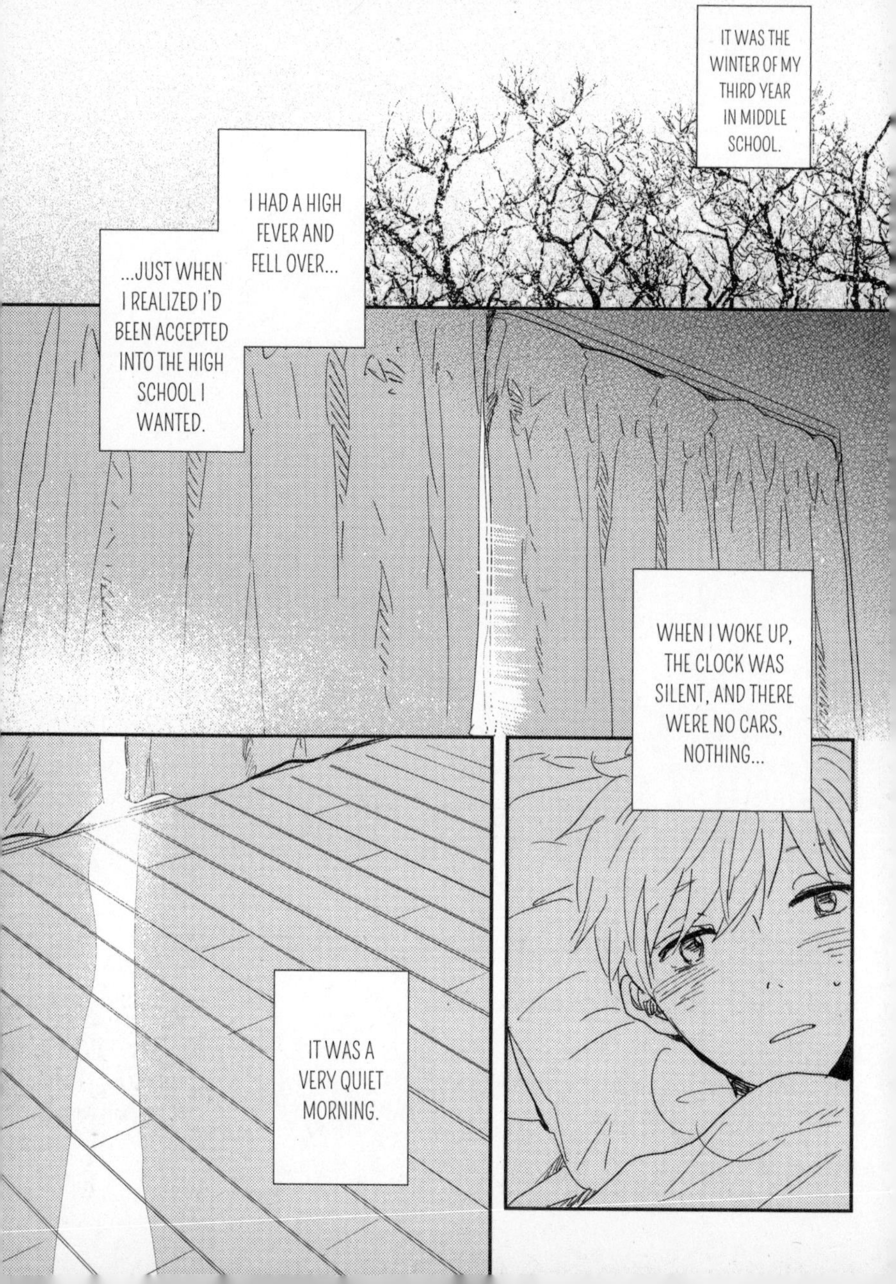
IT WAS THE WINTER OF MY THIRD YEAR IN MIDDLE SCHOOL.
I HAD A HIGH FEVER AND FELL OVER...
...JUST WHEN I REALIZED I'D BEEN ACCEPTED INTO THE HIGH SCHOOL I WANTED.
WHEN I WOKE UP, THE CLOCK WAS SILENT, AND THERE WERE NO CARS, NOTHING...
IT WAS A VERY QUIET MORNING.

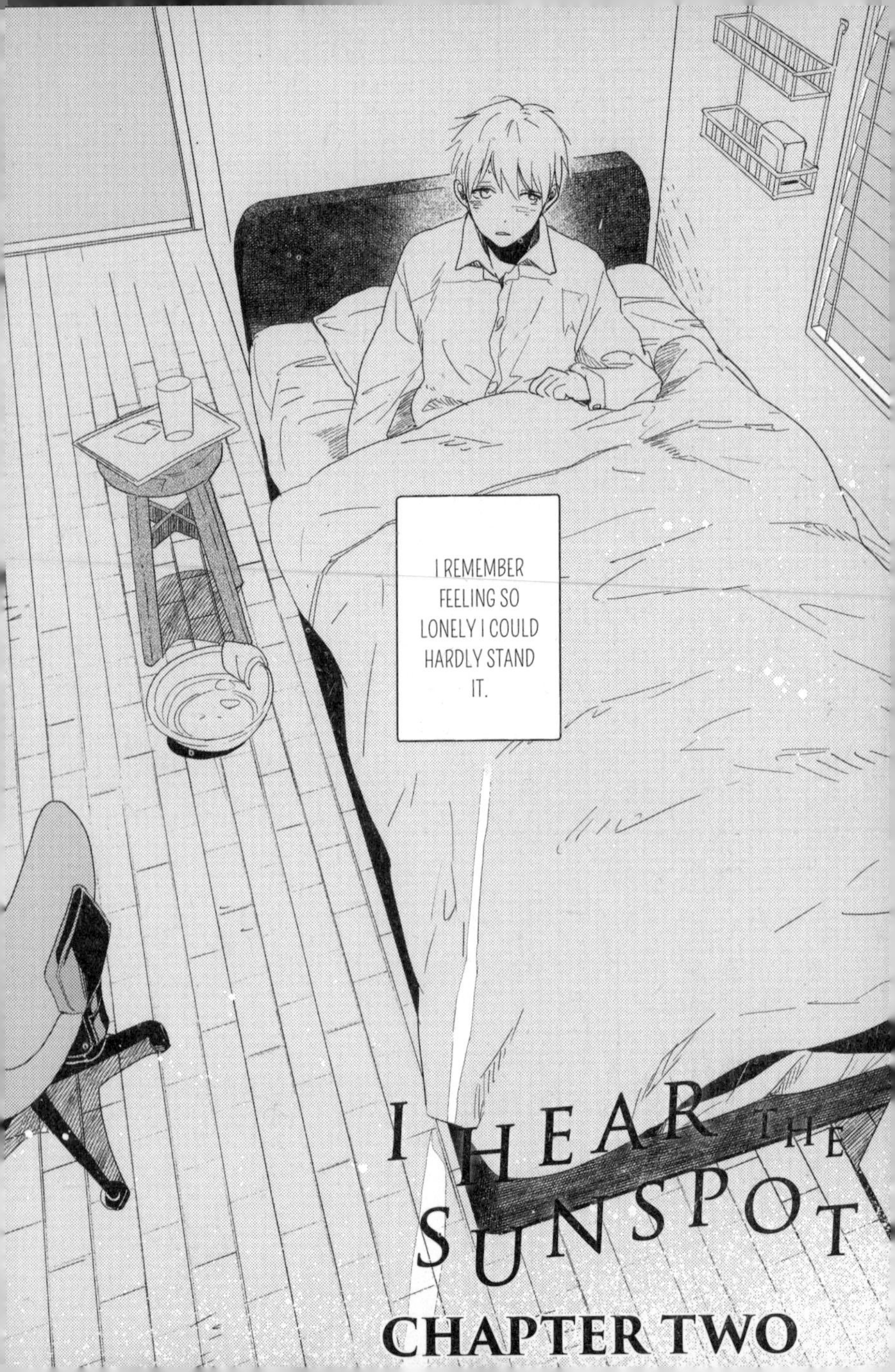
I REMEMBER FEELING SO LONELY I COULD HARDLY STAND IT.
I HEAR THE SUNSPOT
CHAPTER TWO

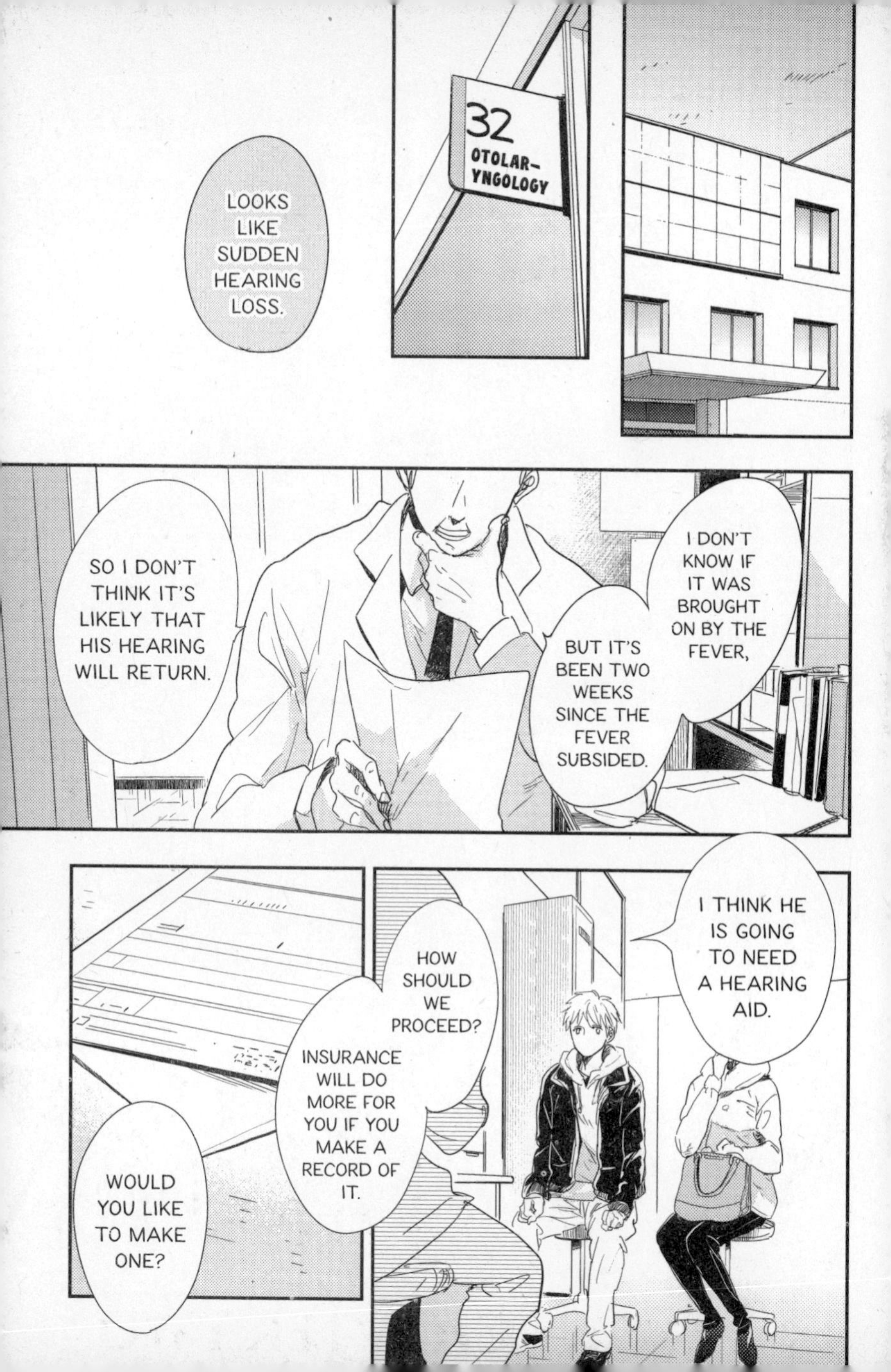
32
OTOLAR-YNGOLOGY
LOOKS LIKE SUDDEN HEARING LOSS.
I DON'T KNOW IF IT WAS BROUGHT ON BY THE FEVER,
BUT IT'S BEEN TWO WEEKS SINCE THE FEVER SUBSIDED.
SO I DON'T THINK IT'S LIKELY THAT HIS HEARING WILL RETURN.
I THINK HE IS GOING TO NEED A HEARING AID.
HOW SHOULD WE PROCEED?
INSURANCE WILL DO MORE FOR YOU IF YOU MAKE A RECORD OF IT.
WOULD YOU LIKE TO MAKE ONE?

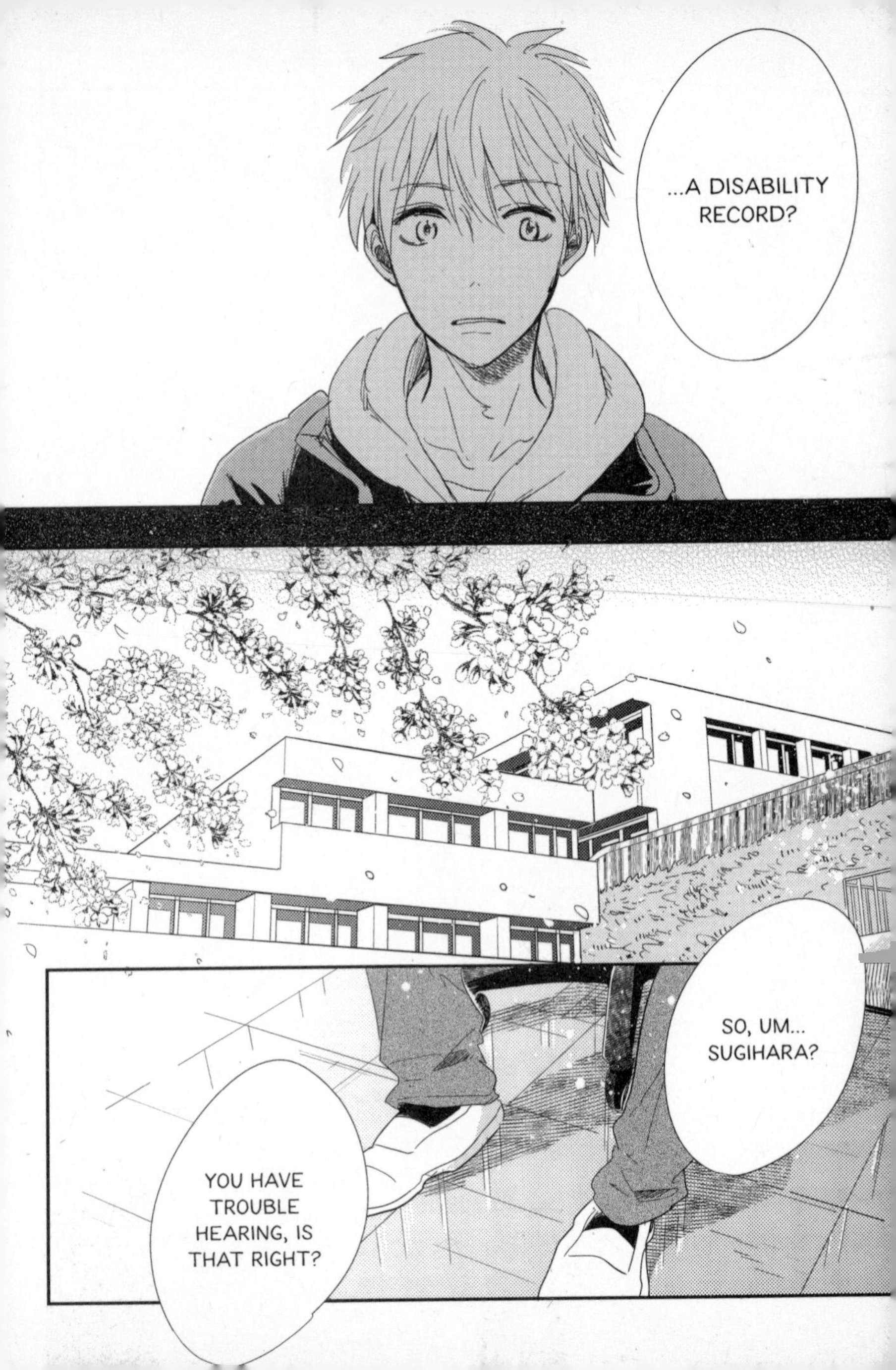
...A DISABILITY RECORD?
SO, UM... SUGIHARA?
YOU HAVE TROUBLE HEARING, IS THAT RIGHT?

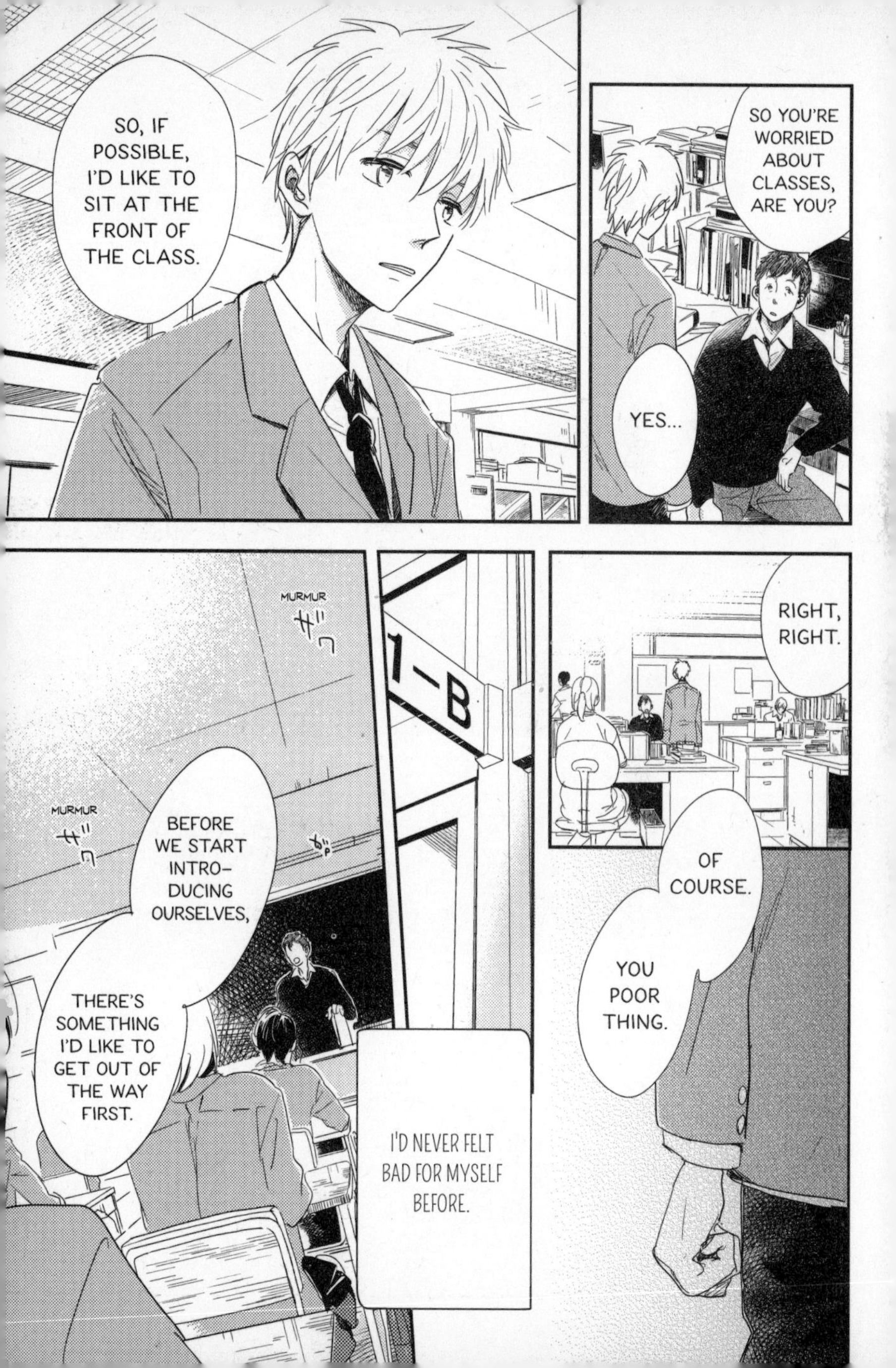
SO YOU'RE WORRIED ABOUT CLASSES, ARE YOU?
YES...
SO, IF POSSIBLE, I'D LIKE TO SIT AT THE FRONT OF THE CLASS.
RIGHT, RIGHT.
OF COURSE.
YOU POOR THING.
I'D NEVER FELT BAD FOR MYSELF BEFORE.
1-B
MURMUR
BEFORE WE START INTRO-DUCING OURSELVES,
MURMUR
THERE'S SOMETHING I'D LIKE TO GET OUT OF THE WAY FIRST.

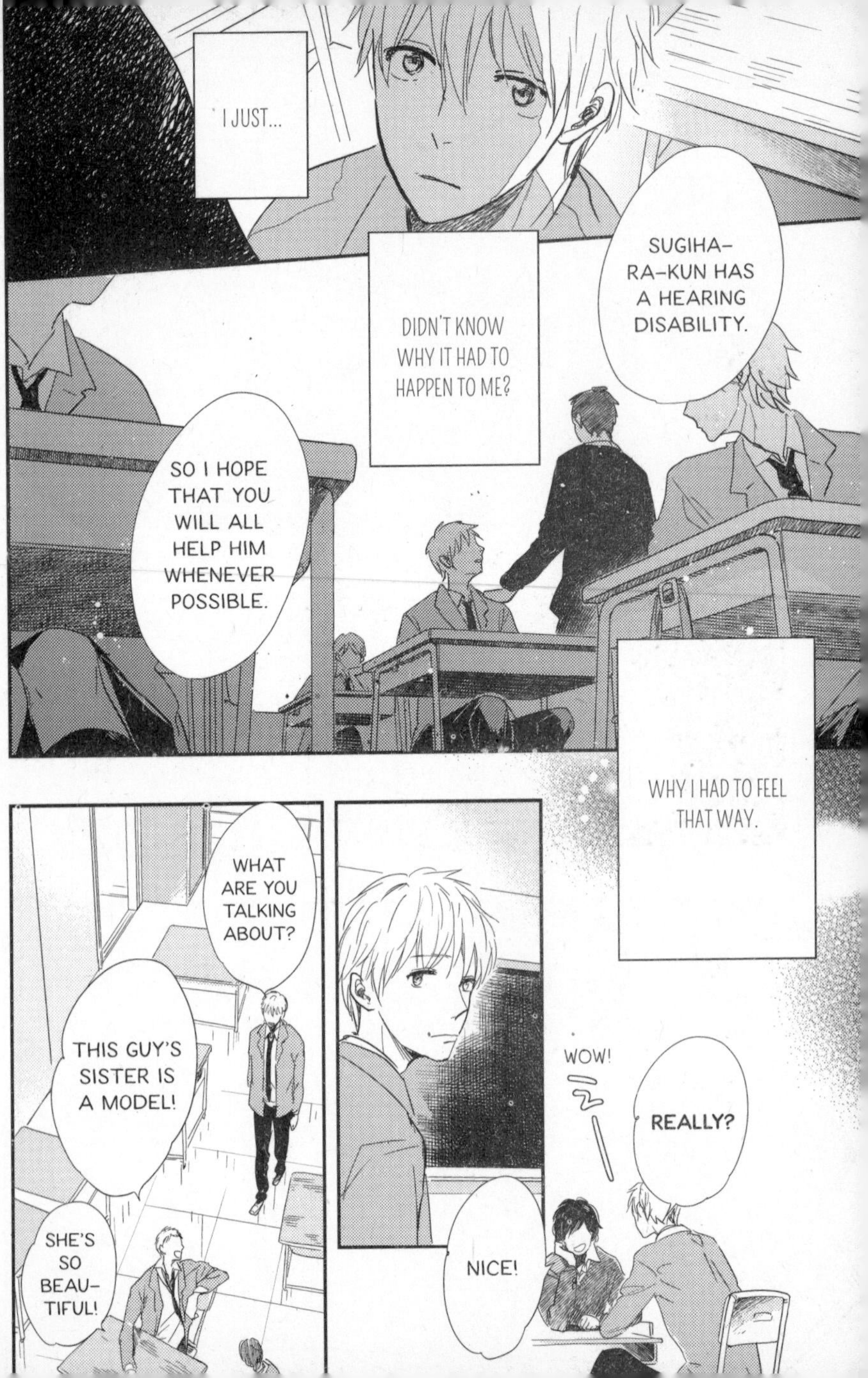
I JUST...
SUGIHA-RA-KUN HAS A HEARING DISABILITY.
DIDN'T KNOW WHY IT HAD TO HAPPEN TO ME?
SO I HOPE THAT YOU WILL ALL HELP HIM WHENEVER POSSIBLE.
WHY I HAD TO FEEL THAT WAY.
WOW!
REALLY?
NICE!
WHAT ARE YOU TALKING ABOUT?
THIS GUY'S SISTER IS A MODEL!
SHE'S SO BEAU-TIFUL!

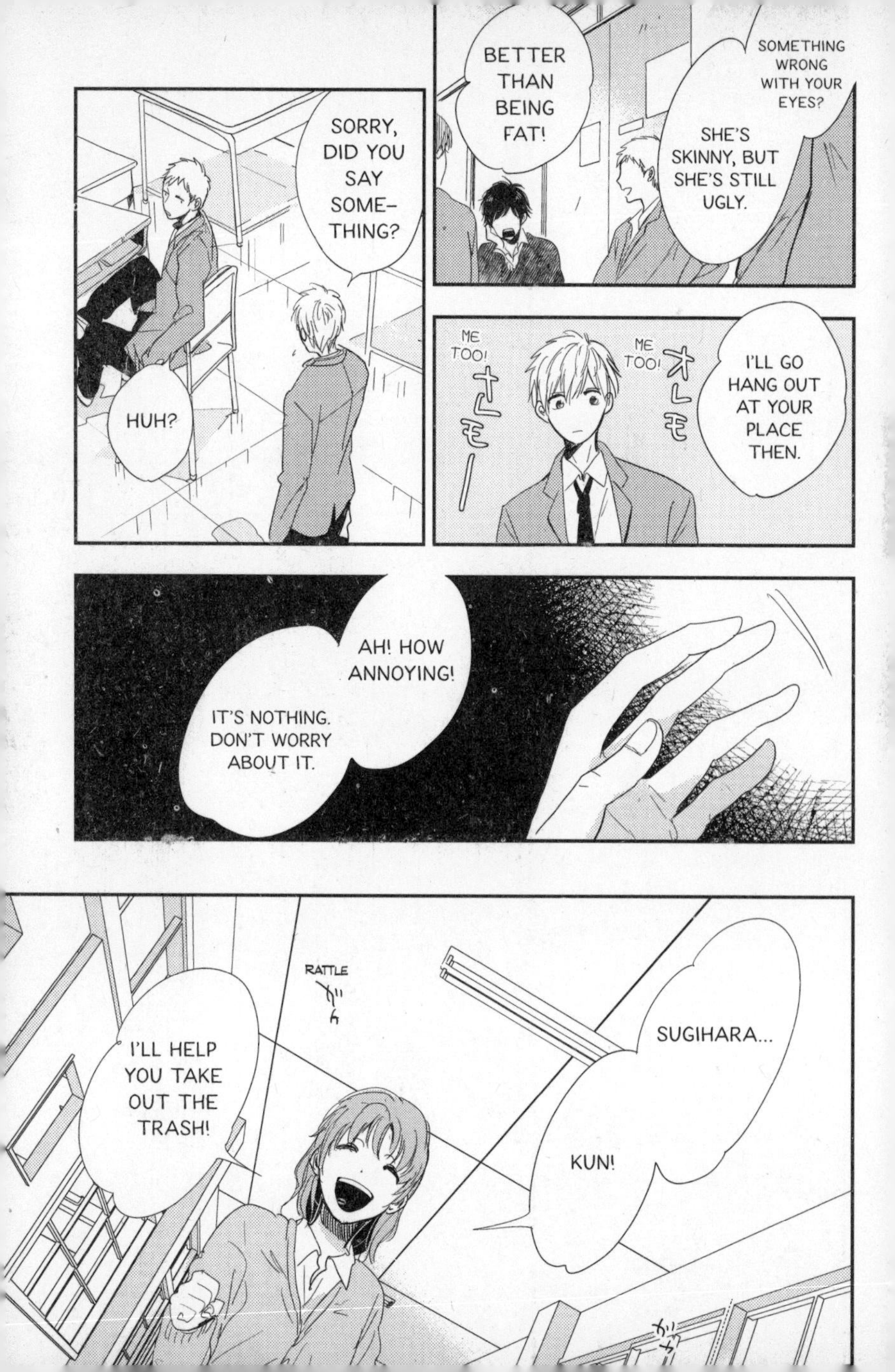
SOMETHING WRONG WITH YOUR EYES?
SHE'S SKINNY, BUT SHE'S STILL UGLY.
BETTER THAN BEING FAT!
I'LL GO HANG OUT AT YOUR PLACE THEN.
ME TOO! オレモ
ME TOO! オレモー
SORRY, DID YOU SAY SOMETHING?
HUH?
AH! HOW ANNOYING!
IT'S NOTHING. DON'T WORRY ABOUT IT.
SUGIHARA...
KUN!
RATTLE
I'LL HELP YOU TAKE OUT THE TRASH!

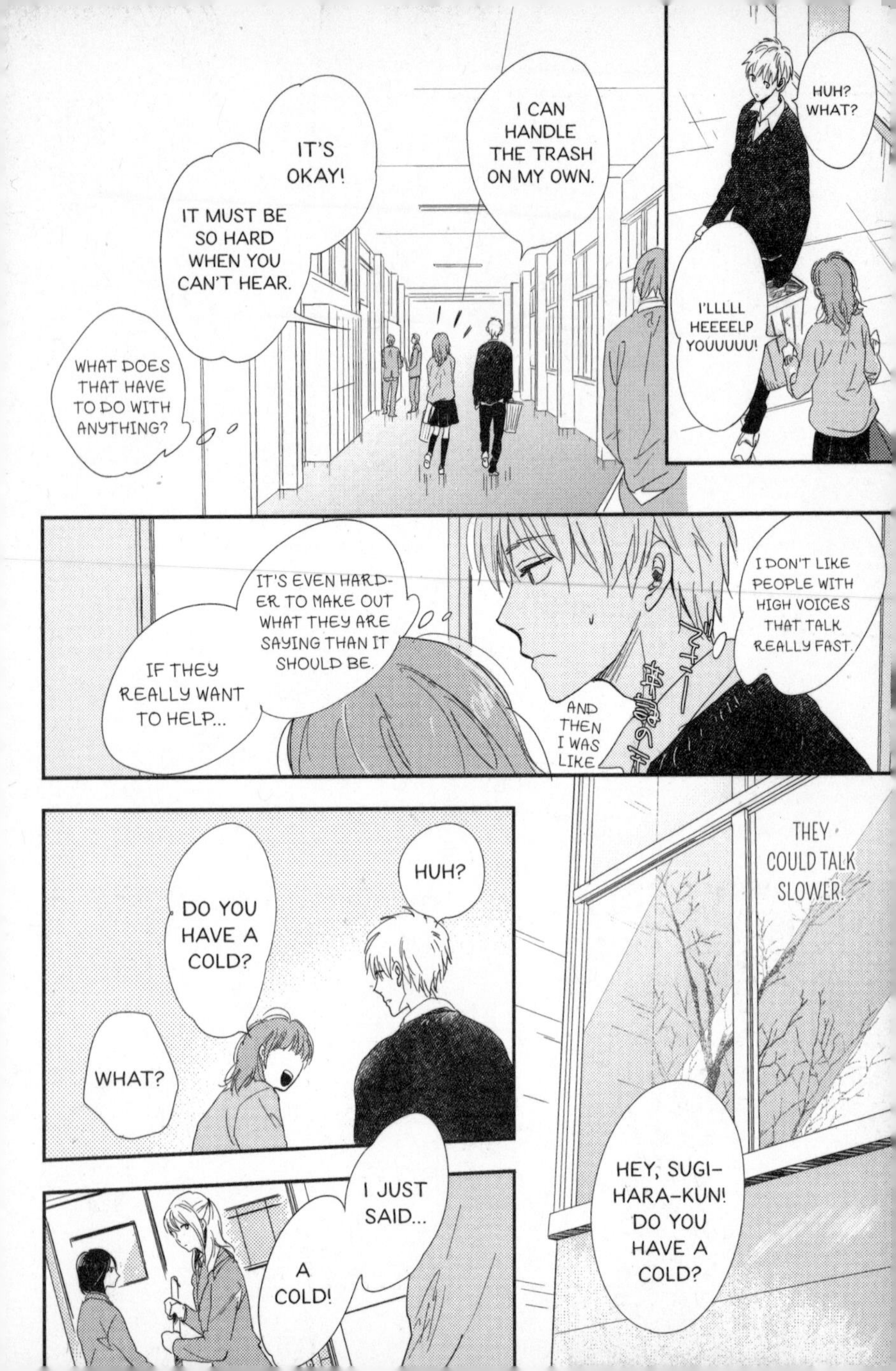
HUH? WHAT?
I'LLLLL HEEEELP YOUUUUU!
I CAN HANDLE THE TRASH ON MY OWN.
IT'S OKAY!
IT MUST BE SO HARD WHEN YOU CAN'T HEAR.
WHAT DOES THAT HAVE TO DO WITH ANYTHING?
I DON'T LIKE PEOPLE WITH HIGH VOICES THAT TALK REALLY FAST.
AND THEN I WAS LIKE
IT'S EVEN HARDER TO MAKE OUT WHAT THEY ARE SAYING THAN IT SHOULD BE.
IF THEY REALLY WANT TO HELP...
THEY COULD TALK SLOWER.
HEY, SUGI-HARA-KUN! DO YOU HAVE A COLD?
HUH?
DO YOU HAVE A COLD?
WHAT?
I JUST SAID...
A COLD!

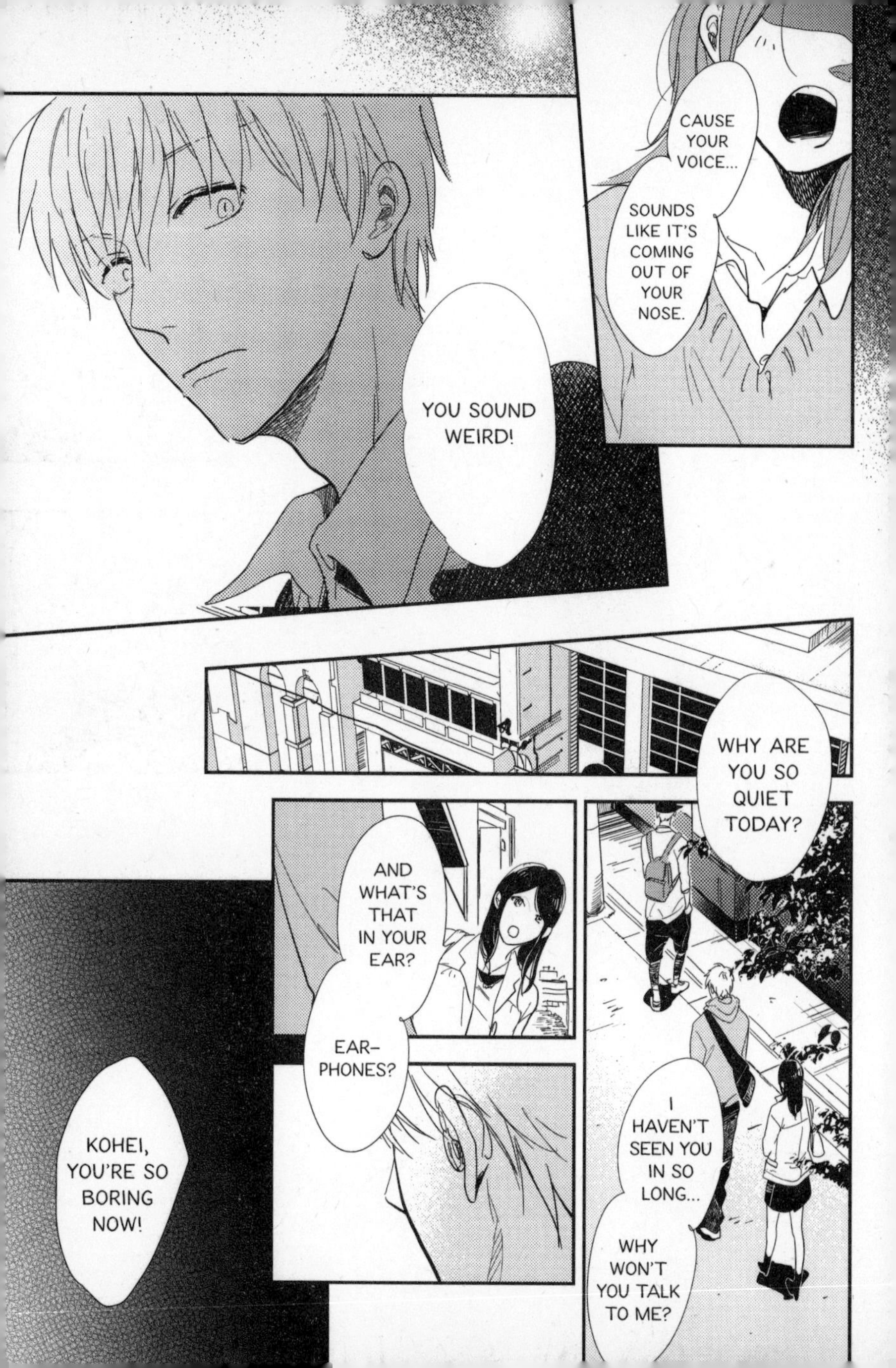
CAUSE YOUR VOICE...
SOUNDS LIKE IT'S COMING OUT OF YOUR NOSE.
YOU SOUND WEIRD!
WHY ARE YOU SO QUIET TODAY?
I HAVEN'T SEEN YOU IN SO LONG...
WHY WON'T YOU TALK TO ME?
AND WHAT'S THAT IN YOUR EAR?
EAR-PHONES?
KOHEI, YOU'RE SO BORING NOW!

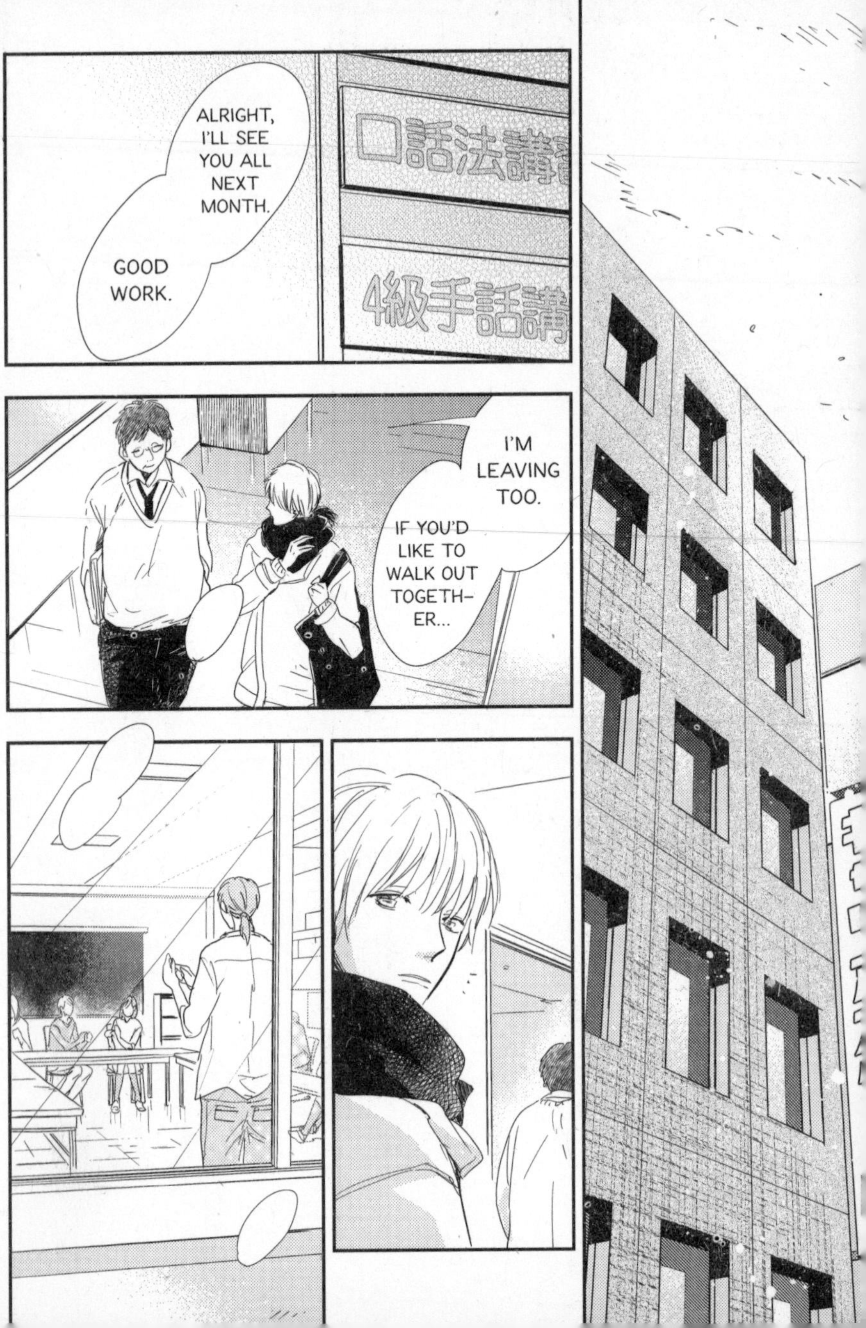
口話法講
4級手話講
ALRIGHT, I'LL SEE YOU ALL NEXT MONTH.
GOOD WORK.
I'M LEAVING TOO.
IF YOU'D LIKE TO WALK OUT TOGETH-ER...

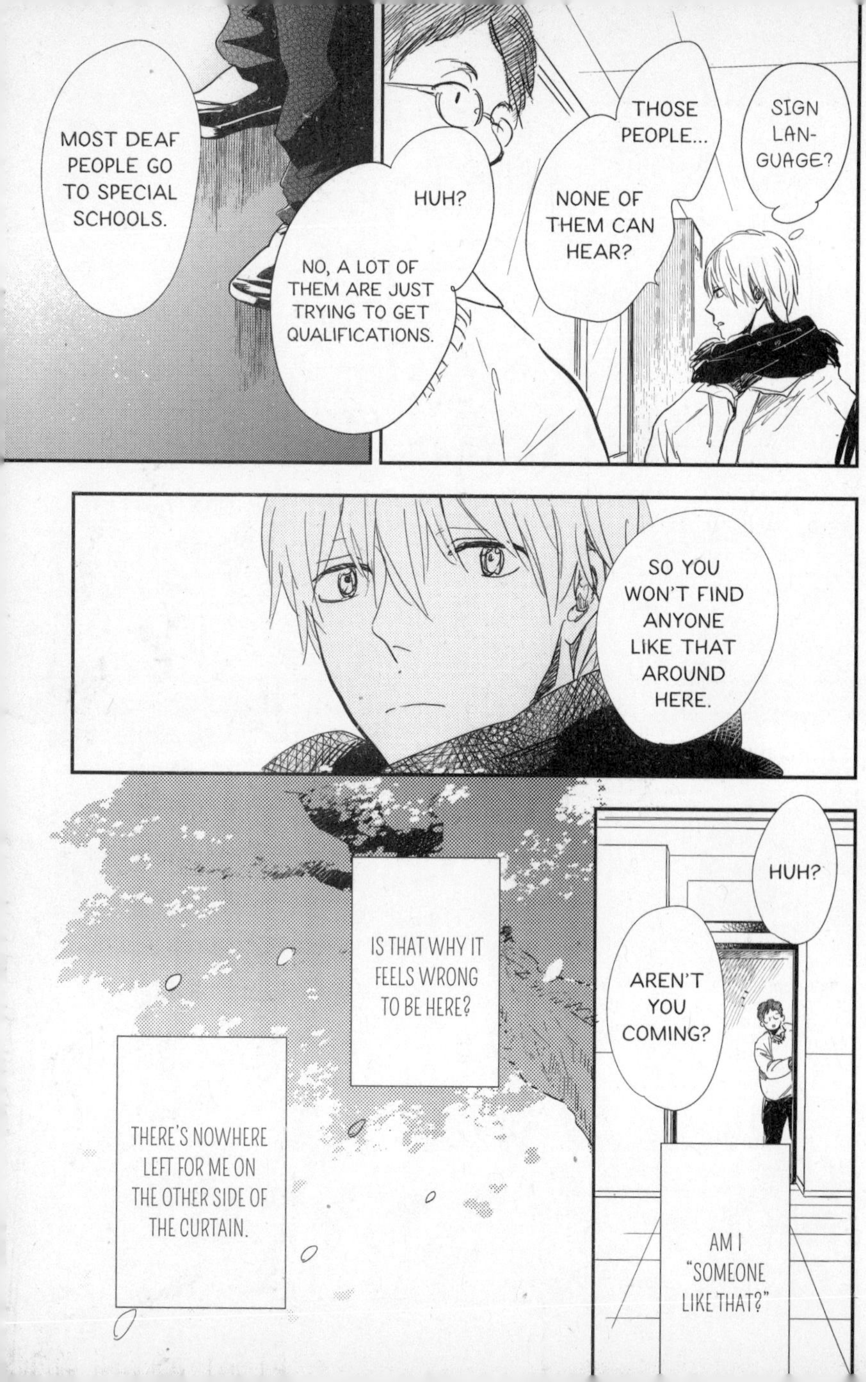
SIGN LAN-GUAGE?
THOSE PEOPLE...
NONE OF THEM CAN HEAR?
HUH?
NO, A LOT OF THEM ARE JUST TRYING TO GET QUALIFICATIONS.
MOST DEAF PEOPLE GO TO SPECIAL SCHOOLS.
SO YOU WON'T FIND ANYONE LIKE THAT AROUND HERE.
HUH?
AREN'T YOU COMING?
AM I "SOMEONE LIKE THAT?"
IS THAT WHY IT FEELS WRONG TO BE HERE?
THERE'S NOWHERE LEFT FOR ME ON THE OTHER SIDE OF THE CURTAIN.

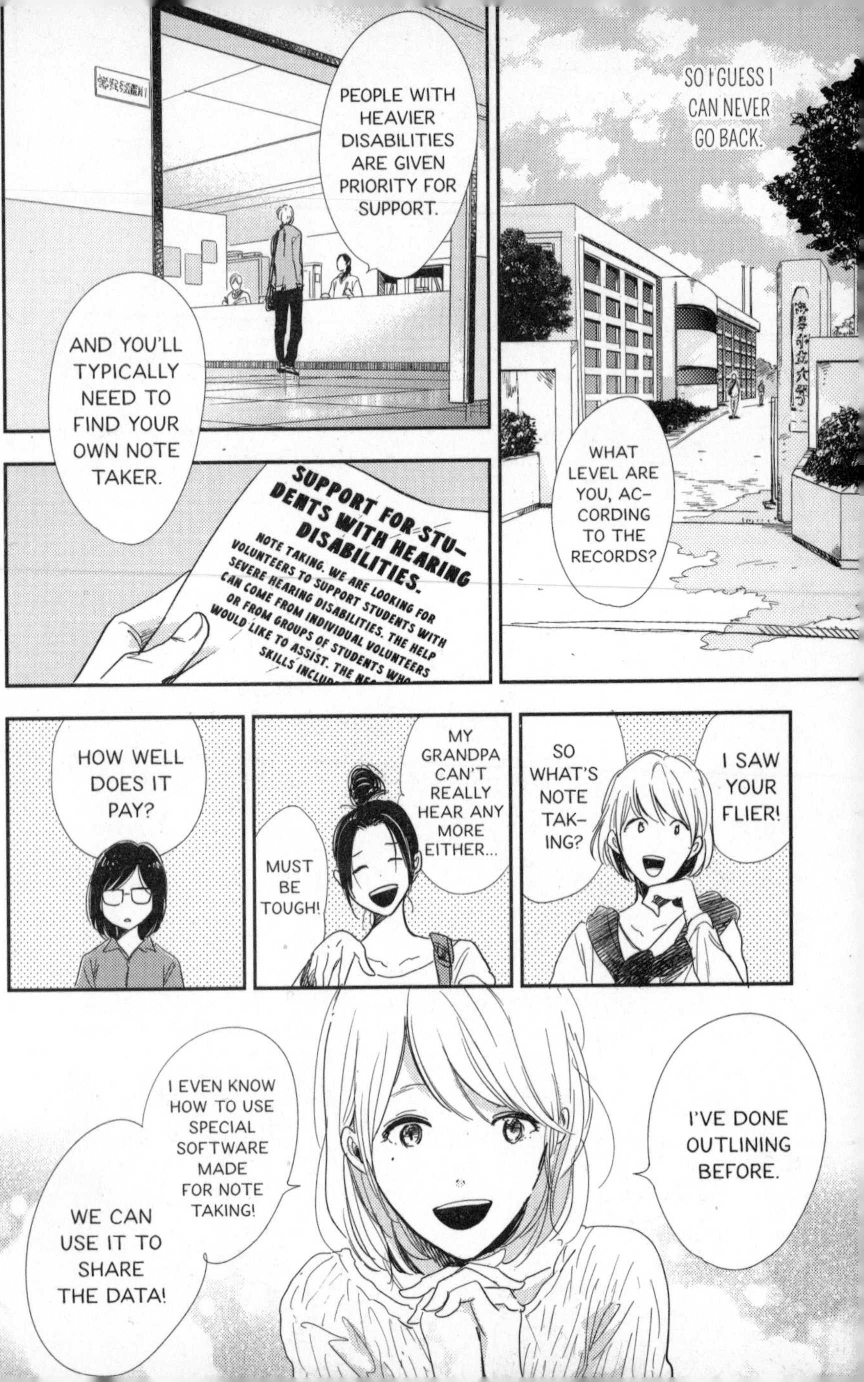
SO I GUESS I CAN NEVER GO BACK.
WHAT LEVEL ARE YOU, AC-CORDING TO THE RECORDS?
PEOPLE WITH HEAVIER DISABILITIES ARE GIVEN PRIORITY FOR SUPPORT.
AND YOU'LL TYPICALLY NEED TO FIND YOUR OWN NOTE TAKER.
SUPPORT FOR STU-DENTS WITH HEARING DISABILITIES.
NOTE TAKING. WE ARE LOOKING FOR VOLUNTEERS TO SUPPORT STUDENTS WITH SEVERE HEARING DISABILITIES. THE HELP CAN COME FROM INDIVIDUAL VOLUNTEERS OR FROM GROUPS OF STUDENTS WHO WOULD LIKE TO ASSIST. THE
I SAW YOUR FLIER!
SO WHAT'S NOTE TAK-ING?
MY GRANDPA CAN'T REALLY HEAR ANY MORE EITHER...
MUST BE TOUGH!
HOW WELL DOES IT PAY?
I'VE DONE OUTLINING BEFORE.
I EVEN KNOW HOW TO USE SPECIAL SOFTWARE MADE FOR NOTE TAKING!
WE CAN USE IT TO SHARE THE DATA!

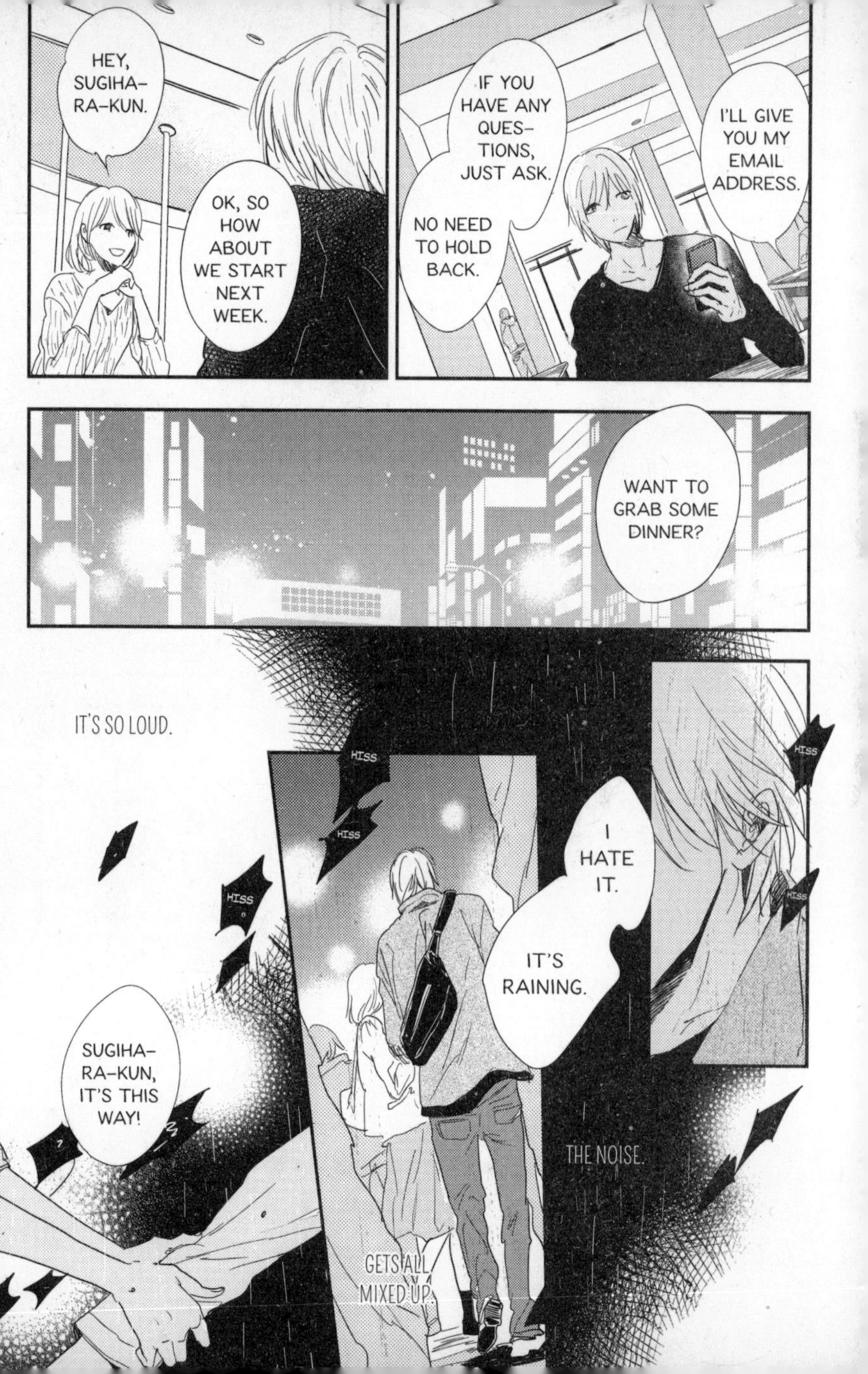
I'LL GIVE YOU MY EMAIL ADDRESS.
IF YOU HAVE ANY QUES-TIONS, JUST ASK.
NO NEED TO HOLD BACK.
HEY, SUGIHA-RA-KUN.
OK, SO HOW ABOUT WE START NEXT WEEK.
WANT TO GRAB SOME DINNER?
HISS
I HATE IT.
IT'S RAINING.
HISS
THE NOISE.
HISS
HISS
IT'S SO LOUD.
HISS
GETS ALL MIXED UP.
SUGIHA-RA-KUN, IT'S THIS WAY!

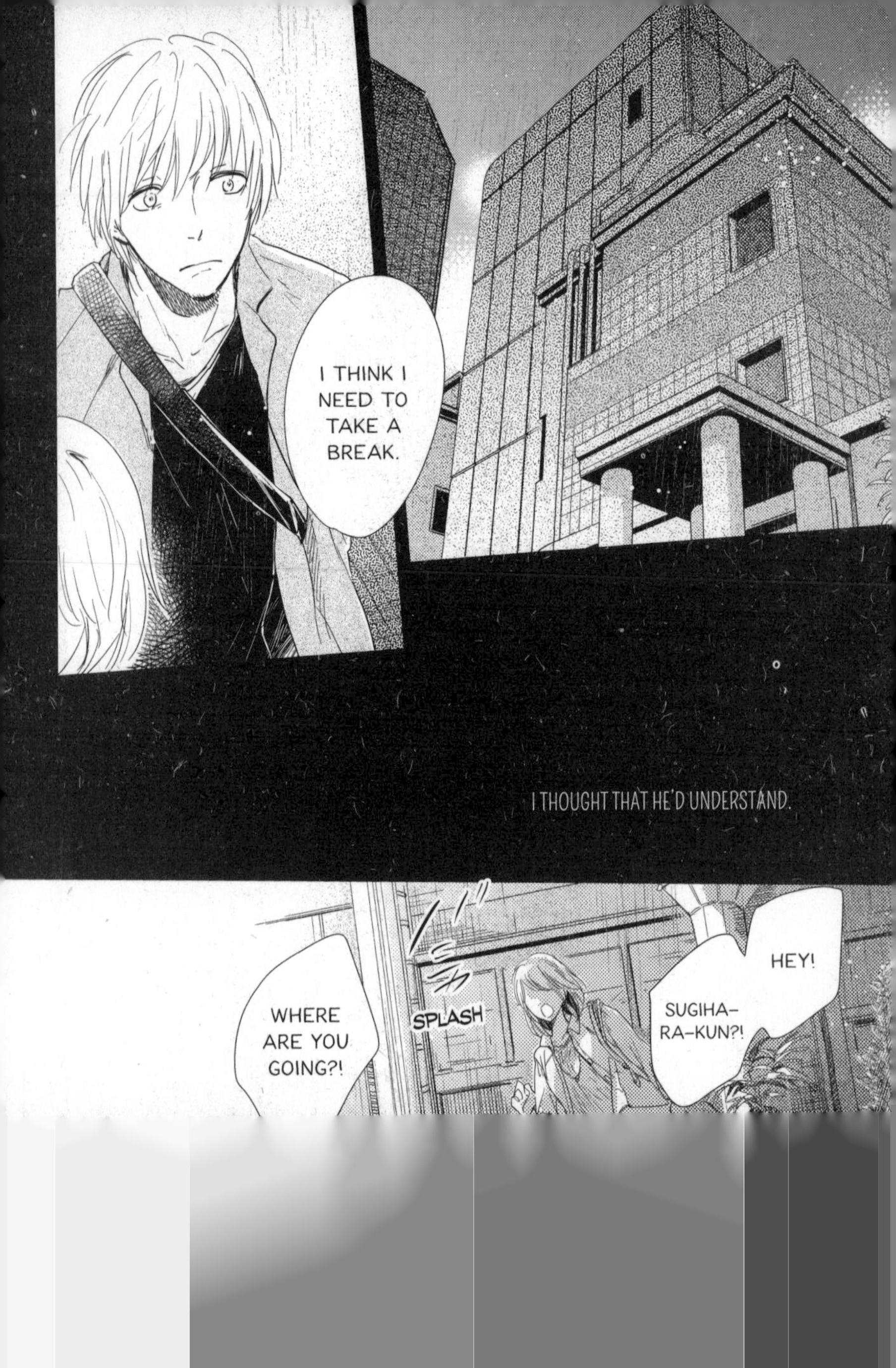
I THINK I NEED TO TAKE A BREAK.
I THOUGHT THAT HE'D UNDERSTAND.
HEY!
SUGIHA-RA-KUN?!
SPLASH
WHERE ARE YOU GOING?!

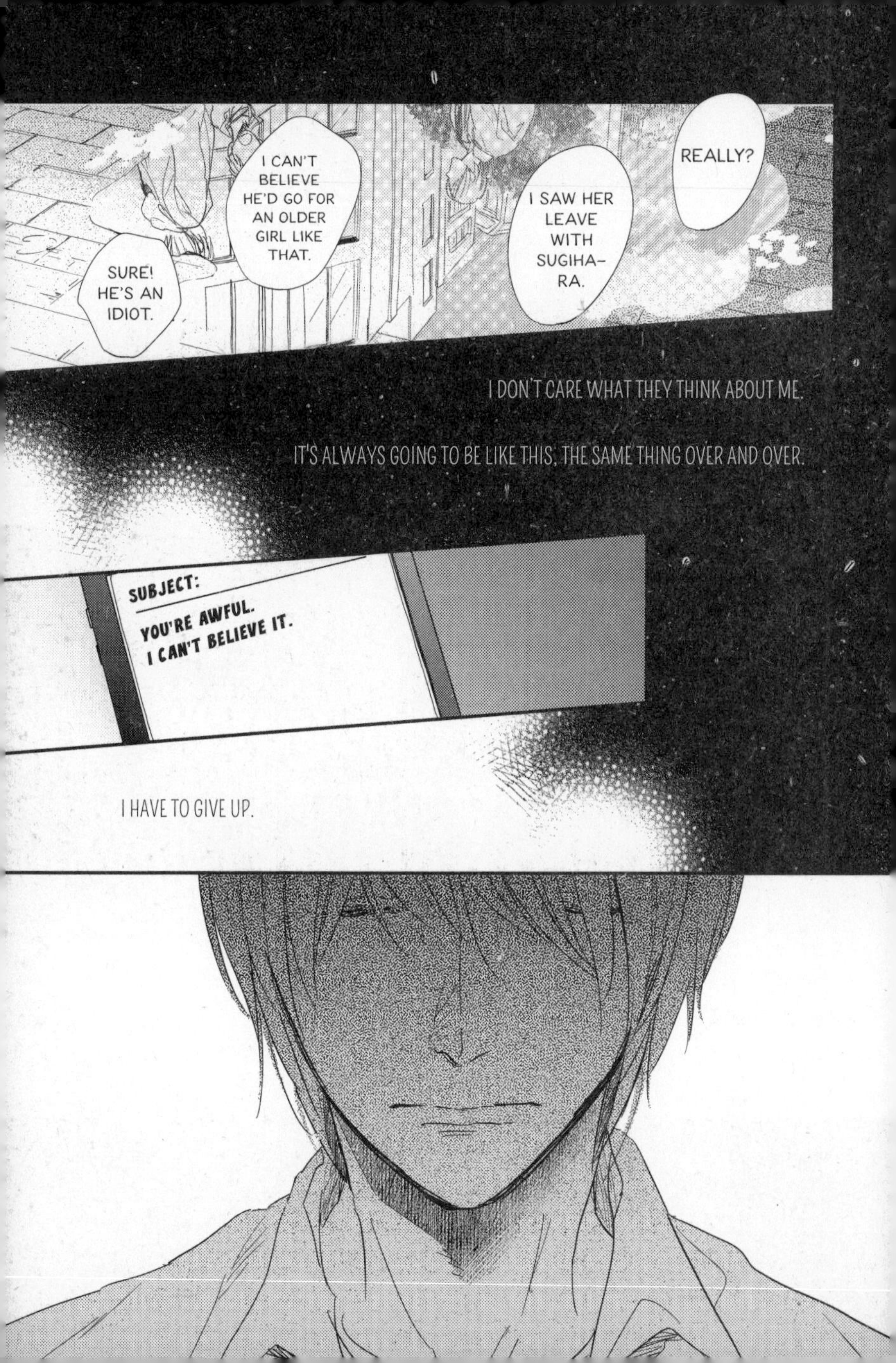
REALLY?
I SAW HER LEAVE WITH SUGIHA-RA.
I CAN'T BELIEVE HE'D GO FOR AN OLDER GIRL LIKE THAT.
SURE! HE'S AN IDIOT.
I DON'T CARE WHAT THEY THINK ABOUT ME.
IT'S ALWAYS GOING TO BE LIKE THIS, THE SAME THING OVER AND OVER.
SUBJECT:
YOU'RE AWFUL. I CAN'T BELIEVE IT.
I HAVE TO GIVE UP.

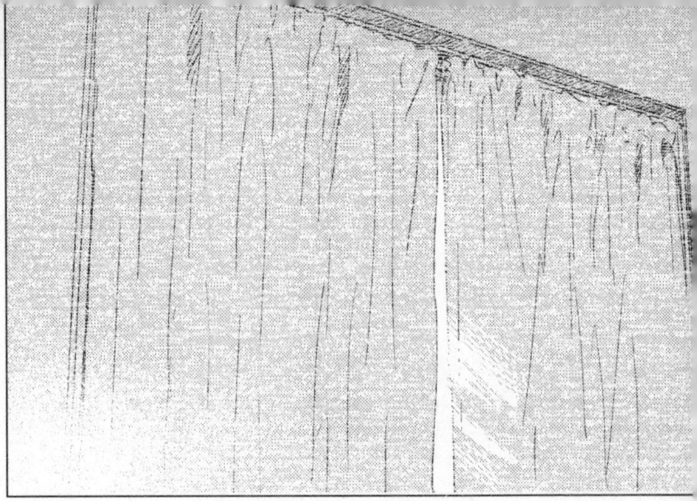

I'LL NEVER GET OUT OF THAT ROOM AGAIN.

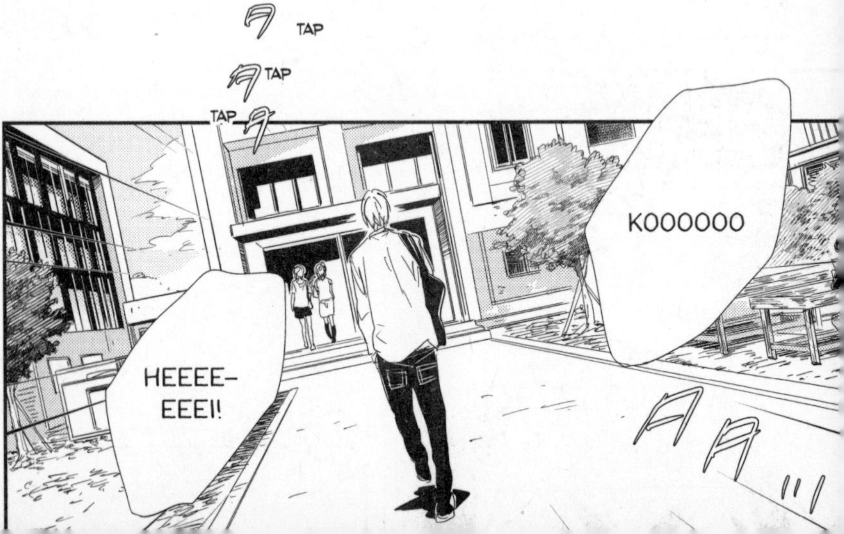
TAP
TAP
TAP
KOOOOOO
HEEEE-EEEI!

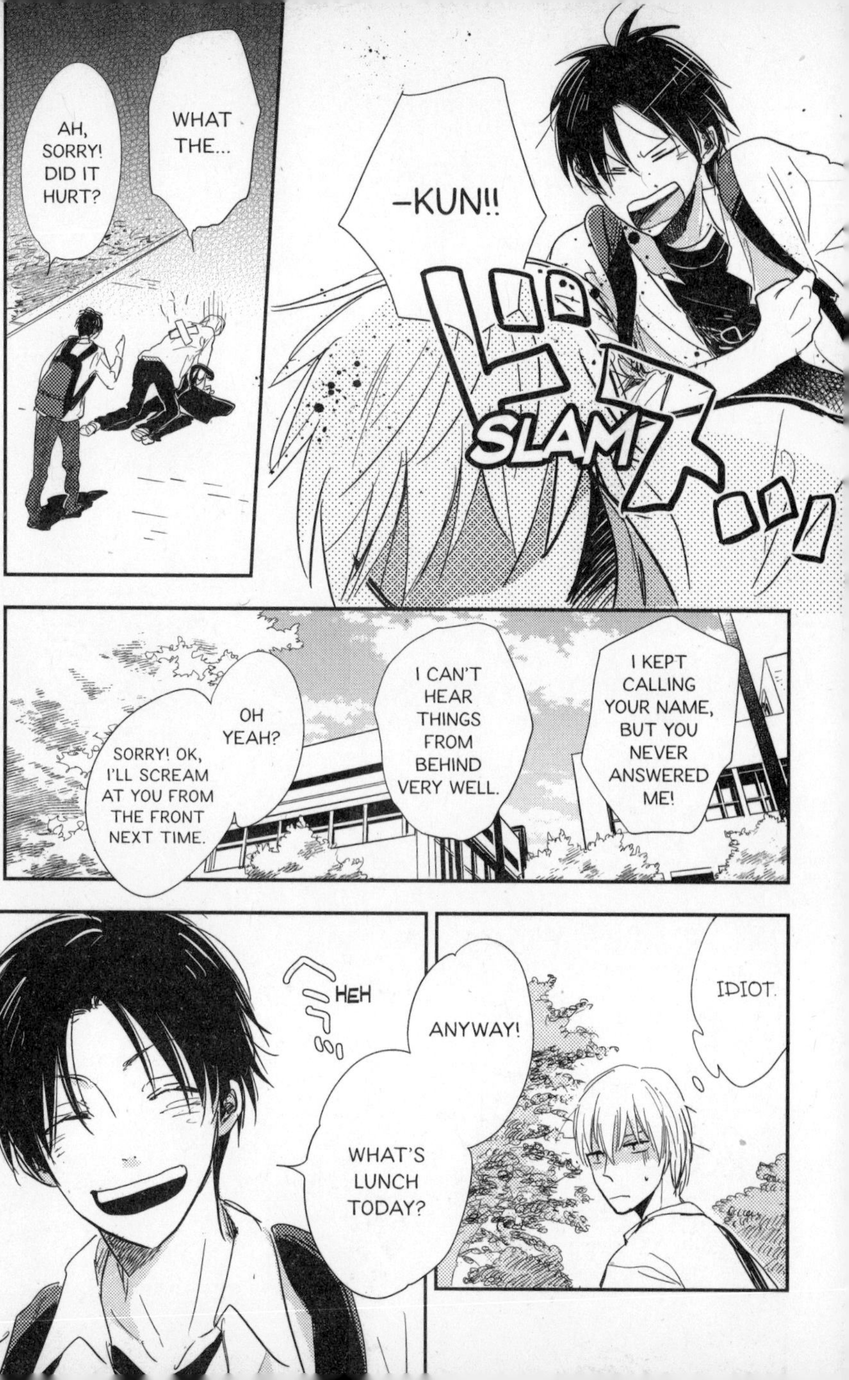
-KUN!!
SLAM
WHAT THE...
AH, SORRY! DID IT HURT?
I KEPT CALLING YOUR NAME, BUT YOU NEVER ANSWERED ME!
I CAN'T HEAR THINGS FROM BEHIND VERY WELL.
OH YEAH?
SORRY! OK, I'LL SCREAM AT YOU FROM THE FRONT NEXT TIME.
IDIOT.
HEH
ANYWAY!
WHAT'S LUNCH TODAY?

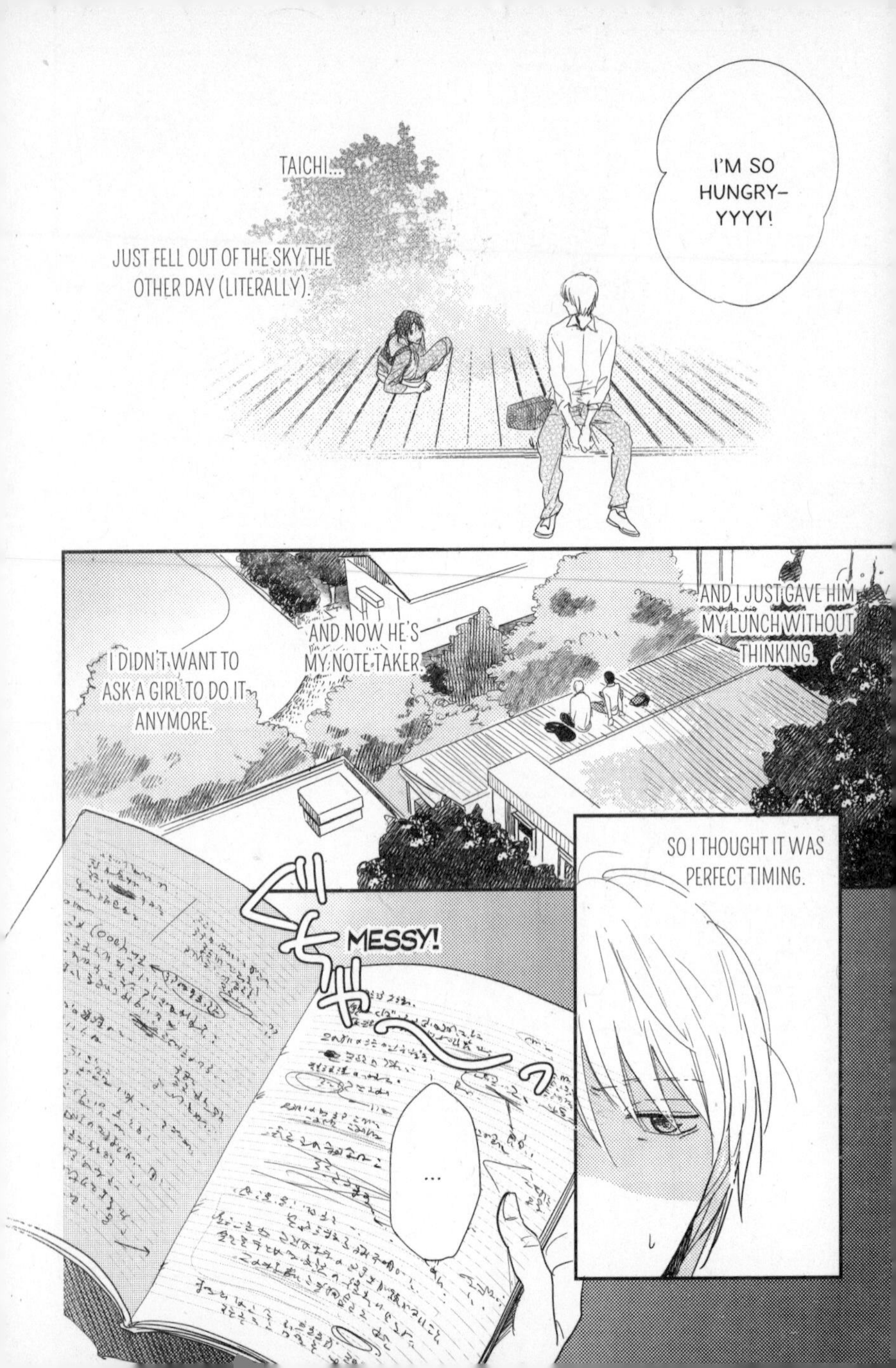
I'M SO HUNGRY–YYYY!
TAICHI...
JUST FELL OUT OF THE SKY THE OTHER DAY (LITERALLY).
AND I JUST GAVE HIM MY LUNCH WITHOUT THINKING.
AND NOW HE'S MY NOTE TAKER.
I DIDN'T WANT TO ASK A GIRL TO DO IT ANYMORE.
SO I THOUGHT IT WAS PERFECT TIMING.
...
MESSY!

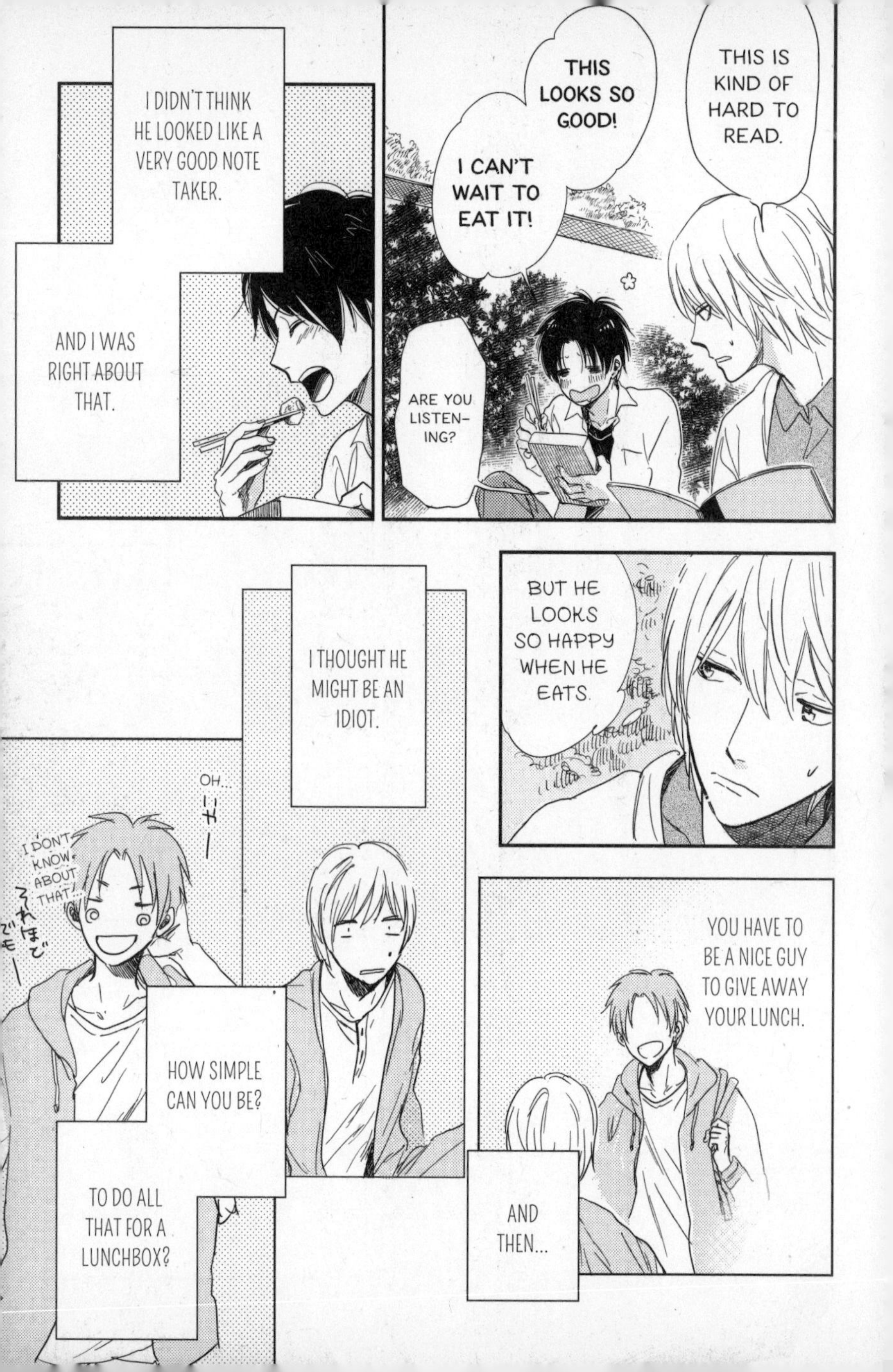
THIS IS KIND OF HARD TO READ.
THIS LOOKS SO GOOD!
I CAN'T WAIT TO EAT IT!
ARE YOU LISTENING?
I DIDN'T THINK HE LOOKED LIKE A VERY GOOD NOTE TAKER.
AND I WAS RIGHT ABOUT THAT.
BUT HE LOOKS SO HAPPY WHEN HE EATS.
I THOUGHT HE MIGHT BE AN IDIOT.
YOU HAVE TO BE A NICE GUY TO GIVE AWAY YOUR LUNCH.
AND THEN...
OH...
ほー
I DON'T KNOW ABOUT THAT!
それほどでもー
HOW SIMPLE CAN YOU BE?
TO DO ALL THAT FOR A LUNCHBOX?

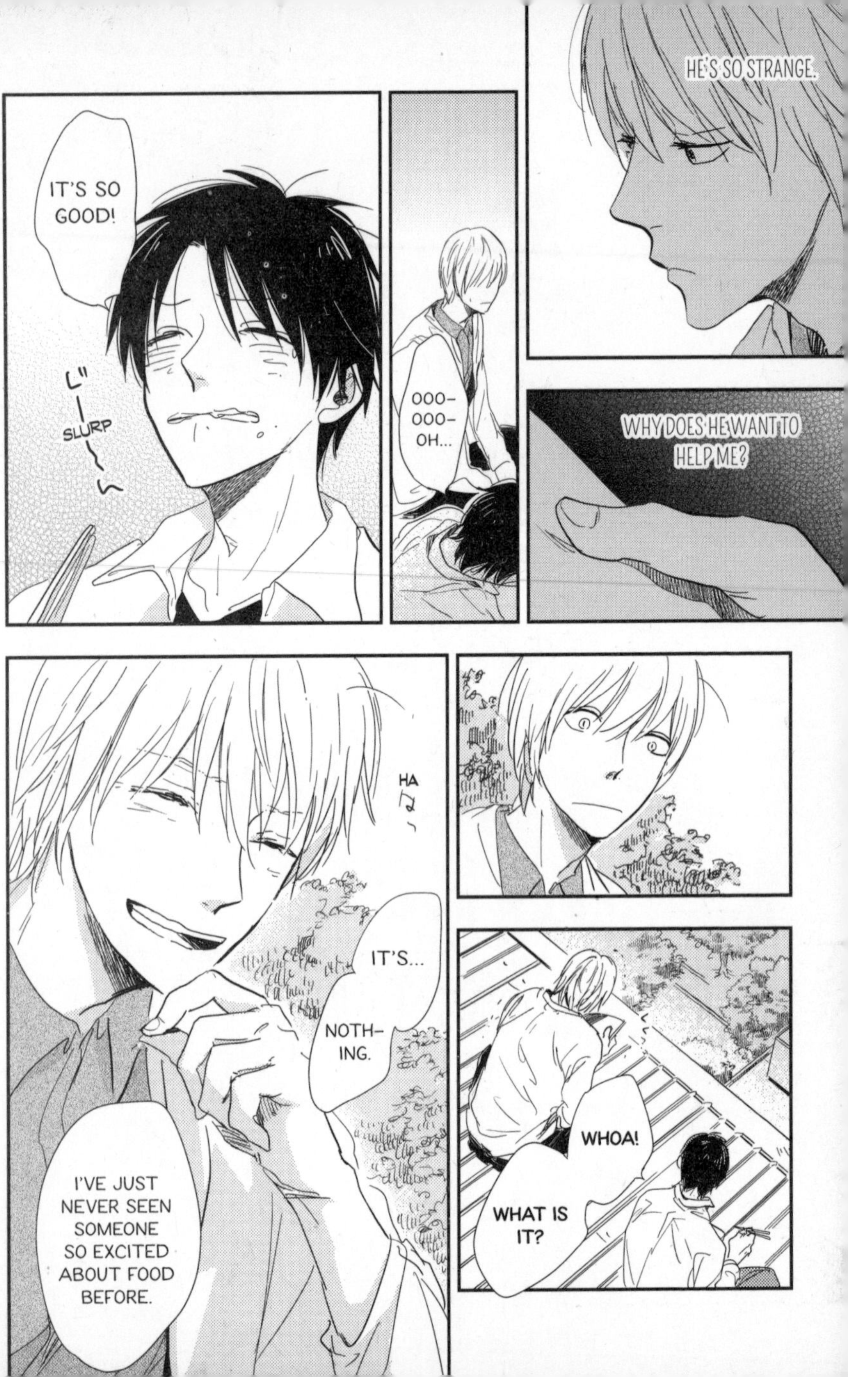
HE'S SO STRANGE.
WHY DOES HE WANT TO HELP ME?
OOO-OOO-OH...
IT'S SO GOOD!
SLURP
WHOA!
WHAT IS IT?
HA
IT'S... NOTHING.
I'VE JUST NEVER SEEN SOMEONE SO EXCITED ABOUT FOOD BEFORE.

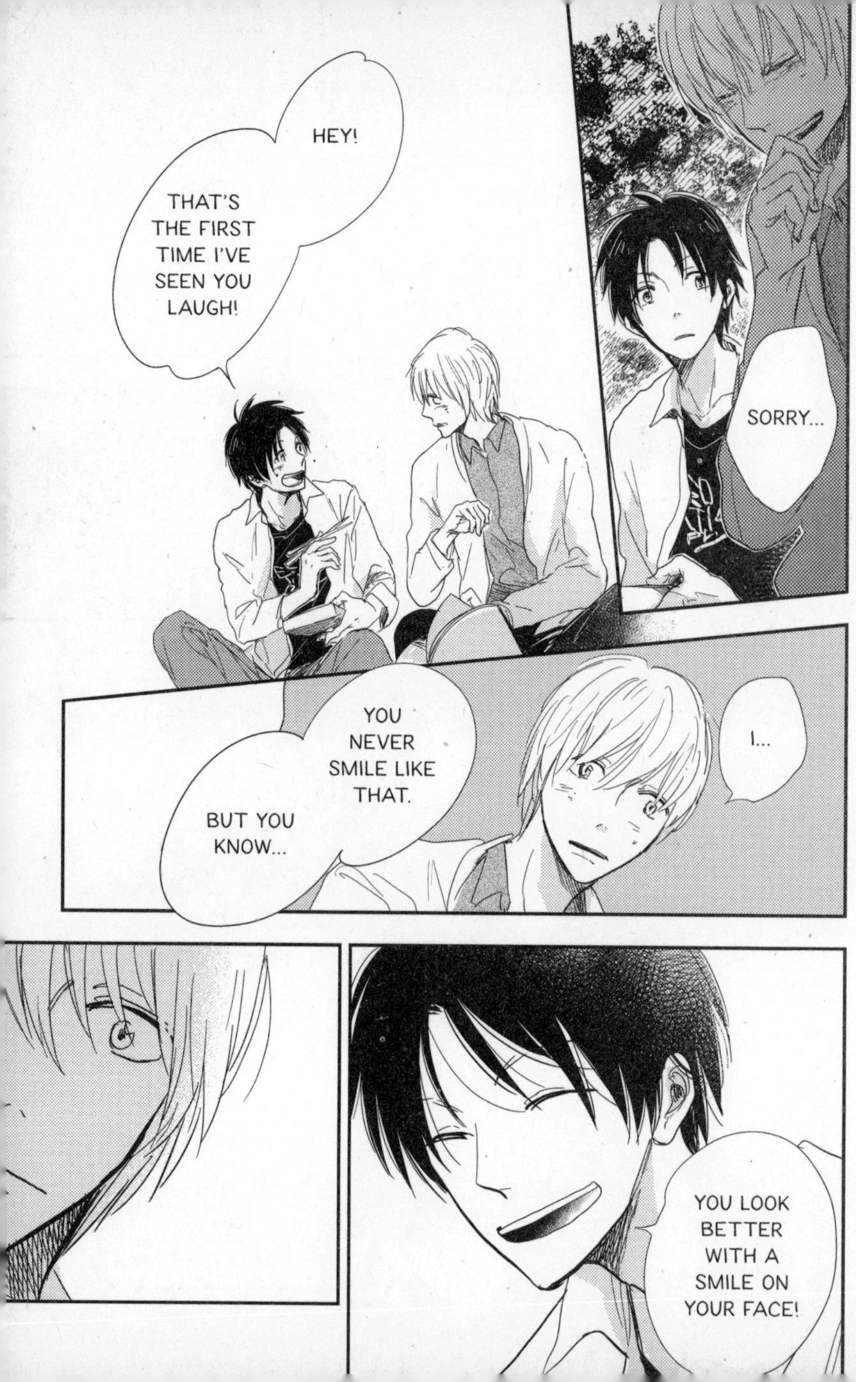
SORRY...
HEY!
THAT'S THE FIRST TIME I'VE SEEN YOU LAUGH!
I...
YOU NEVER SMILE LIKE THAT.
BUT YOU KNOW...
YOU LOOK BETTER WITH A SMILE ON YOUR FACE!

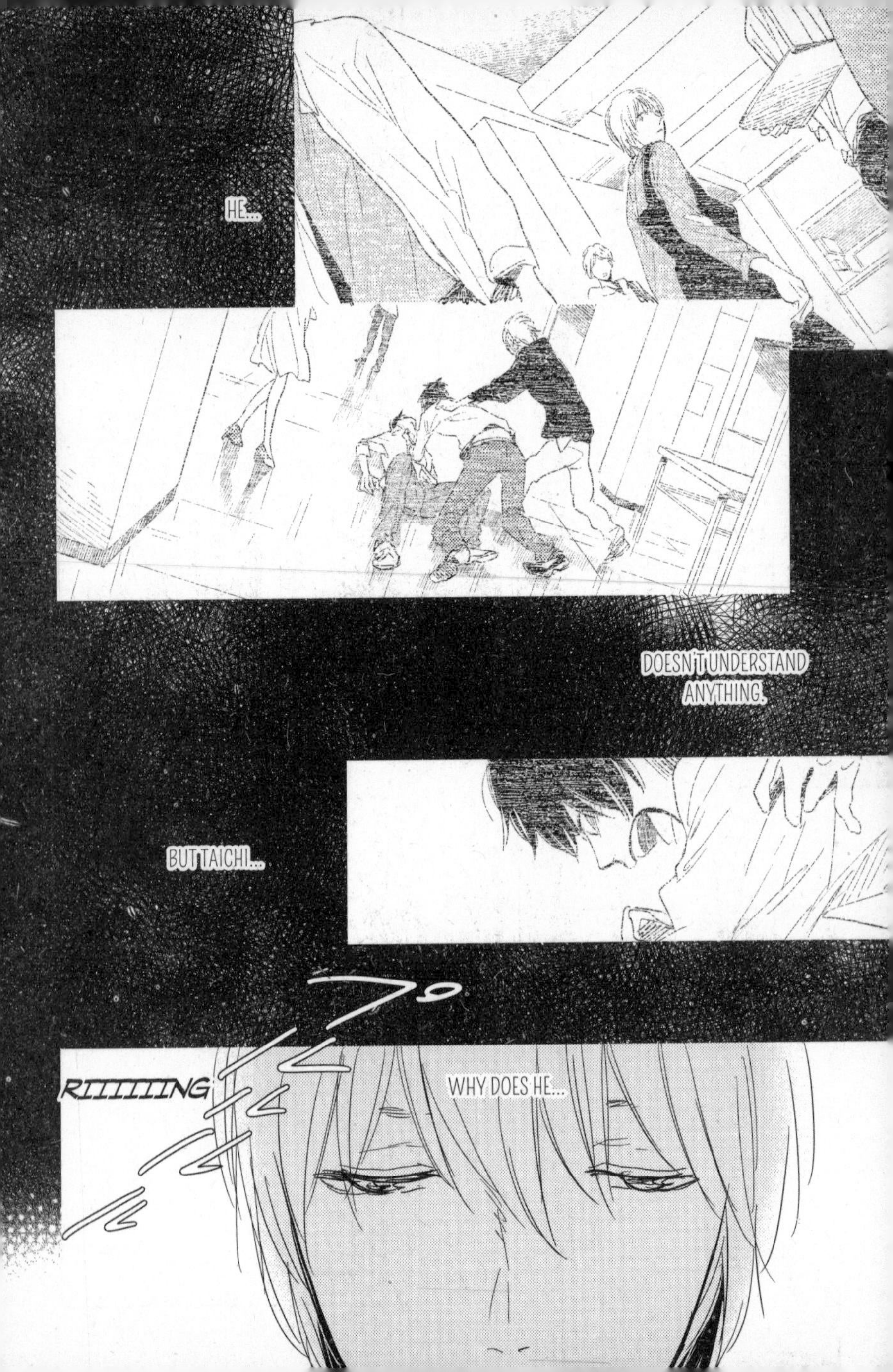
HE...
DOESN'T UNDERSTAND ANYTHING.
BUT TAICHI...
RIIIIIING
WHY DOES HE...

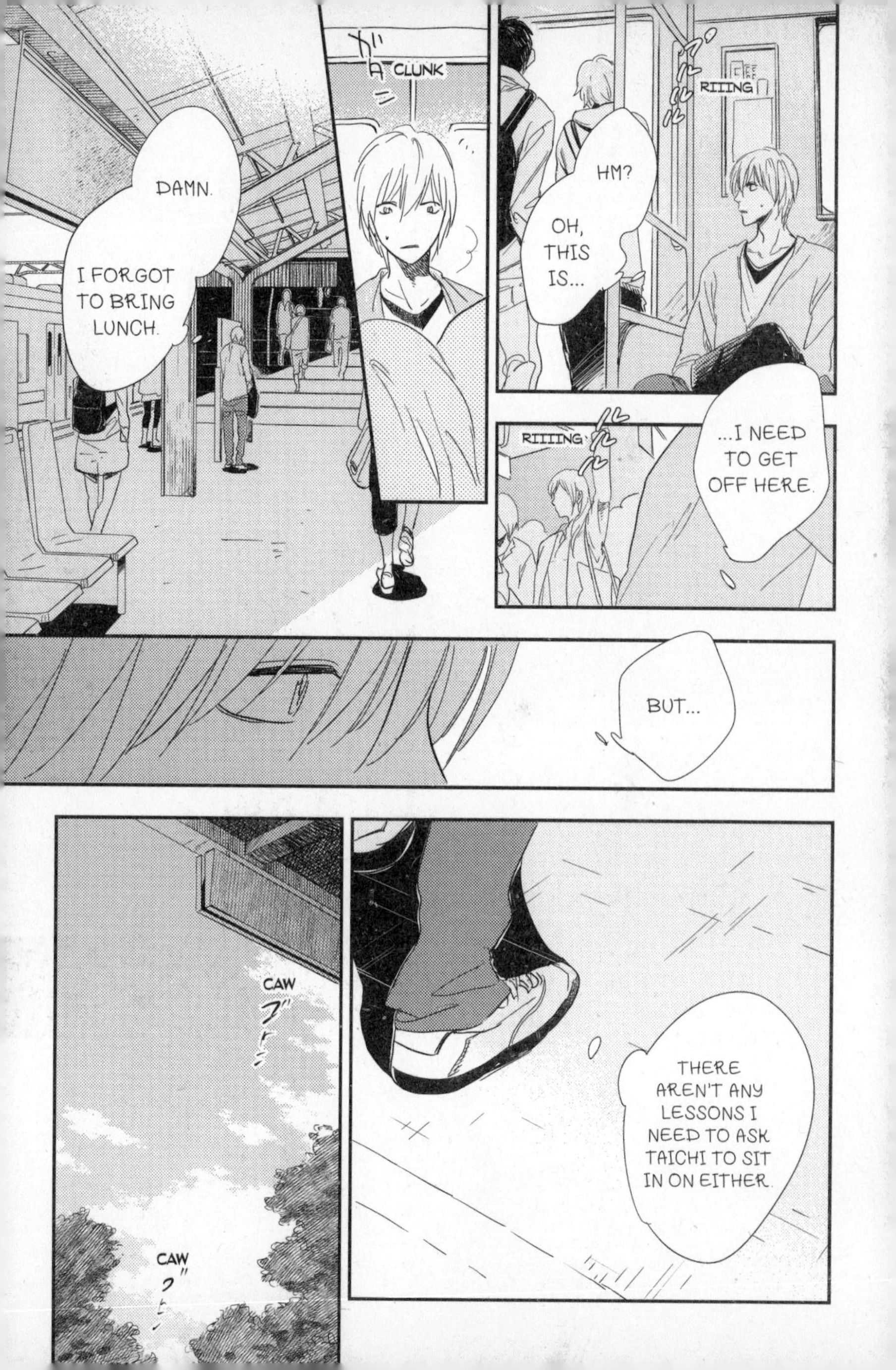
RIIING
HM?
OH, THIS IS...
RIIING
...I NEED TO GET OFF HERE.
CLUNK
DAMN.
I FORGOT TO BRING LUNCH.
BUT...
THERE AREN'T ANY LESSONS I NEED TO ASK TAICHI TO SIT IN ON EITHER.
CAW
CAW

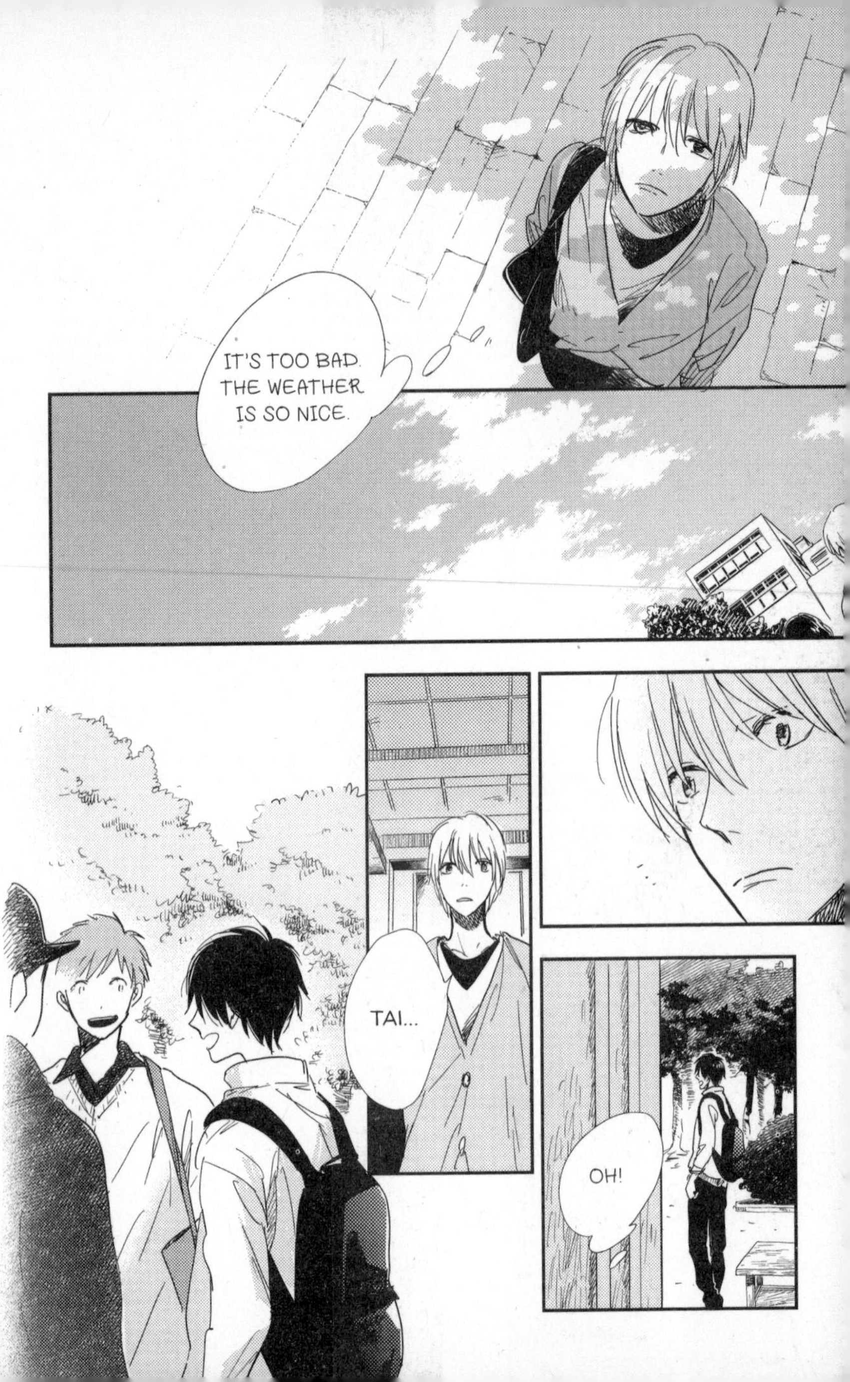
IT'S TOO BAD. THE WEATHER IS SO NICE.
OH!
TAI...

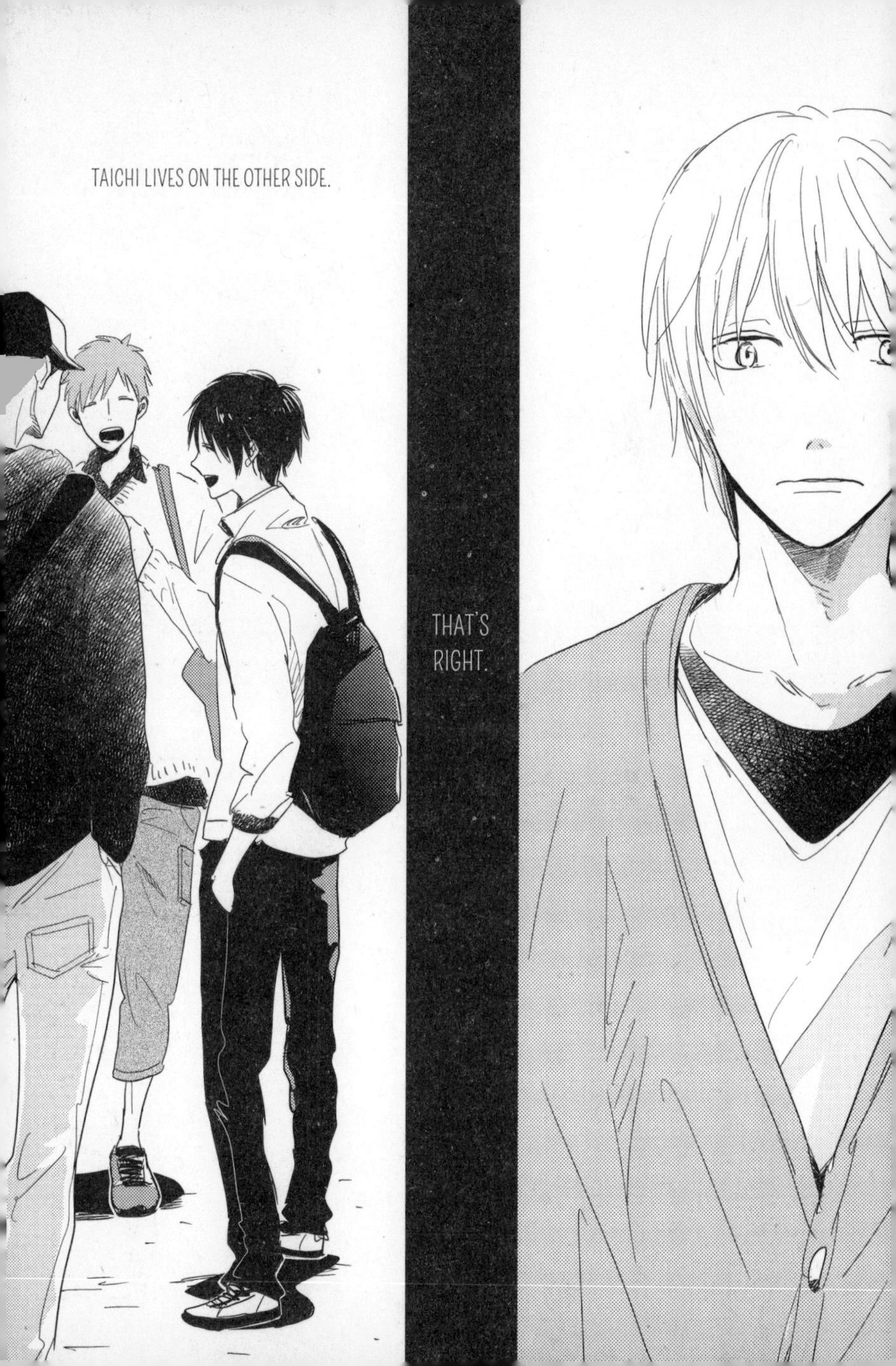
THAT'S RIGHT.
TAICHI LIVES ON THE OTHER SIDE.

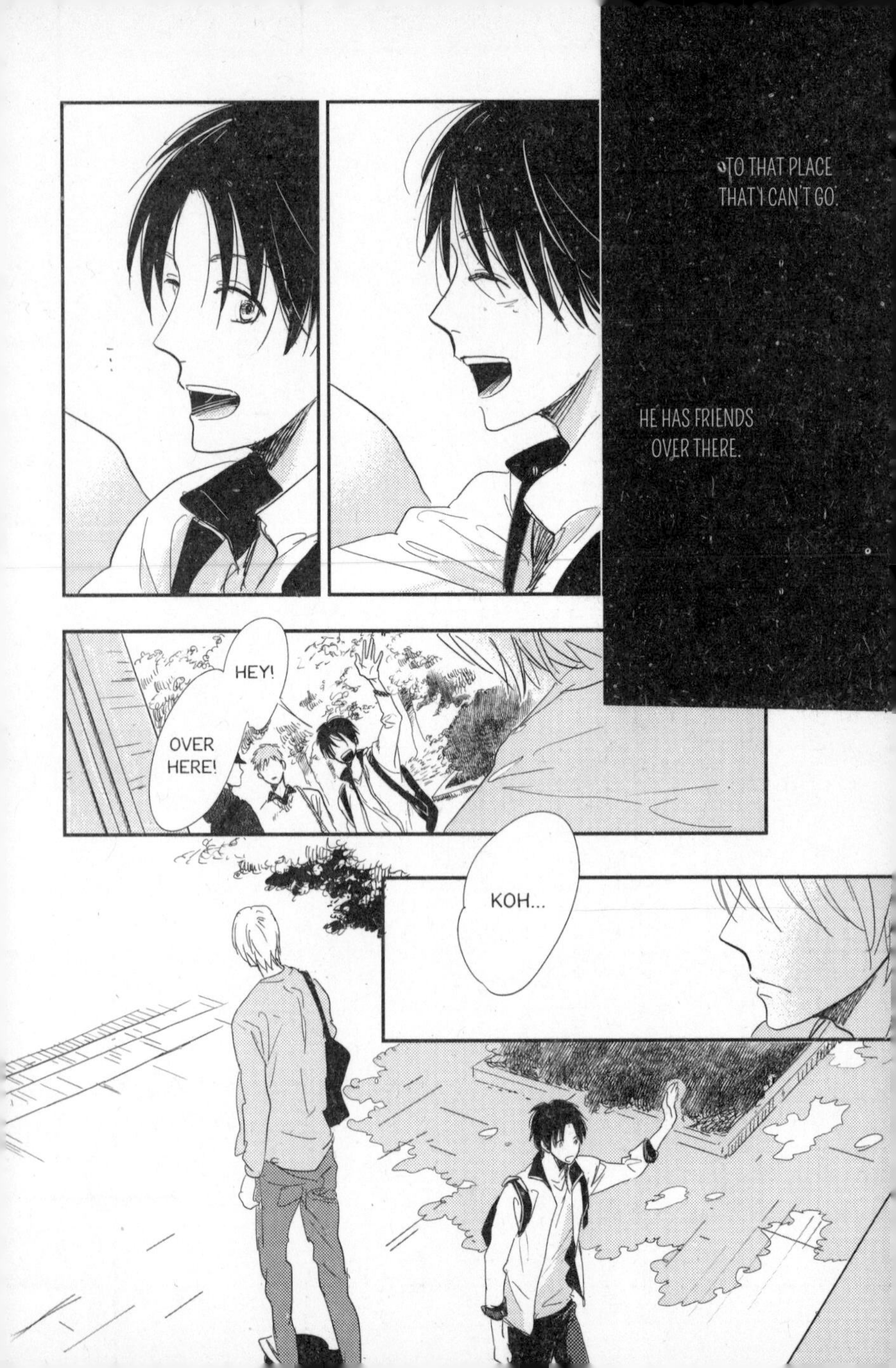
TO THAT PLACE THAT I CAN'T GO.
HE HAS FRIENDS OVER THERE.
HEY!
OVER HERE!
KOH...

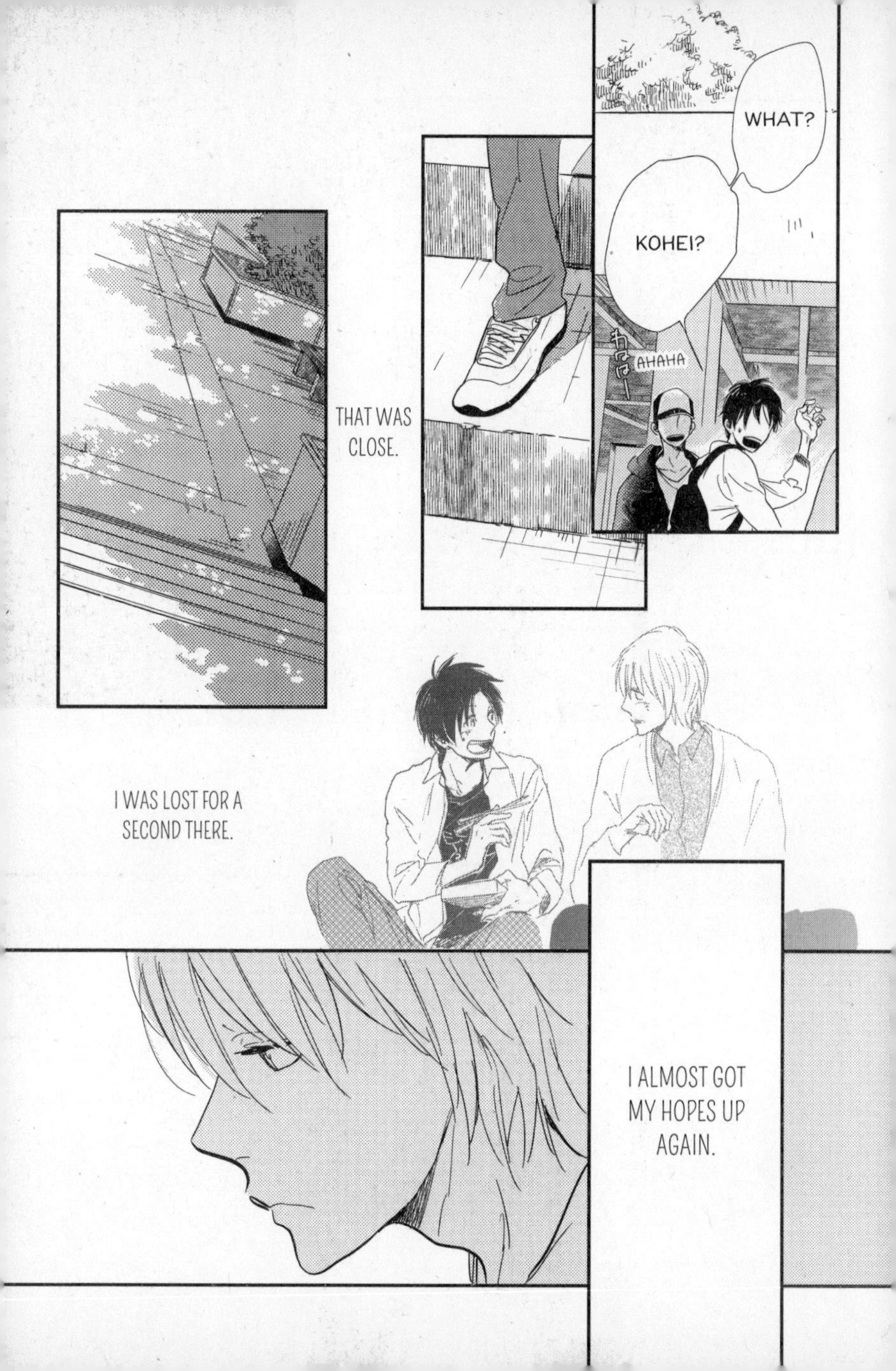
WHAT?
KOHEI?
AHAHA
THAT WAS CLOSE.
I WAS LOST FOR A SECOND THERE.
I ALMOST GOT MY HOPES UP AGAIN.

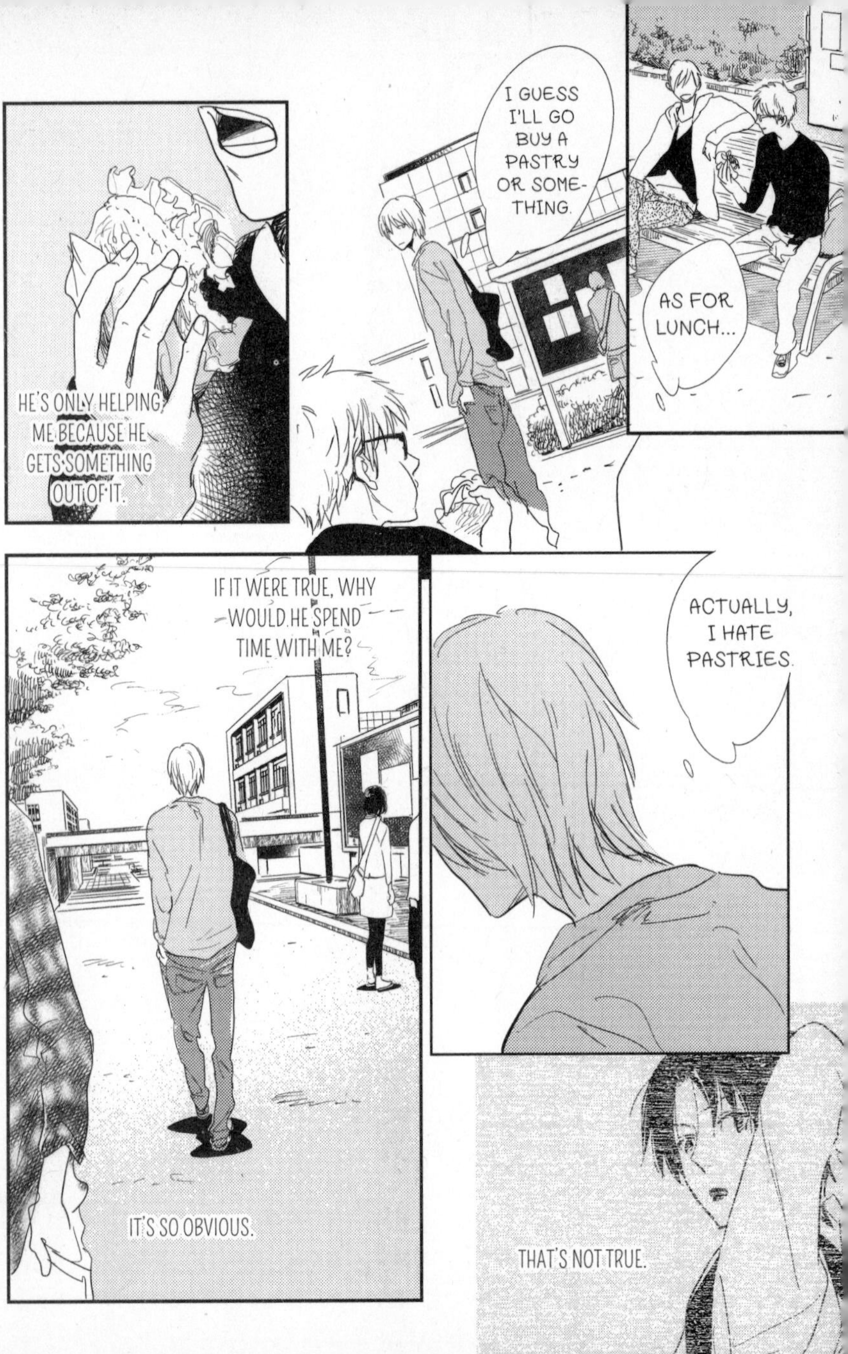
AS FOR LUNCH...
I GUESS I'LL GO BUY A PASTRY OR SOMETHING.
HE'S ONLY HELPING ME BECAUSE HE GETS SOMETHING OUT OF IT.
ACTUALLY, I HATE PASTRIES.
THAT'S NOT TRUE.
IF IT WERE TRUE, WHY WOULD HE SPEND TIME WITH ME?
IT'S SO OBVIOUS.

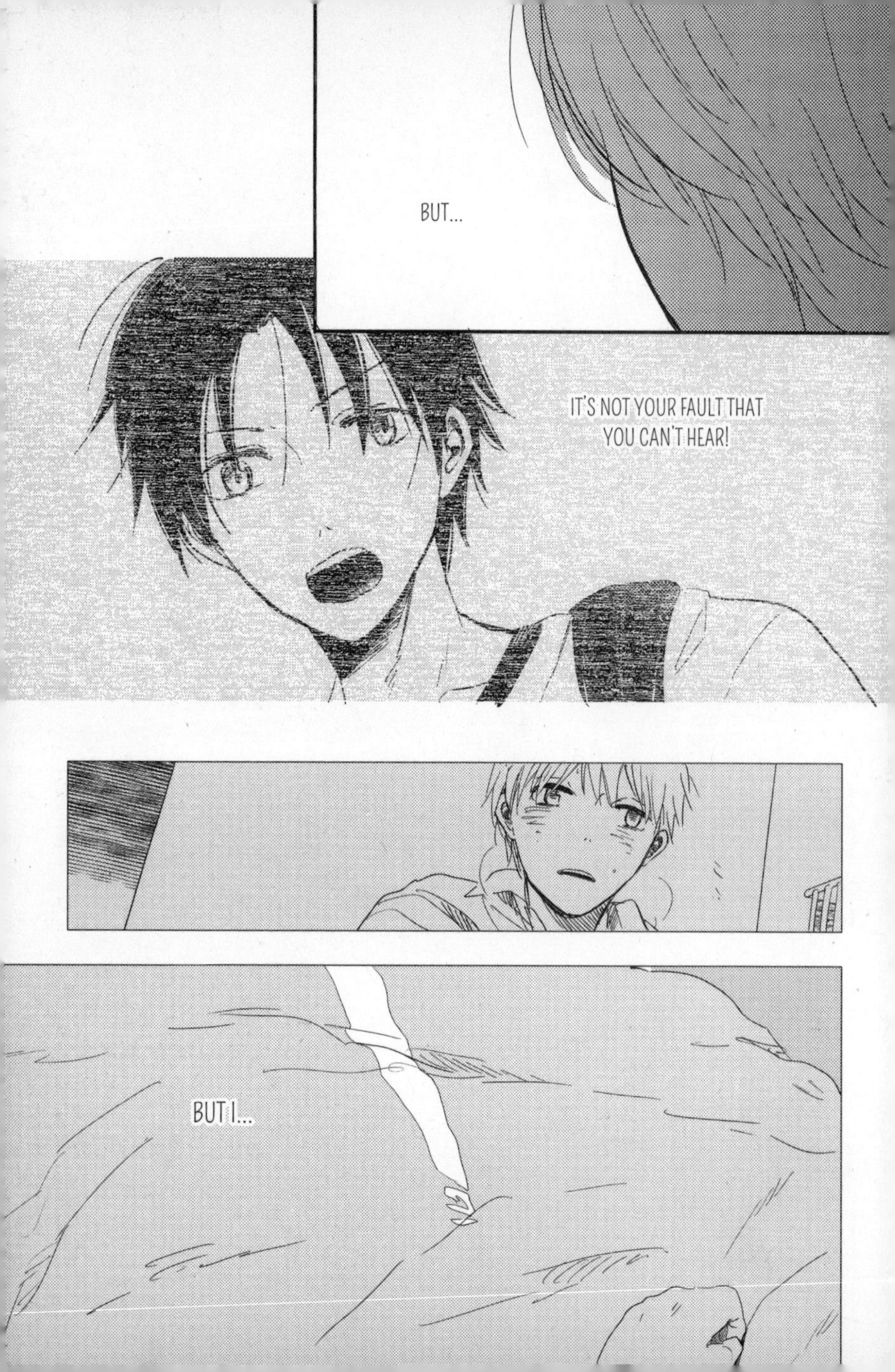
BUT...
IT'S NOT YOUR FAULT THAT YOU CAN'T HEAR!
BUT I...

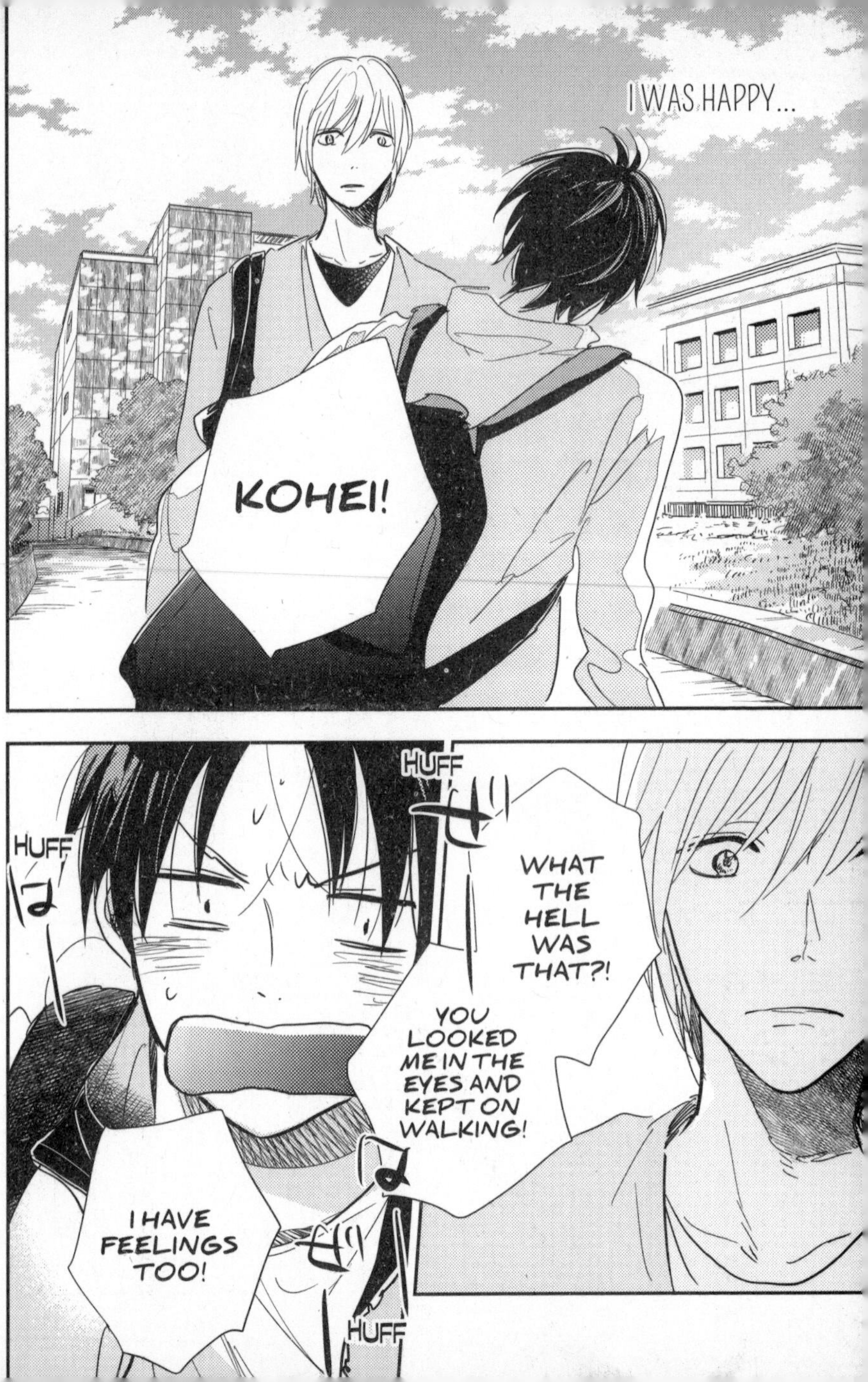
I WAS HAPPY...
KOHEI!
HUFF
WHAT THE HELL WAS THAT?!
YOU LOOKED ME IN THE EYES AND KEPT ON WALKING!
HUFF
I HAVE FEELINGS TOO!
HUFF

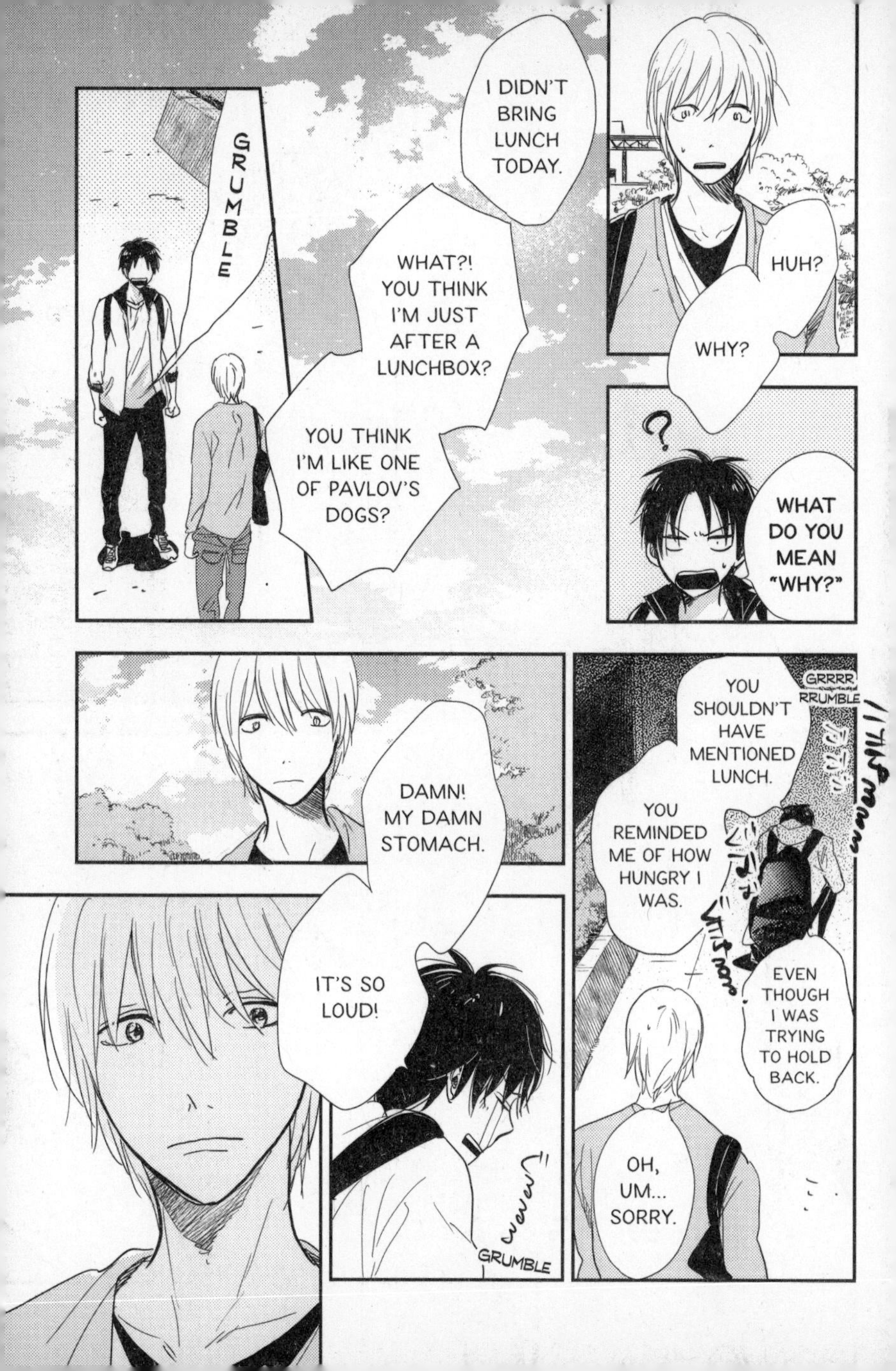
I DIDN'T BRING LUNCH TODAY.
HUH?
WHY?
WHAT DO YOU MEAN "WHY?"
GRUMBLE
WHAT?! YOU THINK I'M JUST AFTER A LUNCHBOX?
YOU THINK I'M LIKE ONE OF PAVLOV'S DOGS?
GRRRR RRUMBLE
YOU SHOULDN'T HAVE MENTIONED LUNCH.
YOU REMINDED ME OF HOW HUNGRY I WAS.
EVEN THOUGH I WAS TRYING TO HOLD BACK.
OH, UM... SORRY.
DAMN! MY DAMN STOMACH.
IT'S SO LOUD!
GRUMBLE

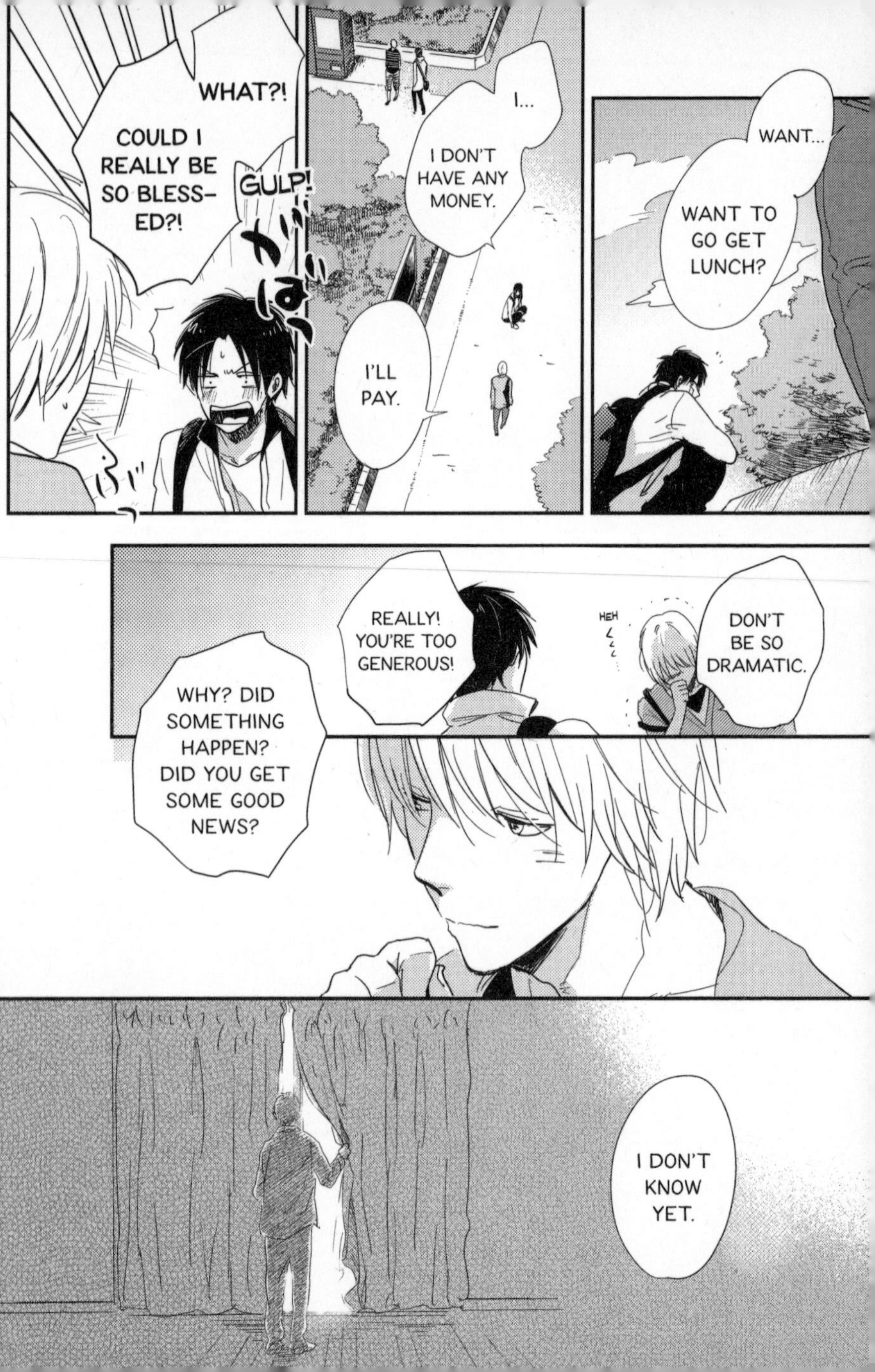
WANT...
WANT TO GO GET LUNCH?
I...
I DON'T HAVE ANY MONEY.
I'LL PAY.
WHAT?!
COULD I REALLY BE SO BLESS-ED?!
GULP!
DON'T BE SO DRAMATIC.
HEH
REALLY! YOU'RE TOO GENEROUS!
WHY? DID SOMETHING HAPPEN? DID YOU GET SOME GOOD NEWS?
I DON'T KNOW YET.

i hear
the
sunspot

i hear the sunspot

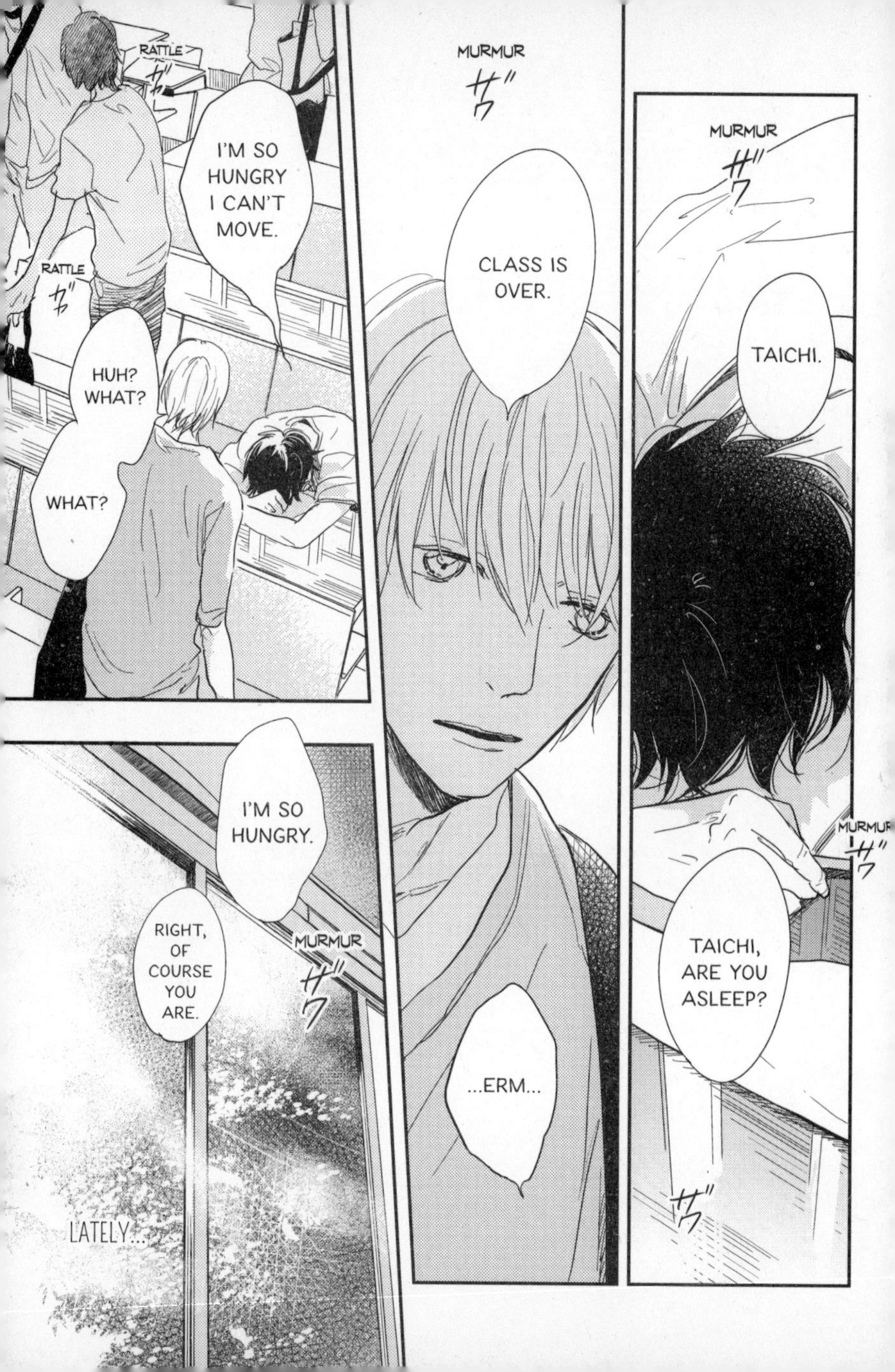
MURMUR
TAICHI.
MURMUR
TAICHI, ARE YOU ASLEEP?
MURMUR
CLASS IS OVER.
...ERM...
RATTLE
I'M SO HUNGRY I CAN'T MOVE.
RATTLE
HUH? WHAT?
WHAT?
I'M SO HUNGRY.
RIGHT, OF COURSE YOU ARE.
MURMUR
LATELY...

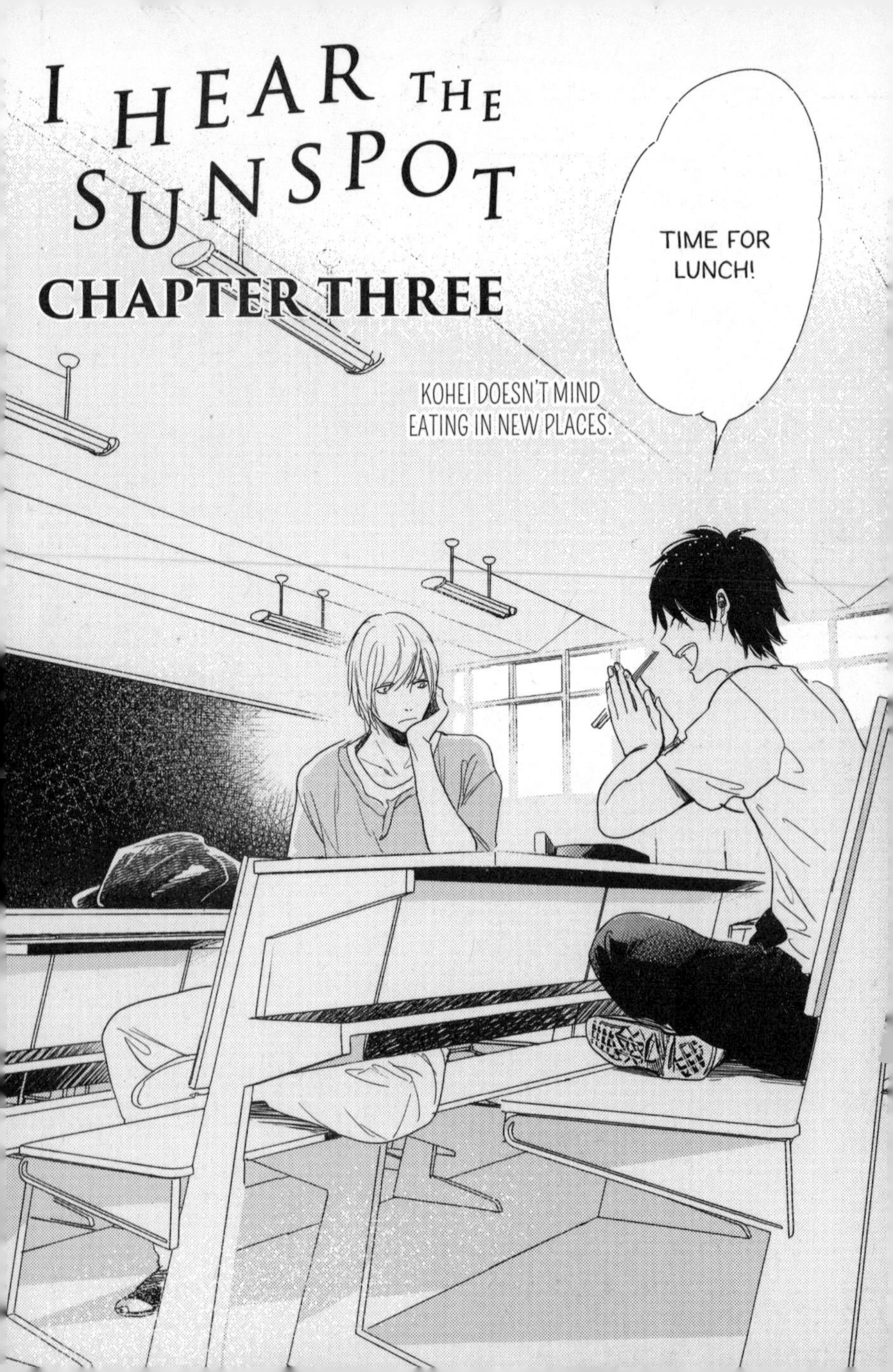
TIME FOR LUNCH!
I HEAR THE SUNSPOT
CHAPTER THREE
KOHEI DOESN'T MIND EATING IN NEW PLACES.

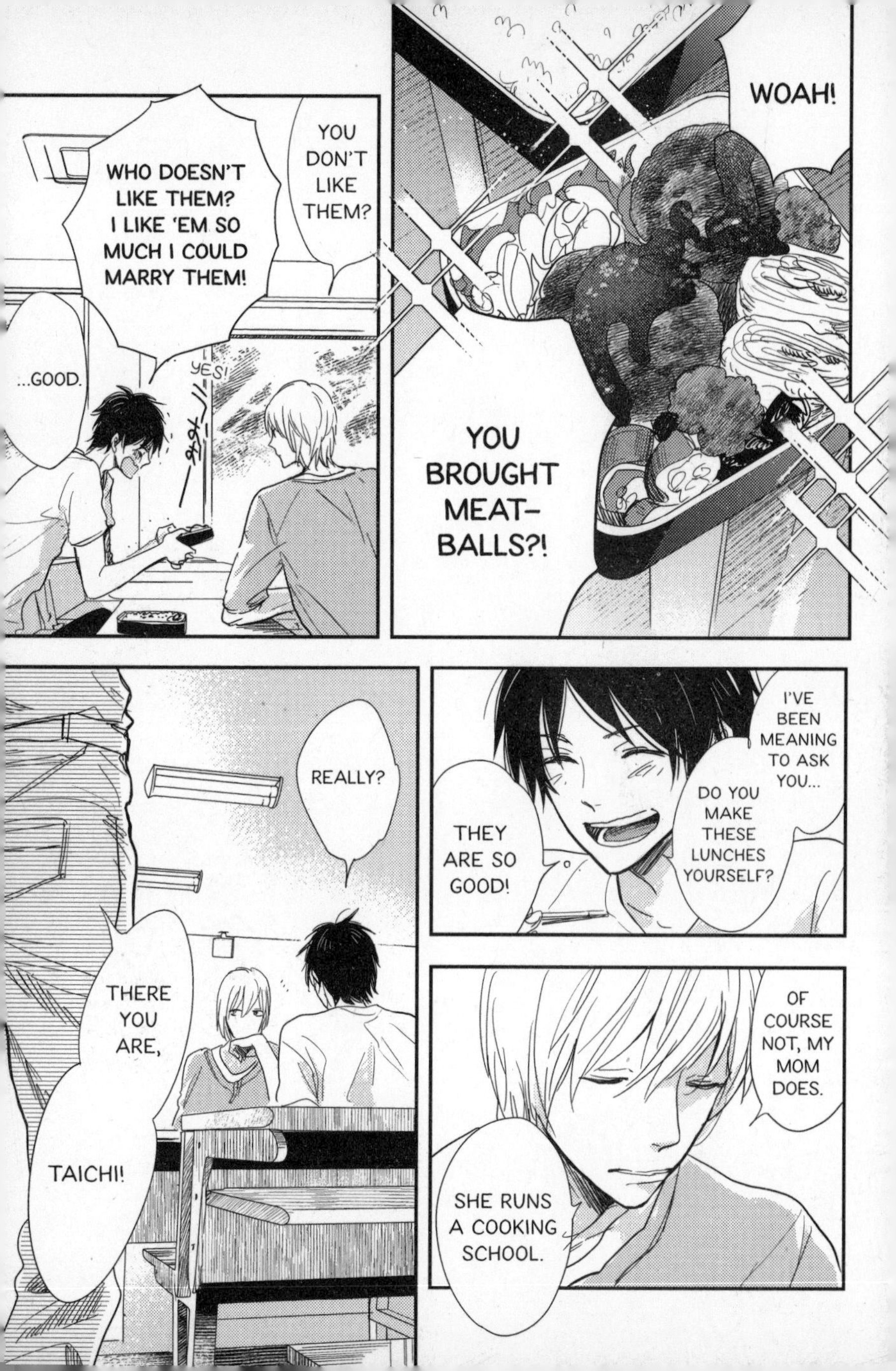
WOAH!
YOU BROUGHT MEAT-BALLS?!
YOU DON'T LIKE THEM?
WHO DOESN'T LIKE THEM? I LIKE 'EM SO MUCH I COULD MARRY THEM!
YES!
...GOOD.
I'VE BEEN MEANING TO ASK YOU...
DO YOU MAKE THESE LUNCHES YOURSELF?
THEY ARE SO GOOD!
OF COURSE NOT, MY MOM DOES.
SHE RUNS A COOKING SCHOOL.
REALLY?
THERE YOU ARE,
TAICHI!

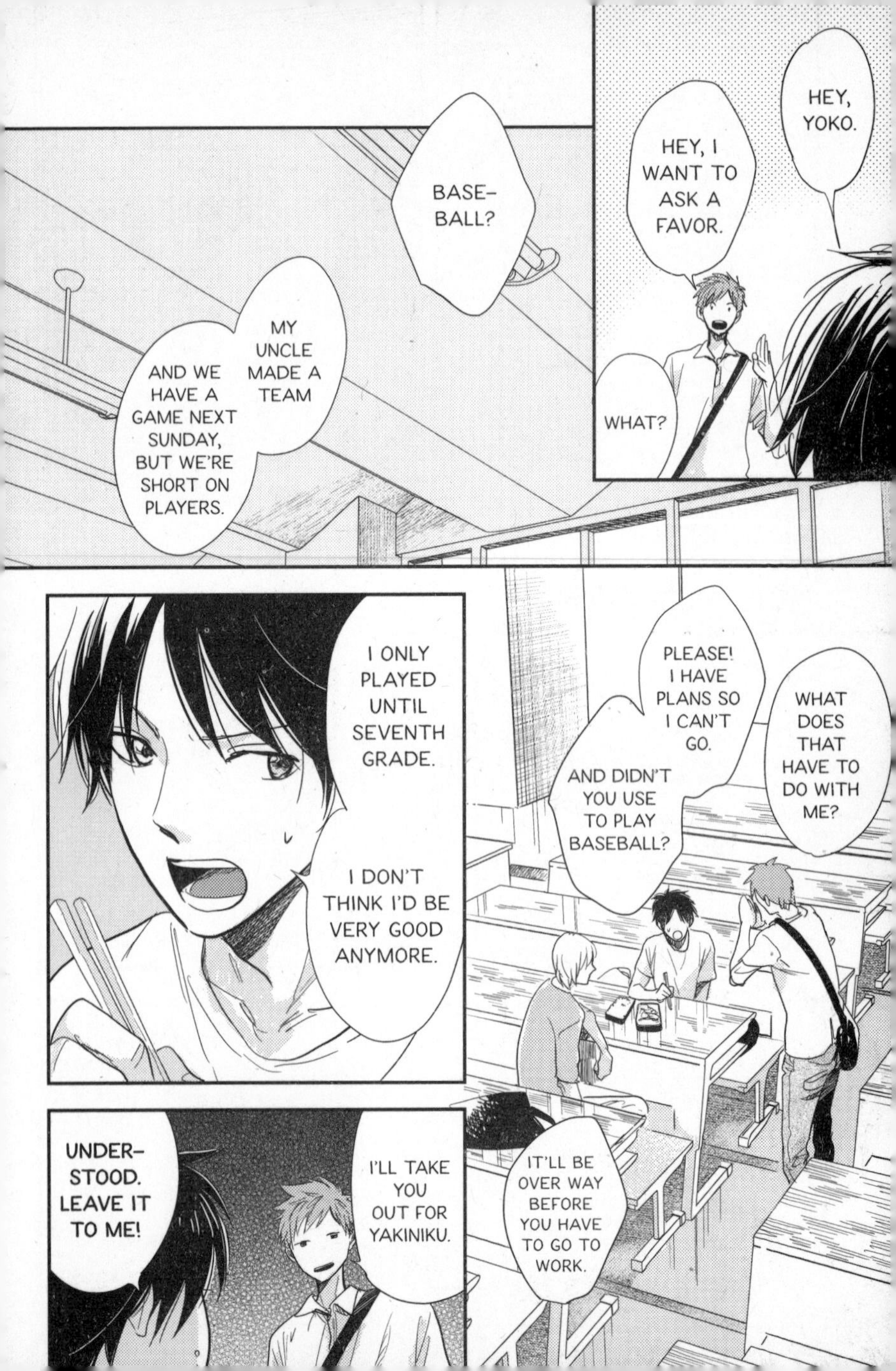
HEY, YOKO.
HEY, I WANT TO ASK A FAVOR.
WHAT?
BASE-BALL?
MY UNCLE MADE A TEAM
AND WE HAVE A GAME NEXT SUNDAY, BUT WE'RE SHORT ON PLAYERS.
WHAT DOES THAT HAVE TO DO WITH ME?
PLEASE! I HAVE PLANS SO I CAN'T GO.
AND DIDN'T YOU USE TO PLAY BASEBALL?
IT'LL BE OVER WAY BEFORE YOU HAVE TO GO TO WORK.
I ONLY PLAYED UNTIL SEVENTH GRADE.
I DON'T THINK I'D BE VERY GOOD ANYMORE.
I'LL TAKE YOU OUT FOR YAKINIKU.
UNDER-STOOD. LEAVE IT TO ME!

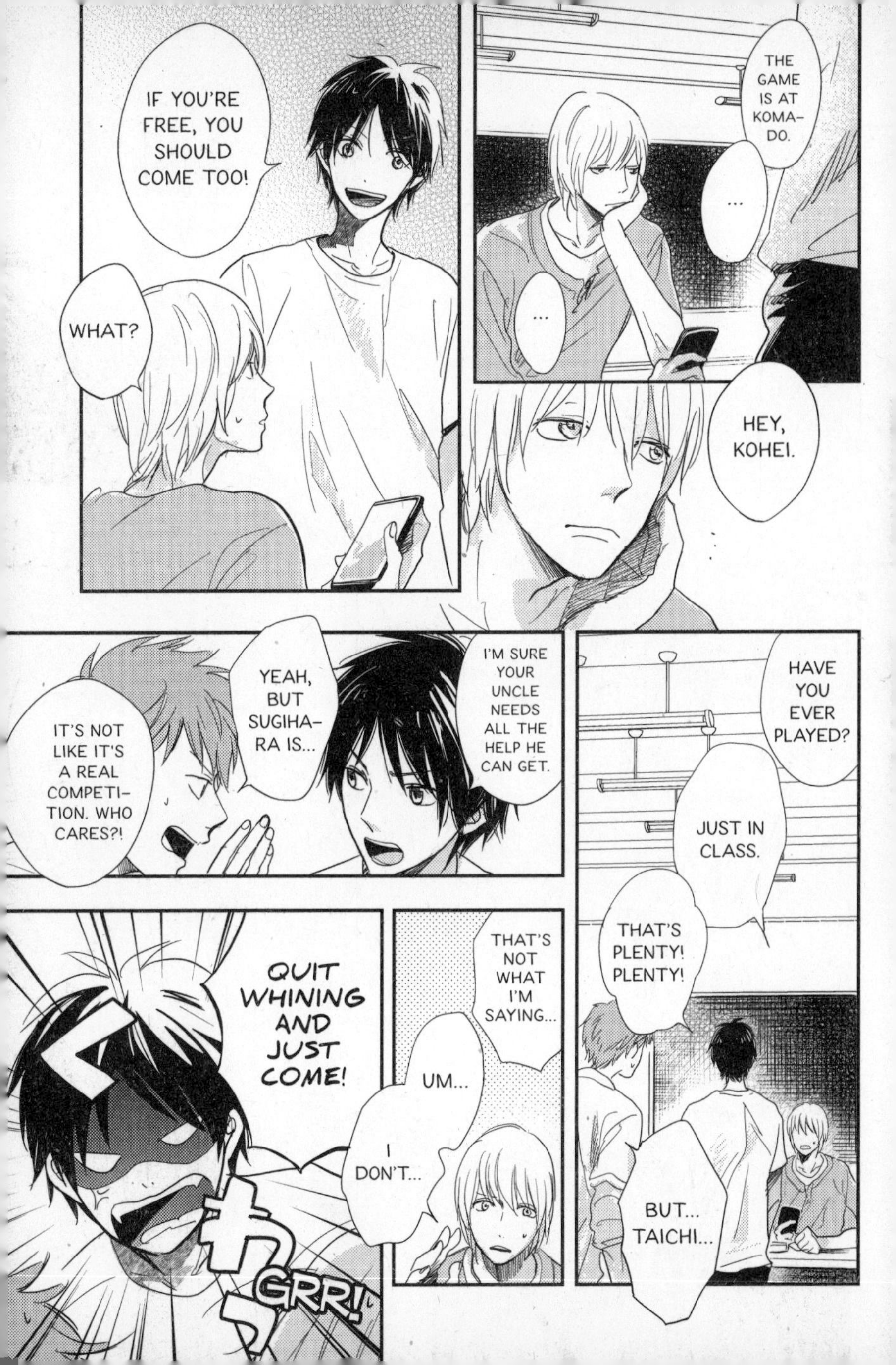
THE GAME IS AT KOMA-DO.
...
...
HEY, KOHEI.
IF YOU'RE FREE, YOU SHOULD COME TOO!
WHAT?
HAVE YOU EVER PLAYED?
JUST IN CLASS.
THAT'S PLENTY! PLENTY!
BUT... TAICHI...
I'M SURE YOUR UNCLE NEEDS ALL THE HELP HE CAN GET.
YEAH, BUT SUGIHARA IS...
IT'S NOT LIKE IT'S A REAL COMPETITION. WHO CARES?!
THAT'S NOT WHAT I'M SAYING...
UM...
I DON'T...
QUIT WHINING AND JUST COME!
GRR!

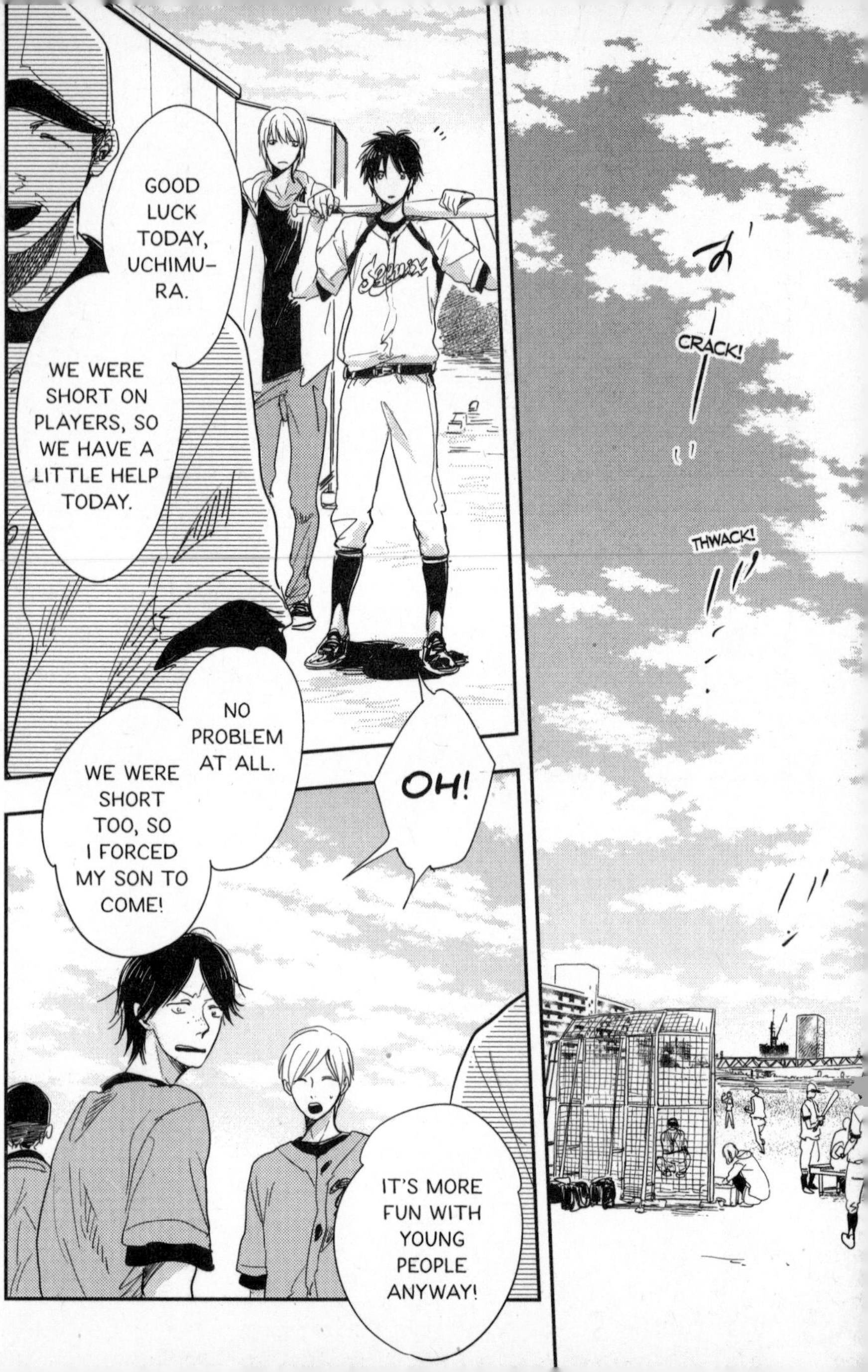
CRACK!
THWACK!
GOOD LUCK TODAY, UCHIMURA.
WE WERE SHORT ON PLAYERS, SO WE HAVE A LITTLE HELP TODAY.
OH!
NO PROBLEM AT ALL.
WE WERE SHORT TOO, SO I FORCED MY SON TO COME!
IT'S MORE FUN WITH YOUNG PEOPLE ANYWAY!

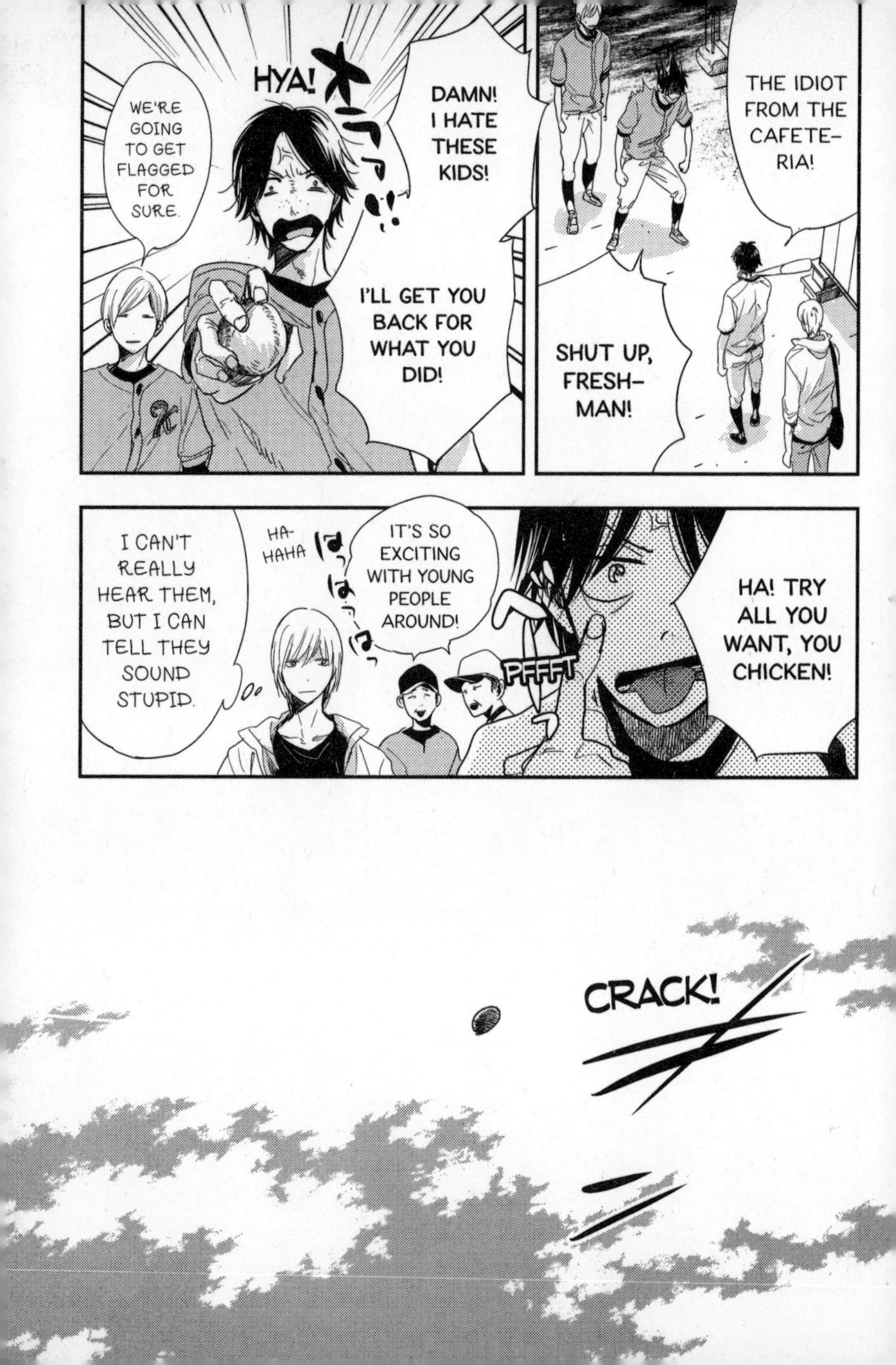
THE IDIOT FROM THE CAFETERIA!
SHUT UP, FRESHMAN!
DAMN! I HATE THESE KIDS!
HYA!
I'LL GET YOU BACK FOR WHAT YOU DID!
WE'RE GOING TO GET FLAGGED FOR SURE.
HA! TRY ALL YOU WANT, YOU CHICKEN!
PFFFT
IT'S SO EXCITING WITH YOUNG PEOPLE AROUND!
HA-HAHA
I CAN'T REALLY HEAR THEM, BUT I CAN TELL THEY SOUND STUPID.
CRACK!

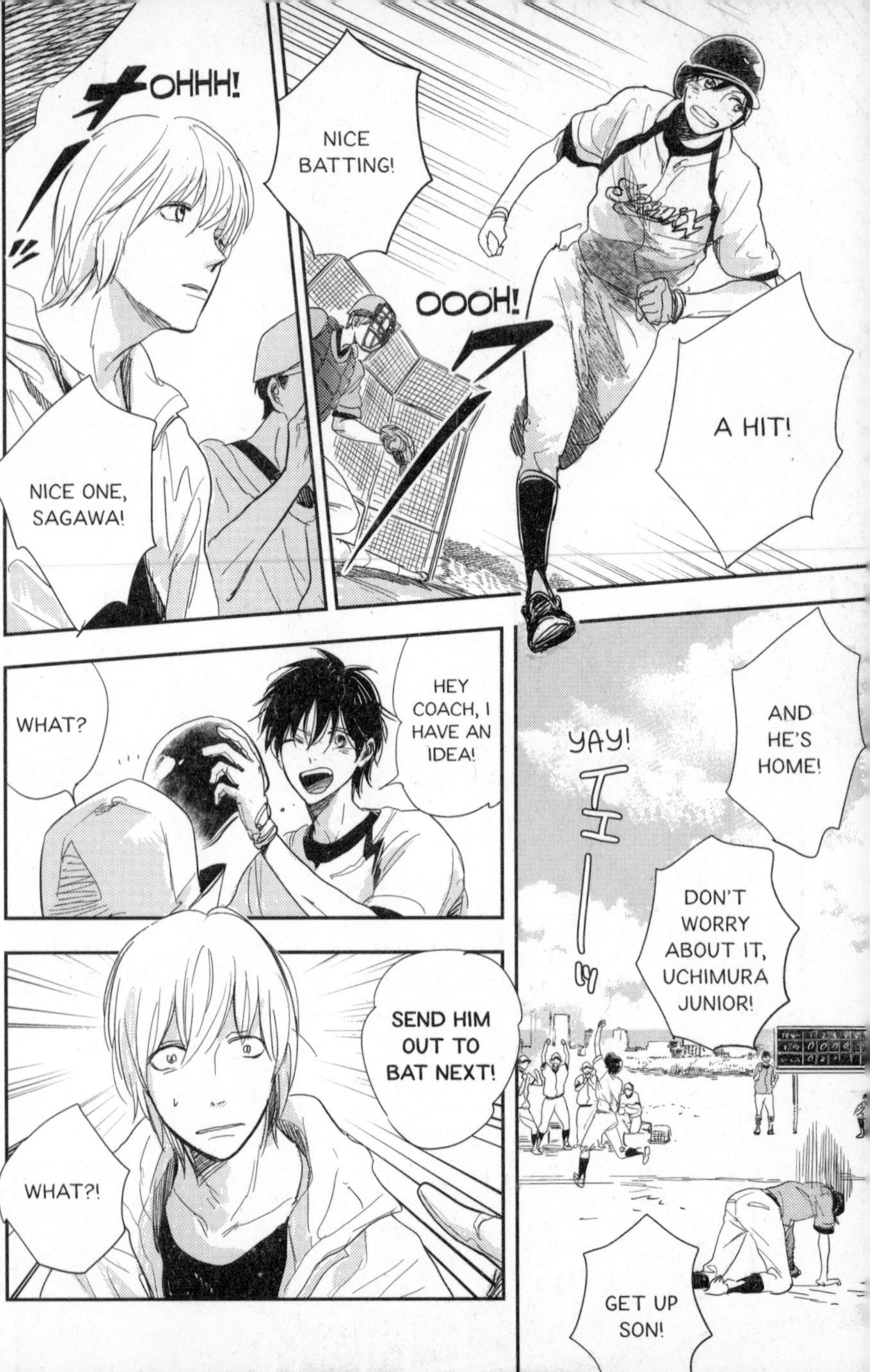
A HIT!
OOOH!
NICE BATTING!
OHHH!
NICE ONE, SAGAWA!
AND HE'S HOME!
YAY!
DON'T WORRY ABOUT IT, UCHIMURA JUNIOR!
GET UP SON!
HEY COACH, I HAVE AN IDEA!
WHAT?
SEND HIM OUT TO BAT NEXT!
WHAT?!

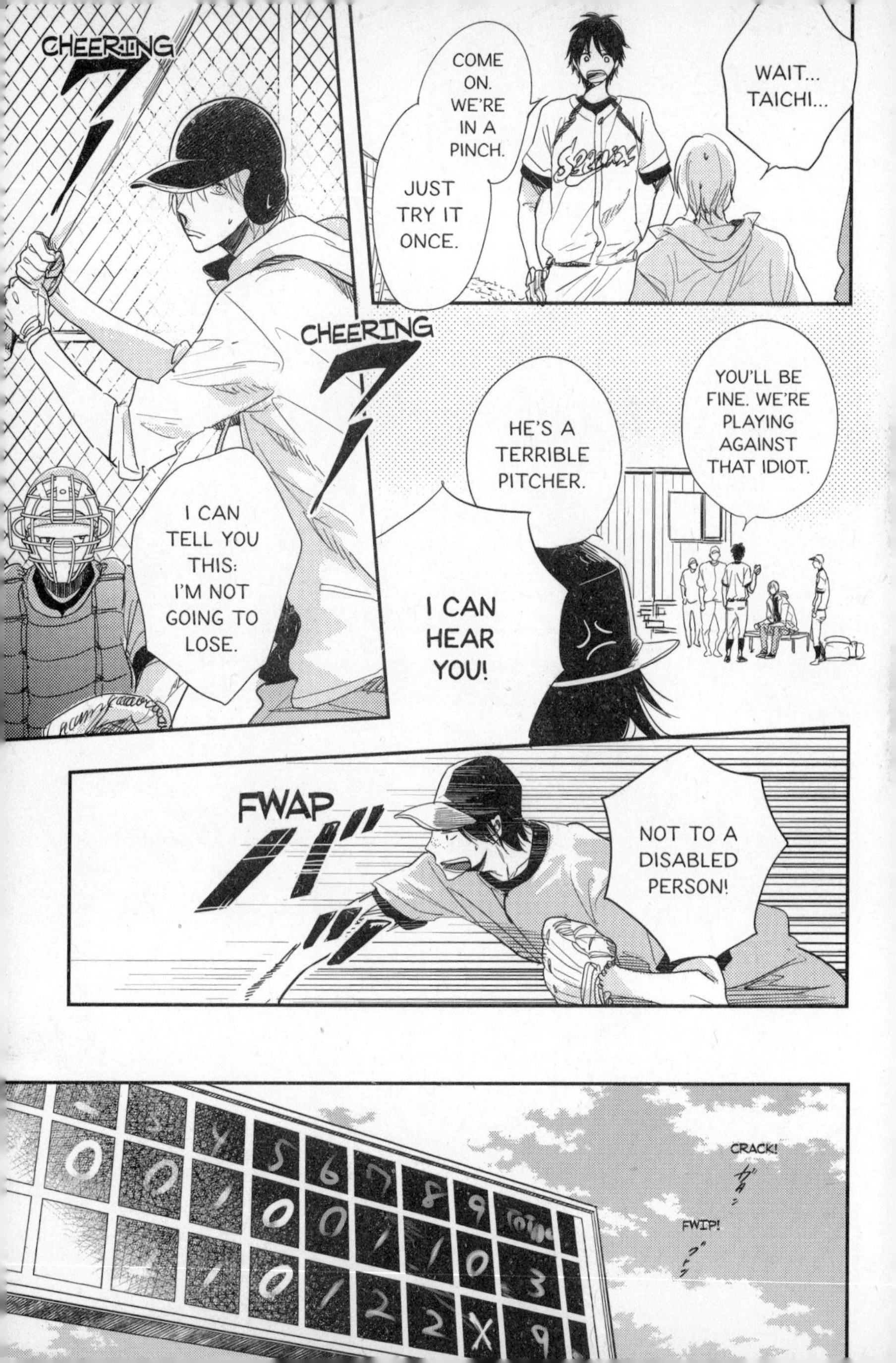
WAIT... TAICHI...
COME ON. WE'RE IN A PINCH.
JUST TRY IT ONCE.
YOU'LL BE FINE. WE'RE PLAYING AGAINST THAT IDIOT.
HE'S A TERRIBLE PITCHER.
CHEERING
I CAN HEAR YOU!
CHEERING
I CAN TELL YOU THIS: I'M NOT GOING TO LOSE.
NOT TO A DISABLED PERSON!
FWAP
CRACK!
FWIP!

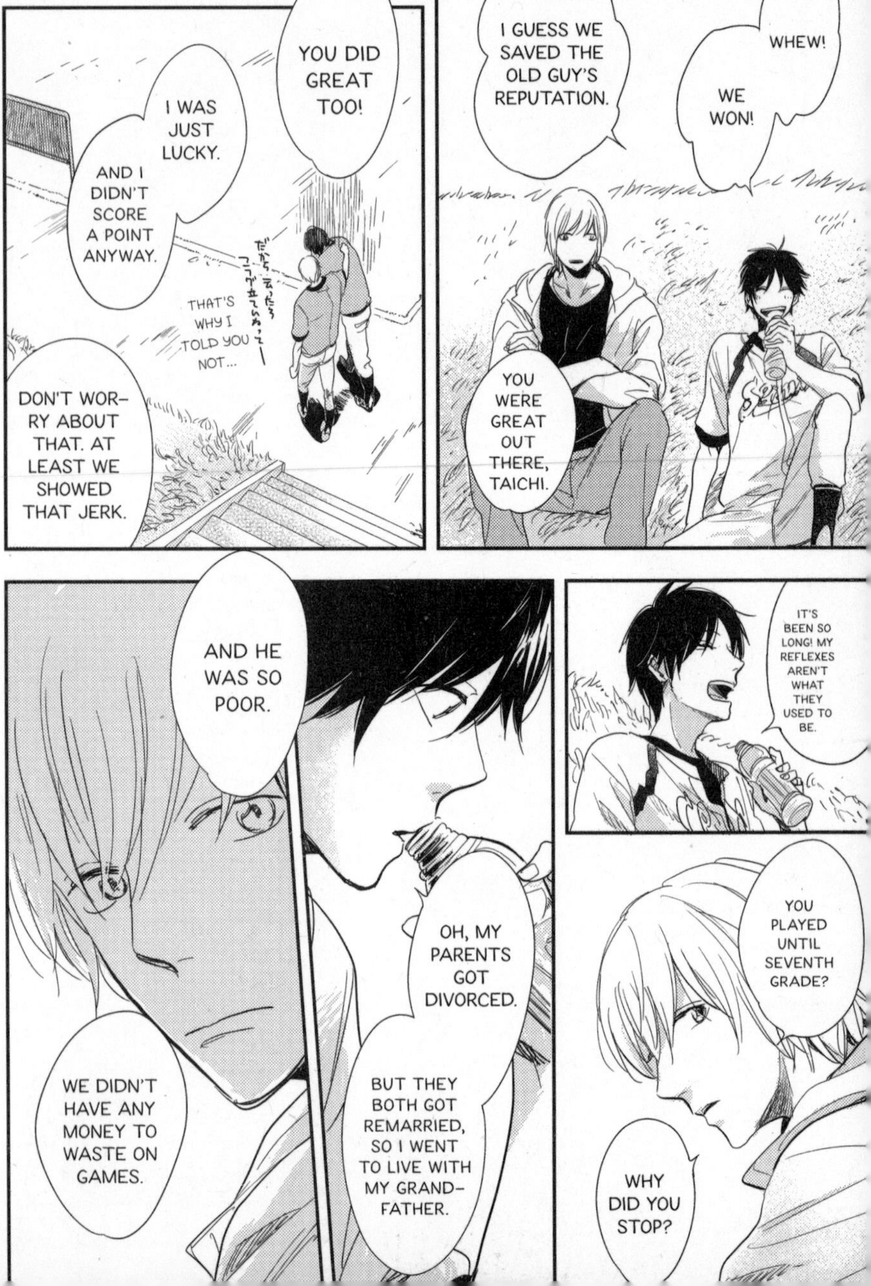
WHEW!
WE WON!
I GUESS WE SAVED THE OLD GUY'S REPUTATION.
YOU WERE GREAT OUT THERE, TAICHI.
YOU DID GREAT TOO!
I WAS JUST LUCKY.
AND I DIDN'T SCORE A POINT ANYWAY.
だから言ったろ フラグ立てんなってー
THAT'S WHY I TOLD YOU NOT...
DON'T WOR-RY ABOUT THAT. AT LEAST WE SHOWED THAT JERK.
IT'S BEEN SO LONG! MY REFLEXES AREN'T WHAT THEY USED TO BE.
YOU PLAYED UNTIL SEVENTH GRADE?
WHY DID YOU STOP?
OH, MY PARENTS GOT DIVORCED.
BUT THEY BOTH GOT REMARRIED, SO I WENT TO LIVE WITH MY GRAND-FATHER.
AND HE WAS SO POOR.
WE DIDN'T HAVE ANY MONEY TO WASTE ON GAMES.

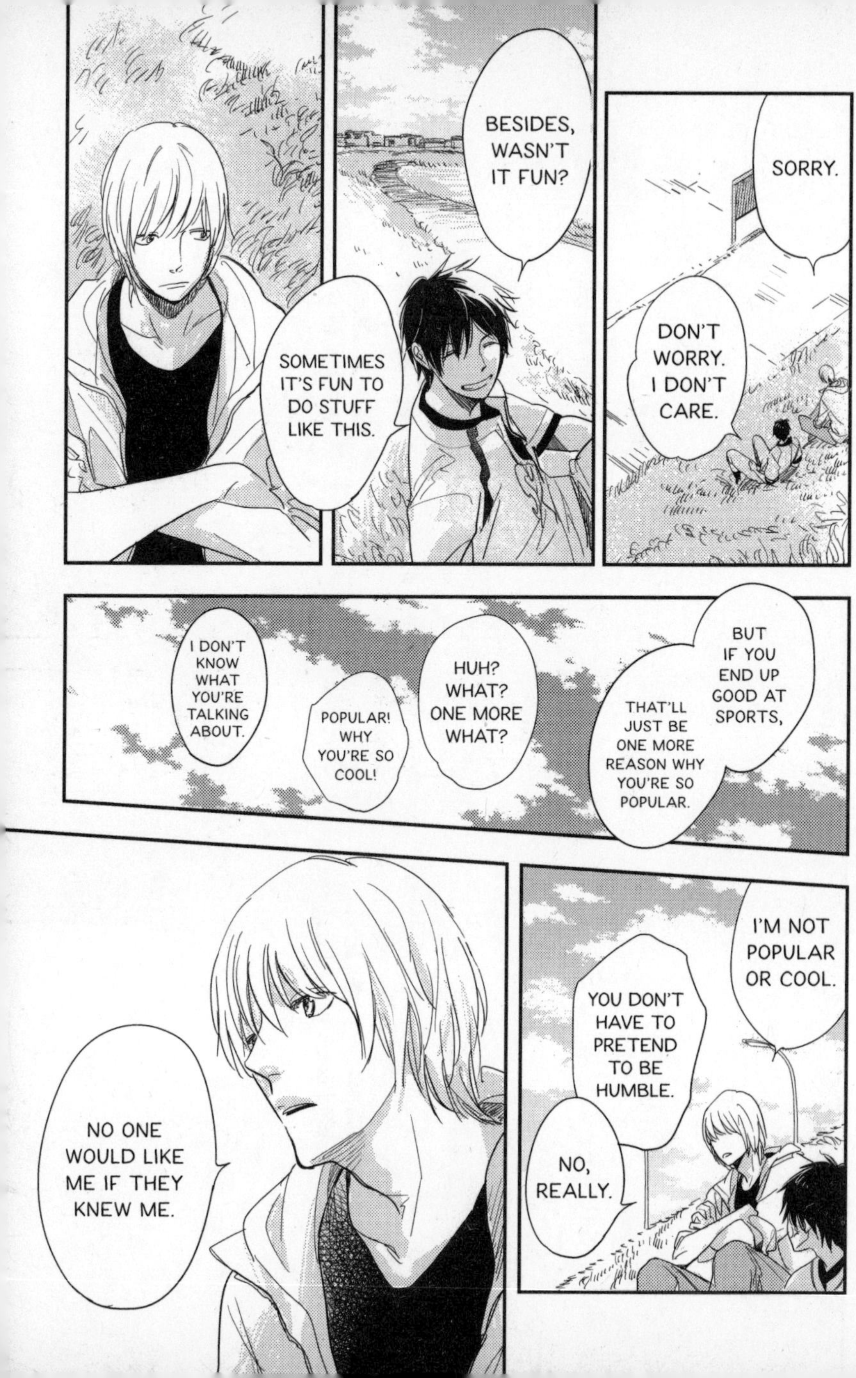
SORRY.
DON'T WORRY. I DON'T CARE.
BESIDES, WASN'T IT FUN?
SOMETIMES IT'S FUN TO DO STUFF LIKE THIS.
BUT IF YOU END UP GOOD AT SPORTS,
THAT'LL JUST BE ONE MORE REASON WHY YOU'RE SO POPULAR.
HUH? WHAT? ONE MORE WHAT?
POPULAR! WHY YOU'RE SO COOL!
I DON'T KNOW WHAT YOU'RE TALKING ABOUT.
I'M NOT POPULAR OR COOL.
YOU DON'T HAVE TO PRETEND TO BE HUMBLE.
NO, REALLY.
NO ONE WOULD LIKE ME IF THEY KNEW ME.

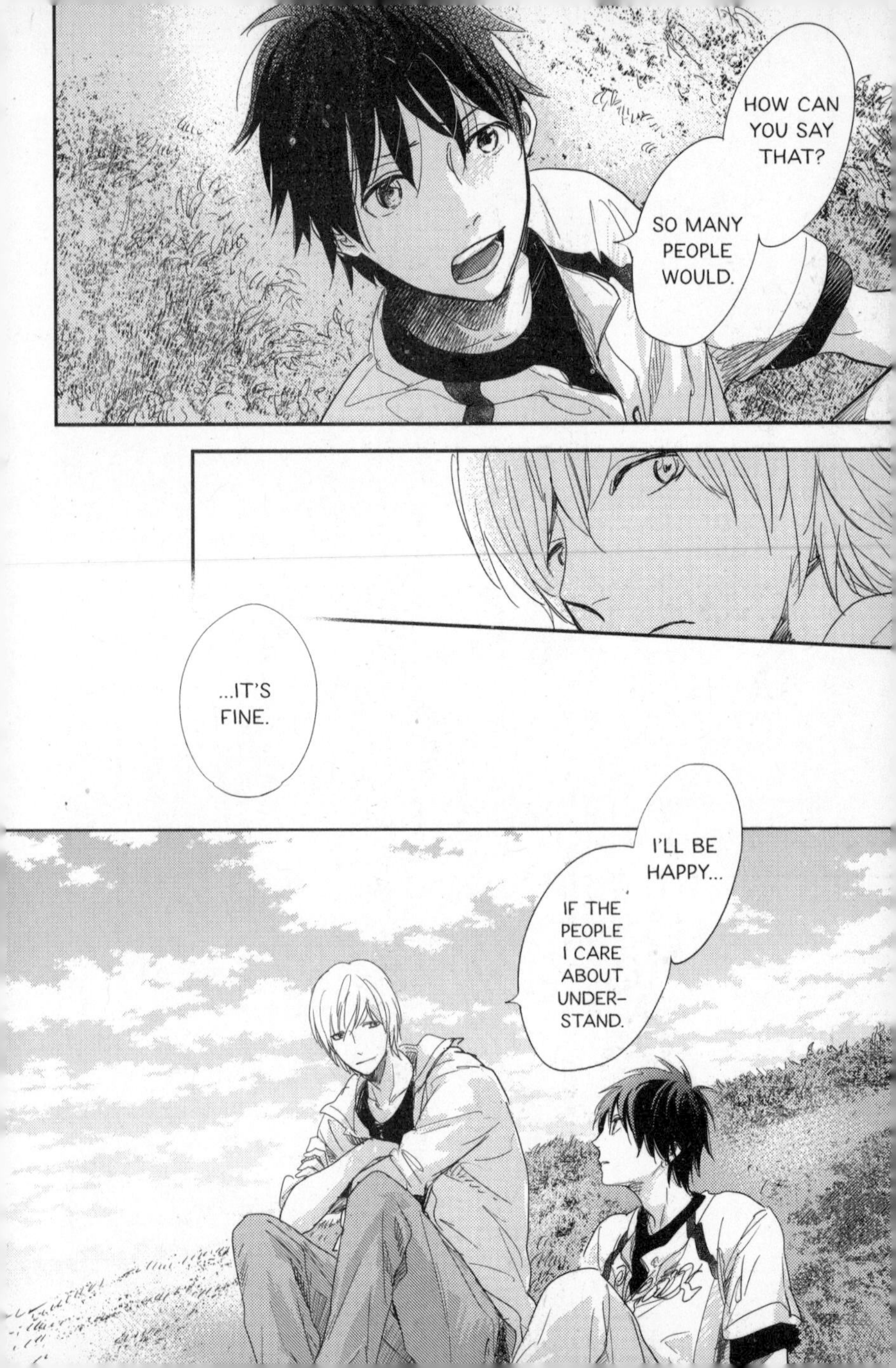
HOW CAN YOU SAY THAT?
SO MANY PEOPLE WOULD.
...IT'S FINE.
I'LL BE HAPPY...
IF THE PEOPLE I CARE ABOUT UNDER-STAND.

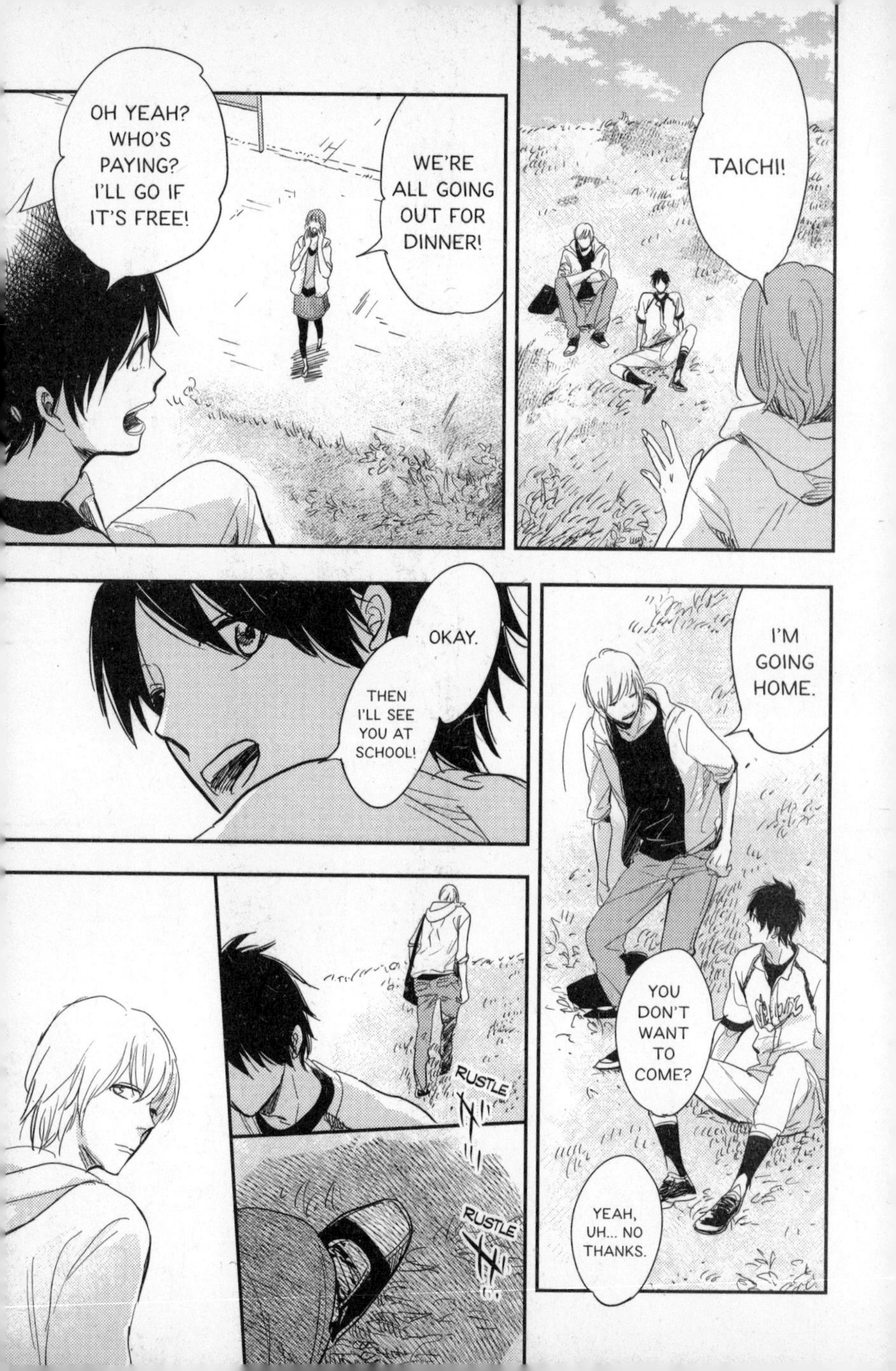
TAICHI!
WE'RE ALL GOING OUT FOR DINNER!
OH YEAH? WHO'S PAYING? I'LL GO IF IT'S FREE!
I'M GOING HOME.
YOU DON'T WANT TO COME?
YEAH, UH... NO THANKS.
OKAY.
THEN I'LL SEE YOU AT SCHOOL!
RUSTLE
RUSTLE

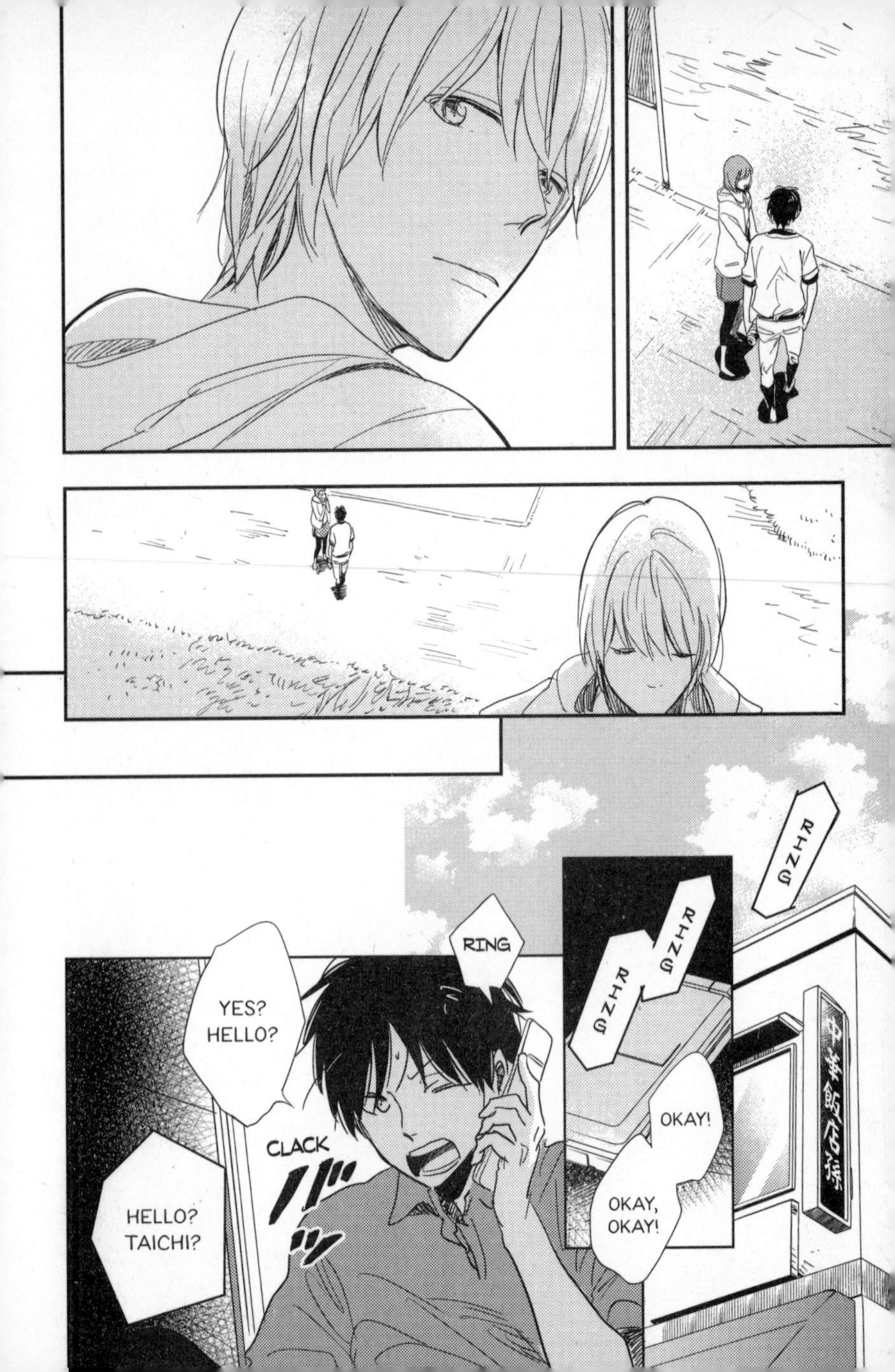
RING
RING
RING
RING
中華飯店孫
OKAY!
OKAY, OKAY!
YES? HELLO?
CLACK
HELLO? TAICHI?

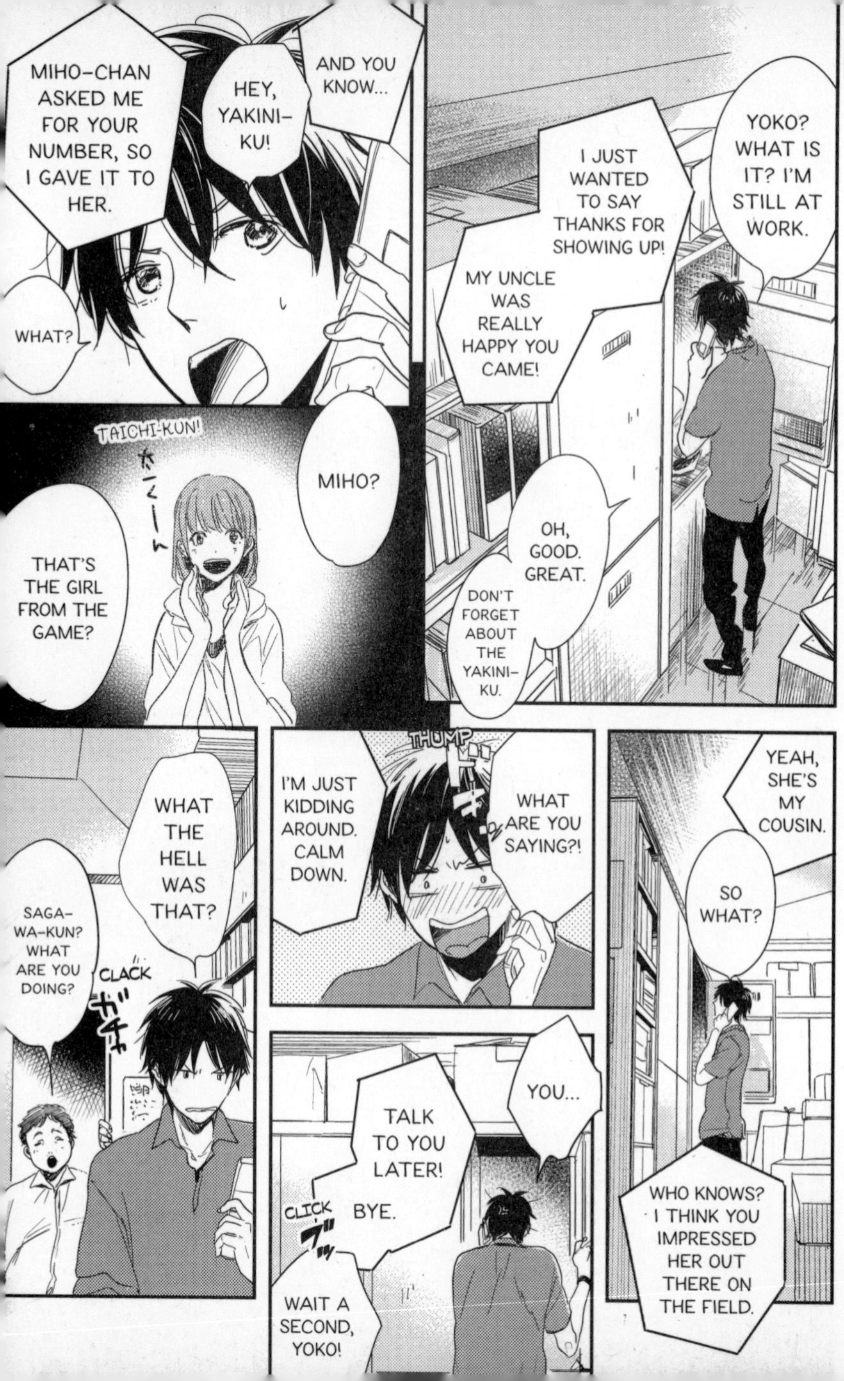
YOKO? WHAT IS IT? I'M STILL AT WORK.
I JUST WANTED TO SAY THANKS FOR SHOWING UP!
MY UNCLE WAS REALLY HAPPY YOU CAME!
OH, GOOD. GREAT.
DON'T FORGET ABOUT THE YAKINI-KU.
AND YOU KNOW...
HEY, YAKINI-KU!
MIHO-CHAN ASKED ME FOR YOUR NUMBER, SO I GAVE IT TO HER.
WHAT?
MIHO?
TAICHI-KUN!
THAT'S THE GIRL FROM THE GAME?
YEAH, SHE'S MY COUSIN.
SO WHAT?
WHO KNOWS? I THINK YOU IMPRESSED HER OUT THERE ON THE FIELD.
WHAT ARE YOU SAYING?!
THUMP
I'M JUST KIDDING AROUND. CALM DOWN.
YOU...
TALK TO YOU LATER!
BYE.
CLICK
WAIT A SECOND, YOKO!
WHAT THE HELL WAS THAT?
CLACK
SAGA-WA-KUN? WHAT ARE YOU DOING?

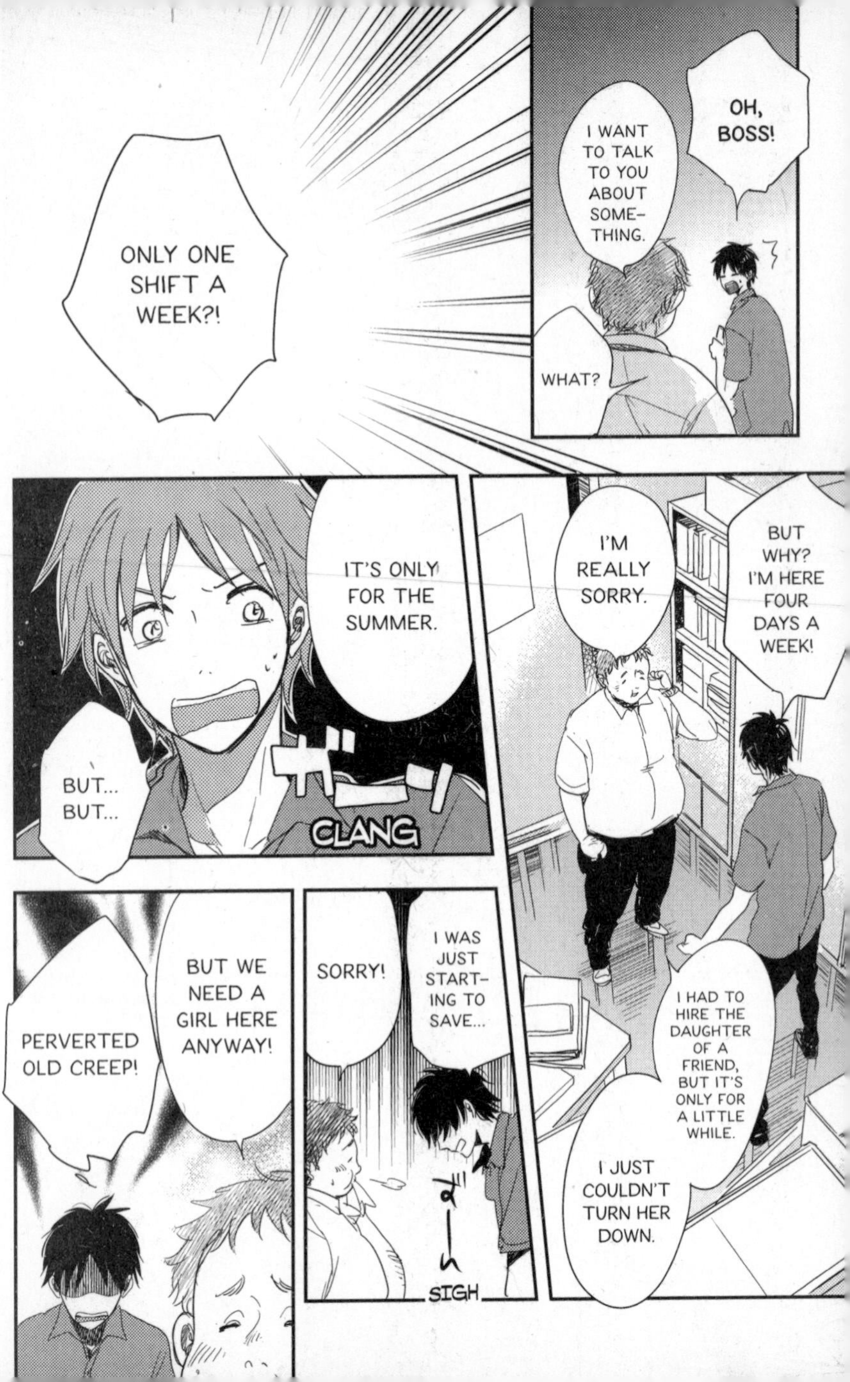
OH, BOSS!
I WANT TO TALK TO YOU ABOUT SOME-THING.
WHAT?
ONLY ONE SHIFT A WEEK?!
BUT WHY? I'M HERE FOUR DAYS A WEEK!
I'M REALLY SORRY.
I HAD TO HIRE THE DAUGHTER OF A FRIEND, BUT IT'S ONLY FOR A LITTLE WHILE.
I JUST COULDN'T TURN HER DOWN.
IT'S ONLY FOR THE SUMMER.
BUT... BUT...
CLANG
I WAS JUST START-ING TO SAVE...
SORRY!
SIGH
BUT WE NEED A GIRL HERE ANYWAY!
PERVERTED OLD CREEP!

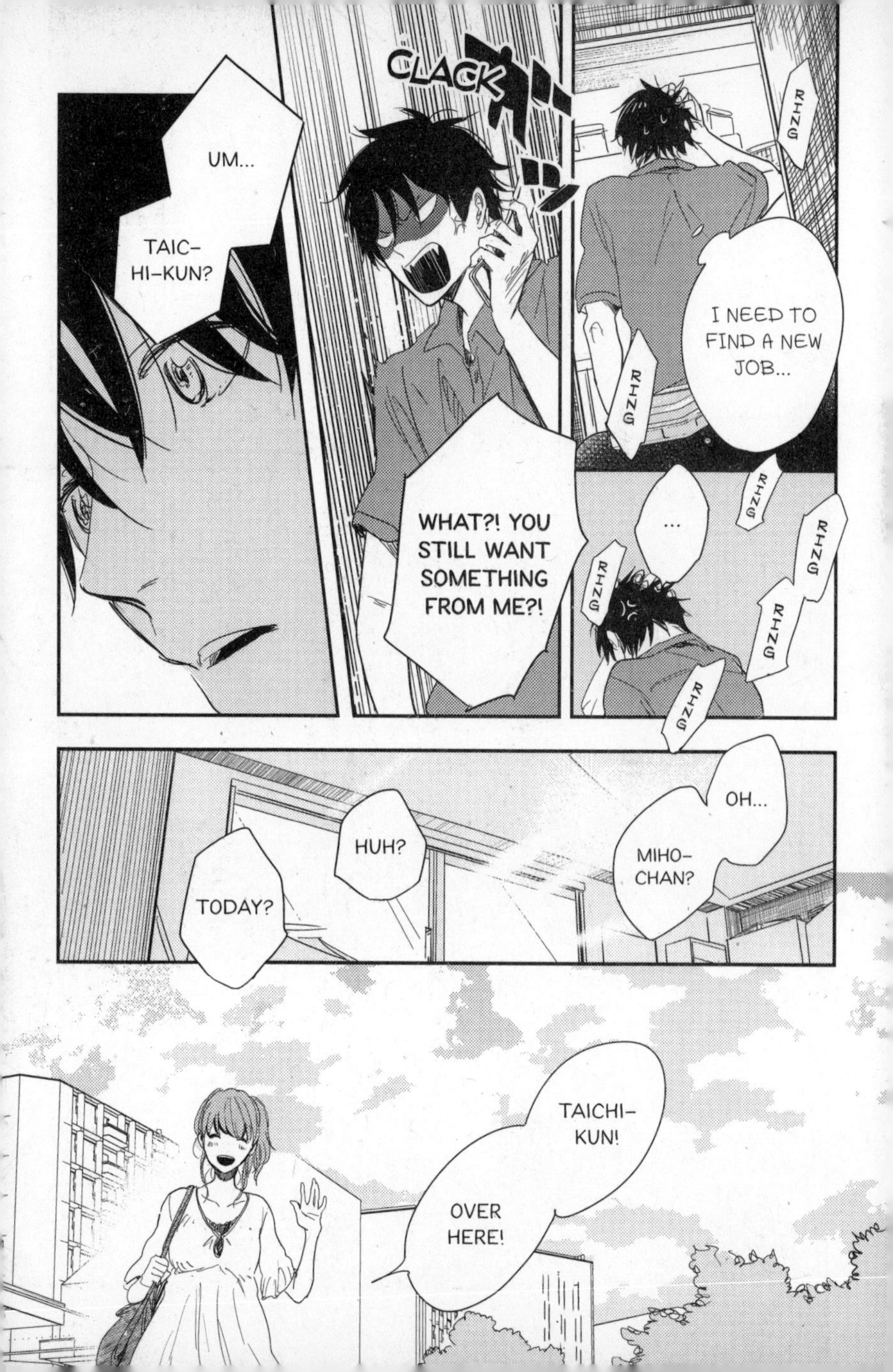
RING
I NEED TO FIND A NEW JOB...
RING
RING
...
RING
RING
RING
RING
CLACK
WHAT?! YOU STILL WANT SOMETHING FROM ME?!
UM...
TAIC-HI-KUN?
OH...
MIHO-CHAN?
HUH?
TODAY?
TAICHI-KUN!
OVER HERE!

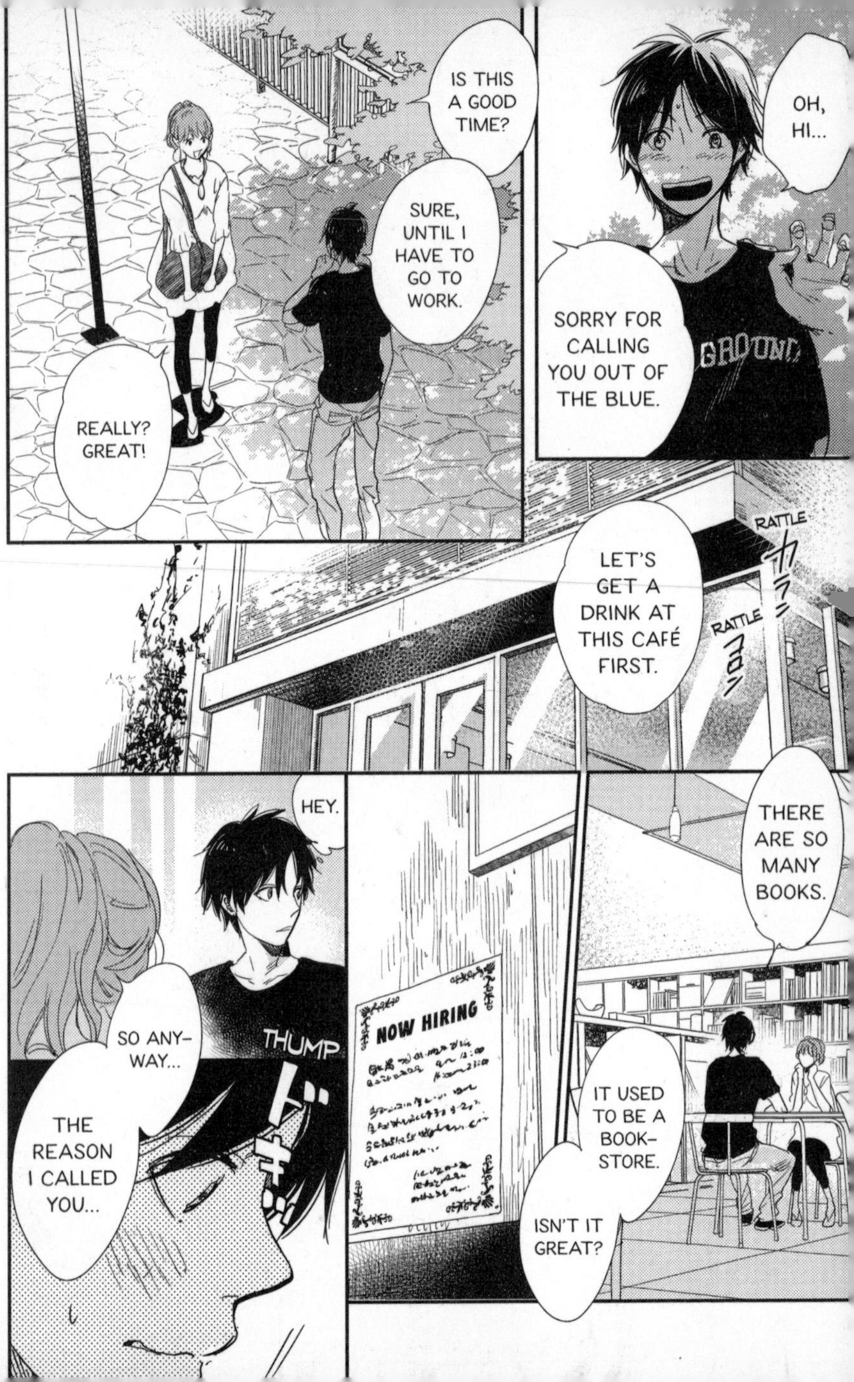

OH, HI...
SORRY FOR CALLING YOU OUT OF THE BLUE.
GROUND
IS THIS A GOOD TIME?
SURE, UNTIL I HAVE TO GO TO WORK.
REALLY? GREAT!
RATTLE
RATTLE
LET'S GET A DRINK AT THIS CAFÉ FIRST.
THERE ARE SO MANY BOOKS.
IT USED TO BE A BOOK-STORE.
ISN'T IT GREAT?
NOW HIRING
HEY.
SO ANY-WAY...
THUMP
THE REASON I CALLED YOU...

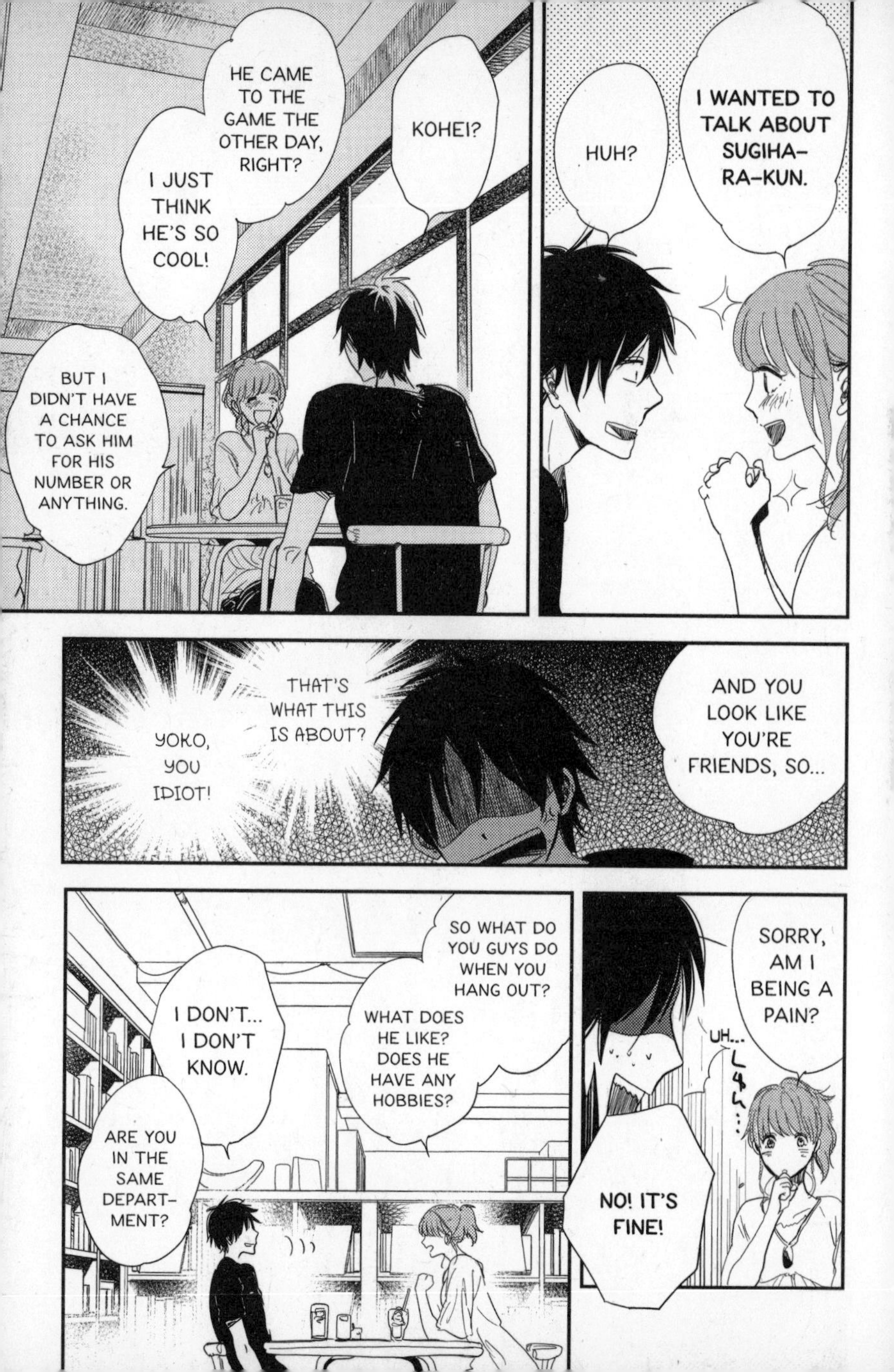
I WANTED TO TALK ABOUT SUGIHA-RA-KUN.
HUH?
KOHEI?
HE CAME TO THE GAME THE OTHER DAY, RIGHT?
I JUST THINK HE'S SO COOL!
BUT I DIDN'T HAVE A CHANCE TO ASK HIM FOR HIS NUMBER OR ANYTHING.
AND YOU LOOK LIKE YOU'RE FRIENDS, SO...
THAT'S WHAT THIS IS ABOUT?
YOKO, YOU IDIOT!
SORRY, AM I BEING A PAIN?
UH...
しゅん...
NO! IT'S FINE!
SO WHAT DO YOU GUYS DO WHEN YOU HANG OUT?
WHAT DOES HE LIKE? DOES HE HAVE ANY HOBBIES?
I DON'T... I DON'T KNOW.
ARE YOU IN THE SAME DEPART-MENT?

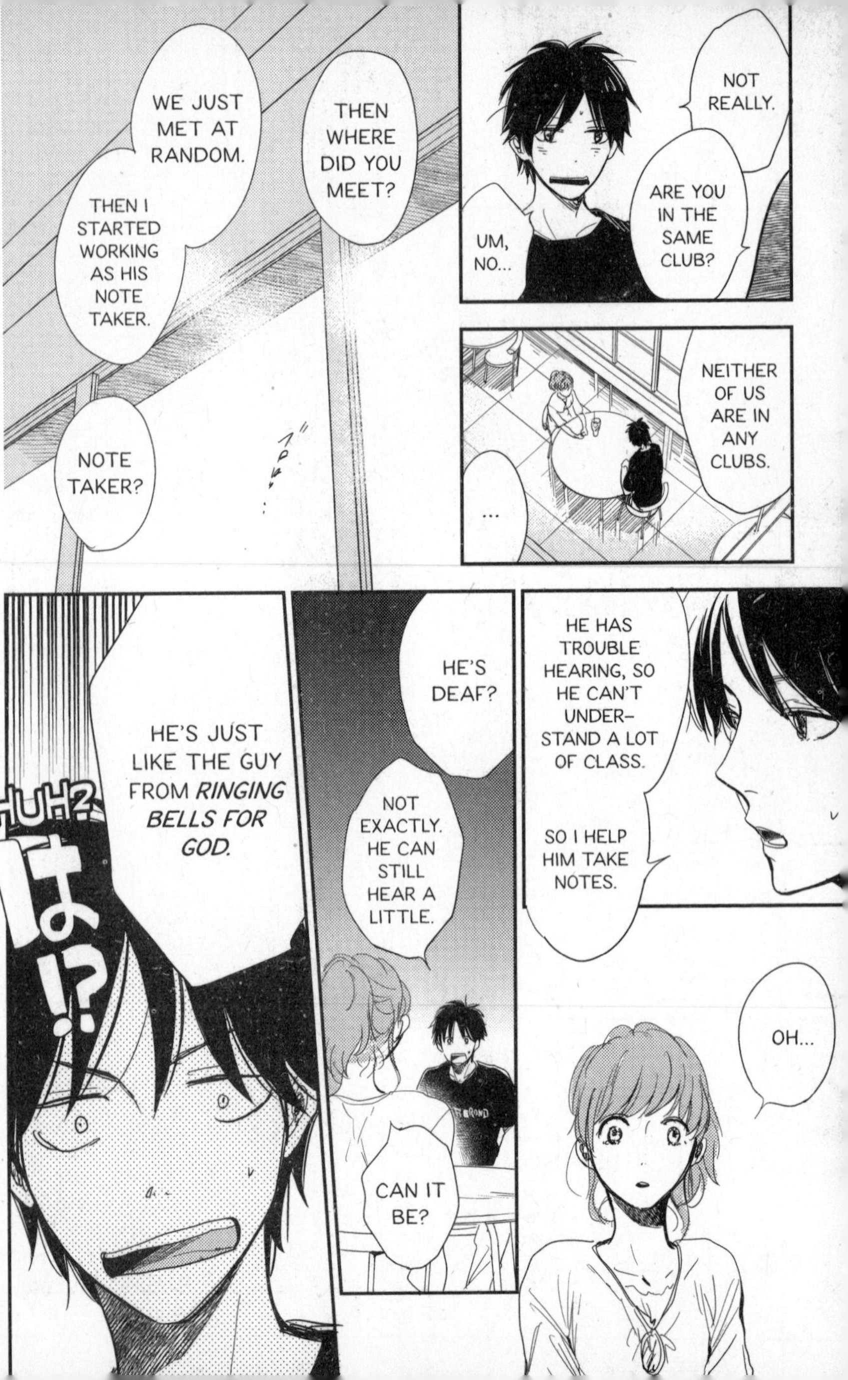
NOT REALLY.
ARE YOU IN THE SAME CLUB?
UM, NO...
NEITHER OF US ARE IN ANY CLUBS.
...
THEN WHERE DID YOU MEET?
WE JUST MET AT RANDOM.
THEN I STARTED WORKING AS HIS NOTE TAKER.
NOTE TAKER?
HE HAS TROUBLE HEARING, SO HE CAN'T UNDER-STAND A LOT OF CLASS.
SO I HELP HIM TAKE NOTES.
OH...
HE'S DEAF?
NOT EXACTLY. HE CAN STILL HEAR A LITTLE.
CAN IT BE?
HE'S JUST LIKE THE GUY FROM *RINGING BELLS FOR GOD.*
HUH?
はあ!?

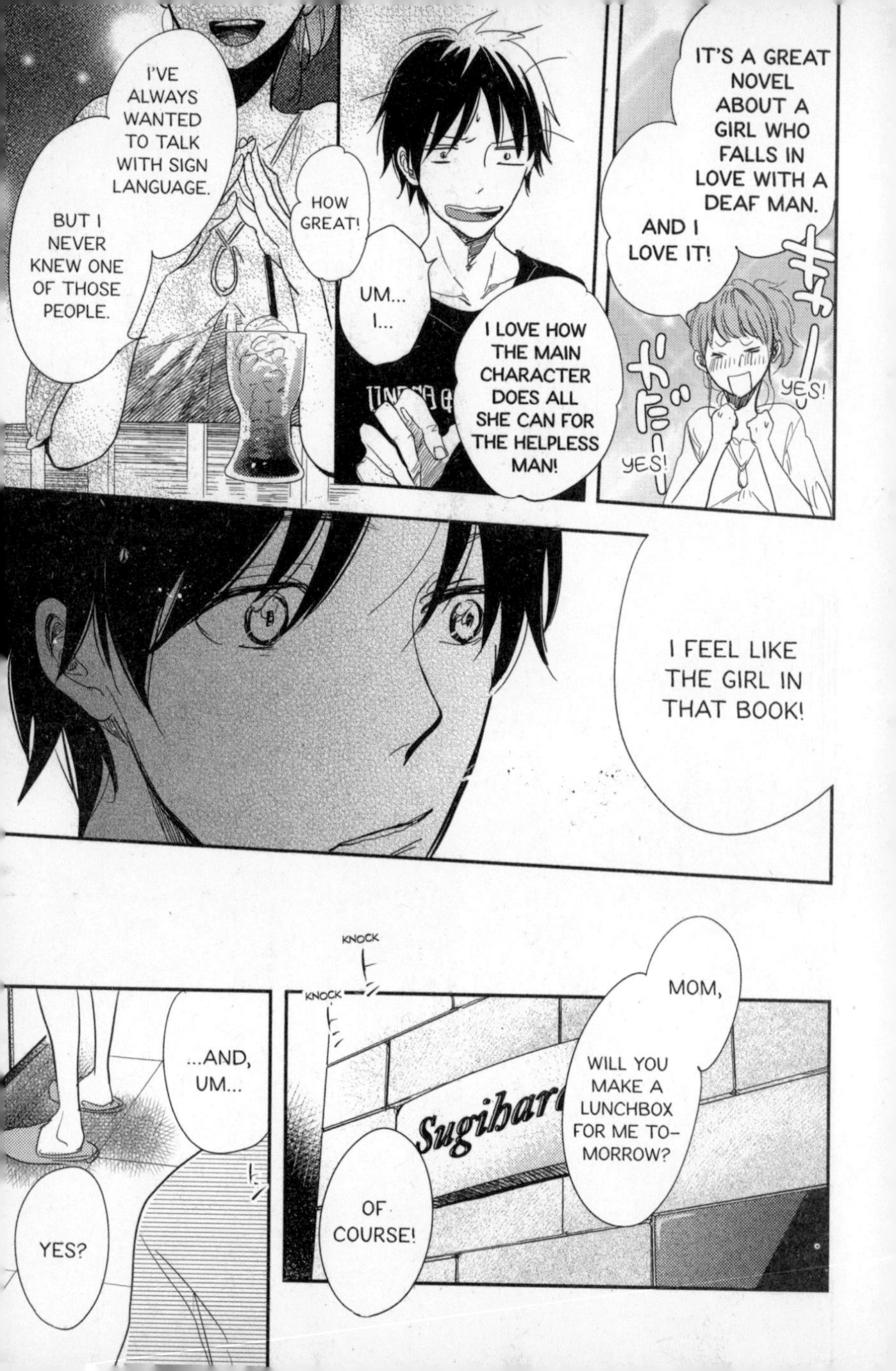

IT'S A GREAT NOVEL ABOUT A GIRL WHO FALLS IN LOVE WITH A DEAF MAN.
AND I LOVE IT!
YES!
YES!
I LOVE HOW THE MAIN CHARACTER DOES ALL SHE CAN FOR THE HELPLESS MAN!
HOW GREAT!
UM... I...
I'VE ALWAYS WANTED TO TALK WITH SIGN LANGUAGE.
BUT I NEVER KNEW ONE OF THOSE PEOPLE.
I FEEL LIKE THE GIRL IN THAT BOOK!
KNOCK
KNOCK
MOM,
WILL YOU MAKE A LUNCHBOX FOR ME TO-MORROW?
Sugihar
OF COURSE!
...AND, UM...
YES?

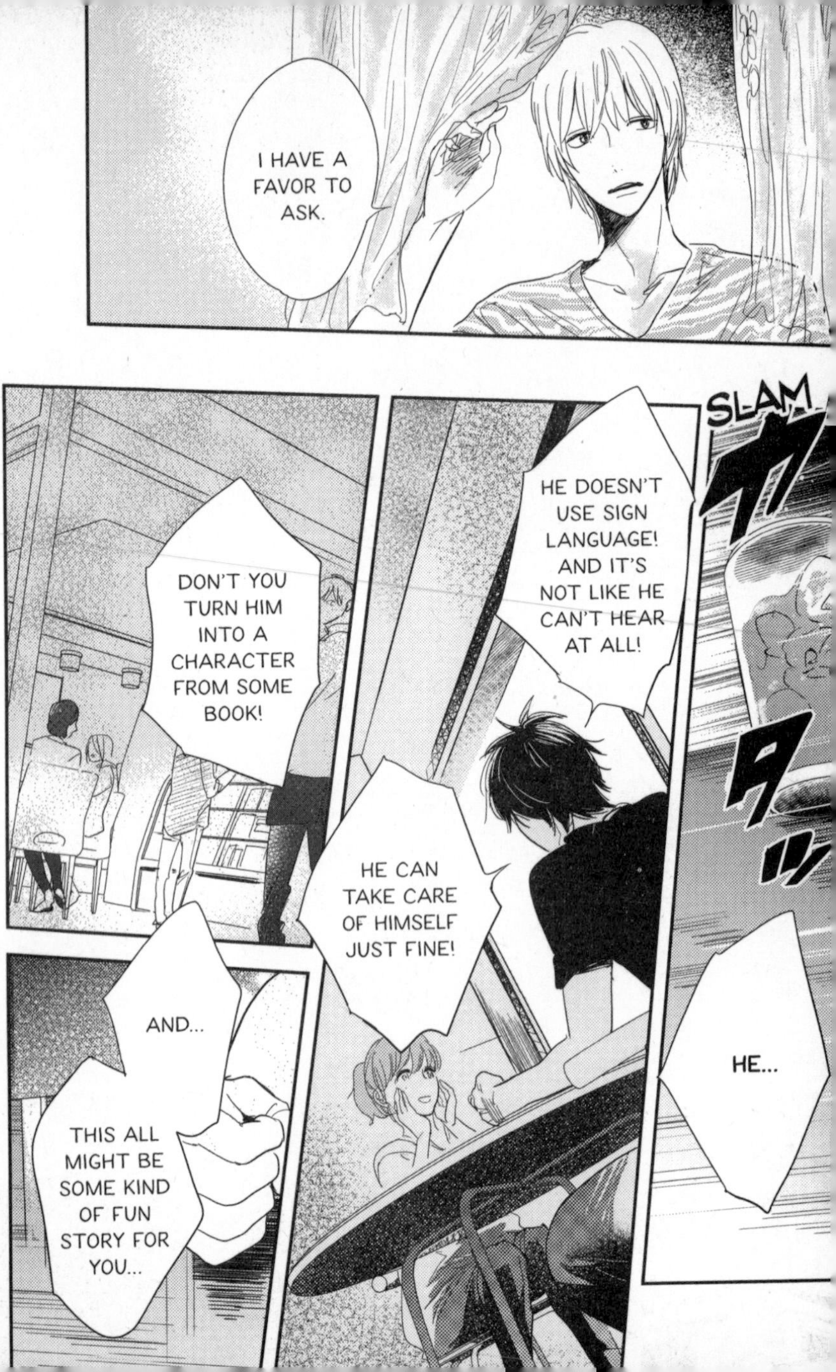
I HAVE A FAVOR TO ASK.
SLAM
HE...
HE DOESN'T USE SIGN LANGUAGE! AND IT'S NOT LIKE HE CAN'T HEAR AT ALL!
HE CAN TAKE CARE OF HIMSELF JUST FINE!
DON'T YOU TURN HIM INTO A CHARACTER FROM SOME BOOK!
AND...
THIS ALL MIGHT BE SOME KIND OF FUN STORY FOR YOU...

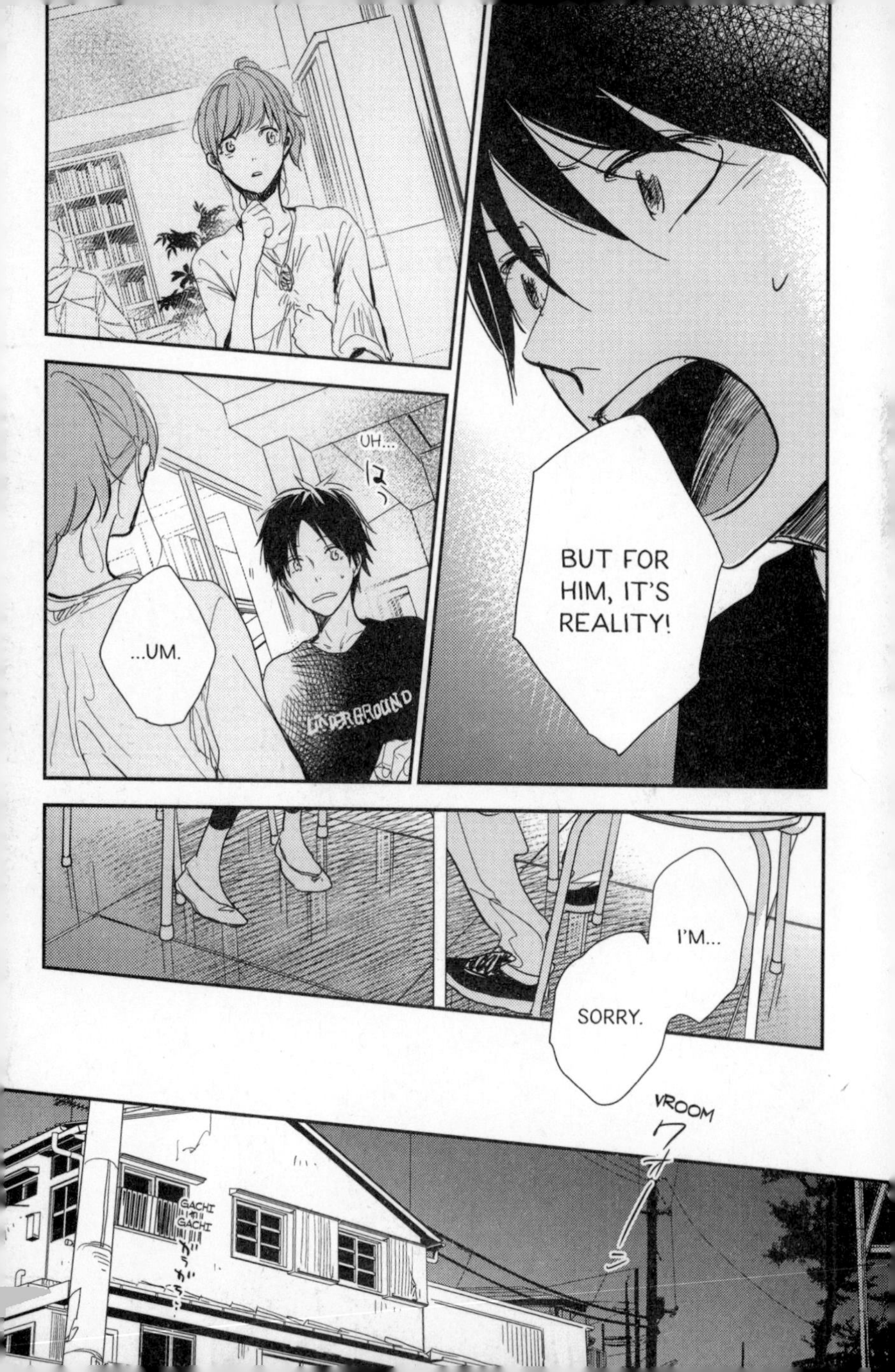
BUT FOR HIM, IT'S REALITY!
UH...
...UM.
I'M...
SORRY.
VROOM
GACHI GACHI

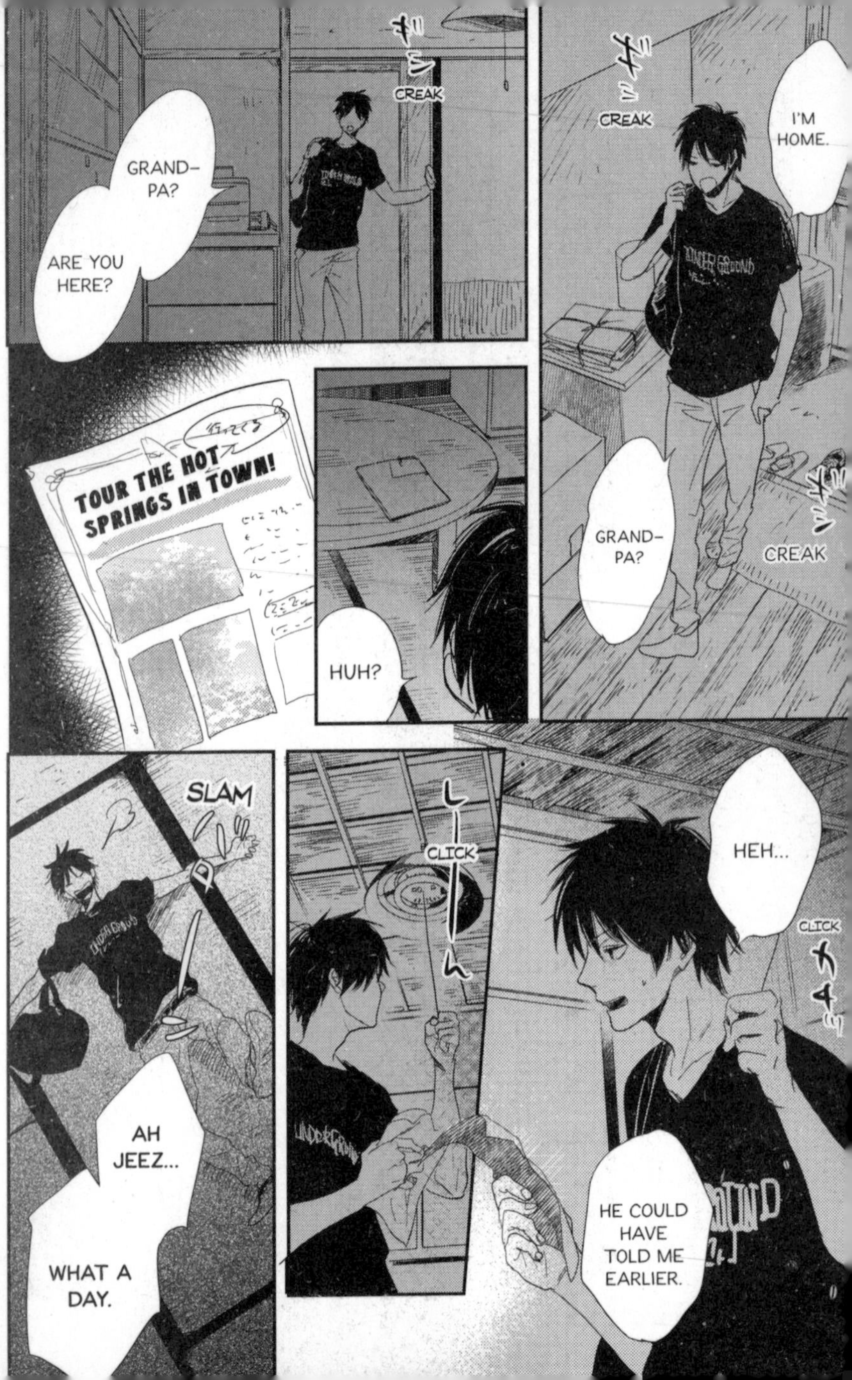
CREAK
I'M HOME.
GRAND-PA?
CREAK
CREAK
GRAND-PA?
ARE YOU HERE?
HUH?
TOUR THE HOT SPRINGS IN TOWN!
HEH...
CLICK
HE COULD HAVE TOLD ME EARLIER.
CLICK
SLAM
AH JEEZ...
WHAT A DAY.

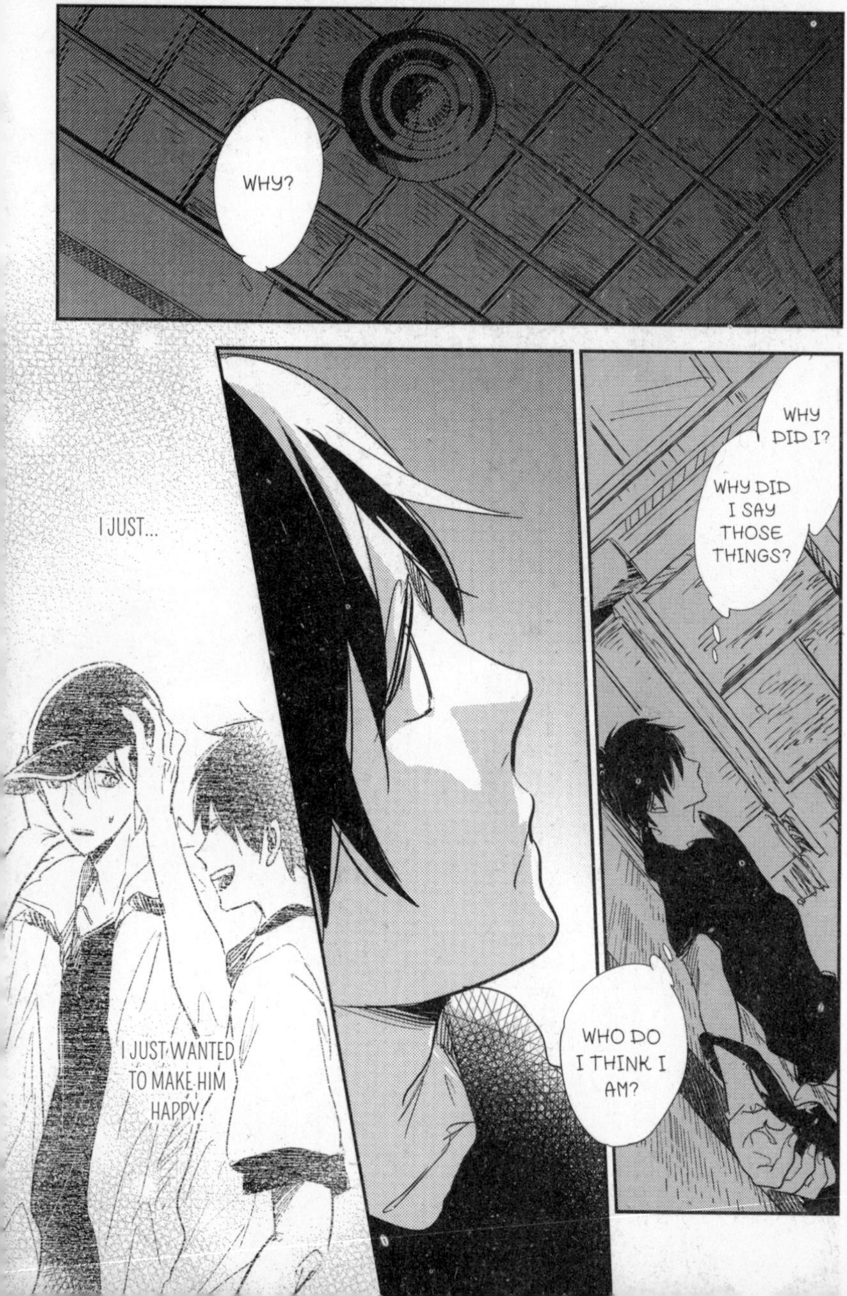
WHY?
WHY DID I?
WHY DID I SAY THOSE THINGS?
WHO DO I THINK I AM?
I JUST...
I JUST WANTED TO MAKE HIM HAPPY.

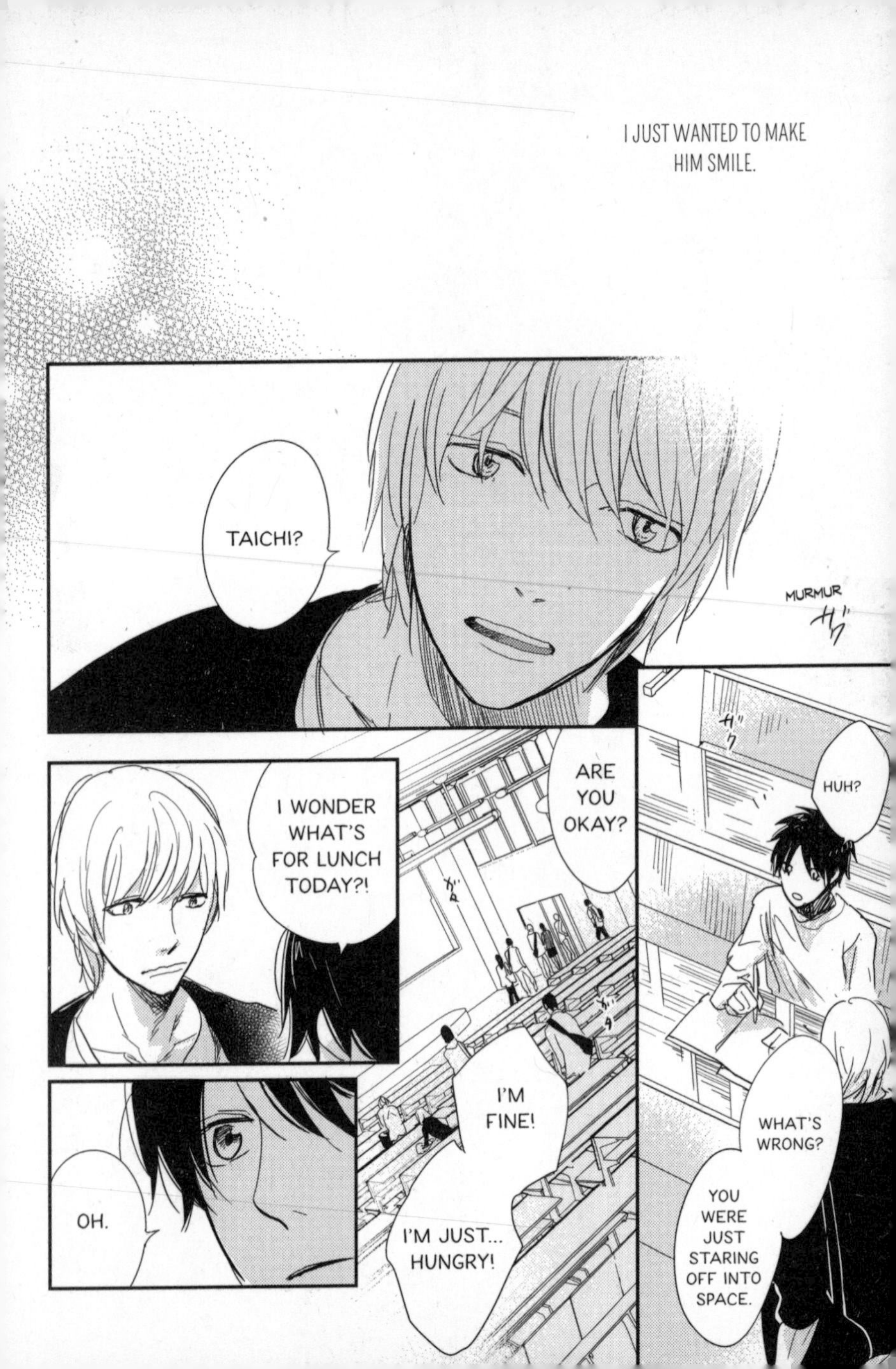
I JUST WANTED TO MAKE HIM SMILE.
TAICHI?
MURMUR
HUH?
WHAT'S WRONG?
YOU WERE JUST STARING OFF INTO SPACE.
ARE YOU OKAY?
I'M FINE!
I'M JUST... HUNGRY!
I WONDER WHAT'S FOR LUNCH TODAY?!
OH.

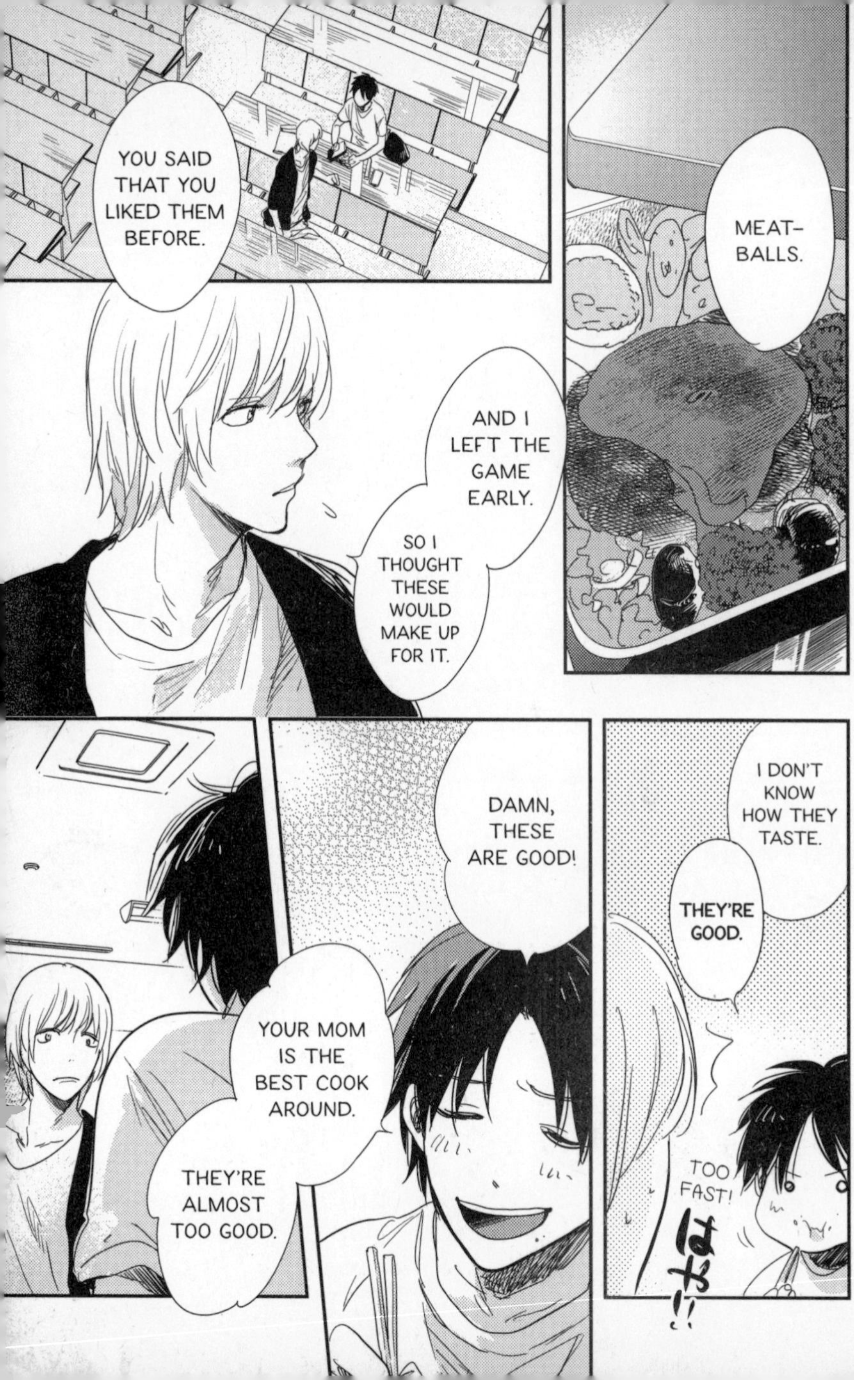
MEAT-BALLS.
YOU SAID THAT YOU LIKED THEM BEFORE.
AND I LEFT THE GAME EARLY.
SO I THOUGHT THESE WOULD MAKE UP FOR IT.
I DON'T KNOW HOW THEY TASTE.
THEY'RE GOOD.
TOO FAST!
はや!!
DAMN, THESE ARE GOOD!
YOUR MOM IS THE BEST COOK AROUND.
THEY'RE ALMOST TOO GOOD.

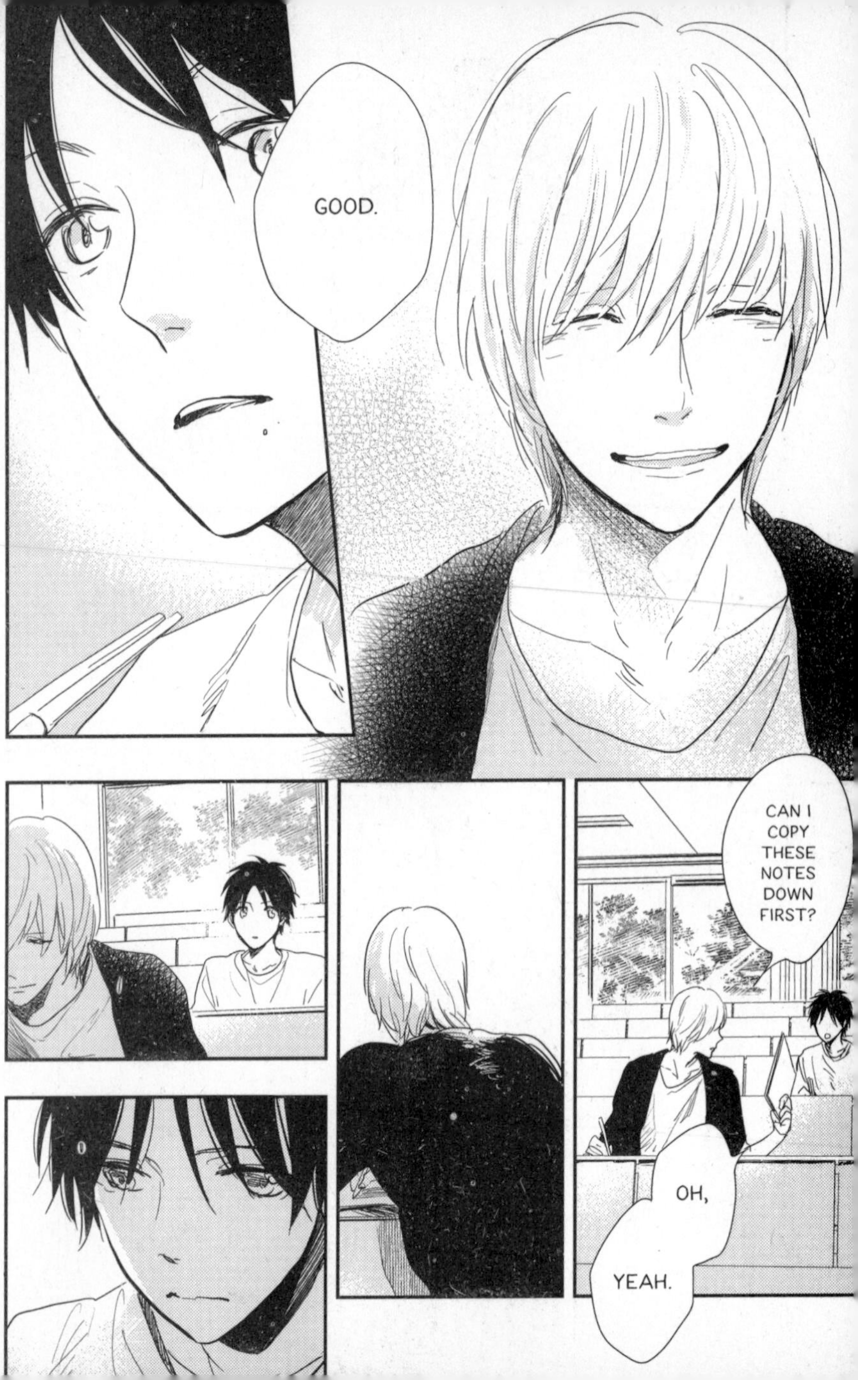
GOOD.
CAN I COPY THESE NOTES DOWN FIRST?
OH, YEAH.

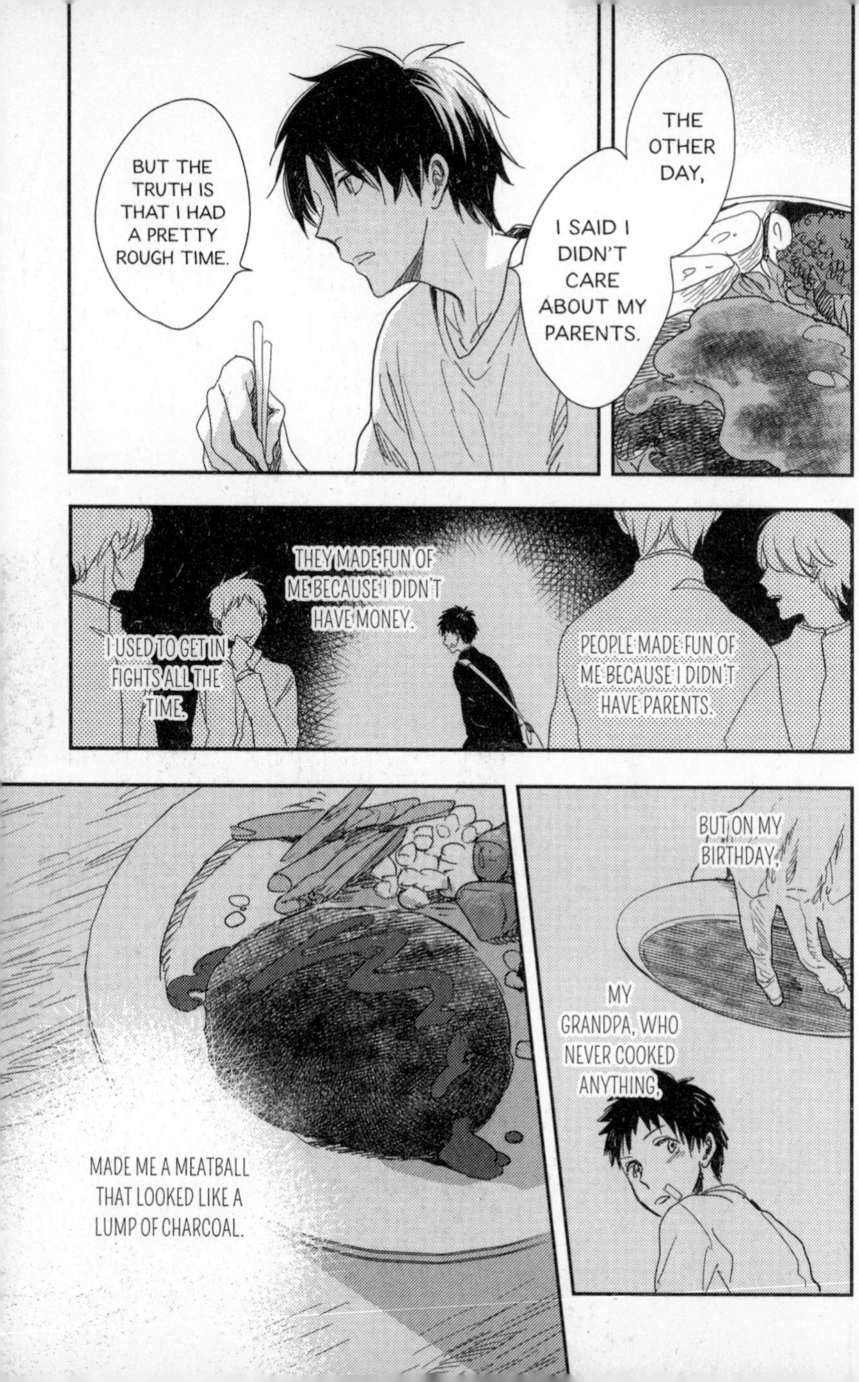
THE OTHER DAY,
I SAID I DIDN'T CARE ABOUT MY PARENTS.
BUT THE TRUTH IS THAT I HAD A PRETTY ROUGH TIME.
PEOPLE MADE FUN OF ME BECAUSE I DIDN'T HAVE PARENTS.
THEY MADE FUN OF ME BECAUSE I DIDN'T HAVE MONEY.
I USED TO GET IN FIGHTS ALL THE TIME.
BUT ON MY BIRTHDAY,
MY GRANDPA, WHO NEVER COOKED ANYTHING,
MADE ME A MEATBALL THAT LOOKED LIKE A LUMP OF CHARCOAL.

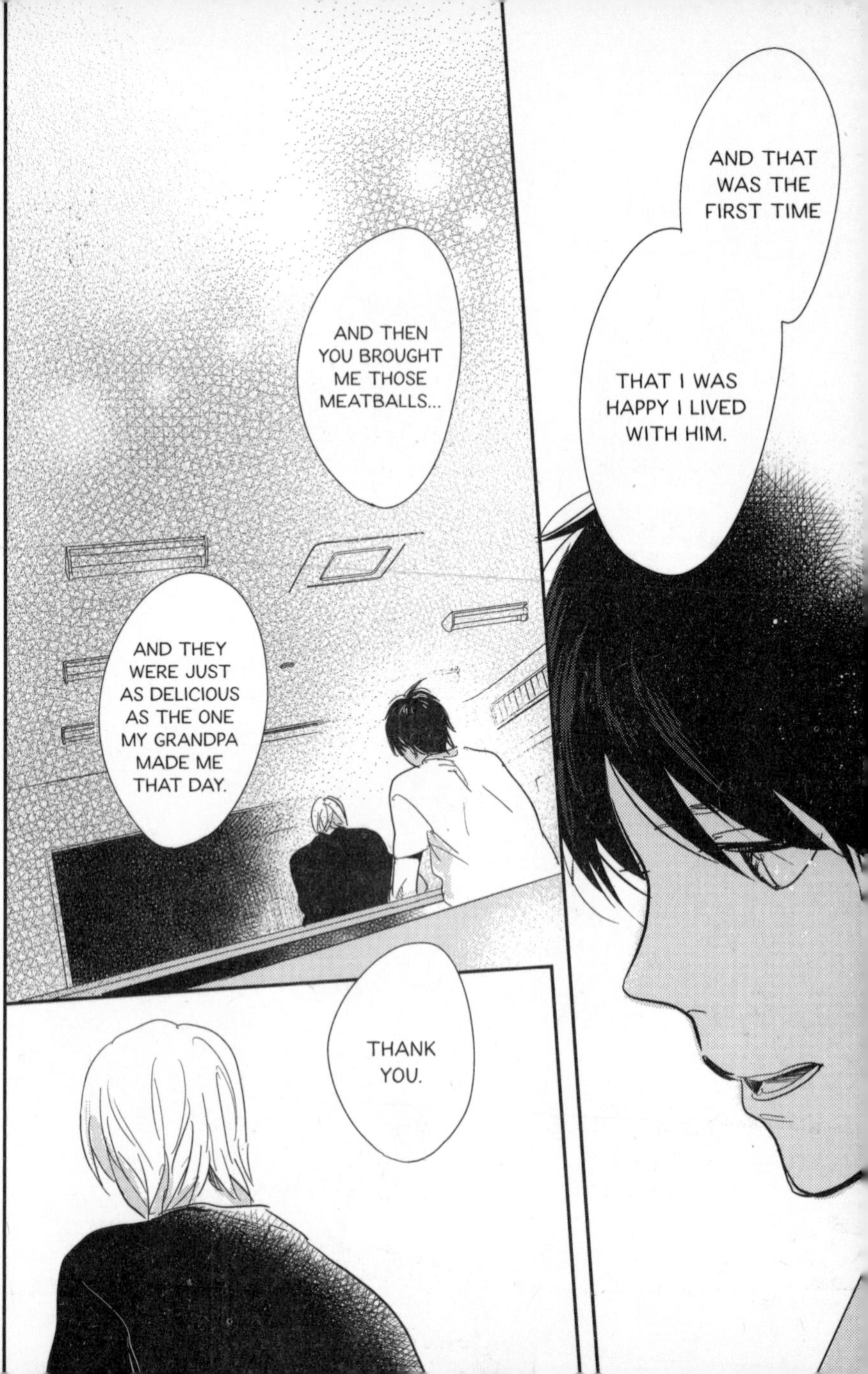
AND THAT WAS THE FIRST TIME
THAT I WAS HAPPY I LIVED WITH HIM.
AND THEN YOU BROUGHT ME THOSE MEATBALLS...
AND THEY WERE JUST AS DELICIOUS AS THE ONE MY GRANDPA MADE ME THAT DAY.
THANK YOU.

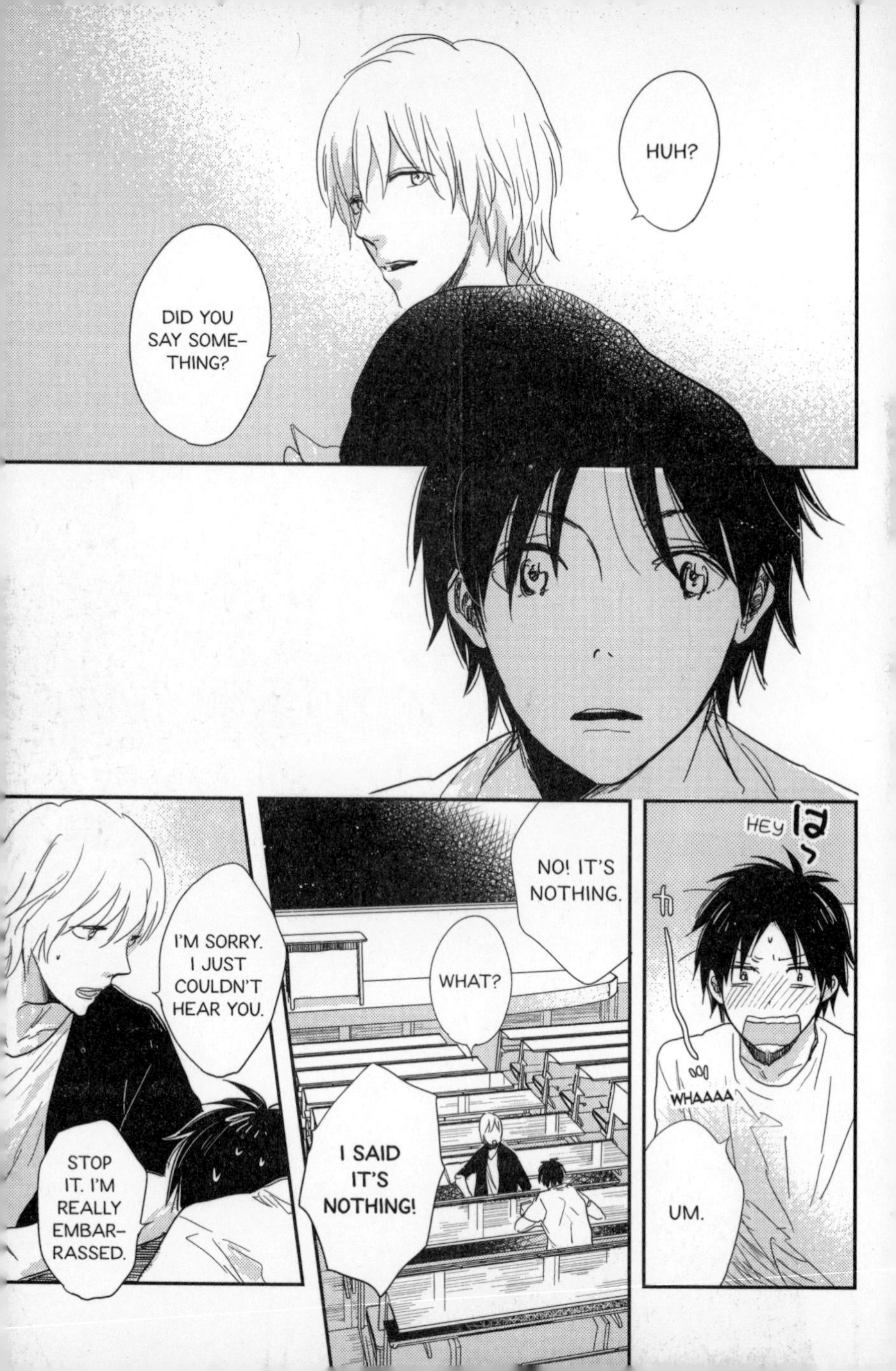
HUH?
DID YOU SAY SOME-THING?
HEY
WHAAAA
UM.
NO! IT'S NOTHING.
WHAT?
I SAID IT'S NOTHING!
I'M SORRY. I JUST COULDN'T HEAR YOU.
STOP IT. I'M REALLY EMBAR-RASSED.

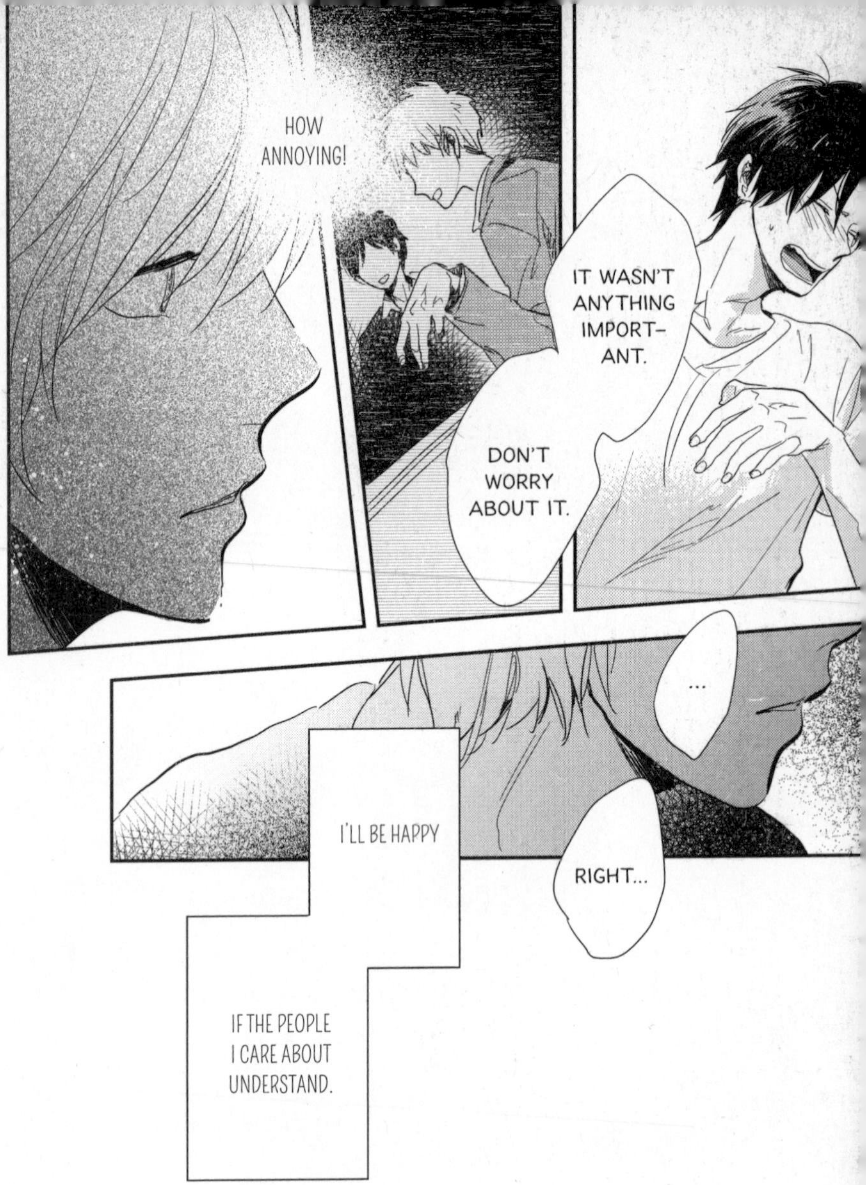
IT WASN'T ANYTHING IMPORT-ANT.
DON'T WORRY ABOUT IT.
HOW ANNOYING!
...
RIGHT...
I'LL BE HAPPY
IF THE PEOPLE I CARE ABOUT UNDERSTAND.

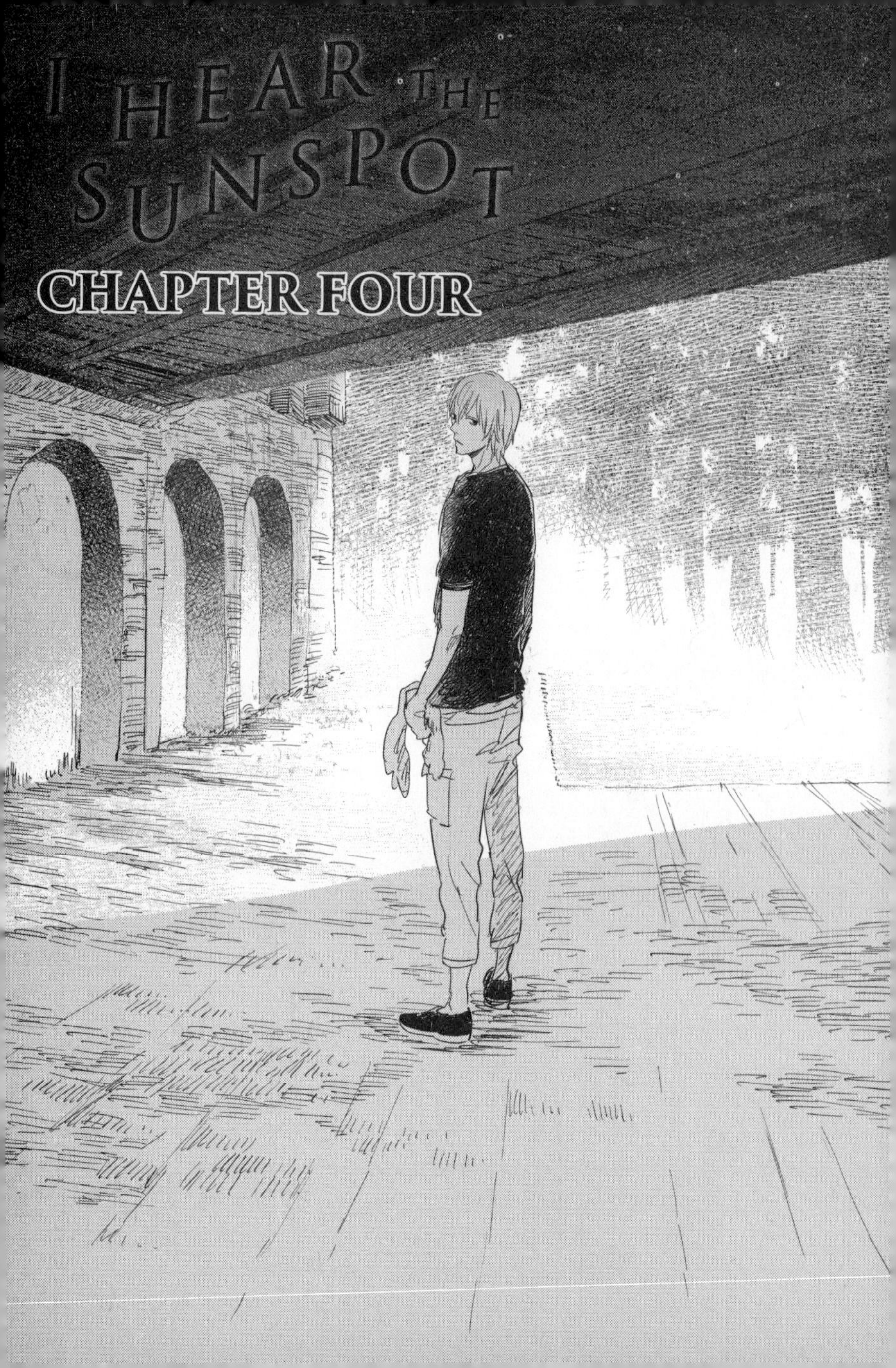
I HEAR THE SUNSPOT
CHAPTER FOUR

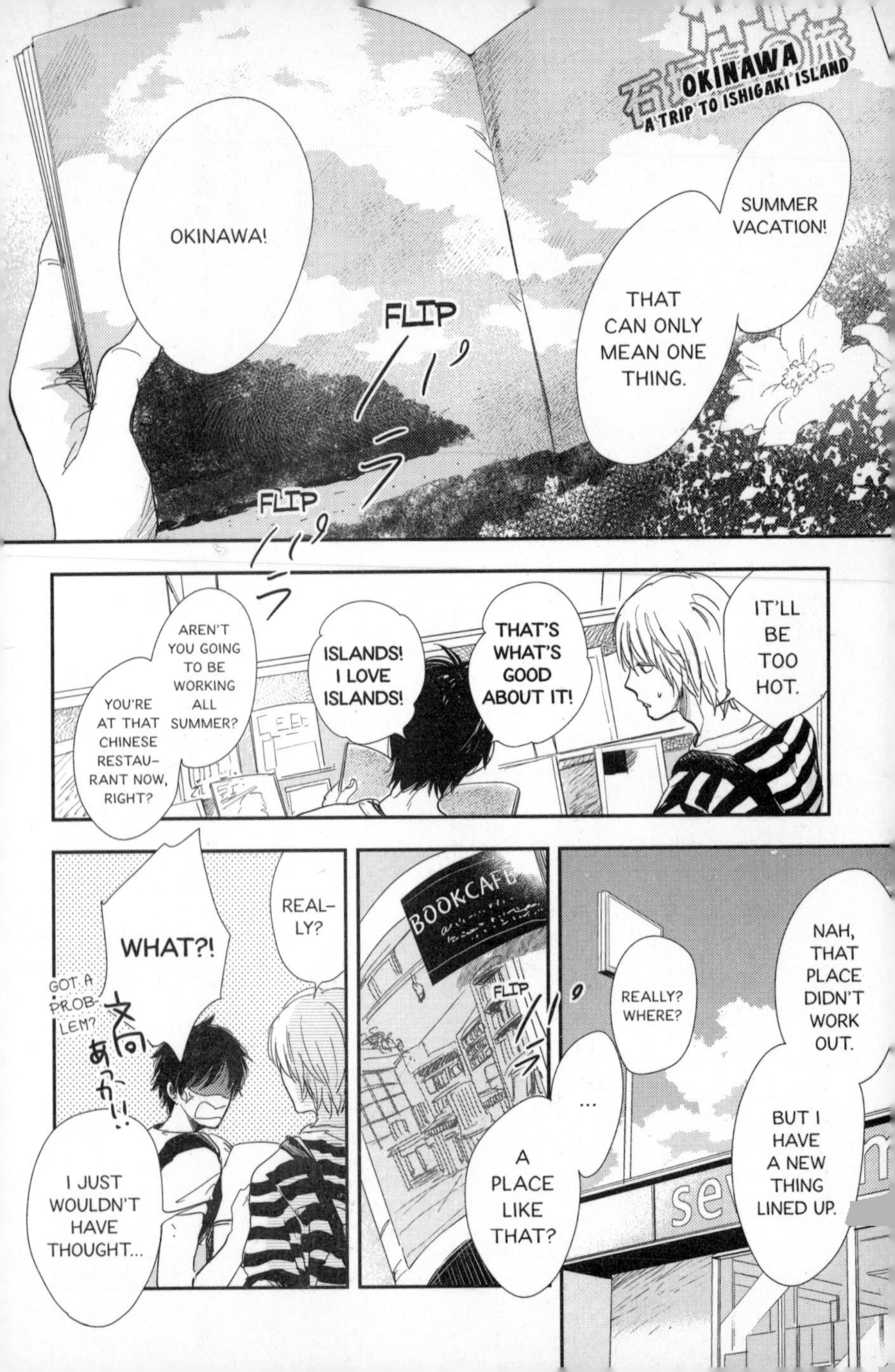
OKINAWA
A TRIP TO ISHIGAKI ISLAND
SUMMER VACATION!
THAT CAN ONLY MEAN ONE THING.
OKINAWA!
FLIP
FLIP
IT'LL BE TOO HOT.
THAT'S WHAT'S GOOD ABOUT IT!
ISLANDS! I LOVE ISLANDS!
AREN'T YOU GOING TO BE WORKING ALL SUMMER?
YOU'RE AT THAT CHINESE RESTAU-RANT NOW, RIGHT?
NAH, THAT PLACE DIDN'T WORK OUT.
BUT I HAVE A NEW THING LINED UP.
REALLY? WHERE?
BOOKCAFE
FLIP
...
A PLACE LIKE THAT?
REAL-LY?
WHAT?!
GOT A PROB-LEM?
I JUST WOULDN'T HAVE THOUGHT...

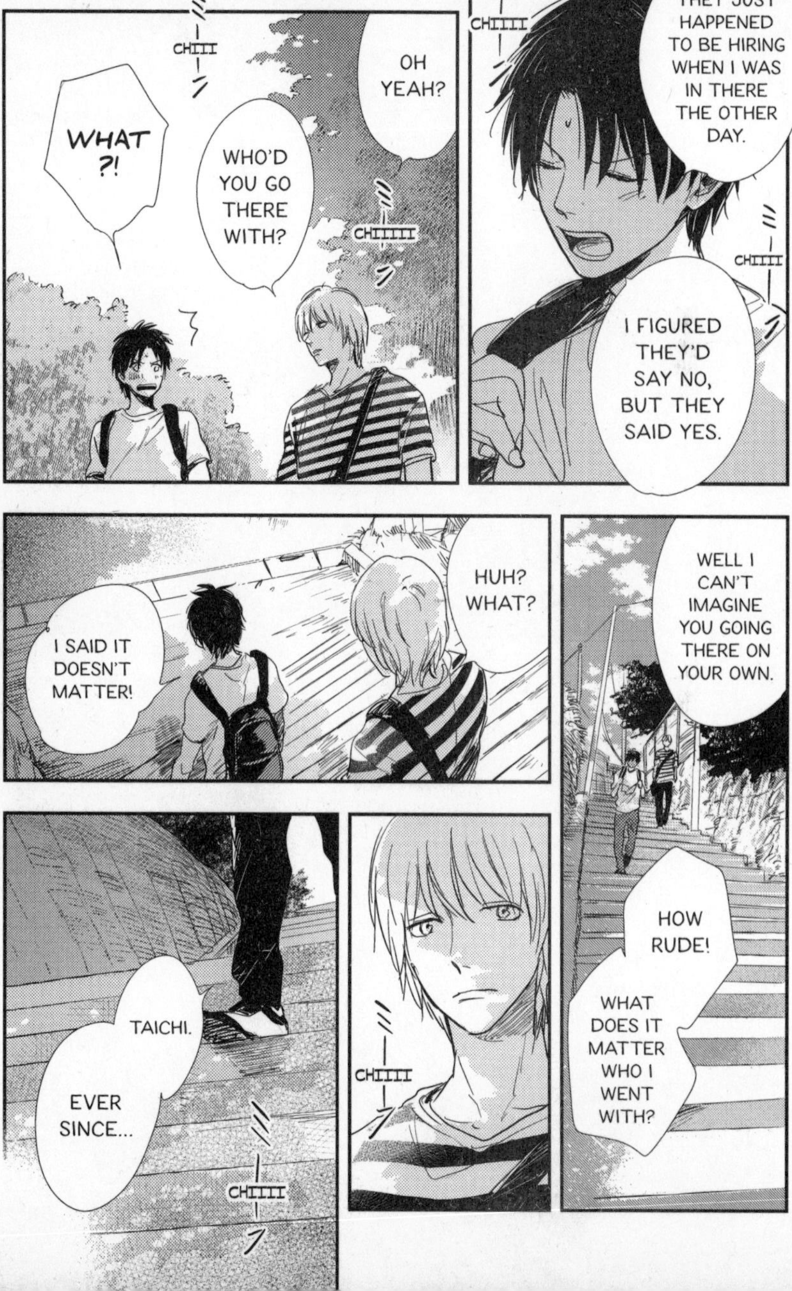
CHIIII
THEY JUST HAPPENED TO BE HIRING WHEN I WAS IN THERE THE OTHER DAY.
CHIIII
I FIGURED THEY'D SAY NO, BUT THEY SAID YES.
OH YEAH?
CHIII
WHO'D YOU GO THERE WITH?
CHIIIII
WHAT ?!
WELL I CAN'T IMAGINE YOU GOING THERE ON YOUR OWN.
HOW RUDE!
WHAT DOES IT MATTER WHO I WENT WITH?
HUH? WHAT?
I SAID IT DOESN'T MATTER!
CHIIII
TAICHI.
EVER SINCE...
CHIIII

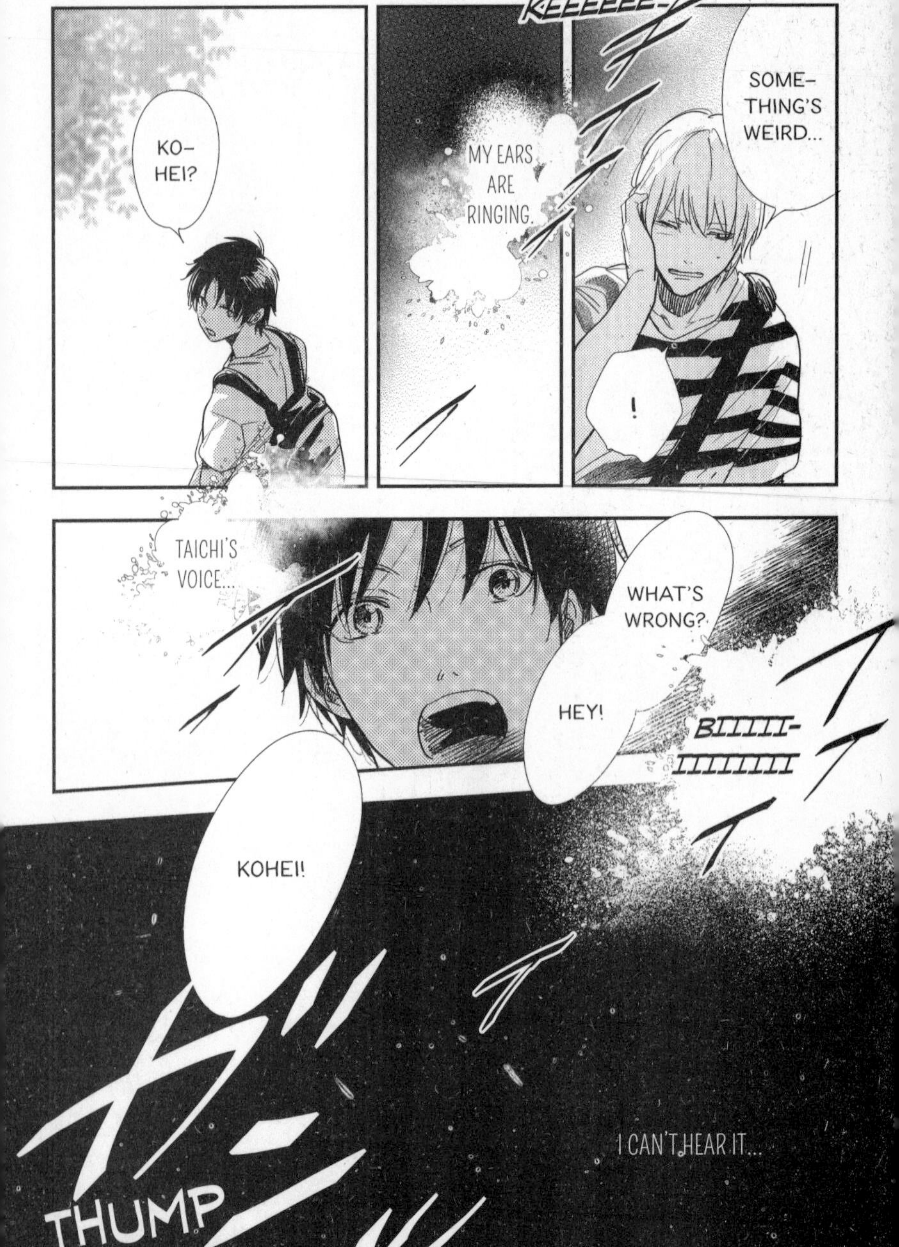
SOME-THING'S WEIRD...
!
KEEEEEEE
MY EARS ARE RINGING.
KO-HEI?
WHAT'S WRONG?
HEY!
BIIIII-IIIIIIII
TAICHI'S VOICE...
KOHEI!
I CAN'T HEAR IT...
THUMP

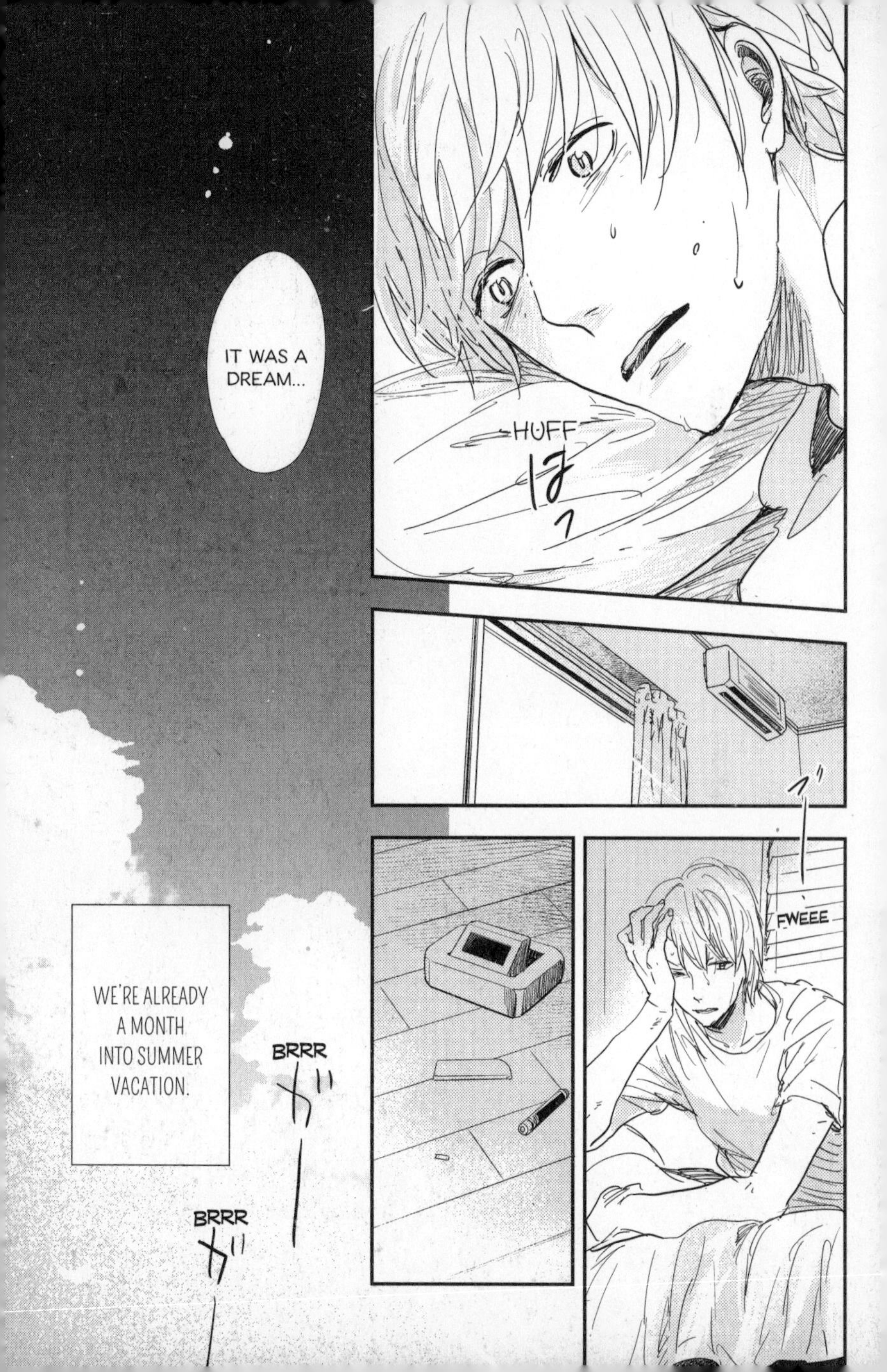
HUFF
はっ
FWEEE
ヴー
IT WAS A DREAM...
WE'RE ALREADY A MONTH INTO SUMMER VACATION.
BRRR
ガー
BRRR
ガー

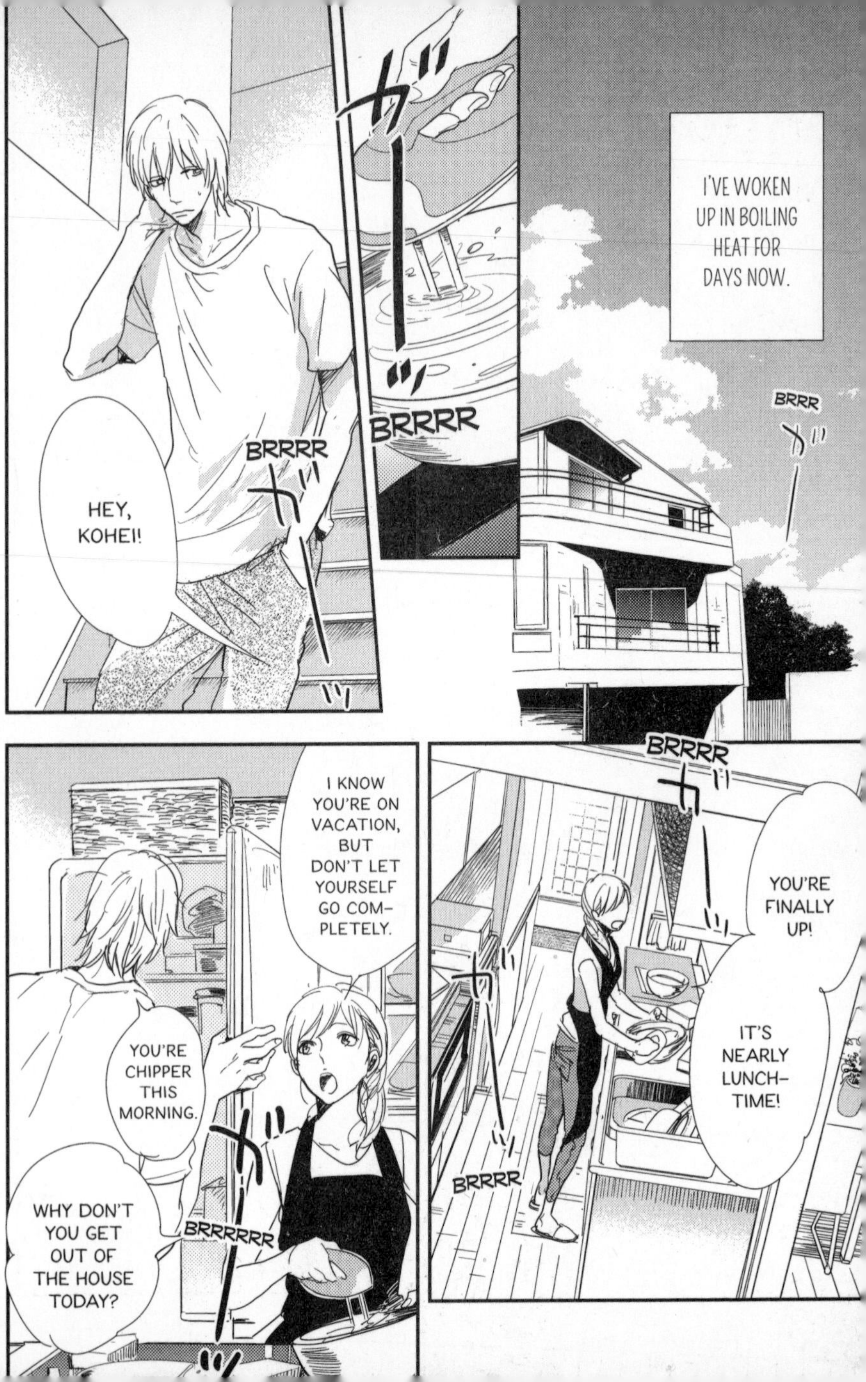
I'VE WOKEN UP IN BOILING HEAT FOR DAYS NOW.
BRRR
BRRRR
BRRRR
HEY, KOHEI!
BRRRR
YOU'RE FINALLY UP!
IT'S NEARLY LUNCH-TIME!
BRRRR
I KNOW YOU'RE ON VACATION, BUT DON'T LET YOURSELF GO COM-PLETELY.
YOU'RE CHIPPER THIS MORNING.
BRRRRRR
WHY DON'T YOU GET OUT OF THE HOUSE TODAY?

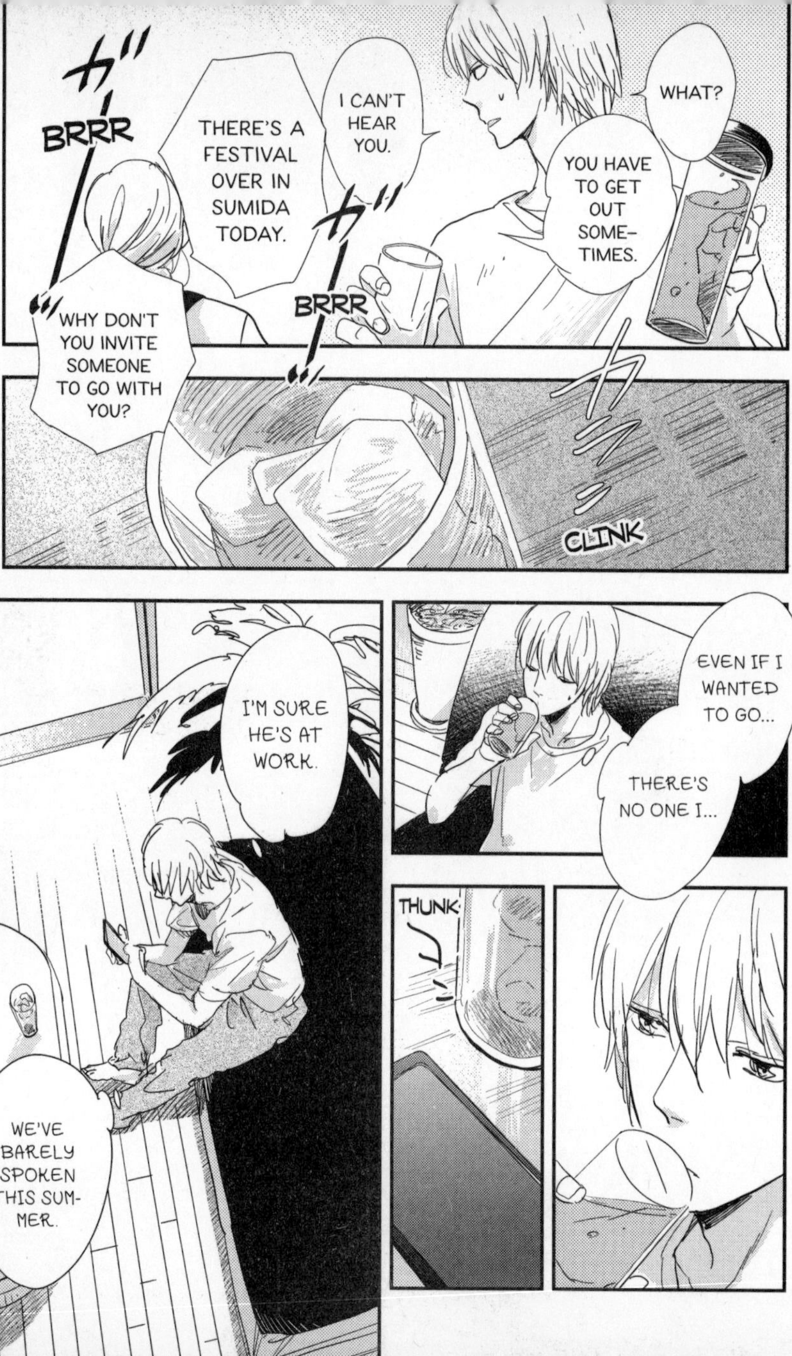
WHAT?
YOU HAVE TO GET OUT SOME-TIMES.
I CAN'T HEAR YOU.
THERE'S A FESTIVAL OVER IN SUMIDA TODAY.
BRRR
BRRR
WHY DON'T YOU INVITE SOMEONE TO GO WITH YOU?
CLINK
EVEN IF I WANTED TO GO...
THERE'S NO ONE I...
THUNK
I'M SURE HE'S AT WORK.
WE'VE BARELY SPOKEN THIS SUM-MER.

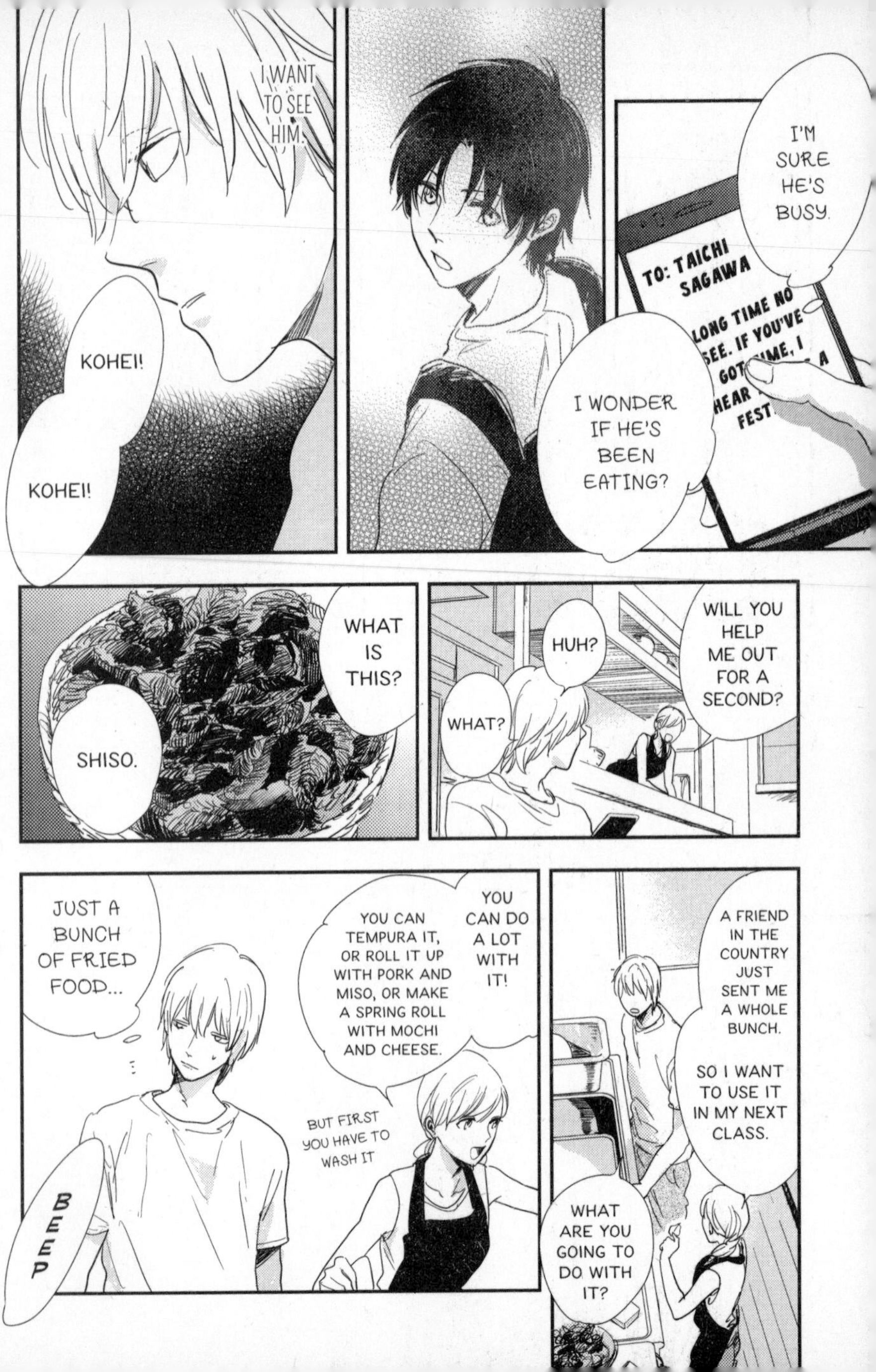
I'M SURE HE'S BUSY.
TO: TAICHI SAGAWA
LONG TIME NO SEE. IF YOU'VE
GOT
TIME, I
HEAR
A
FEST
I WONDER IF HE'S BEEN EATING?
I WANT TO SEE HIM.
KOHEI!
KOHEI!
WILL YOU HELP ME OUT FOR A SECOND?
HUH?
WHAT?
WHAT IS THIS?
SHISO.
A FRIEND IN THE COUNTRY JUST SENT ME A WHOLE BUNCH.
SO I WANT TO USE IT IN MY NEXT CLASS.
WHAT ARE YOU GOING TO DO WITH IT?
YOU CAN DO A LOT WITH IT!
YOU CAN TEMPURA IT, OR ROLL IT UP WITH PORK AND MISO, OR MAKE A SPRING ROLL WITH MOCHI AND CHEESE.
JUST A BUNCH OF FRIED FOOD...
...
BUT FIRST YOU HAVE TO WASH IT
BEEP

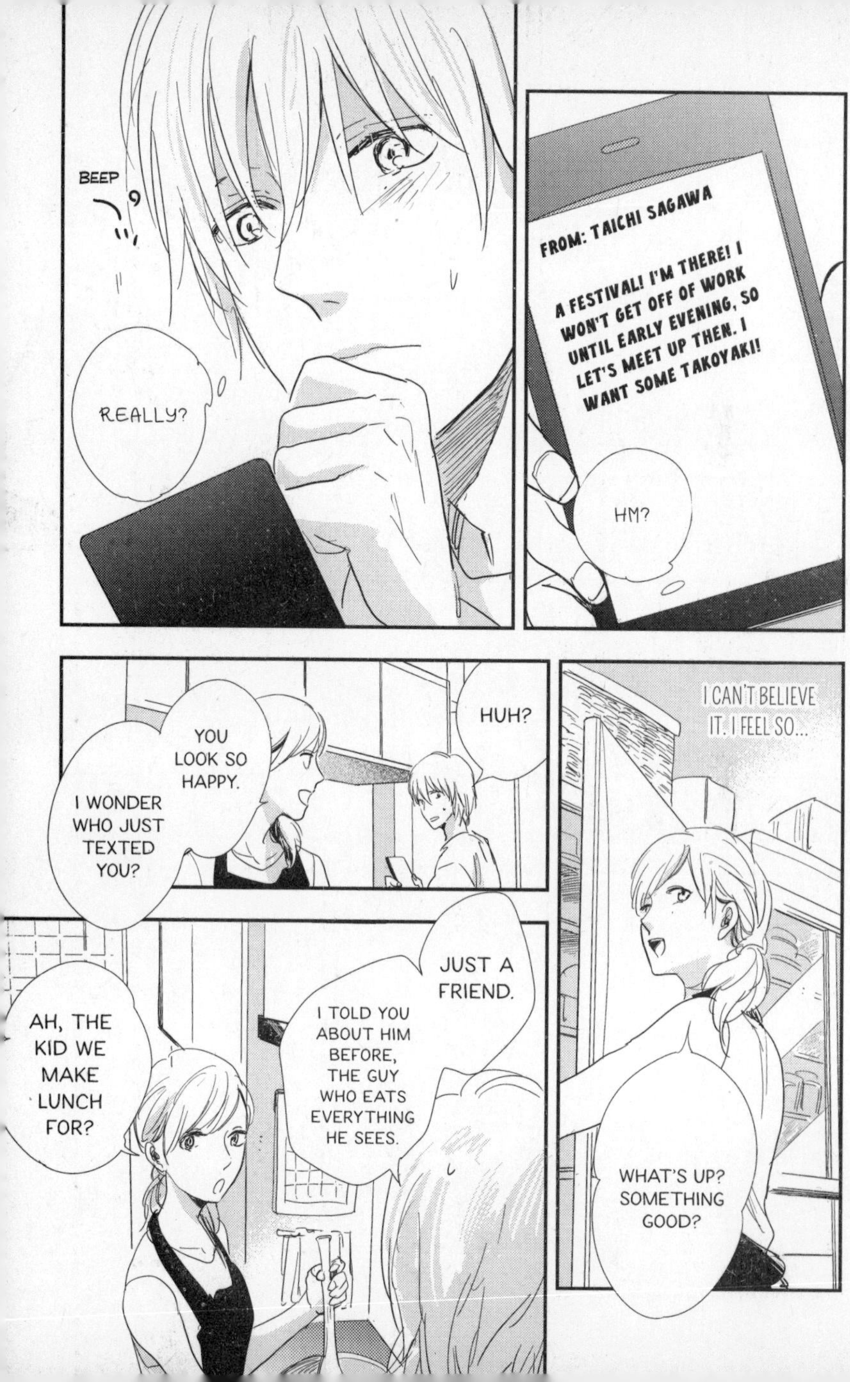

FROM: TAICHI SAGAWA
A FESTIVAL! I'M THERE! I WON'T GET OFF OF WORK UNTIL EARLY EVENING, SO LET'S MEET UP THEN. I WANT SOME TAKOYAKI!
HM?
BEEP
REALLY?
I CAN'T BELIEVE IT. I FEEL SO...
WHAT'S UP? SOMETHING GOOD?
HUH?
YOU LOOK SO HAPPY.
I WONDER WHO JUST TEXTED YOU?
JUST A FRIEND.
I TOLD YOU ABOUT HIM BEFORE, THE GUY WHO EATS EVERYTHING HE SEES.
AH, THE KID WE MAKE LUNCH FOR?

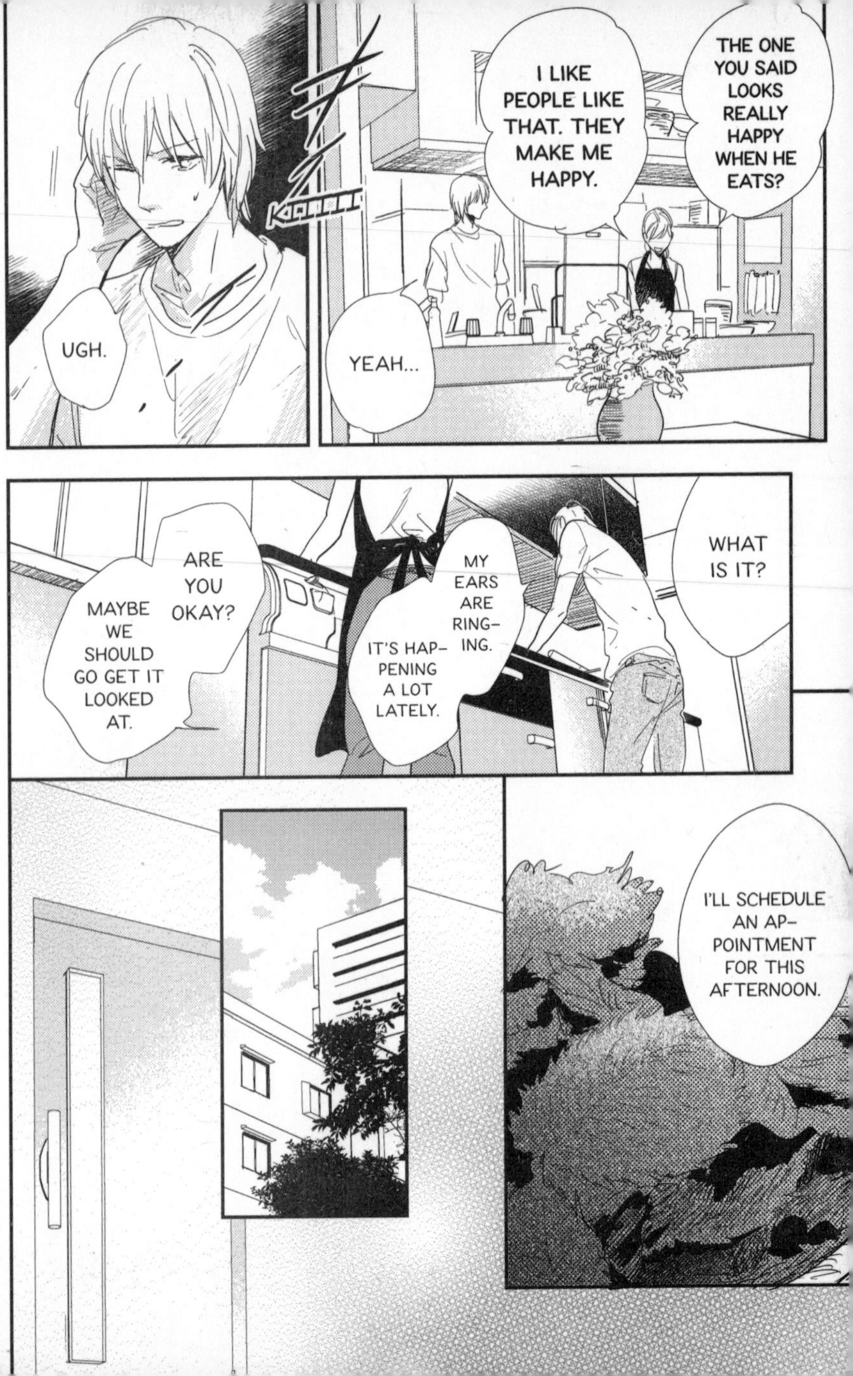
THE ONE YOU SAID LOOKS REALLY HAPPY WHEN HE EATS?
I LIKE PEOPLE LIKE THAT. THEY MAKE ME HAPPY.
YEAH...
UGH.
WHAT IS IT?
MY EARS ARE RING- ING.
IT'S HAP- PENING A LOT LATELY.
ARE YOU OKAY?
MAYBE WE SHOULD GO GET IT LOOKED AT.
I'LL SCHEDULE AN AP- POINTMENT FOR THIS AFTERNOON.

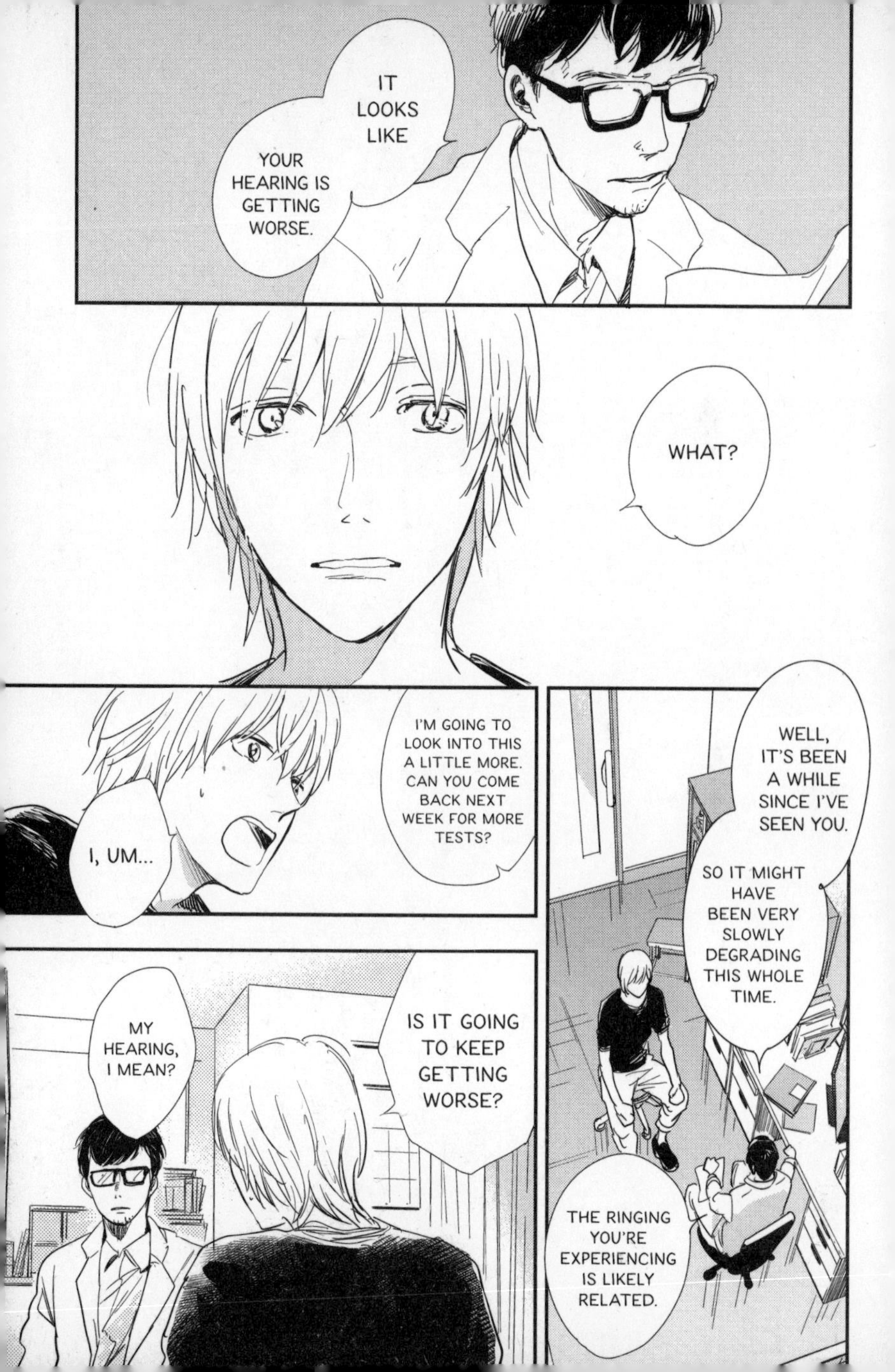
IT LOOKS LIKE
YOUR HEARING IS GETTING WORSE.
WHAT?
WELL, IT'S BEEN A WHILE SINCE I'VE SEEN YOU.
SO IT MIGHT HAVE BEEN VERY SLOWLY DEGRADING THIS WHOLE TIME.
THE RINGING YOU'RE EXPERIENCING IS LIKELY RELATED.
I'M GOING TO LOOK INTO THIS A LITTLE MORE. CAN YOU COME BACK NEXT WEEK FOR MORE TESTS?
I, UM...
IS IT GOING TO KEEP GETTING WORSE?
MY HEARING, I MEAN?

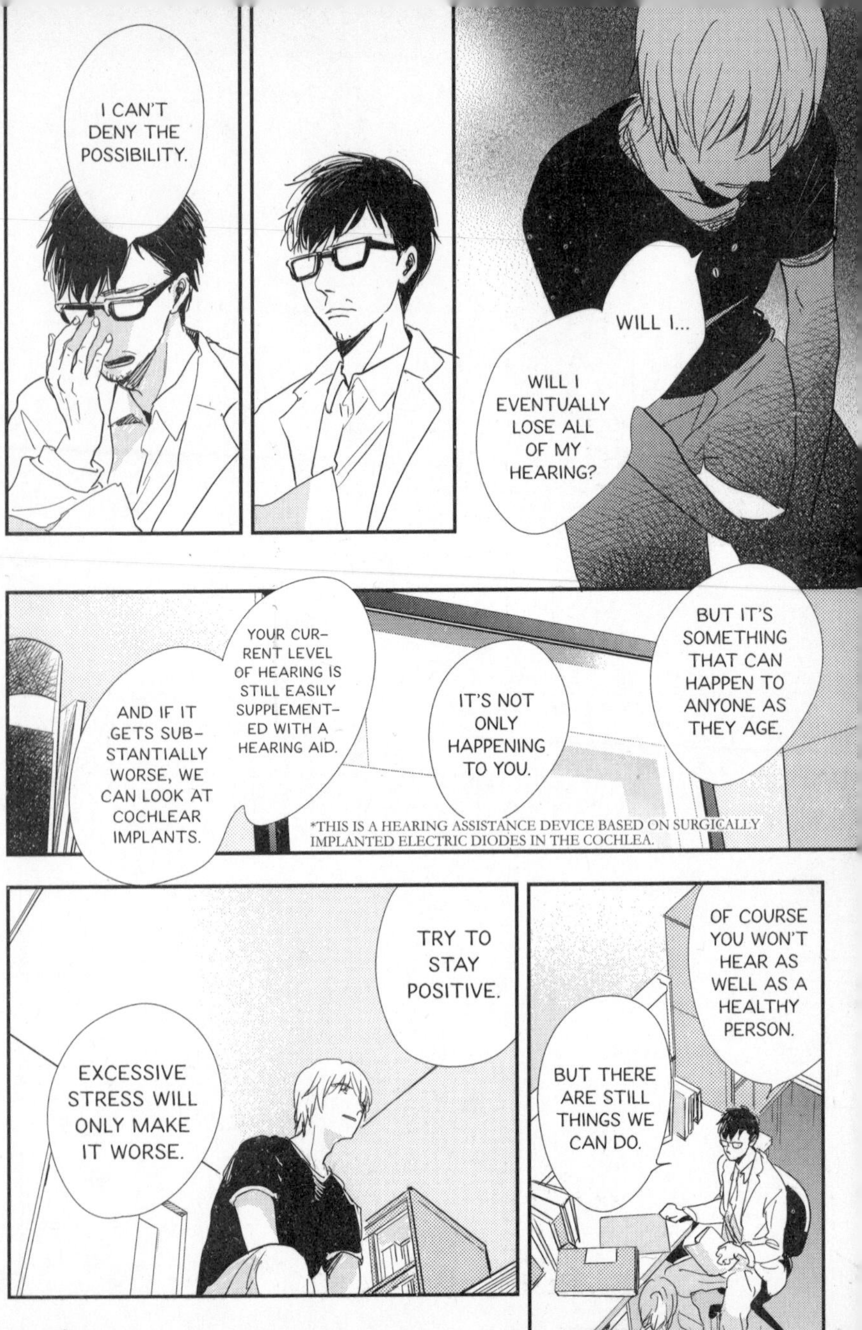
WILL I...
WILL I EVENTUALLY LOSE ALL OF MY HEARING?
I CAN'T DENY THE POSSIBILITY.
BUT IT'S SOMETHING THAT CAN HAPPEN TO ANYONE AS THEY AGE.
IT'S NOT ONLY HAPPENING TO YOU.
YOUR CUR-RENT LEVEL OF HEARING IS STILL EASILY SUPPLEMENT-ED WITH A HEARING AID.
AND IF IT GETS SUB-STANTIALLY WORSE, WE CAN LOOK AT COCHLEAR IMPLANTS.
*THIS IS A HEARING ASSISTANCE DEVICE BASED ON SURGICALLY IMPLANTED ELECTRIC DIODES IN THE COCHLEA.
OF COURSE YOU WON'T HEAR AS WELL AS A HEALTHY PERSON.
BUT THERE ARE STILL THINGS WE CAN DO.
TRY TO STAY POSITIVE.
EXCESSIVE STRESS WILL ONLY MAKE IT WORSE.

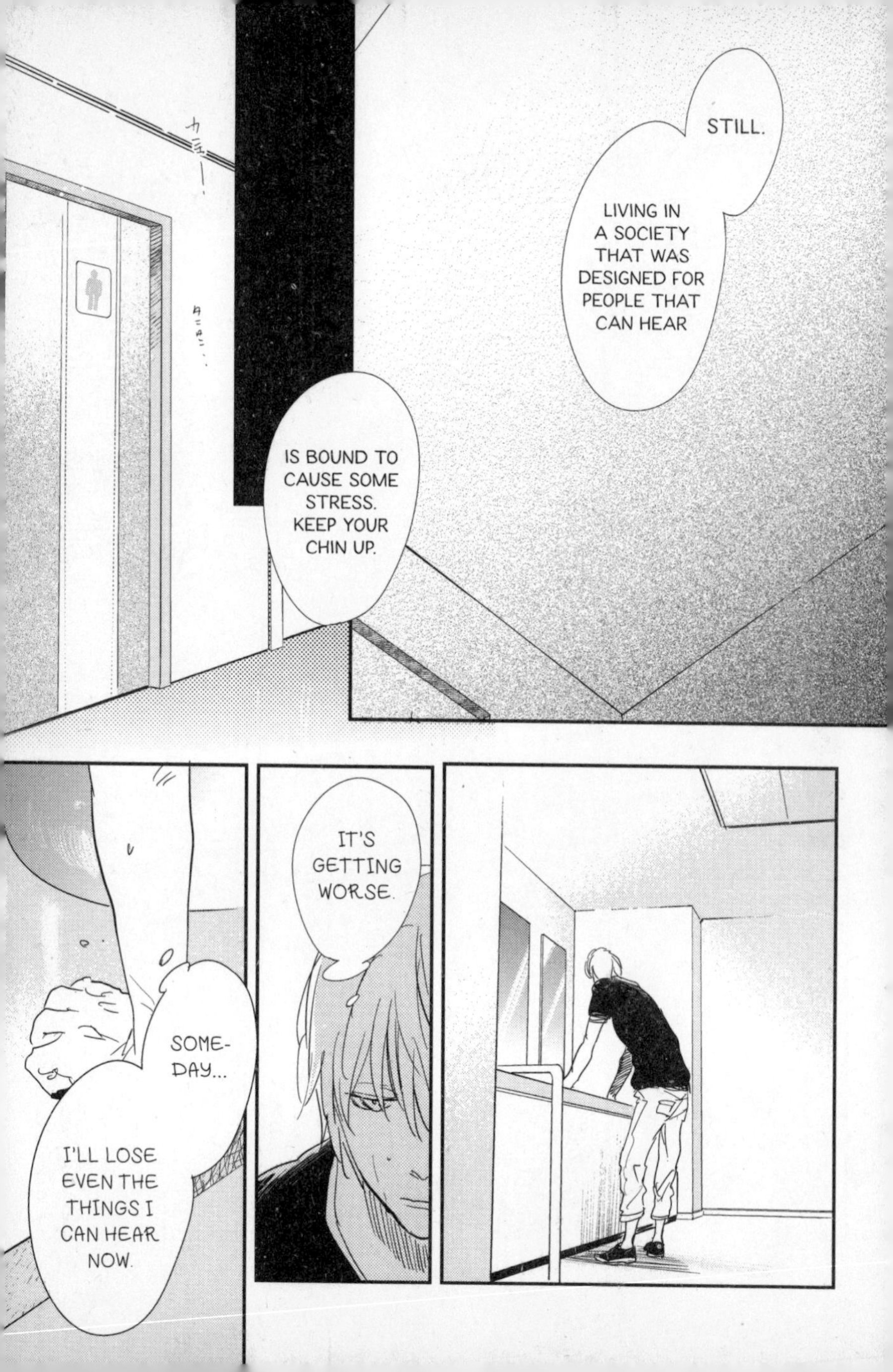
STILL.
LIVING IN A SOCIETY THAT WAS DESIGNED FOR PEOPLE THAT CAN HEAR
IS BOUND TO CAUSE SOME STRESS. KEEP YOUR CHIN UP.
IT'S GETTING WORSE.
SOME-DAY...
I'LL LOSE EVEN THE THINGS I CAN HEAR NOW.

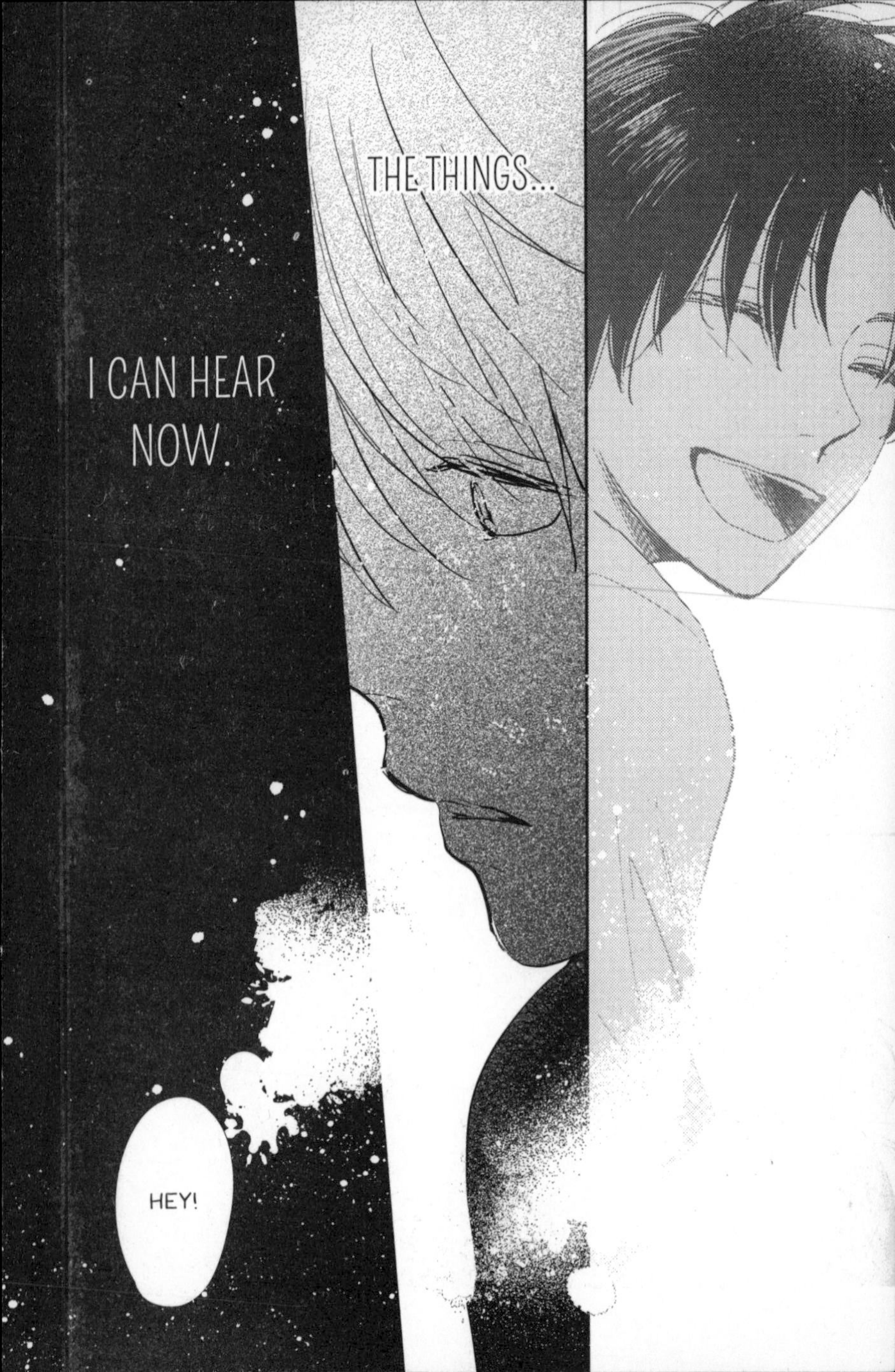
THE THINGS...
I CAN HEAR NOW.
HEY!

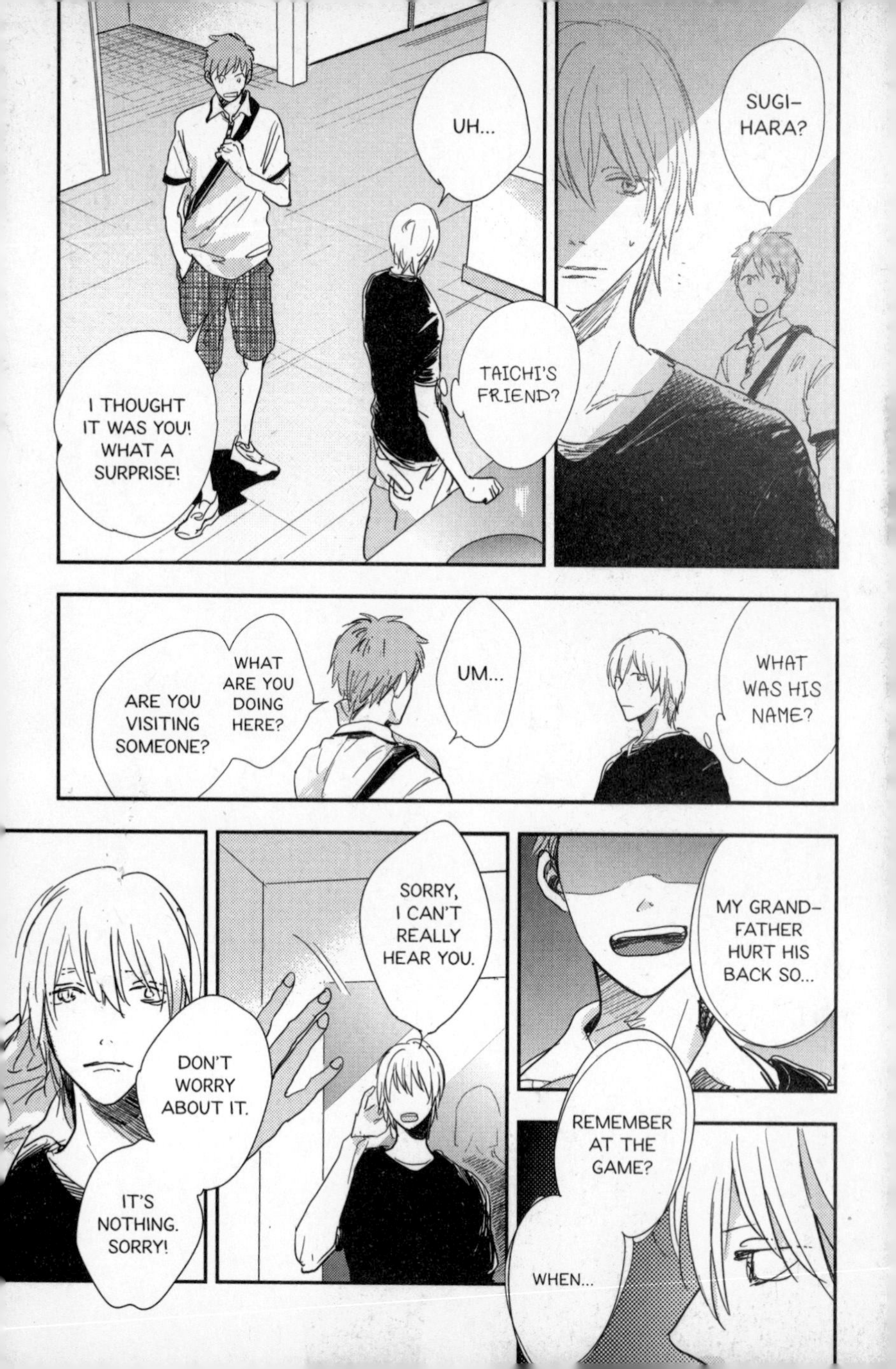
SUGI-HARA?
UH...
TAICHI'S FRIEND?
I THOUGHT IT WAS YOU! WHAT A SURPRISE!
WHAT WAS HIS NAME?
UM...
WHAT ARE YOU DOING HERE?
ARE YOU VISITING SOMEONE?
MY GRAND-FATHER HURT HIS BACK SO...
REMEMBER AT THE GAME?
WHEN...
SORRY, I CAN'T REALLY HEAR YOU.
DON'T WORRY ABOUT IT.
IT'S NOTHING. SORRY!

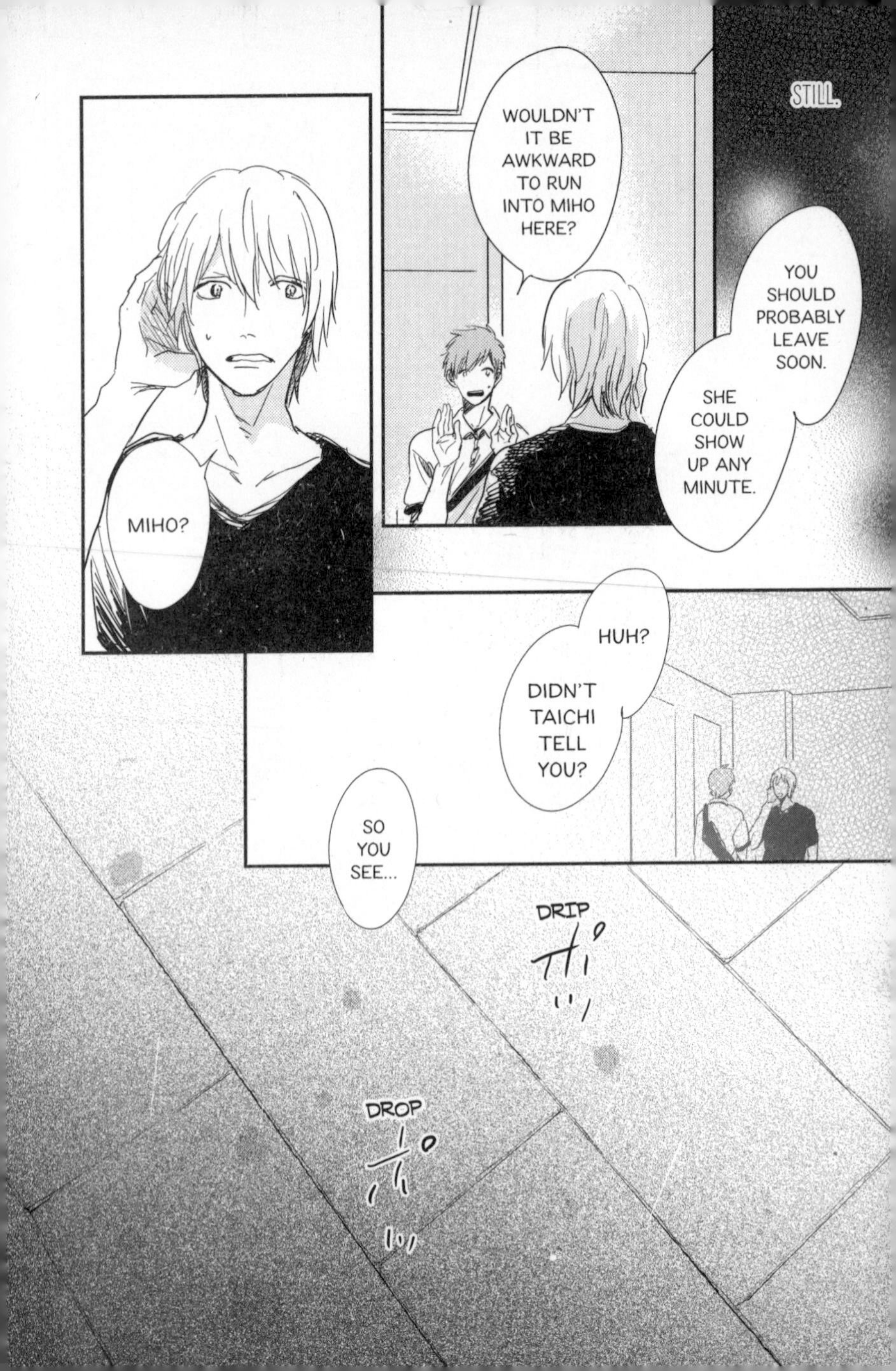
STILL.
WOULDN'T IT BE AWKWARD TO RUN INTO MIHO HERE?
YOU SHOULD PROBABLY LEAVE SOON.
SHE COULD SHOW UP ANY MINUTE.
MIHO?
HUH?
DIDN'T TAICHI TELL YOU?
SO YOU SEE...
DRIP
DROP

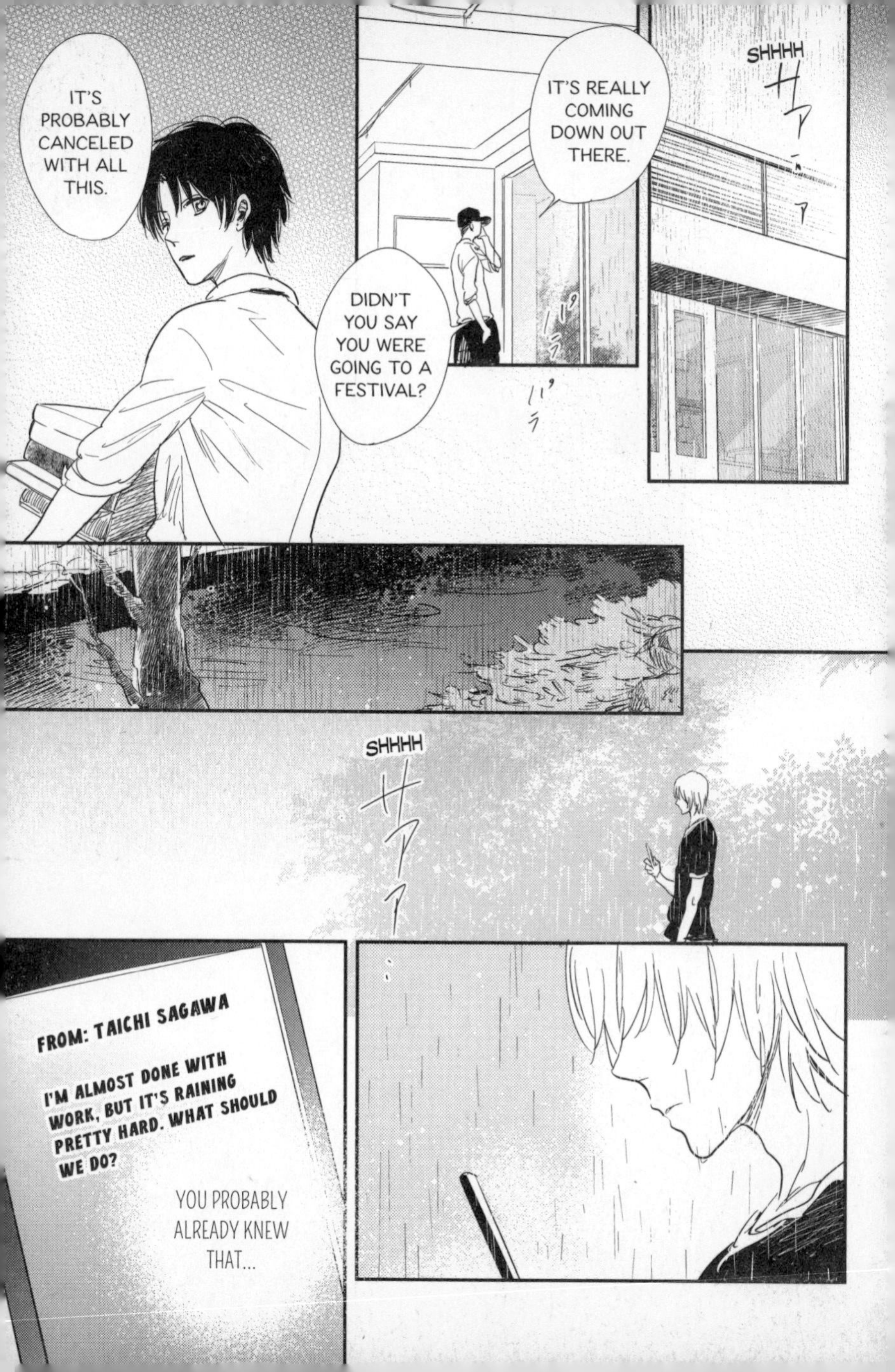
SHHHH
IT'S REALLY COMING DOWN OUT THERE.
DIDN'T YOU SAY YOU WERE GOING TO A FESTIVAL?
IT'S PROBABLY CANCELED WITH ALL THIS.
SHHHH
FROM: TAICHI SAGAWA
I'M ALMOST DONE WITH WORK, BUT IT'S RAINING PRETTY HARD. WHAT SHOULD WE DO?
YOU PROBABLY ALREADY KNEW THAT...

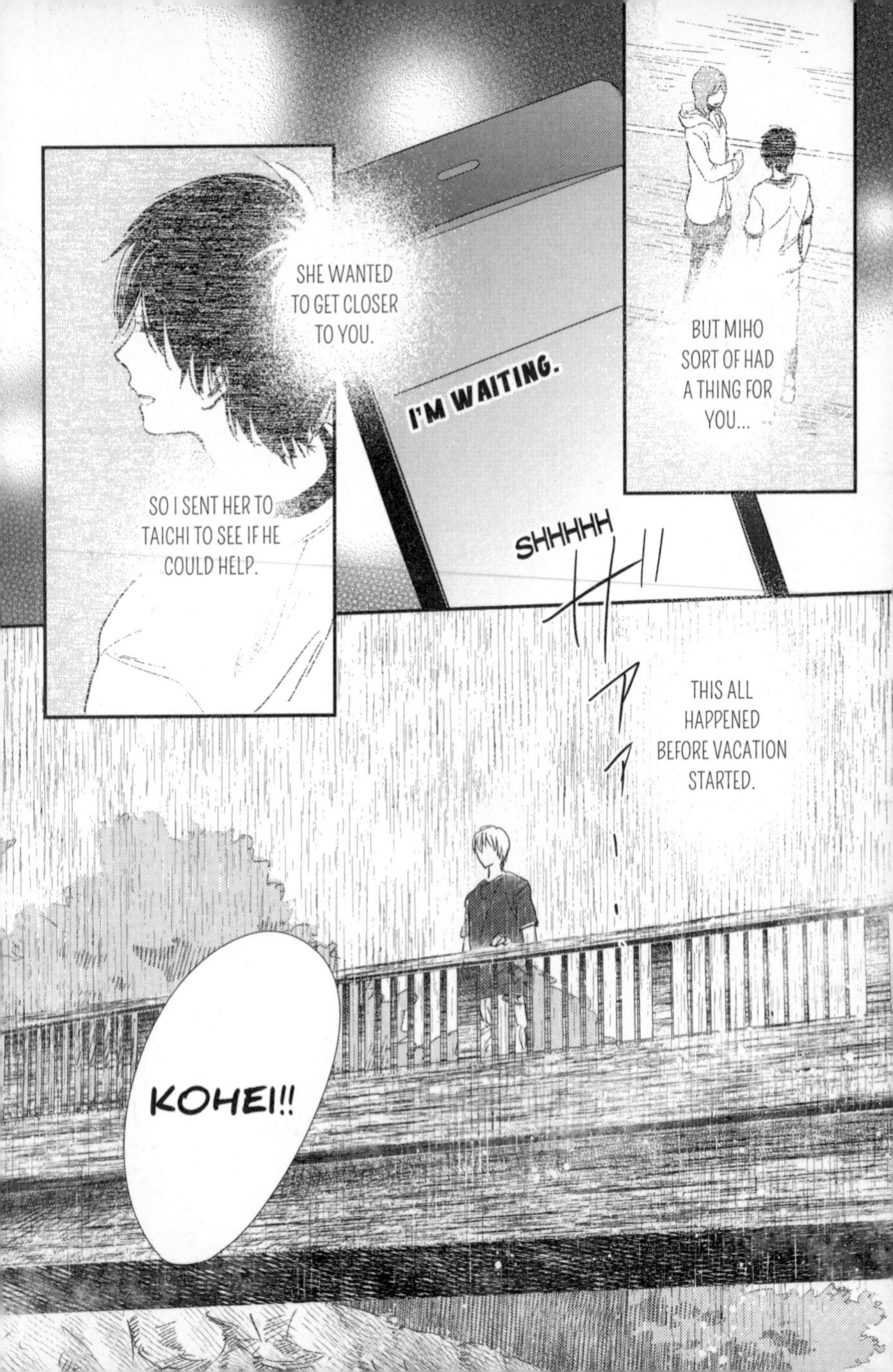
BUT MIHO SORT OF HAD A THING FOR YOU...
SHE WANTED TO GET CLOSER TO YOU.
SO I SENT HER TO TAICHI TO SEE IF HE COULD HELP.
I'M WAITING.
SHHHHH
THIS ALL HAPPENED BEFORE VACATION STARTED.
KOHEI!!

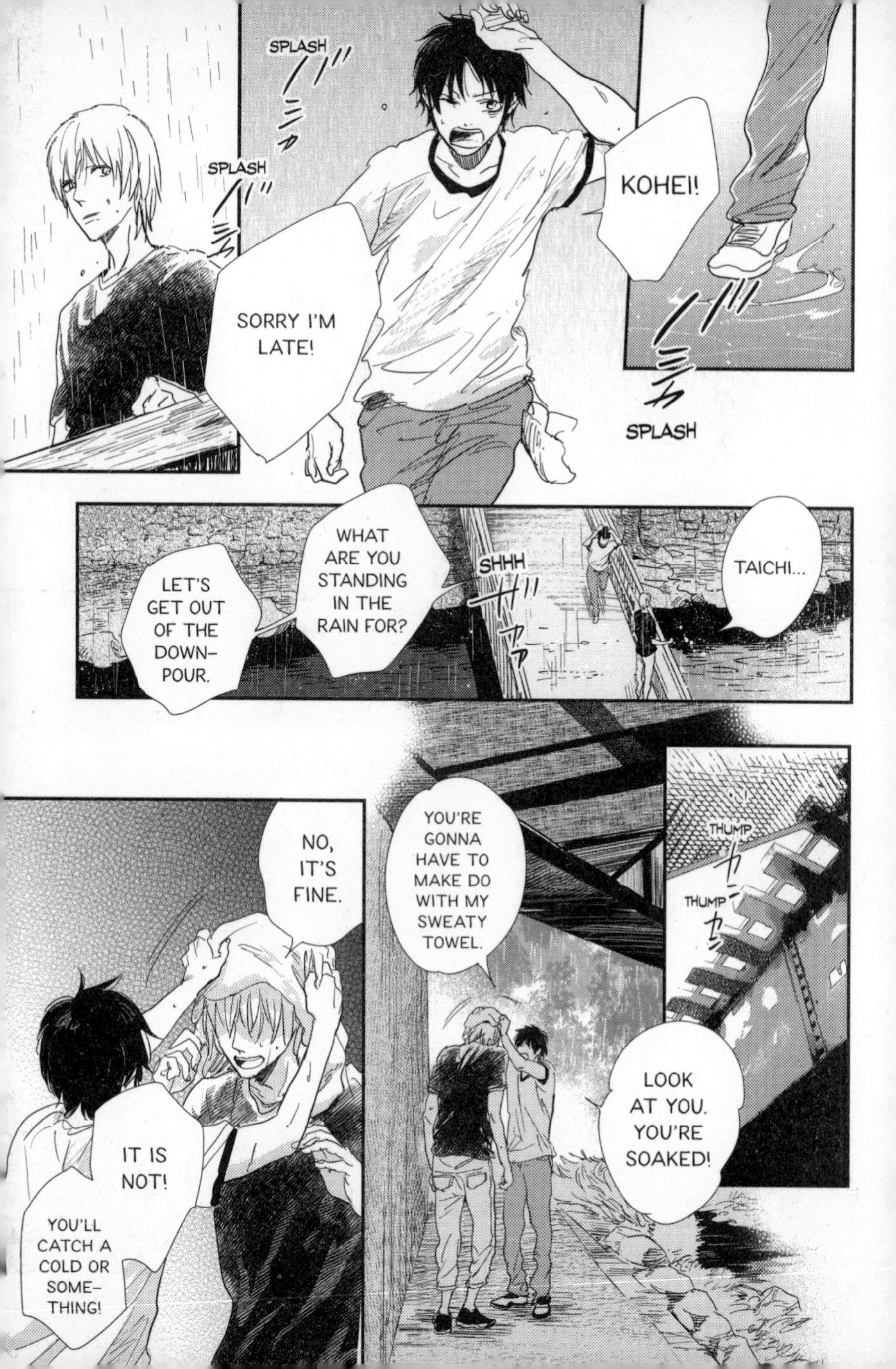
KOHEI!
SPLASH
SPLASH
SPLASH
SORRY I'M LATE!
TAICHI...
SHHH
WHAT ARE YOU STANDING IN THE RAIN FOR?
LET'S GET OUT OF THE DOWN-POUR.
THUMP
THUMP
LOOK AT YOU. YOU'RE SOAKED!
YOU'RE GONNA HAVE TO MAKE DO WITH MY SWEATY TOWEL.
NO, IT'S FINE.
IT IS NOT!
YOU'LL CATCH A COLD OR SOME-THING!

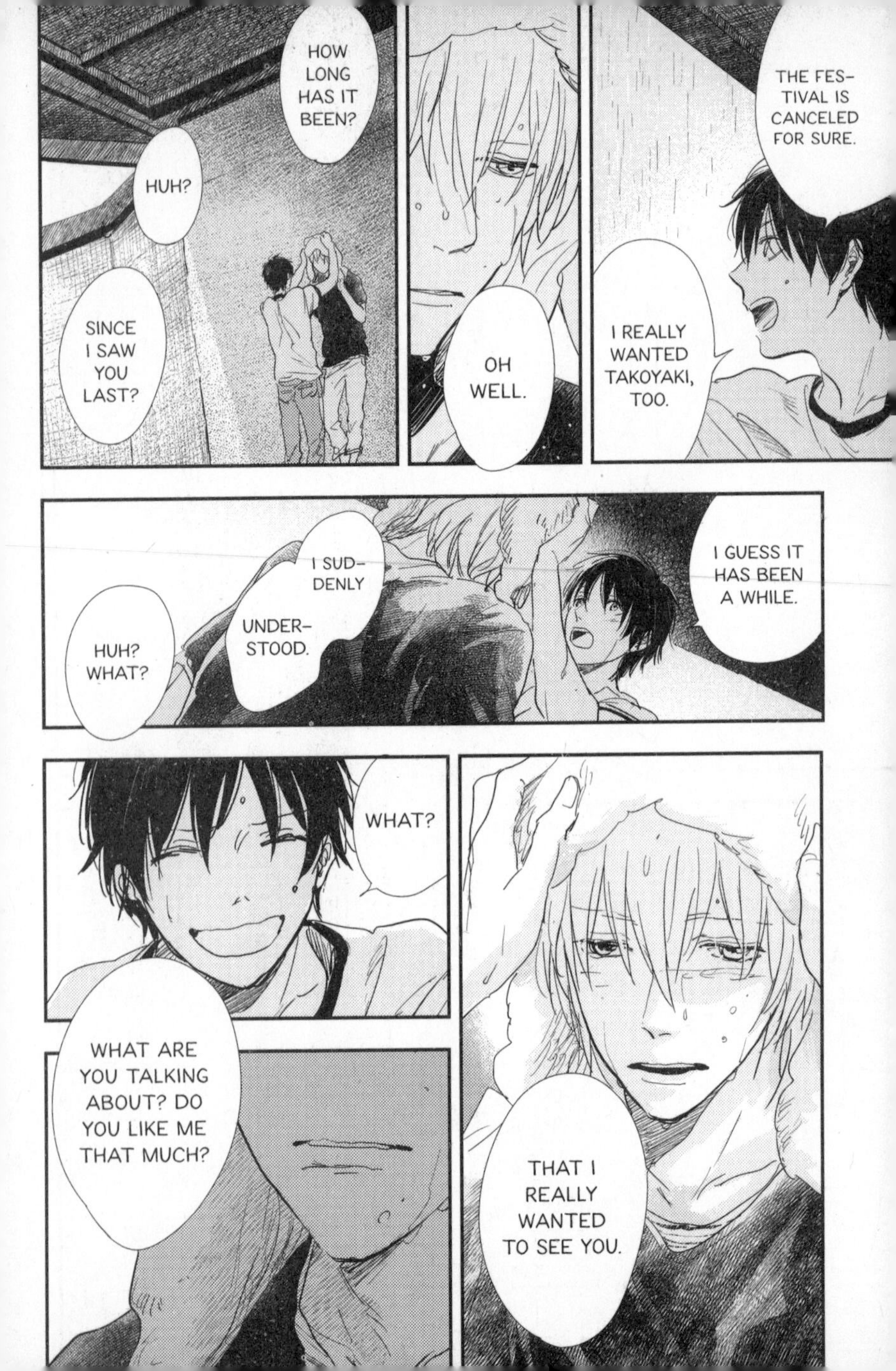
THE FES-
TIVAL IS
CANCELED
FOR SURE.
I REALLY
WANTED
TAKOYAKI,
TOO.
OH
WELL.
HOW
LONG
HAS IT
BEEN?
HUH?
SINCE
I SAW
YOU
LAST?
I GUESS IT
HAS BEEN
A WHILE.
I SUD-
DENLY
UNDER-
STOOD.
HUH?
WHAT?
THAT I
REALLY
WANTED
TO SEE YOU.
WHAT?
WHAT ARE
YOU TALKING
ABOUT? DO
YOU LIKE ME
THAT MUCH?

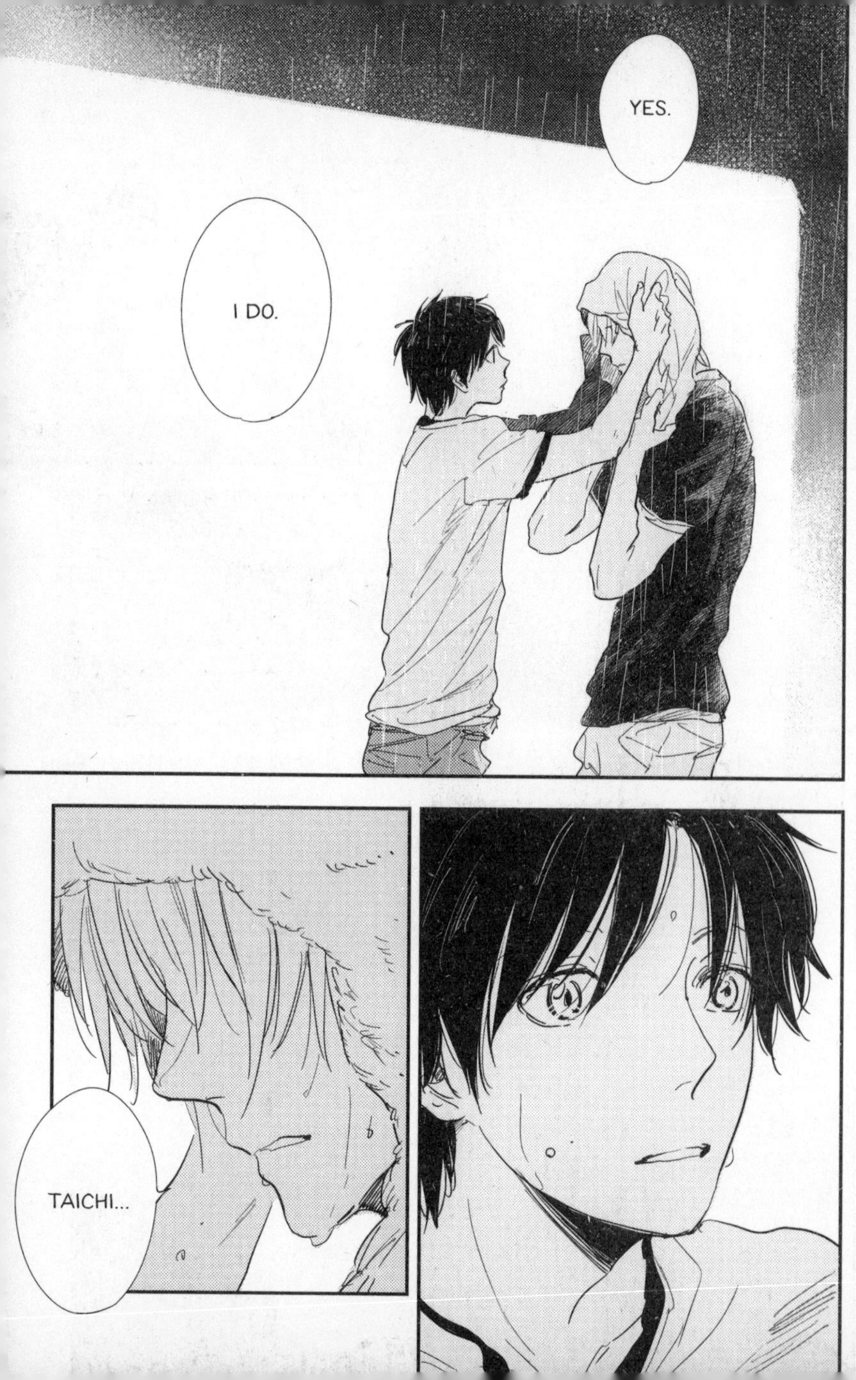
YES.
I DO.
TAICHI...

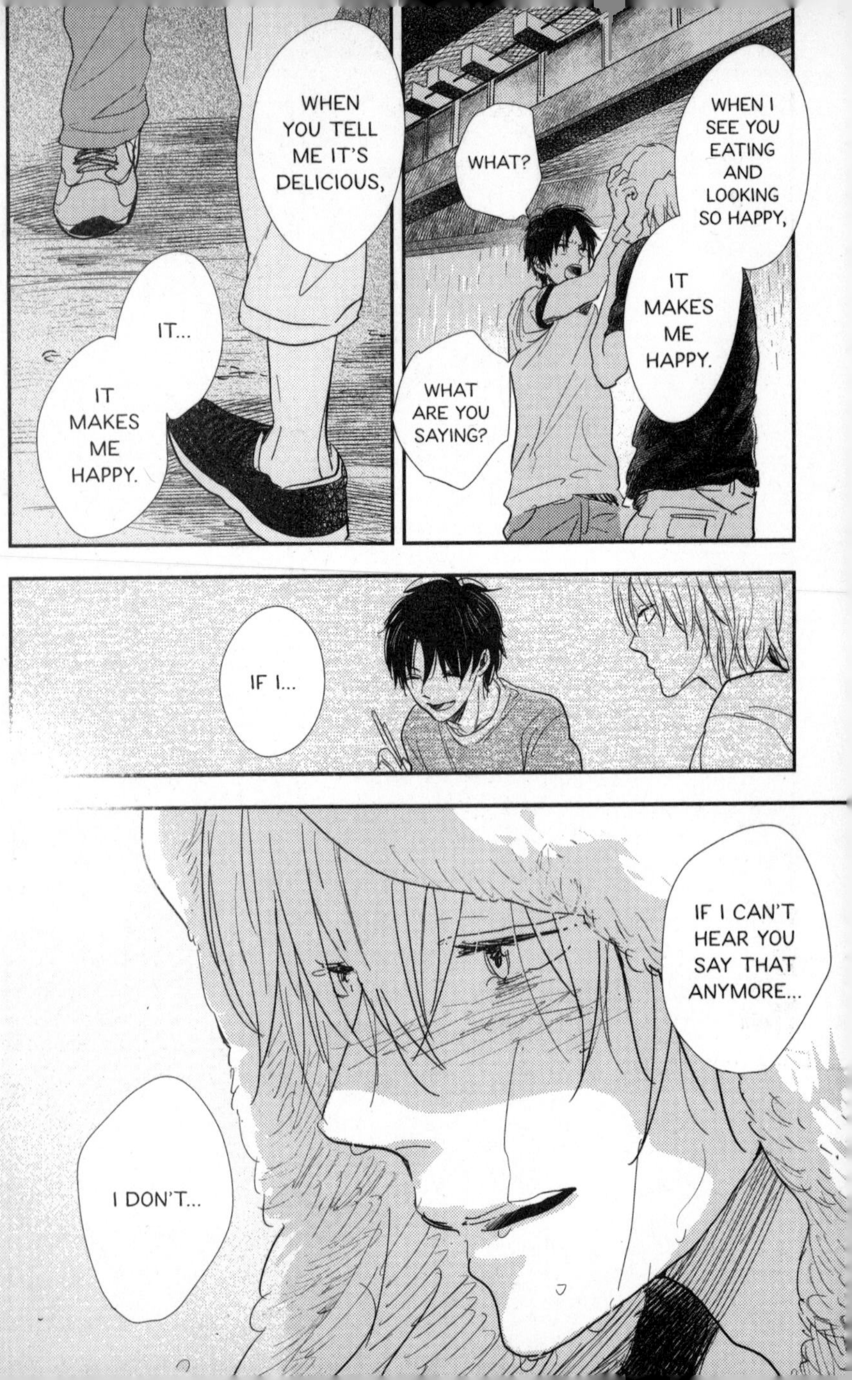
WHEN I SEE YOU EATING AND LOOKING SO HAPPY,
WHAT?
IT MAKES ME HAPPY.
WHAT ARE YOU SAYING?
WHEN YOU TELL ME IT'S DELICIOUS,
IT...
IT MAKES ME HAPPY.
IF I...
IF I CAN'T HEAR YOU SAY THAT ANYMORE...
I DON'T...

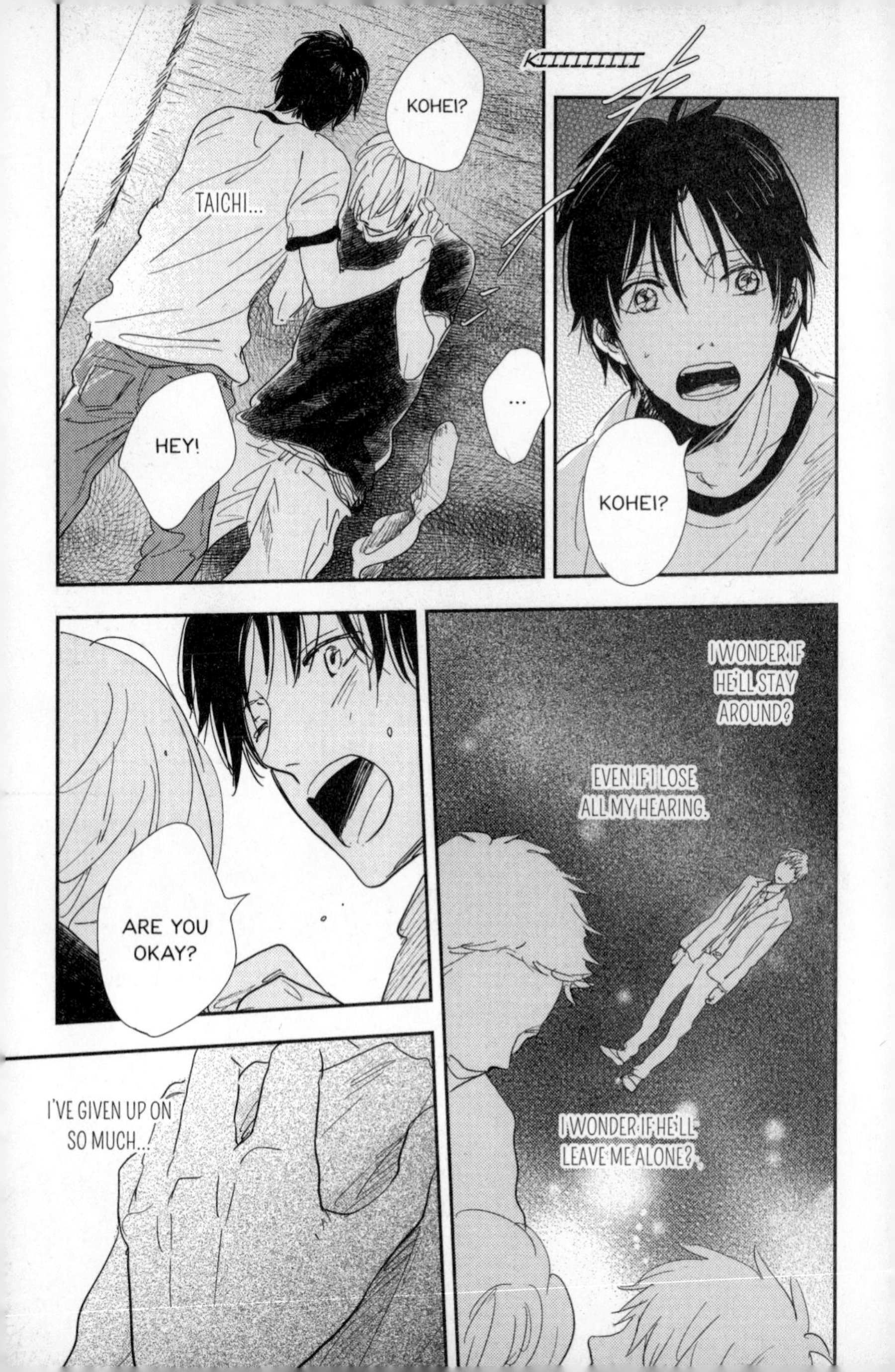
KIIIIIIIII
KOHEI?
KOHEI?
TAICHI...
...
HEY!
I WONDER IF HE'LL STAY AROUND?
EVEN IF I LOSE ALL MY HEARING.
I WONDER IF HE'LL LEAVE ME ALONE?
ARE YOU OKAY?
I'VE GIVEN UP ON SO MUCH...!

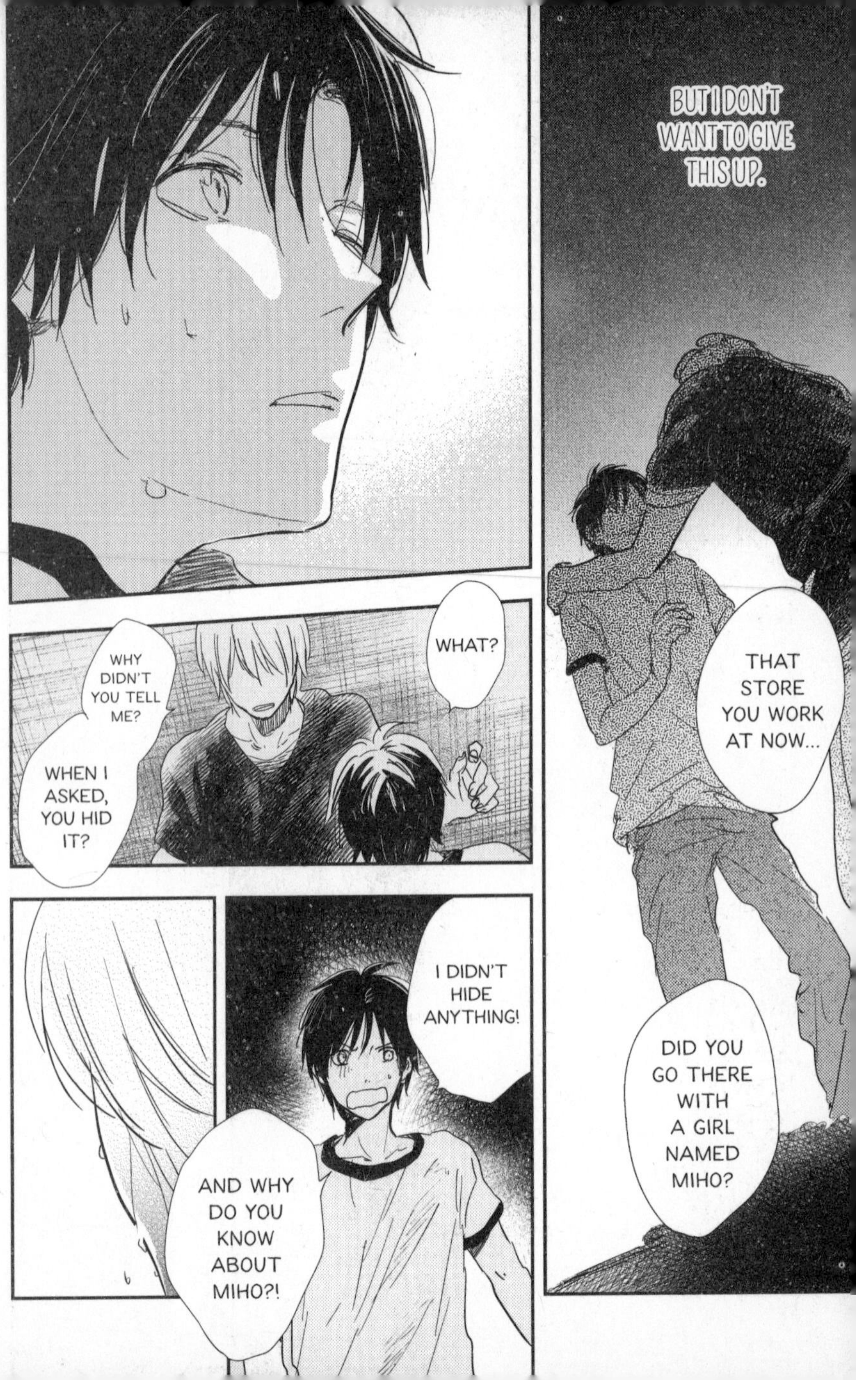
BUT I DON'T WANT TO GIVE THIS UP.
THAT STORE YOU WORK AT NOW...
DID YOU GO THERE WITH A GIRL NAMED MIHO?
WHAT?
WHY DIDN'T YOU TELL ME?
WHEN I ASKED, YOU HID IT?
I DIDN'T HIDE ANYTHING!
AND WHY DO YOU KNOW ABOUT MIHO?!

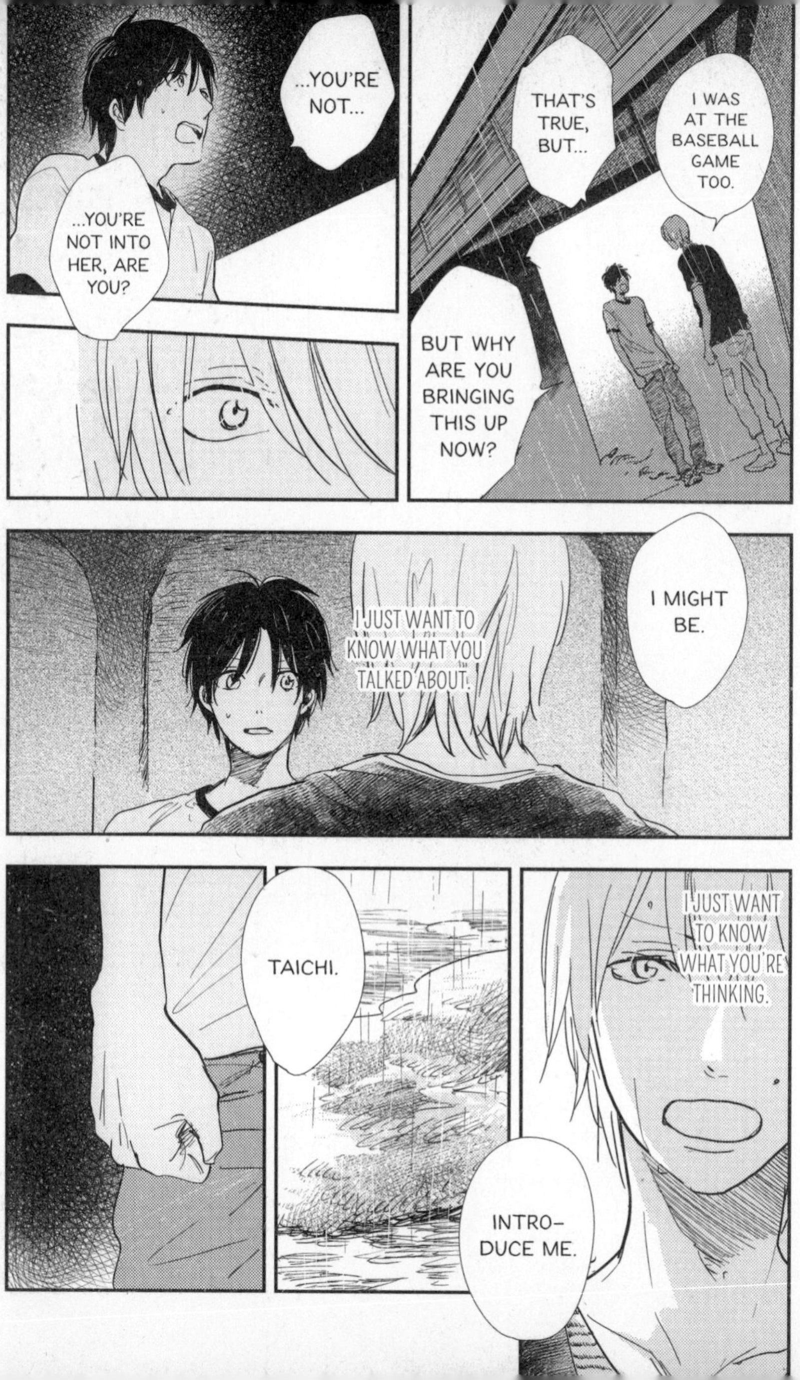
I WAS AT THE BASEBALL GAME TOO.
THAT'S TRUE, BUT...
BUT WHY ARE YOU BRINGING THIS UP NOW?
...YOU'RE NOT...
...YOU'RE NOT INTO HER, ARE YOU?
I MIGHT BE.
I JUST WANT TO KNOW WHAT YOU TALKED ABOUT.
I JUST WANT TO KNOW WHAT YOU'RE THINKING.
INTRO–DUCE ME.
TAICHI.

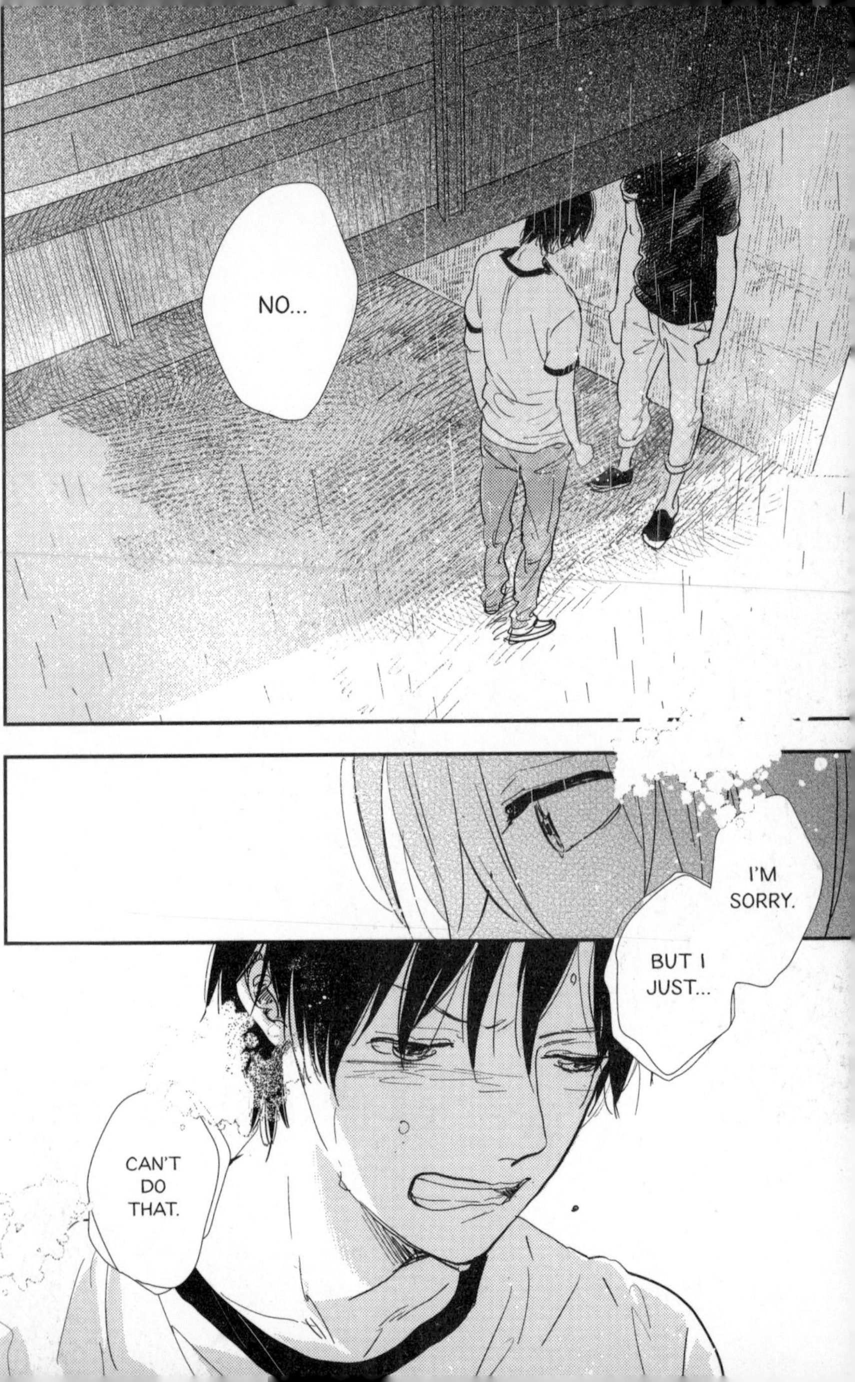
NO...
I'M SORRY.
BUT I JUST...
CAN'T DO THAT.

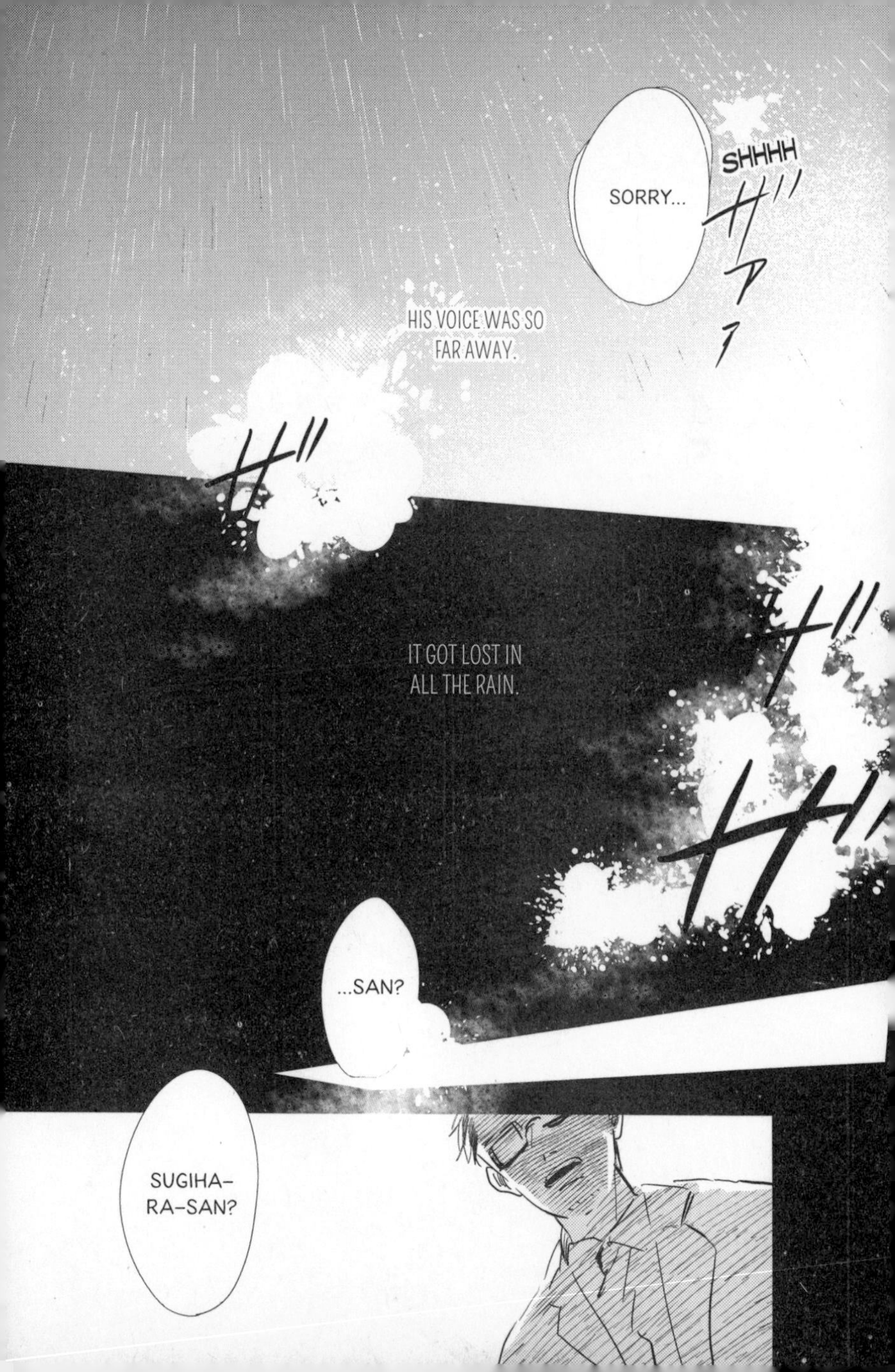
SHHHH
SORRY...
HIS VOICE WAS SO FAR AWAY.
IT GOT LOST IN ALL THE RAIN.
...SAN?
SUGIHA-RA-SAN?

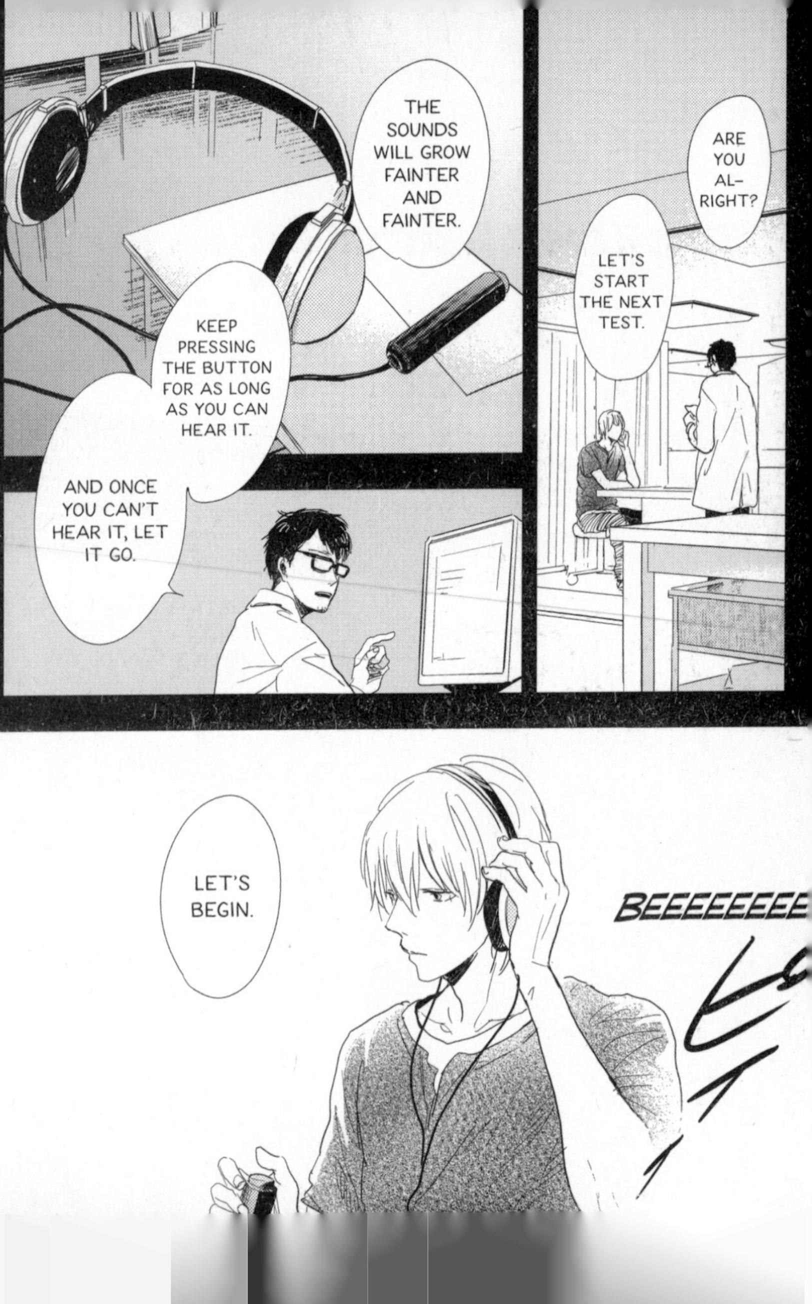
ARE YOU AL-RIGHT?
LET'S START THE NEXT TEST.
THE SOUNDS WILL GROW FAINTER AND FAINTER.
KEEP PRESSING THE BUTTON FOR AS LONG AS YOU CAN HEAR IT.
AND ONCE YOU CAN'T HEAR IT, LET IT GO.
LET'S BEGIN.
BEEEEEEEEE

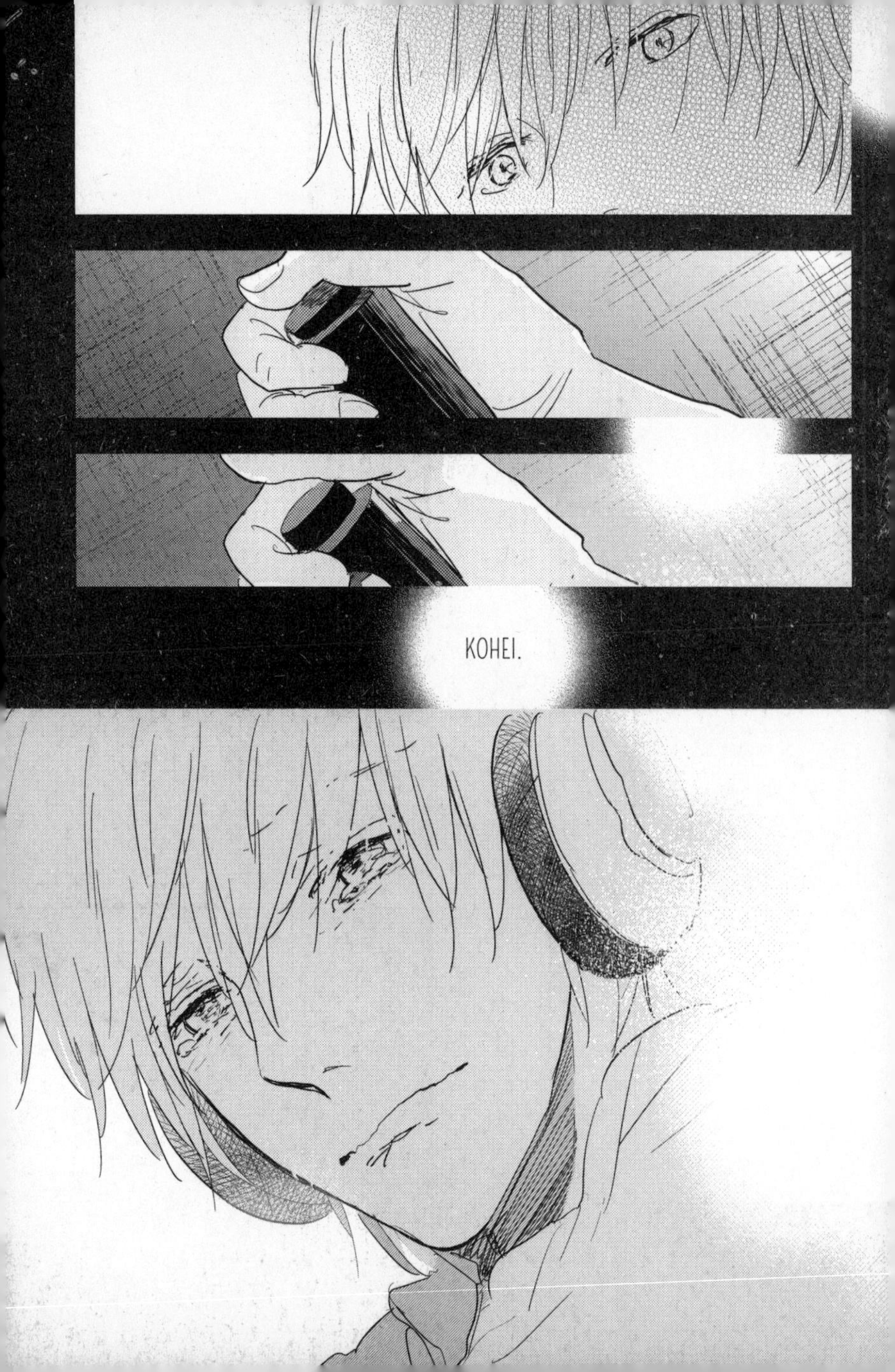
KOHEI.

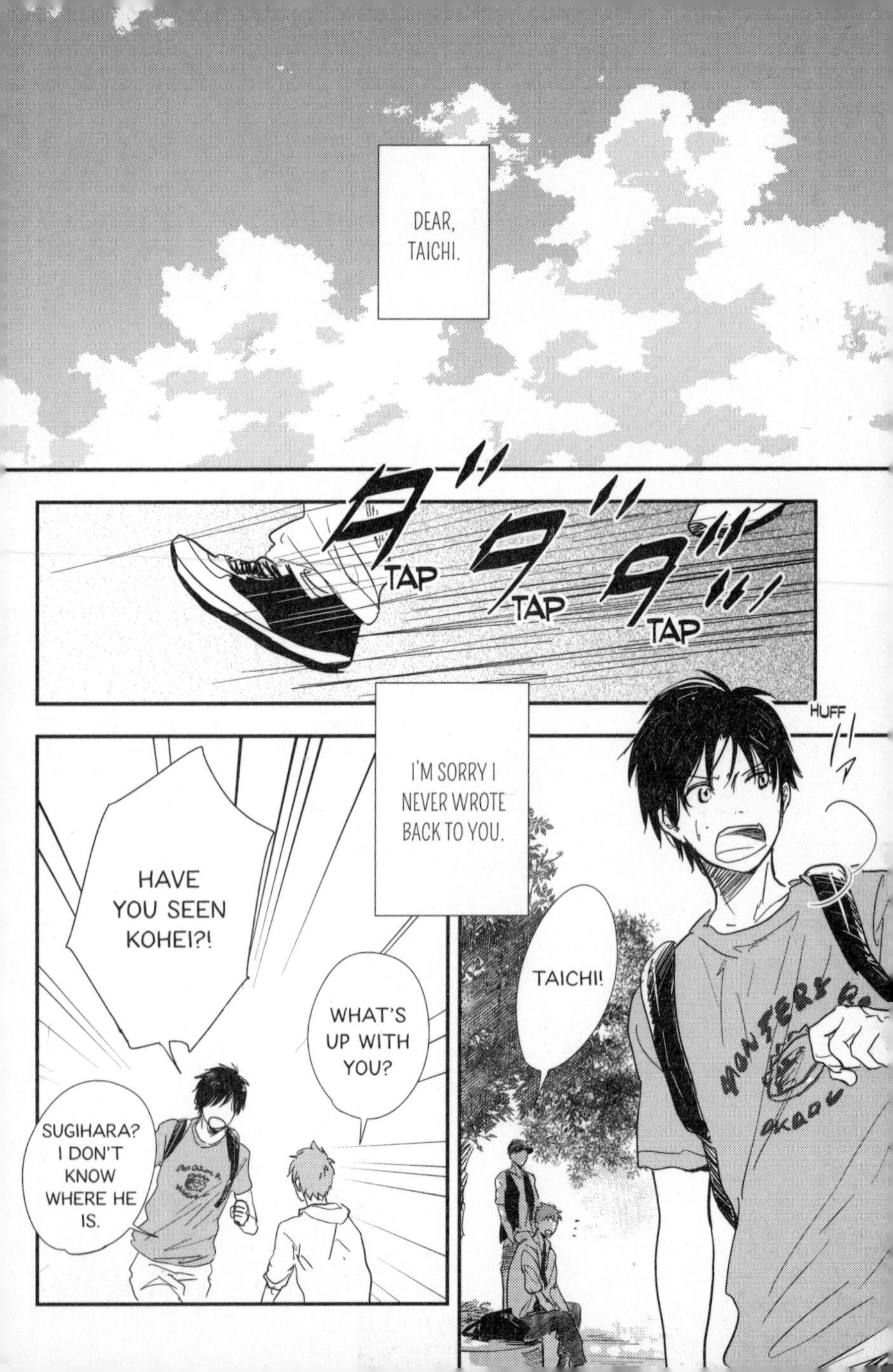
DEAR, TAICHI.
TAP
TAP
TAP
I'M SORRY I NEVER WROTE BACK TO YOU.
HUFF
TAICHI!
HAVE YOU SEEN KOHEI?!
WHAT'S UP WITH YOU?
SUGIHARA? I DON'T KNOW WHERE HE IS.

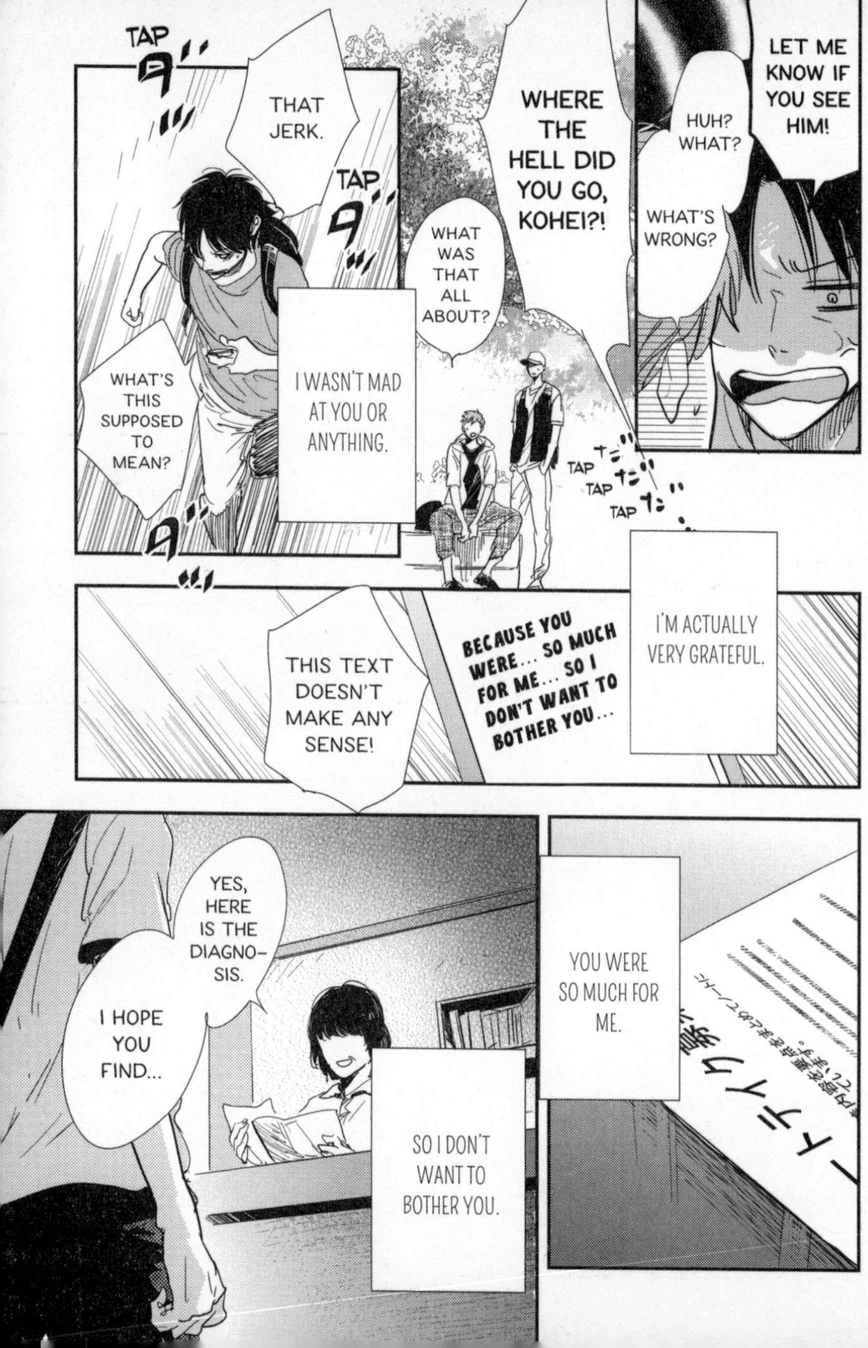
LET ME KNOW IF YOU SEE HIM!
HUH? WHAT?
WHAT'S WRONG?
WHERE THE HELL DID YOU GO, KOHEI?!
WHAT WAS THAT ALL ABOUT?
TAP
TAP
TAP
I WASN'T MAD AT YOU OR ANYTHING.
TAP
THAT JERK.
TAP
WHAT'S THIS SUPPOSED TO MEAN?
I'M ACTUALLY VERY GRATEFUL.
BECAUSE YOU WERE... SO MUCH FOR ME... SO I DON'T WANT TO BOTHER YOU...
THIS TEXT DOESN'T MAKE ANY SENSE!
YOU WERE SO MUCH FOR ME.
SO I DON'T WANT TO BOTHER YOU.
YES, HERE IS THE DIAGNOSIS.
I HOPE YOU FIND...

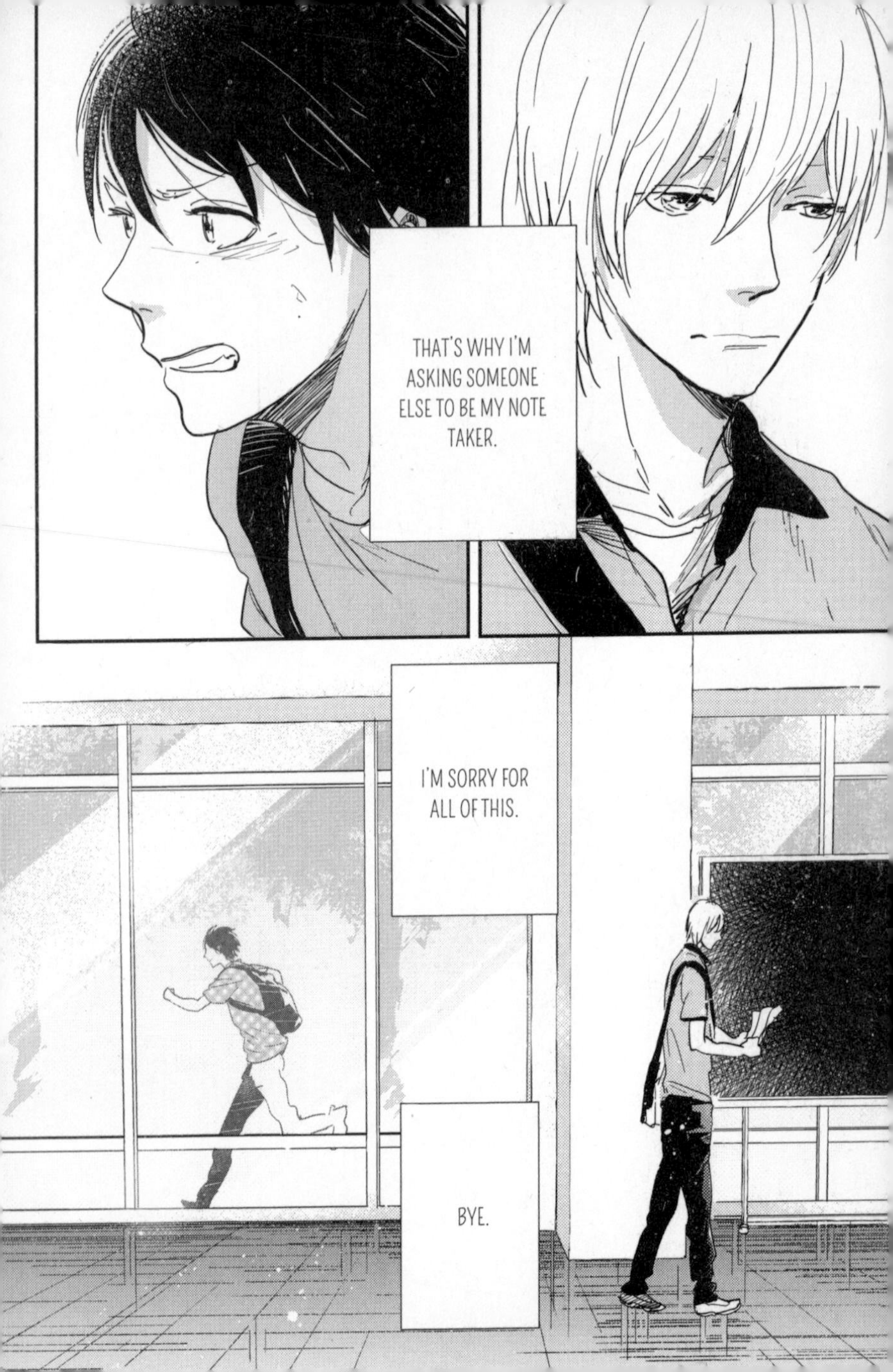
THAT'S WHY I'M ASKING SOMEONE ELSE TO BE MY NOTE TAKER.
I'M SORRY FOR ALL OF THIS.
BYE.

i hear
the
sunspot

i hear the sunspot

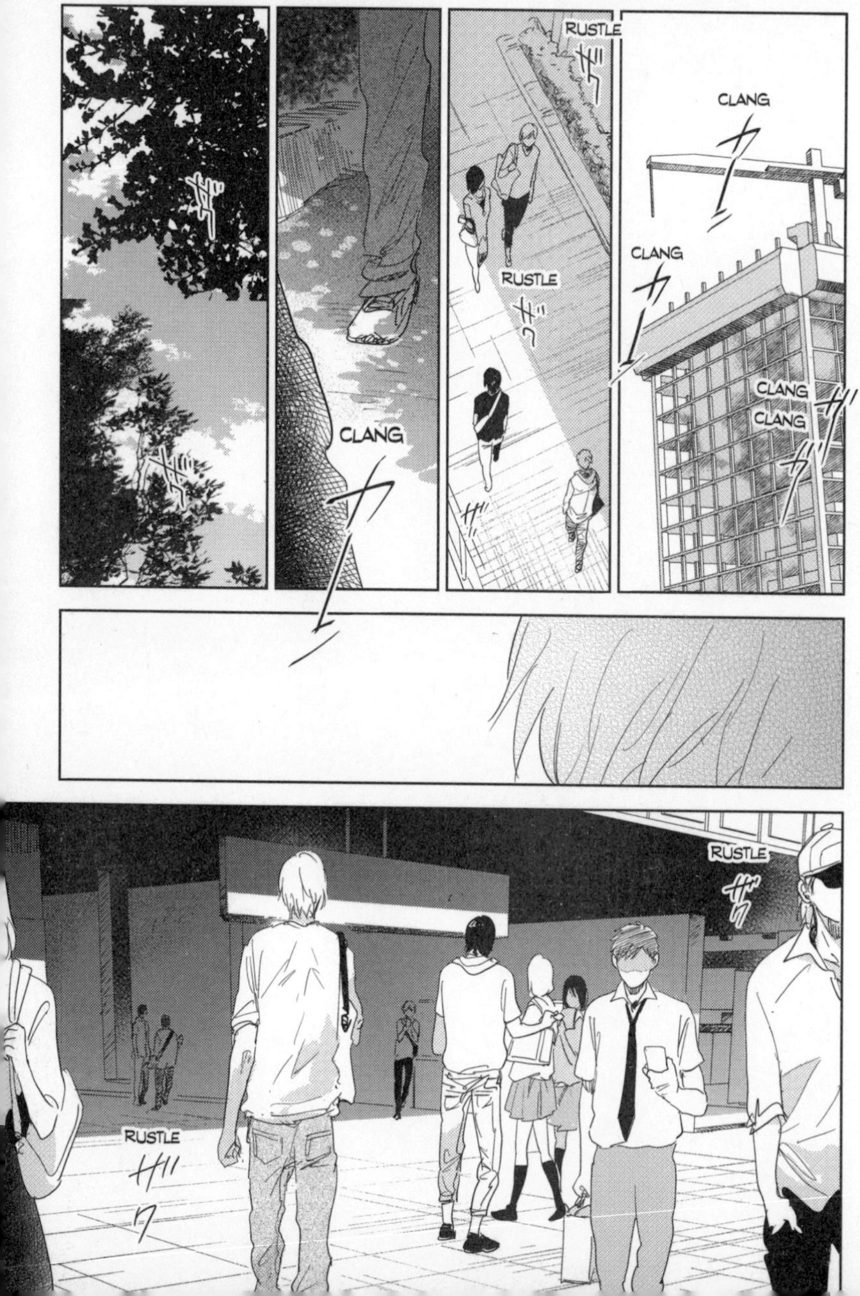
CLANG
CLANG
CLANG
CLANG
RUSTLE
RUSTLE
CLANG
RUSTLE
RUSTLE

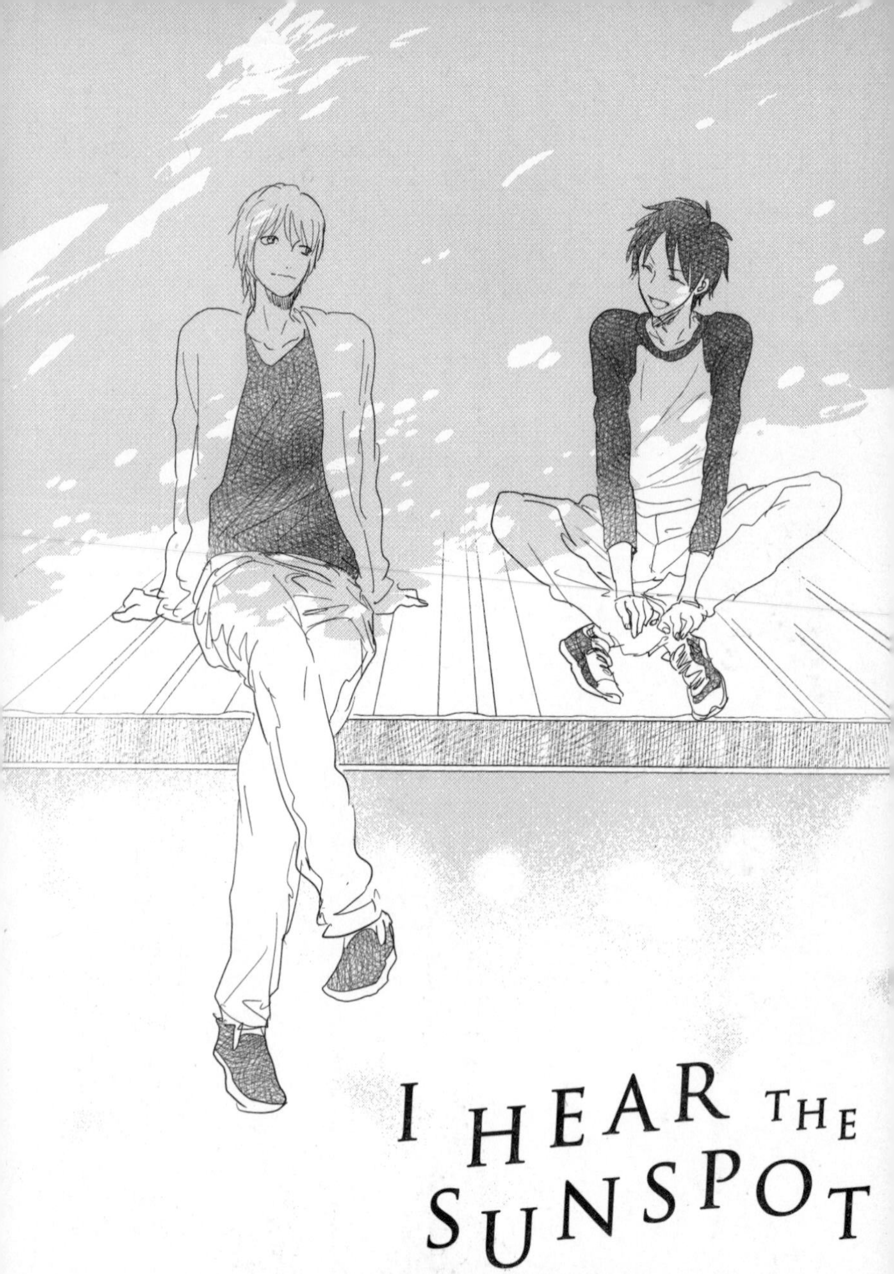

I HEAR THE SUNSPOT

CHAPTER FIVE

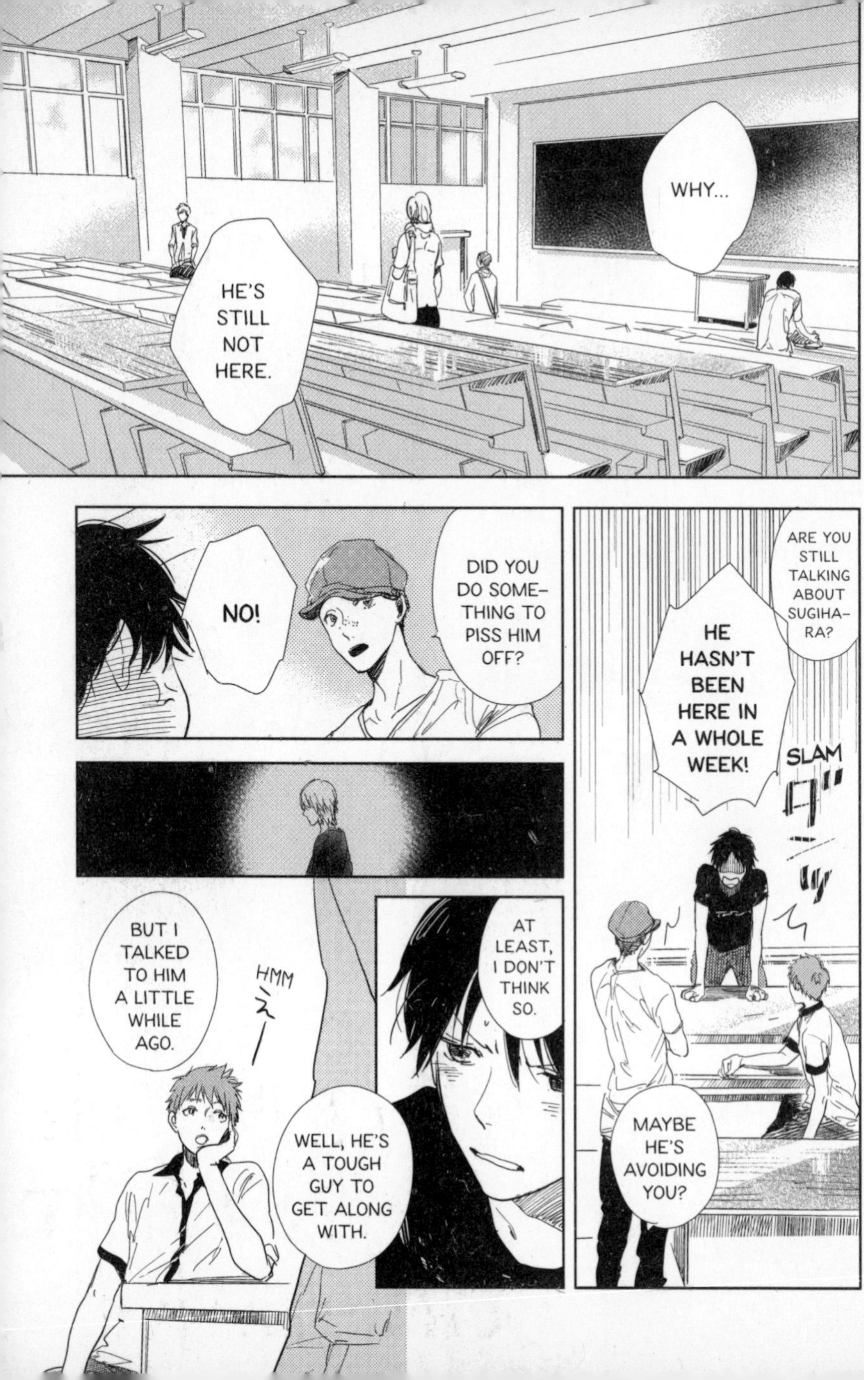
WHY...
HE'S STILL NOT HERE.
ARE YOU STILL TALKING ABOUT SUGIHARA?
HE HASN'T BEEN HERE IN A WHOLE WEEK!
SLAM
MAYBE HE'S AVOIDING YOU?
DID YOU DO SOME-THING TO PISS HIM OFF?
NO!
AT LEAST, I DON'T THINK SO.
BUT I TALKED TO HIM A LITTLE WHILE AGO.
HMM
WELL, HE'S A TOUGH GUY TO GET ALONG WITH.

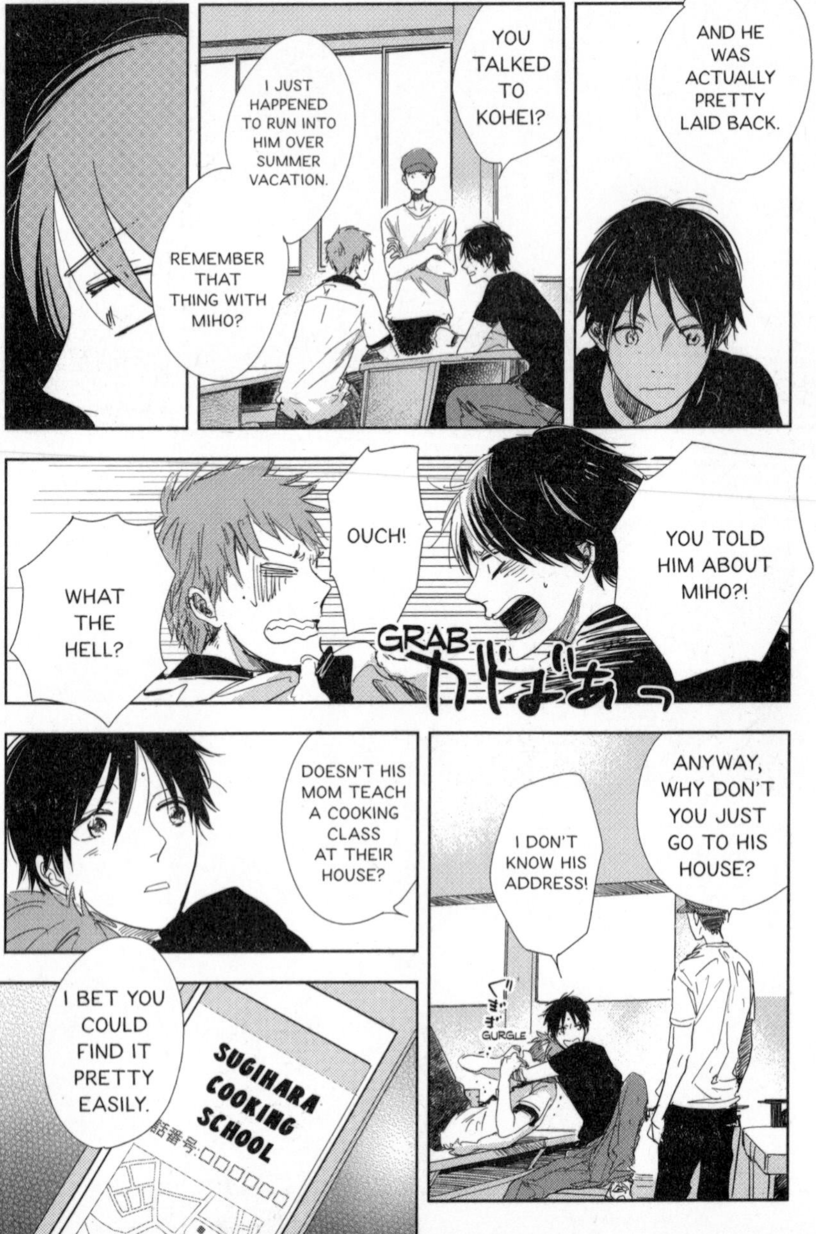
AND HE WAS ACTUALLY PRETTY LAID BACK.
YOU TALKED TO KOHEI?
I JUST HAPPENED TO RUN INTO HIM OVER SUMMER VACATION.
REMEMBER THAT THING WITH MIHO?
YOU TOLD HIM ABOUT MIHO?!
GRAB
OUCH!
WHAT THE HELL?
ANYWAY, WHY DON'T YOU JUST GO TO HIS HOUSE?
I DON'T KNOW HIS ADDRESS!
GURGLE
DOESN'T HIS MOM TEACH A COOKING CLASS AT THEIR HOUSE?
I BET YOU COULD FIND IT PRETTY EASILY.
SUGIHARA COOKING SCHOOL

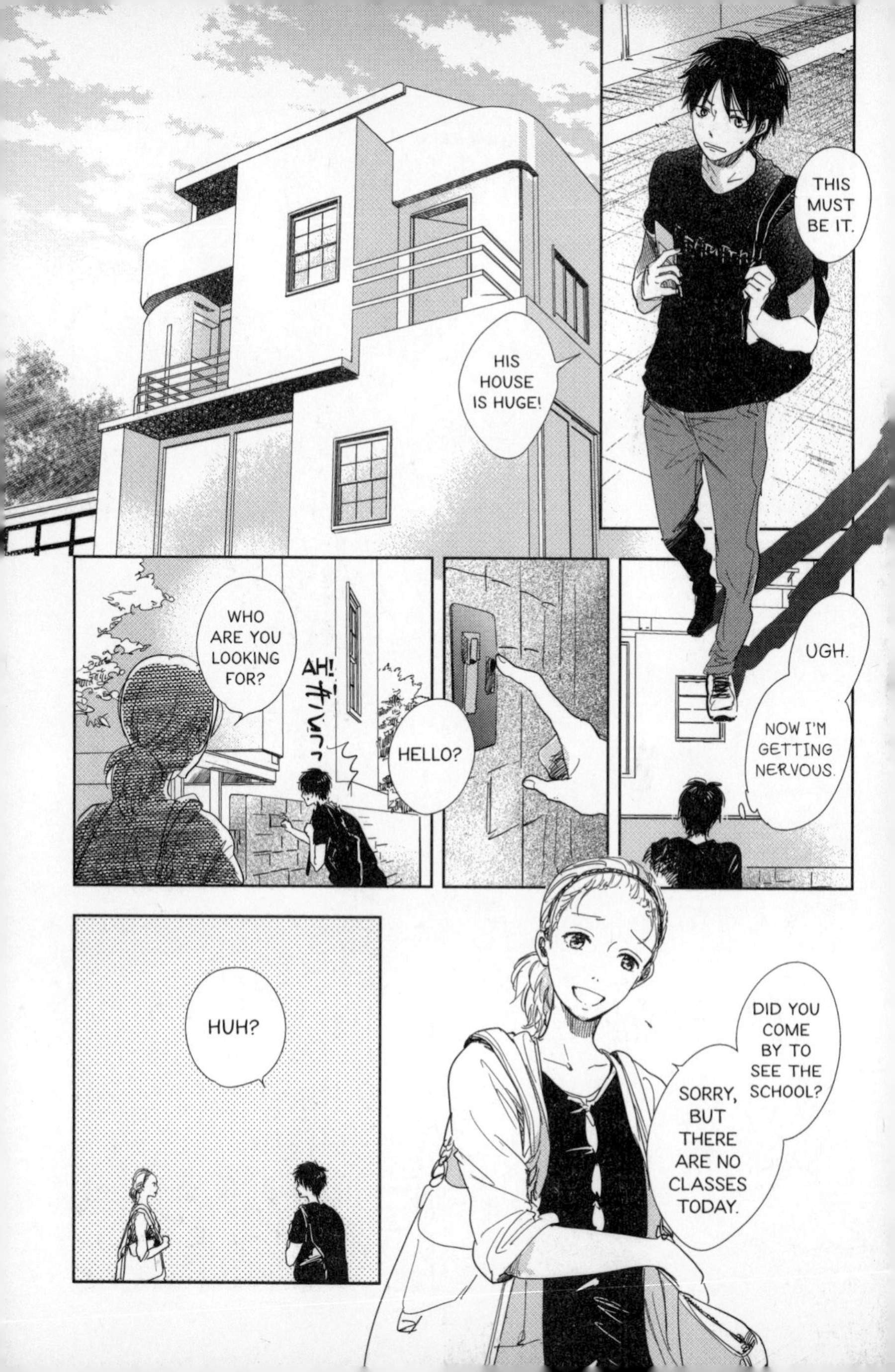
THIS MUST BE IT.
HIS HOUSE IS HUGE!
UGH.
NOW I'M GETTING NERVOUS.
HELLO?
AH!
WHO ARE YOU LOOKING FOR?
DID YOU COME BY TO SEE THE SCHOOL?
SORRY, BUT THERE ARE NO CLASSES TODAY.
HUH?

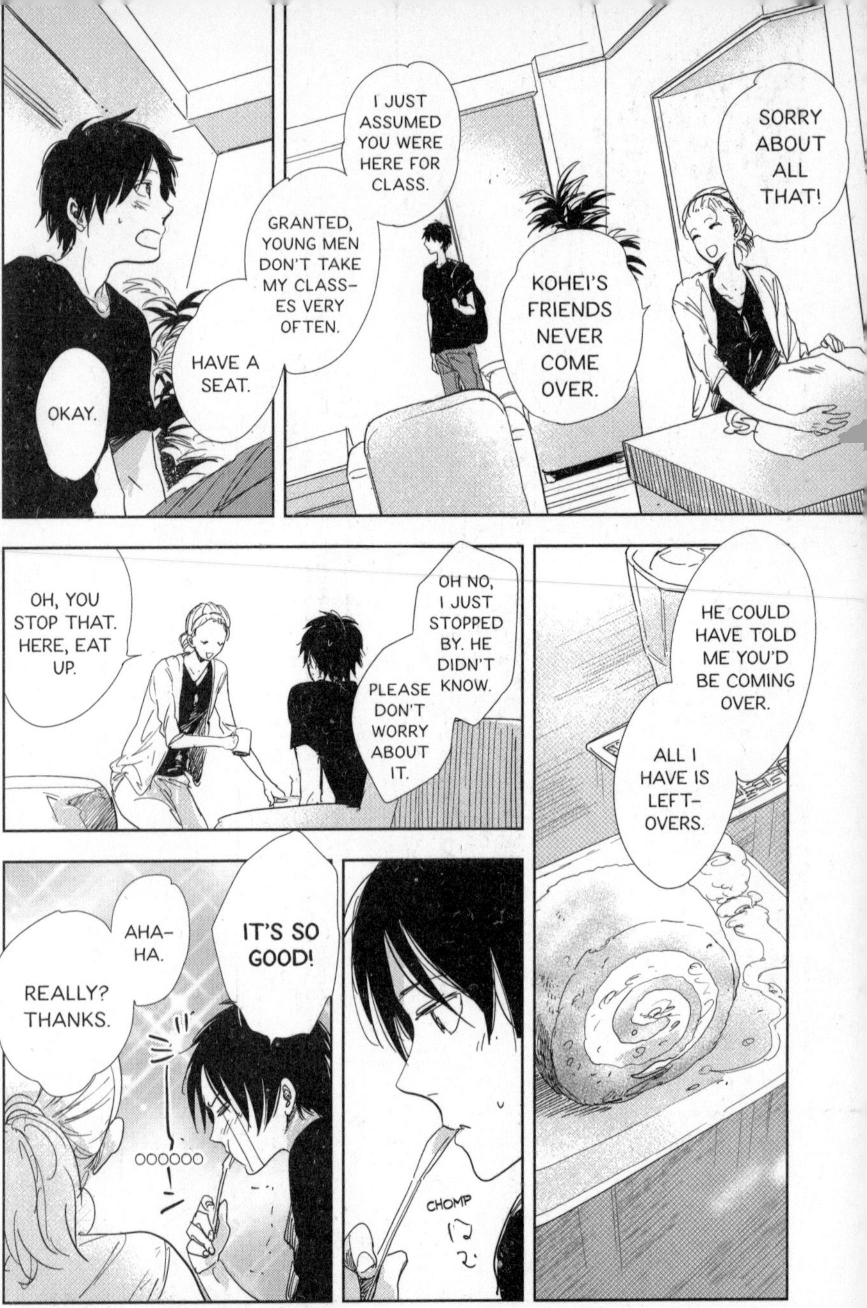
SORRY ABOUT ALL THAT!
KOHEI'S FRIENDS NEVER COME OVER.
I JUST ASSUMED YOU WERE HERE FOR CLASS.
GRANTED, YOUNG MEN DON'T TAKE MY CLASS-ES VERY OFTEN.
HAVE A SEAT.
OKAY.
HE COULD HAVE TOLD ME YOU'D BE COMING OVER.
ALL I HAVE IS LEFT-OVERS.
OH NO, I JUST STOPPED BY. HE DIDN'T KNOW.
PLEASE DON'T WORRY ABOUT IT.
OH, YOU STOP THAT. HERE, EAT UP.
CHOMP
IT'S SO GOOD!
OOOOOO
AHA-HA.
REALLY? THANKS.

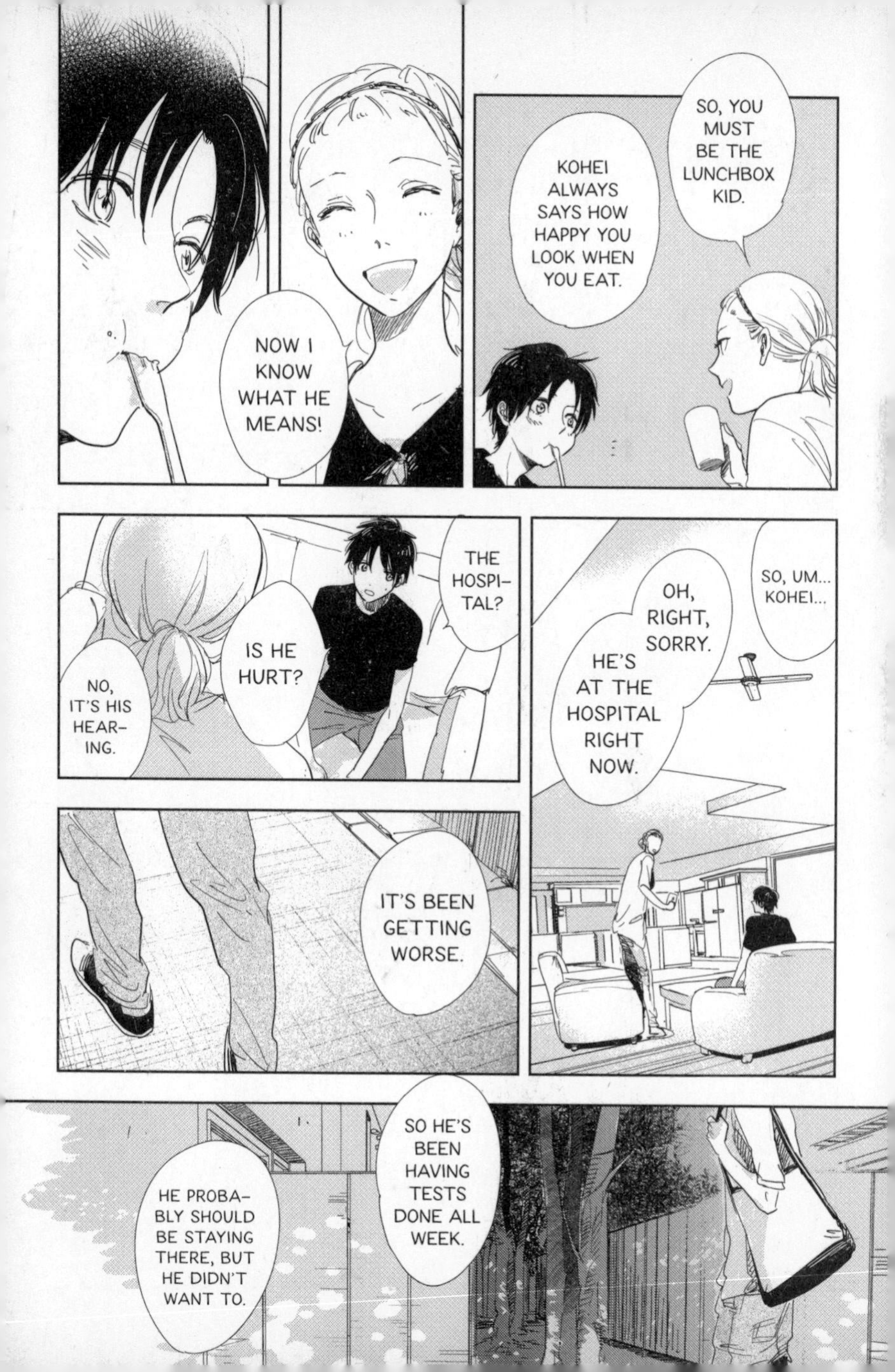
SO, YOU MUST BE THE LUNCHBOX KID.
KOHEI ALWAYS SAYS HOW HAPPY YOU LOOK WHEN YOU EAT.
NOW I KNOW WHAT HE MEANS!
SO, UM... KOHEI...
OH, RIGHT, SORRY.
HE'S AT THE HOSPITAL RIGHT NOW.
THE HOSPITAL?
IS HE HURT?
NO, IT'S HIS HEARING.
IT'S BEEN GETTING WORSE.
SO HE'S BEEN HAVING TESTS DONE ALL WEEK.
HE PROBABLY SHOULD BE STAYING THERE, BUT HE DIDN'T WANT TO.

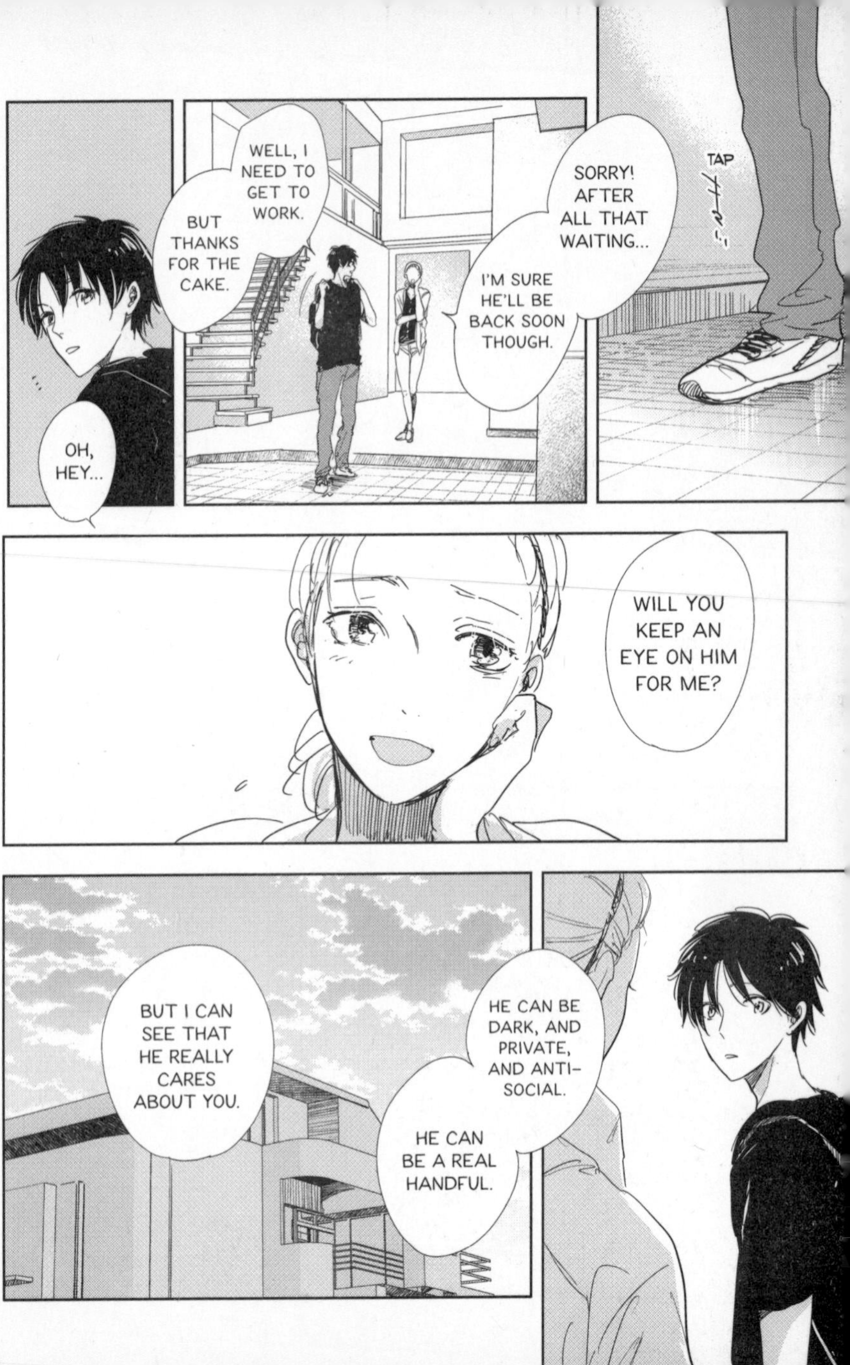
TAP
SORRY! AFTER ALL THAT WAITING...
I'M SURE HE'LL BE BACK SOON THOUGH.
WELL, I NEED TO GET TO WORK.
BUT THANKS FOR THE CAKE.
OH, HEY...
WILL YOU KEEP AN EYE ON HIM FOR ME?
HE CAN BE DARK, AND PRIVATE, AND ANTI-SOCIAL.
HE CAN BE A REAL HANDFUL.
BUT I CAN SEE THAT HE REALLY CARES ABOUT YOU.

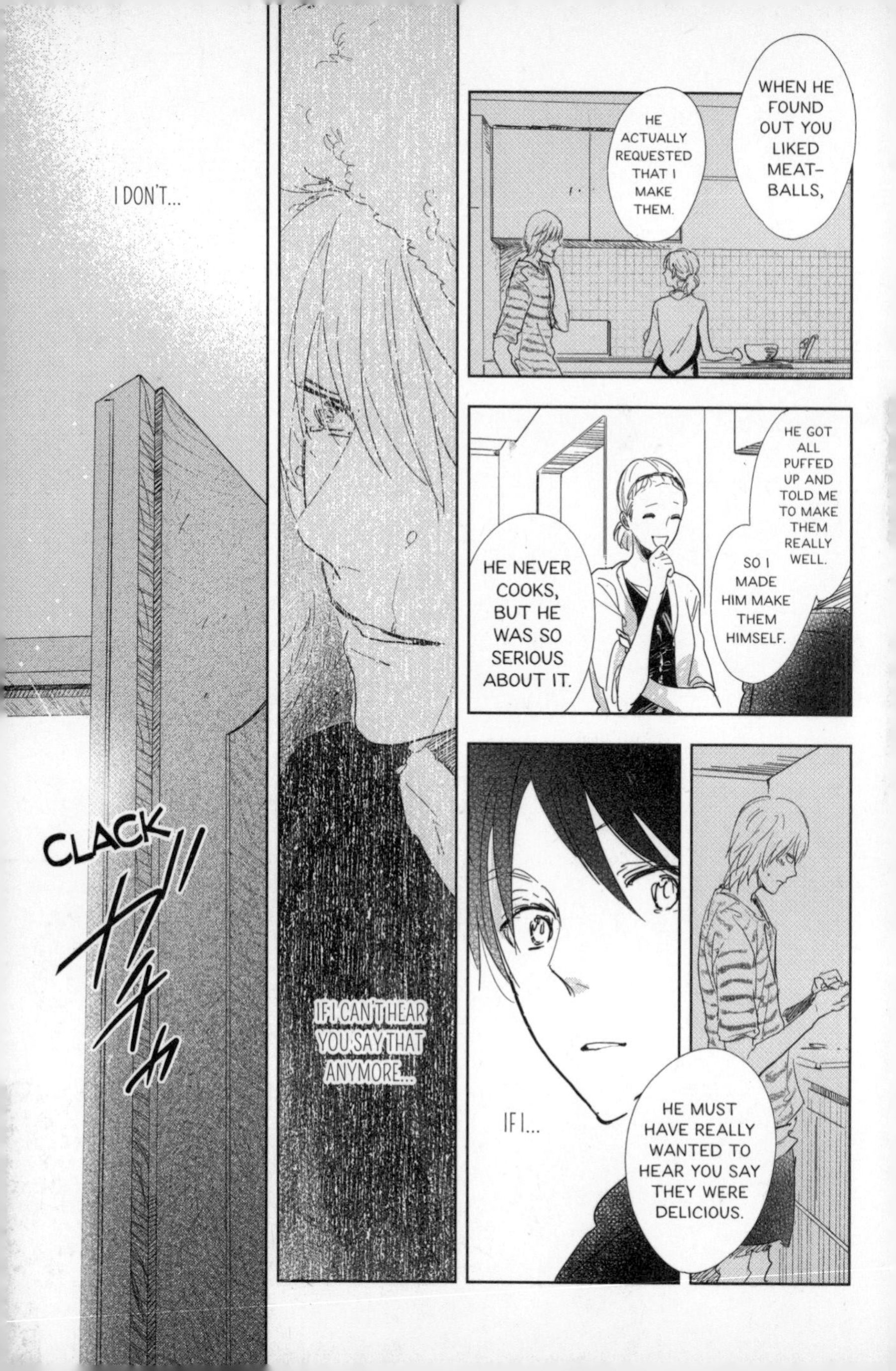
WHEN HE FOUND OUT YOU LIKED MEAT-BALLS,
HE ACTUALLY REQUESTED THAT I MAKE THEM.
HE GOT ALL PUFFED UP AND TOLD ME TO MAKE THEM REALLY WELL.
SO I MADE HIM MAKE THEM HIMSELF.
HE NEVER COOKS, BUT HE WAS SO SERIOUS ABOUT IT.
HE MUST HAVE REALLY WANTED TO HEAR YOU SAY THEY WERE DELICIOUS.
IF I...
IF I CAN'T HEAR YOU SAY THAT ANYMORE...
I DON'T...
CLACK

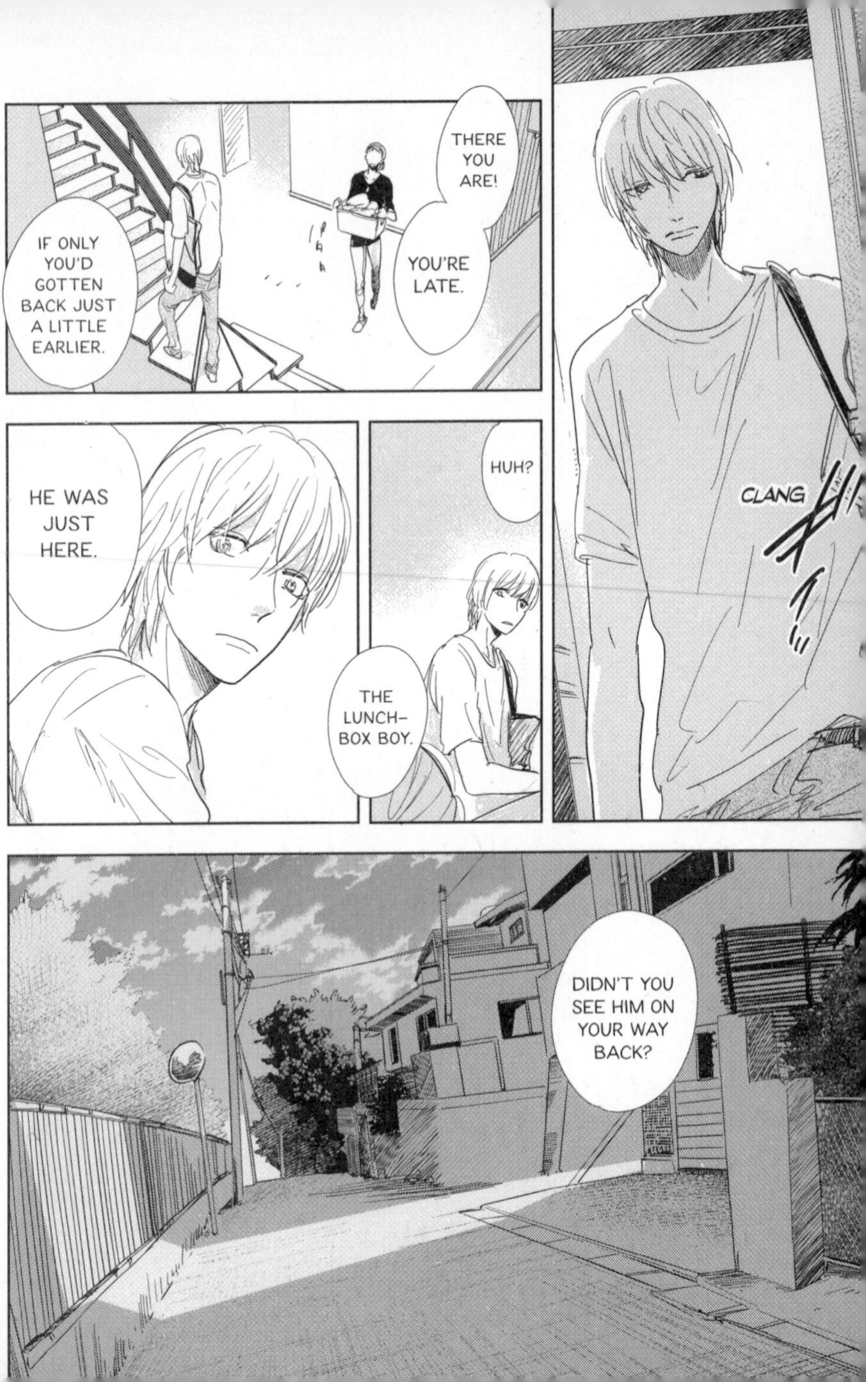
CLANG
THERE YOU ARE!
YOU'RE LATE.
IF ONLY YOU'D GOTTEN BACK JUST A LITTLE EARLIER.
HUH?
THE LUNCH-BOX BOY.
HE WAS JUST HERE.
DIDN'T YOU SEE HIM ON YOUR WAY BACK?

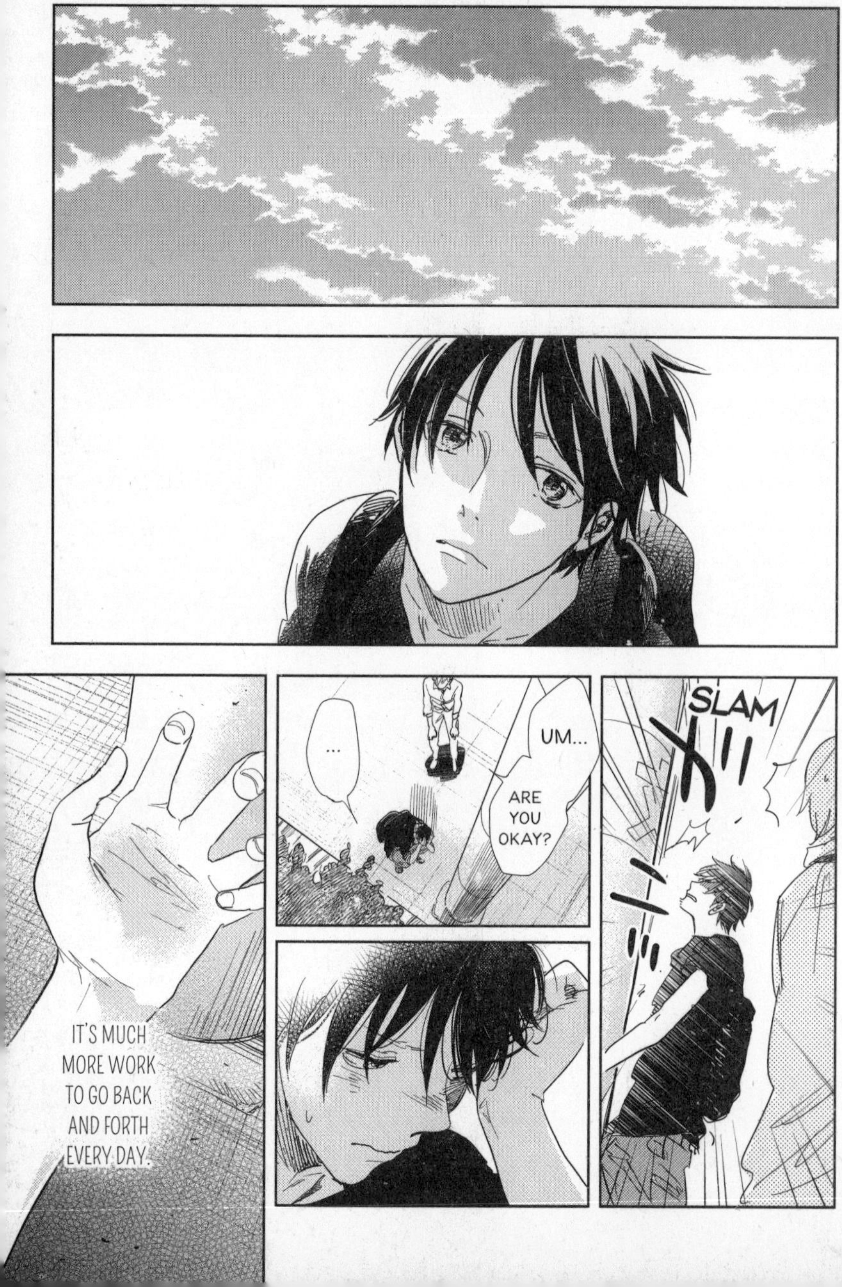
SLAM
UM...
ARE YOU OKAY?
...
IT'S MUCH MORE WORK TO GO BACK AND FORTH EVERY DAY.

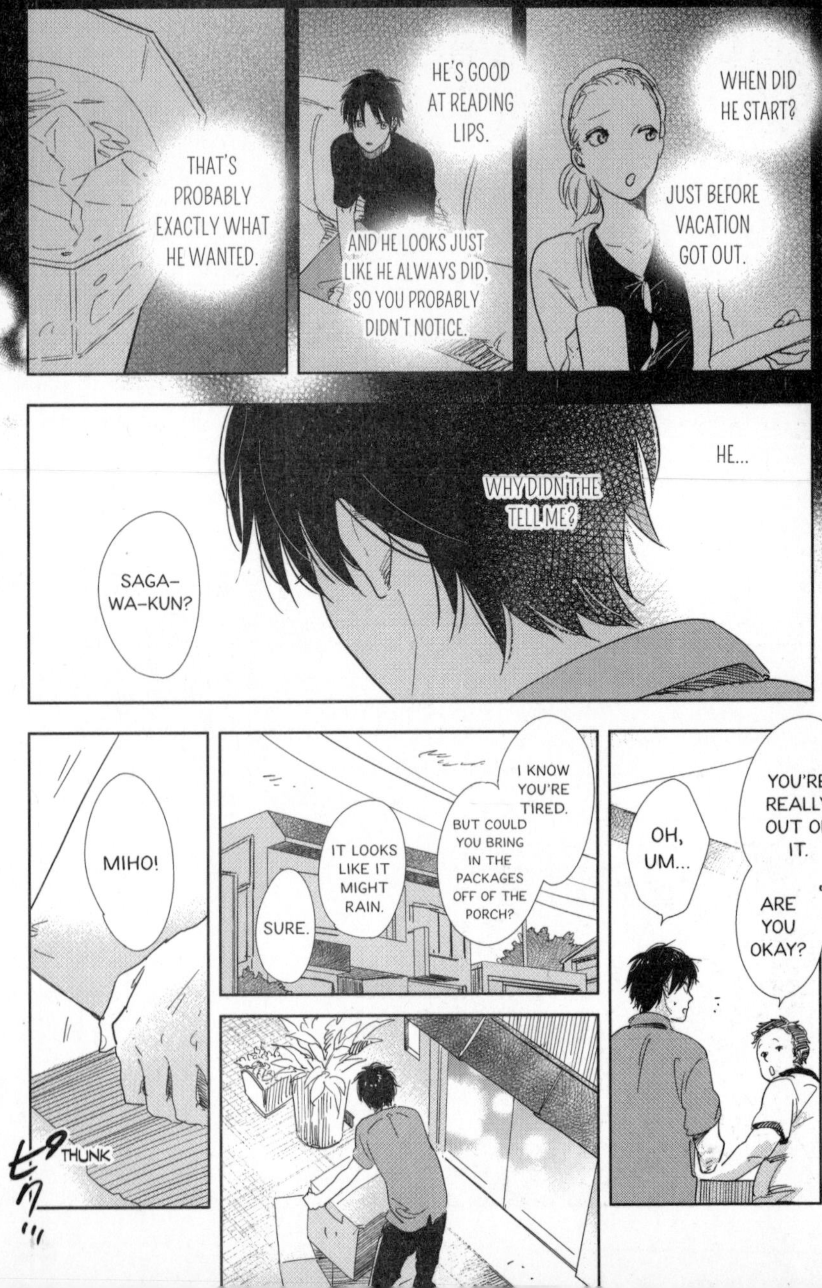

WHEN DID HE START?
JUST BEFORE VACATION GOT OUT.
HE'S GOOD AT READING LIPS.
AND HE LOOKS JUST LIKE HE ALWAYS DID, SO YOU PROBABLY DIDN'T NOTICE.
THAT'S PROBABLY EXACTLY WHAT HE WANTED.
HE...
WHY DIDN'T HE TELL ME?
SAGA-WA-KUN?
YOU'RE REALLY OUT OF IT.
ARE YOU OKAY?
OH, UM...
I KNOW YOU'RE TIRED.
BUT COULD YOU BRING IN THE PACKAGES OFF OF THE PORCH?
IT LOOKS LIKE IT MIGHT RAIN.
SURE.
MIHO!
THUNK

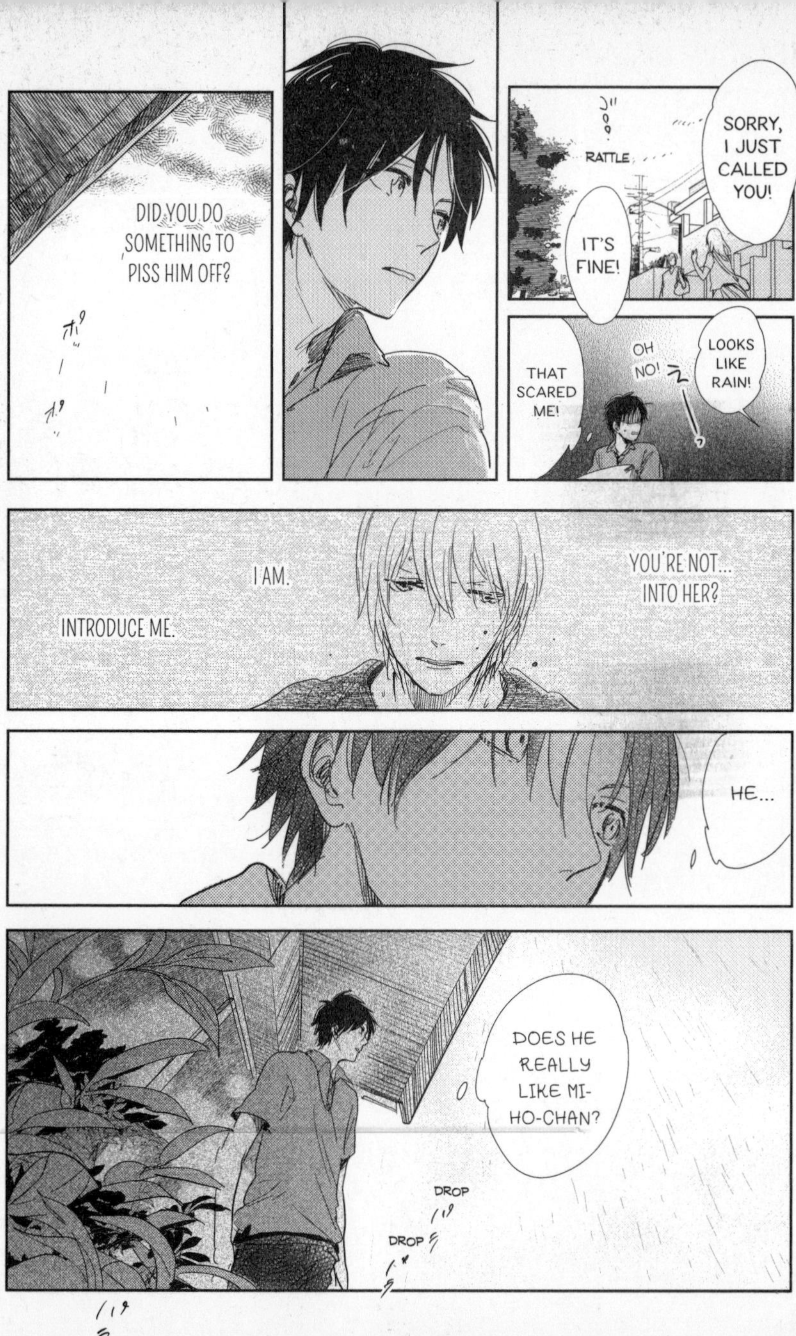
SORRY, I JUST CALLED YOU!
RATTLE
IT'S FINE!
LOOKS LIKE RAIN!
OH NO!
THAT SCARED ME!
DID YOU DO SOMETHING TO PISS HIM OFF?
YOU'RE NOT... INTO HER?
I AM.
INTRODUCE ME.
HE...
DOES HE REALLY LIKE MI-HO-CHAN?
DROP
DROP

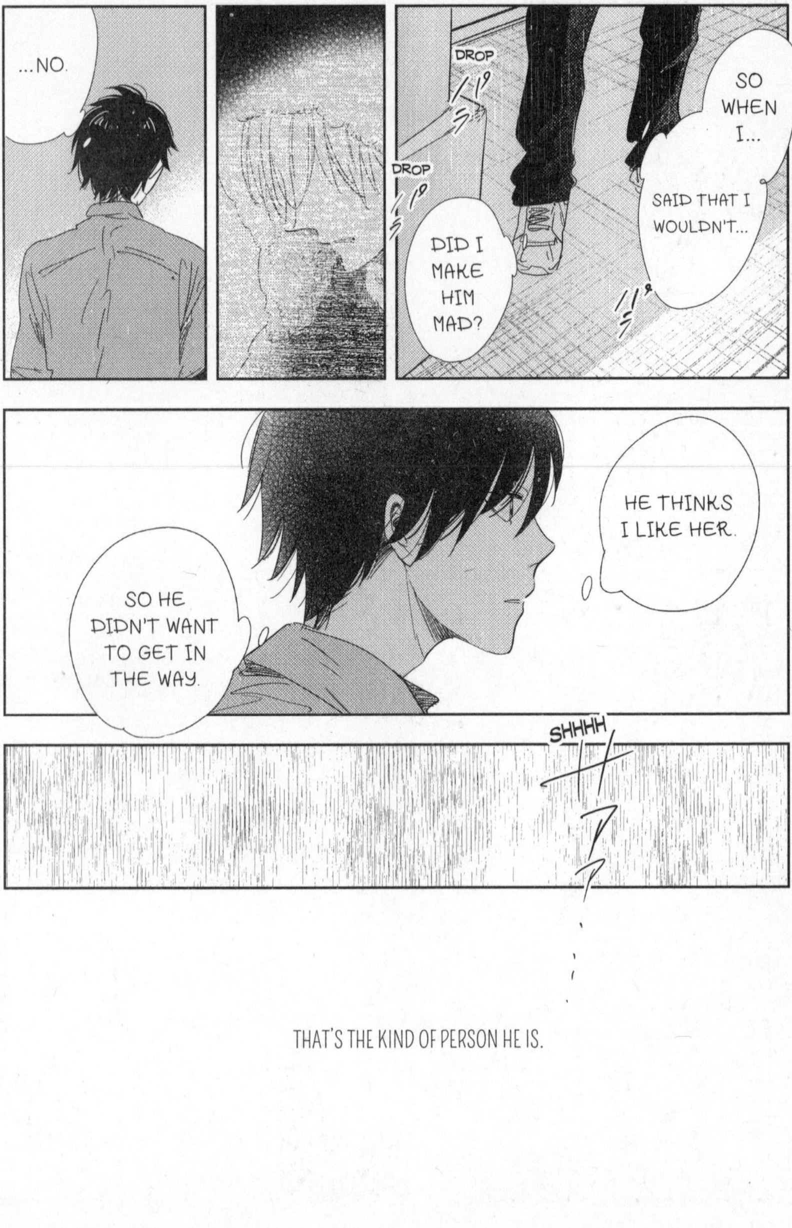
SO WHEN I...
SAID THAT I WOULDN'T...
DROP
DROP
DID I MAKE HIM MAD?
...NO.
HE THINKS I LIKE HER.
SO HE DIDN'T WANT TO GET IN THE WAY.
SHHHH
THAT'S THE KIND OF PERSON HE IS.

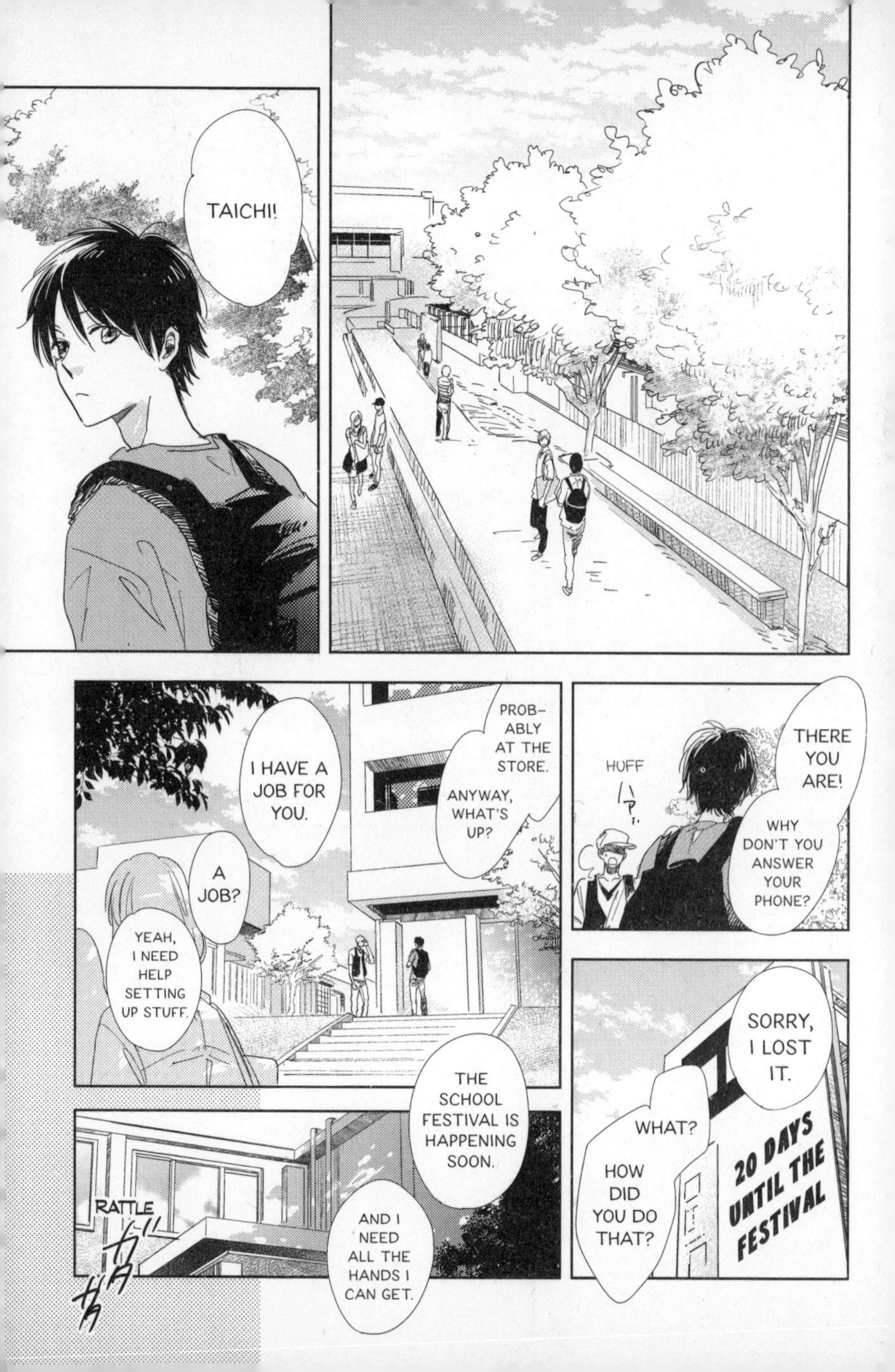
TAICHI!
THERE YOU ARE!
HUFF
WHY DON'T YOU ANSWER YOUR PHONE?
SORRY, I LOST IT.
WHAT?
HOW DID YOU DO THAT?
20 DAYS UNTIL THE FESTIVAL
PROB-ABLY AT THE STORE.
ANYWAY, WHAT'S UP?
I HAVE A JOB FOR YOU.
A JOB?
YEAH, I NEED HELP SETTING UP STUFF.
THE SCHOOL FESTIVAL IS HAPPENING SOON.
AND I NEED ALL THE HANDS I CAN GET.
RATTLE

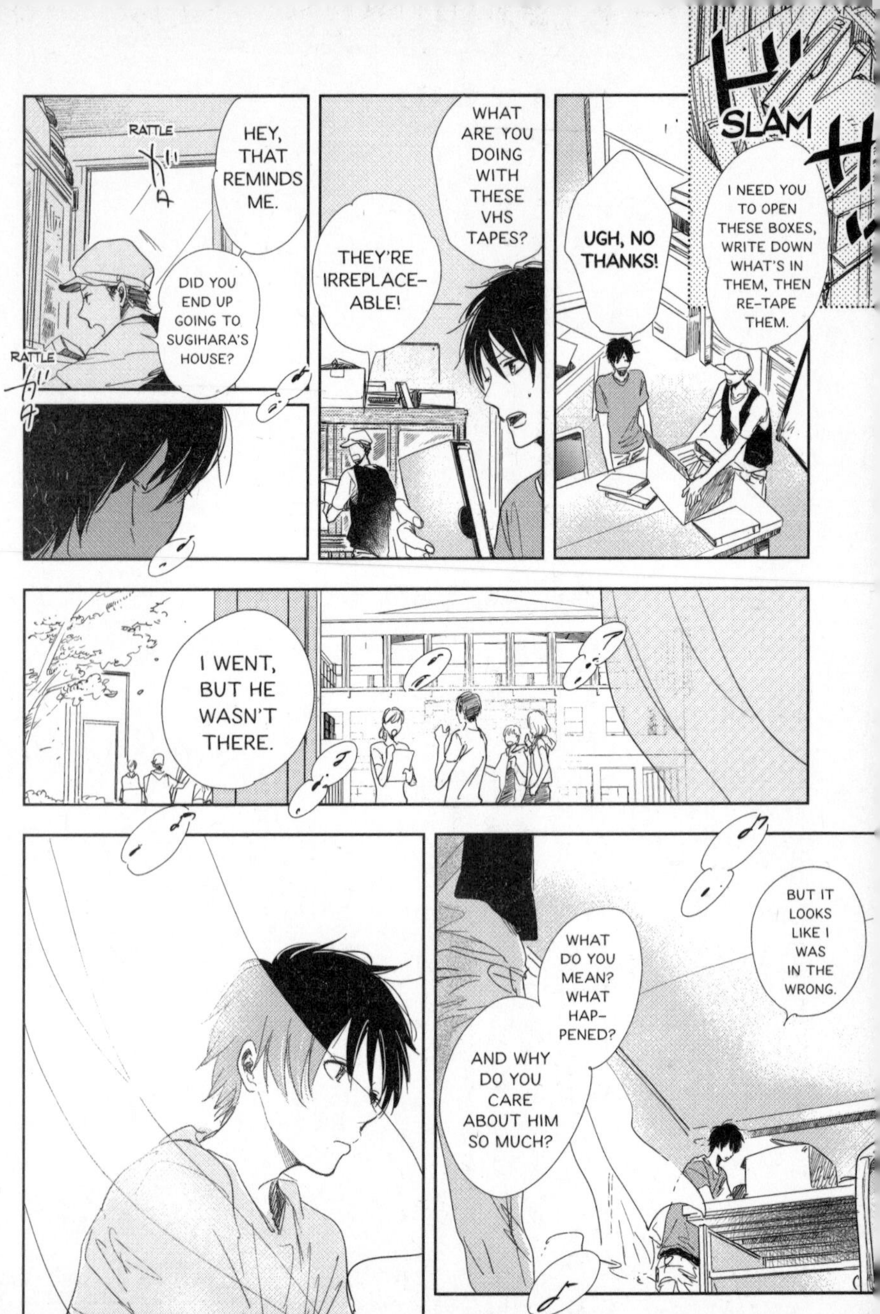
SLAM
I NEED YOU TO OPEN THESE BOXES, WRITE DOWN WHAT'S IN THEM, THEN RE-TAPE THEM.
UGH, NO THANKS!
WHAT ARE YOU DOING WITH THESE VHS TAPES?
THEY'RE IRREPLACE-ABLE!
RATTLE
HEY, THAT REMINDS ME.
DID YOU END UP GOING TO SUGIHARA'S HOUSE?
RATTLE
I WENT, BUT HE WASN'T THERE.
BUT IT LOOKS LIKE I WAS IN THE WRONG.
WHAT DO YOU MEAN? WHAT HAP-PENED?
AND WHY DO YOU CARE ABOUT HIM SO MUCH?

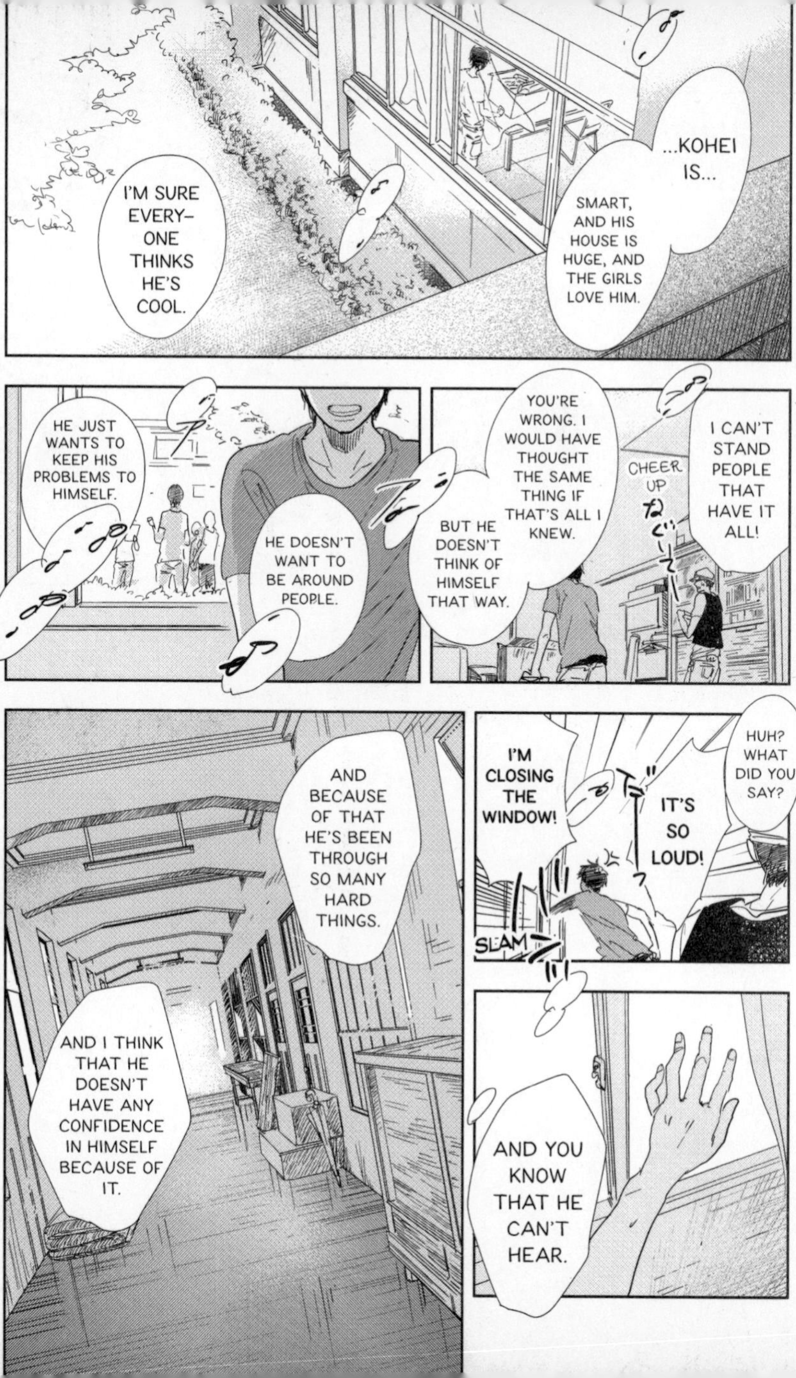
...KOHEI IS...
SMART, AND HIS HOUSE IS HUGE, AND THE GIRLS LOVE HIM.
I'M SURE EVERY-ONE THINKS HE'S COOL.
I CAN'T STAND PEOPLE THAT HAVE IT ALL!
CHEER UP
YOU'RE WRONG. I WOULD HAVE THOUGHT THE SAME THING IF THAT'S ALL I KNEW.
BUT HE DOESN'T THINK OF HIMSELF THAT WAY.
HE DOESN'T WANT TO BE AROUND PEOPLE.
HE JUST WANTS TO KEEP HIS PROBLEMS TO HIMSELF.
HUH? WHAT DID YOU SAY?
IT'S SO LOUD!
I'M CLOSING THE WINDOW!
SLAM
AND YOU KNOW THAT HE CAN'T HEAR.
AND BECAUSE OF THAT HE'S BEEN THROUGH SO MANY HARD THINGS.
AND I THINK THAT HE DOESN'T HAVE ANY CONFIDENCE IN HIMSELF BECAUSE OF IT.

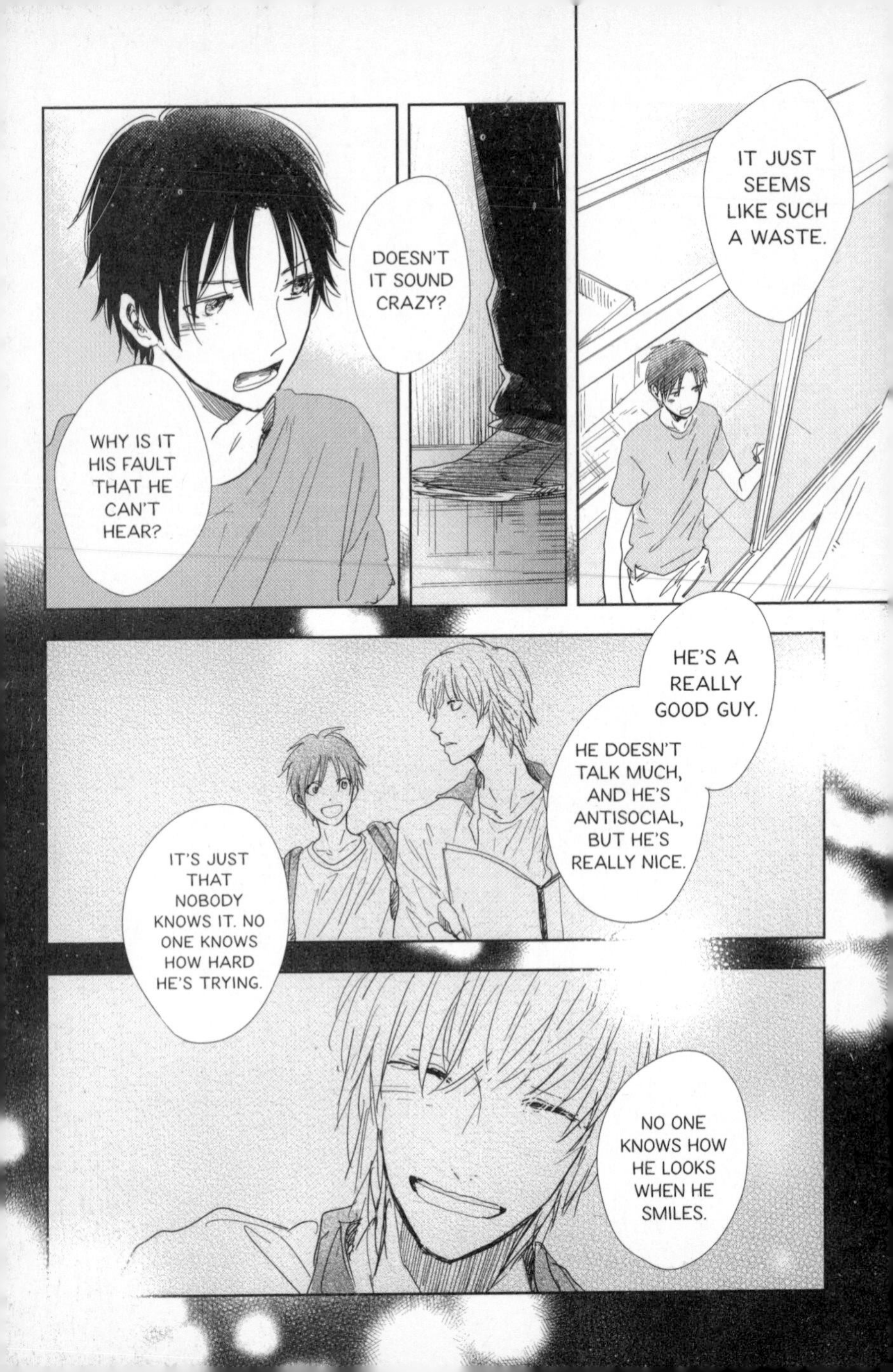
IT JUST SEEMS LIKE SUCH A WASTE.
DOESN'T IT SOUND CRAZY?
WHY IS IT HIS FAULT THAT HE CAN'T HEAR?
HE'S A REALLY GOOD GUY.
HE DOESN'T TALK MUCH, AND HE'S ANTISOCIAL, BUT HE'S REALLY NICE.
IT'S JUST THAT NOBODY KNOWS IT. NO ONE KNOWS HOW HARD HE'S TRYING.
NO ONE KNOWS HOW HE LOOKS WHEN HE SMILES.

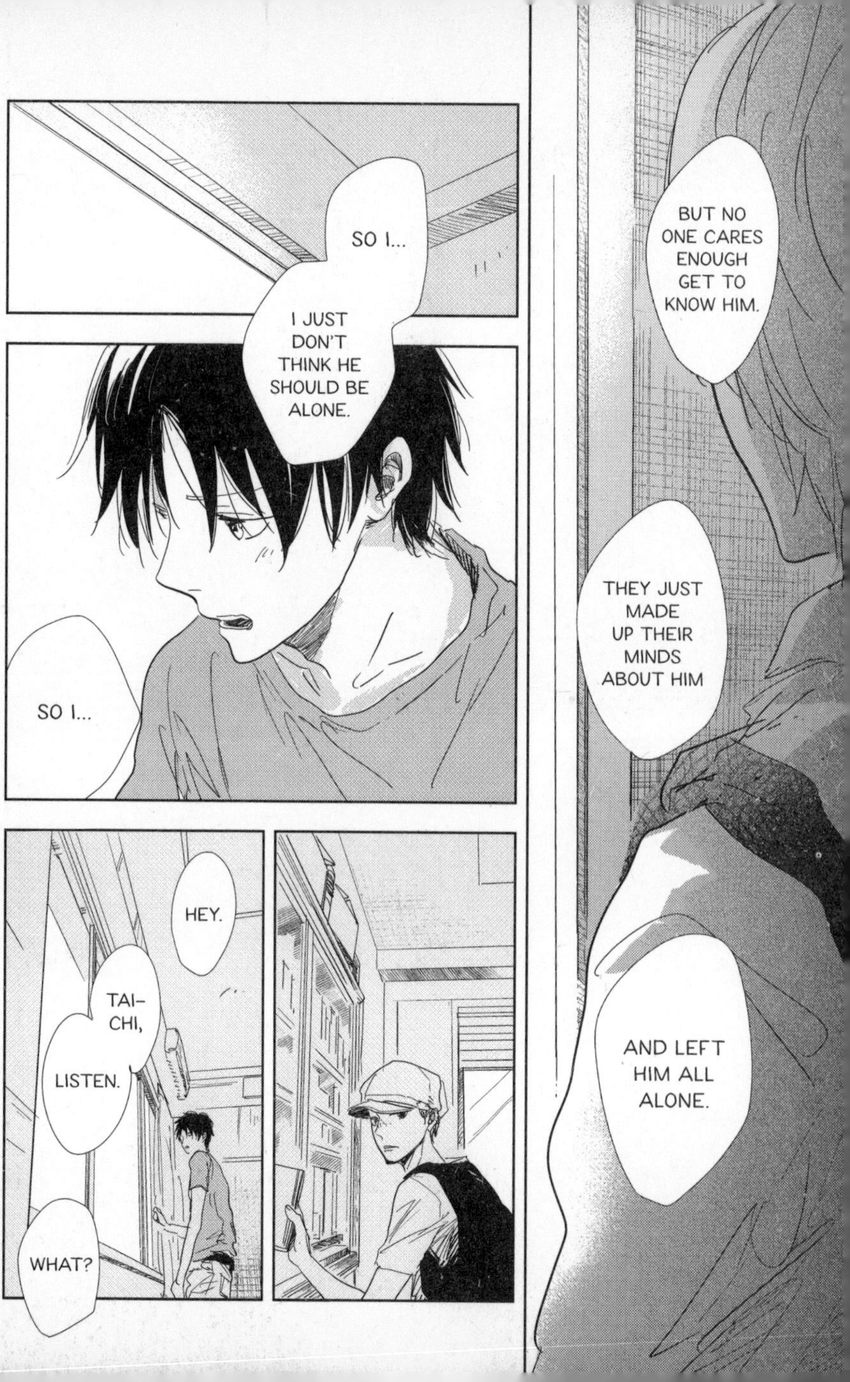
BUT NO ONE CARES ENOUGH GET TO KNOW HIM.
THEY JUST MADE UP THEIR MINDS ABOUT HIM
AND LEFT HIM ALL ALONE.
SO I...
I JUST DON'T THINK HE SHOULD BE ALONE.
SO I...
HEY.
TAI-CHI,
LISTEN.
WHAT?

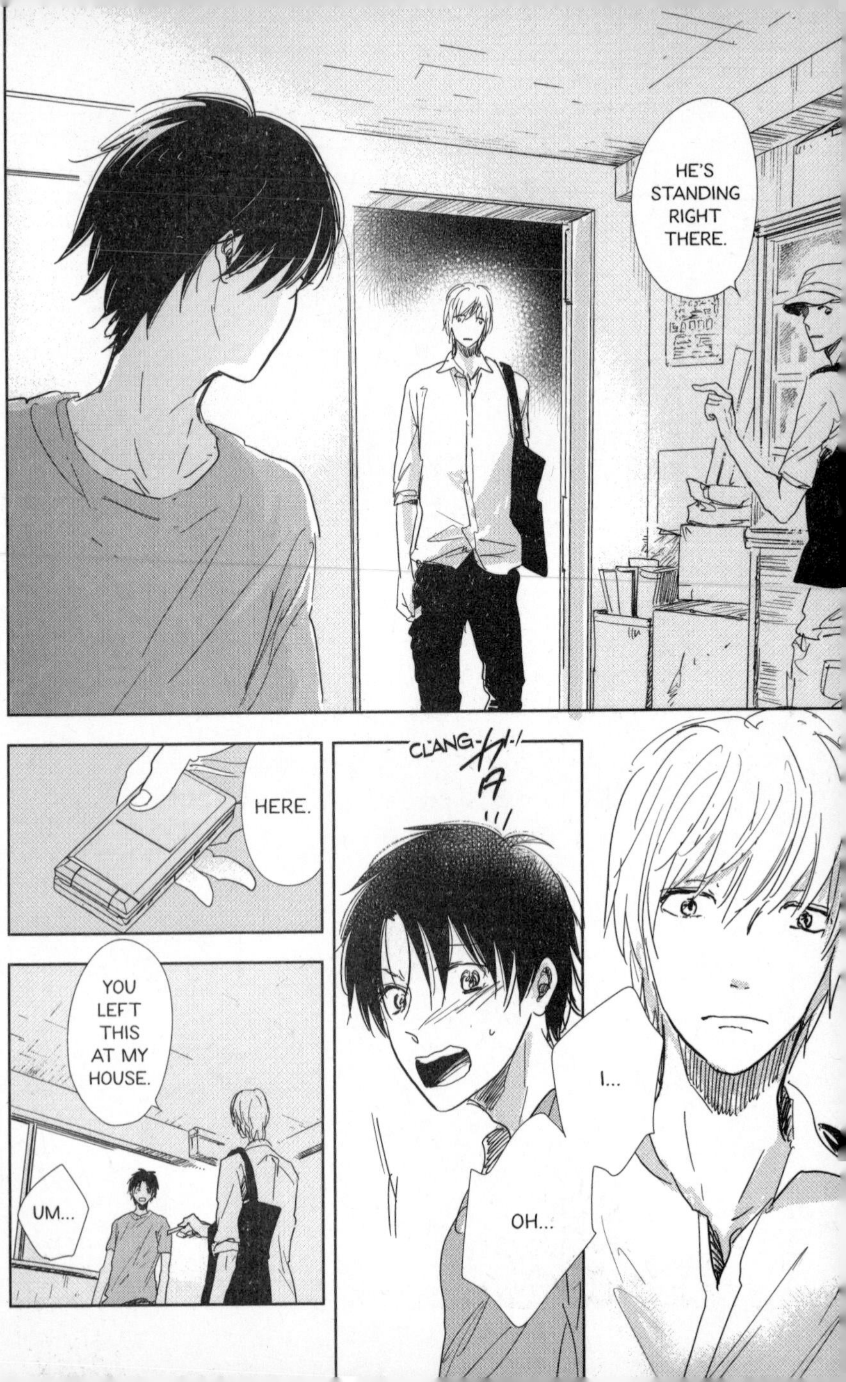
HE'S STANDING RIGHT THERE.
CLANG
I...
OH...
HERE.
YOU LEFT THIS AT MY HOUSE.
UM...

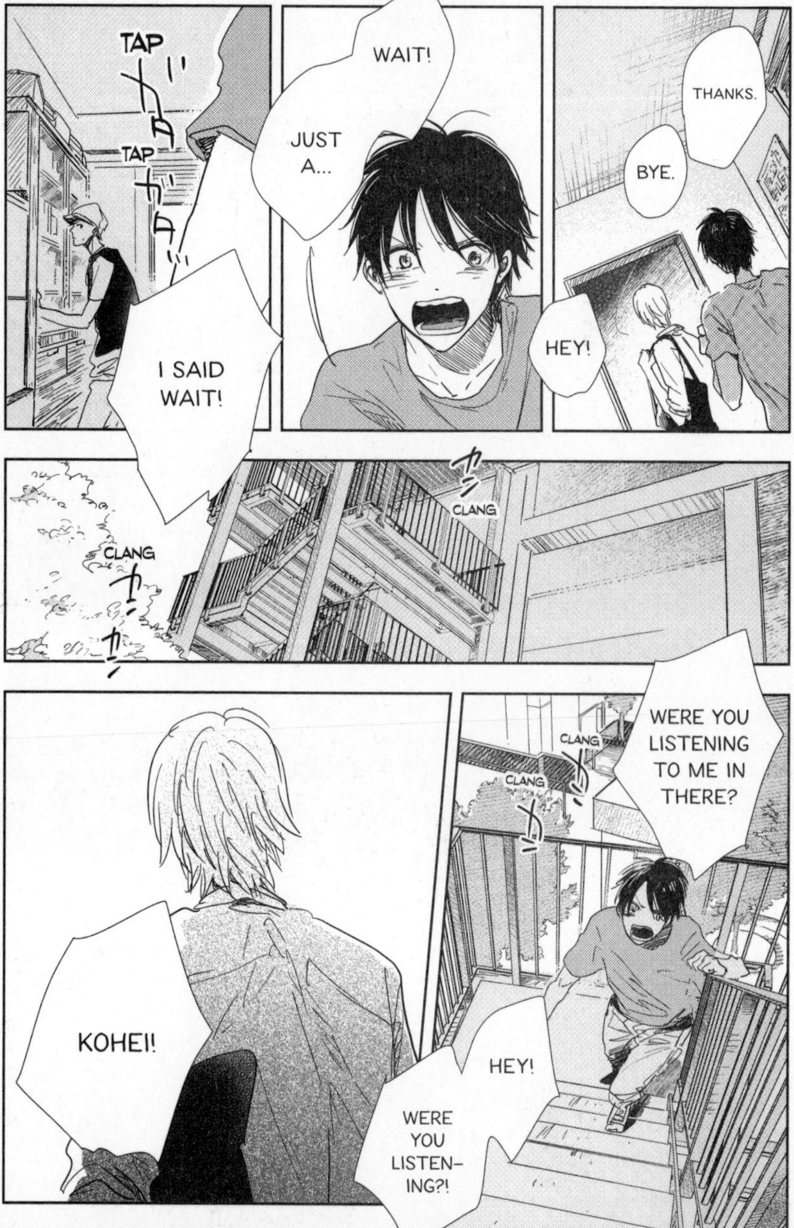
THANKS.
BYE.
HEY!
WAIT!
JUST A...
TAP
TAP
I SAID WAIT!
CLANG
CLANG
WERE YOU LISTENING TO ME IN THERE?
CLANG
CLANG
HEY!
WERE YOU LISTENING?!
KOHEI!

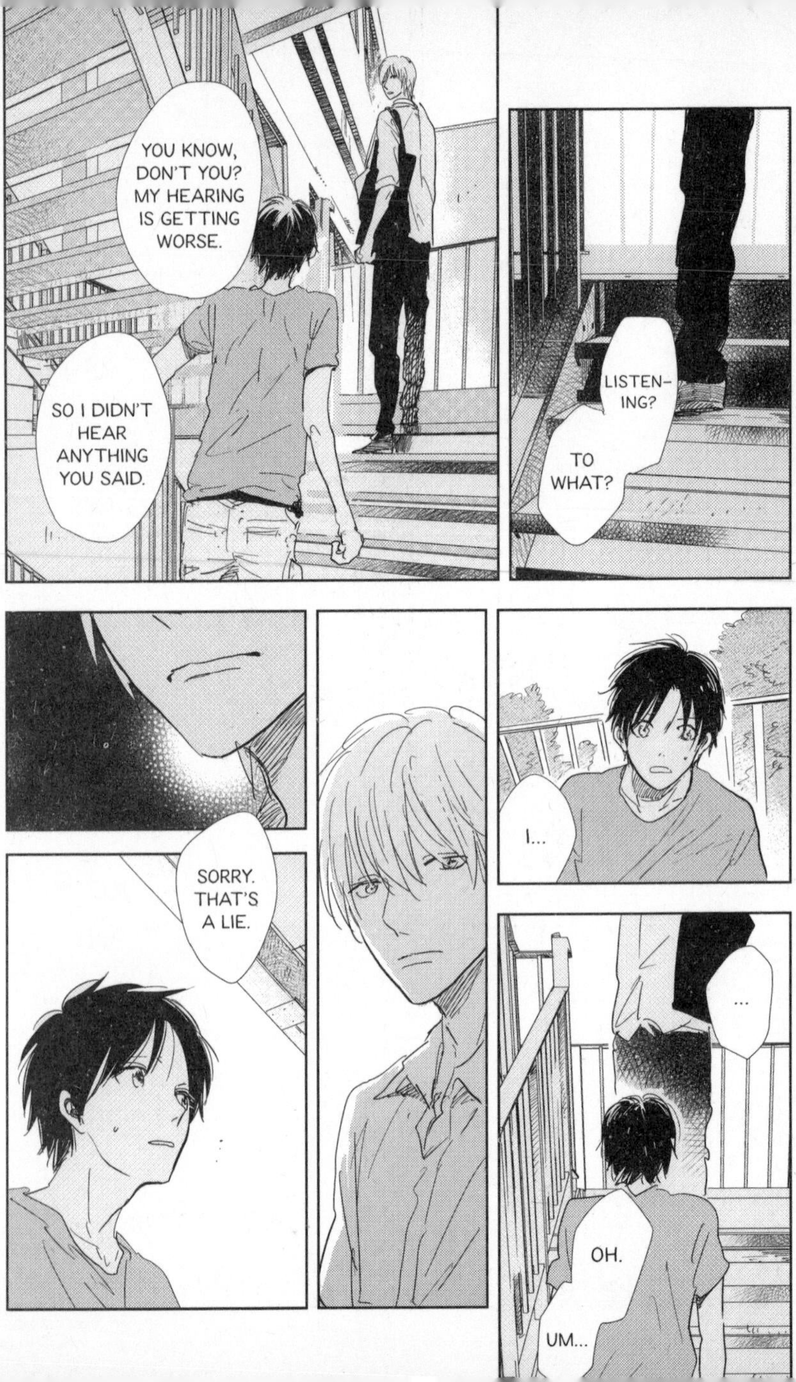
LISTENING?
TO WHAT?
YOU KNOW, DON'T YOU? MY HEARING IS GETTING WORSE.
SO I DIDN'T HEAR ANYTHING YOU SAID.
I...
...
OH.
UM...
SORRY. THAT'S A LIE.

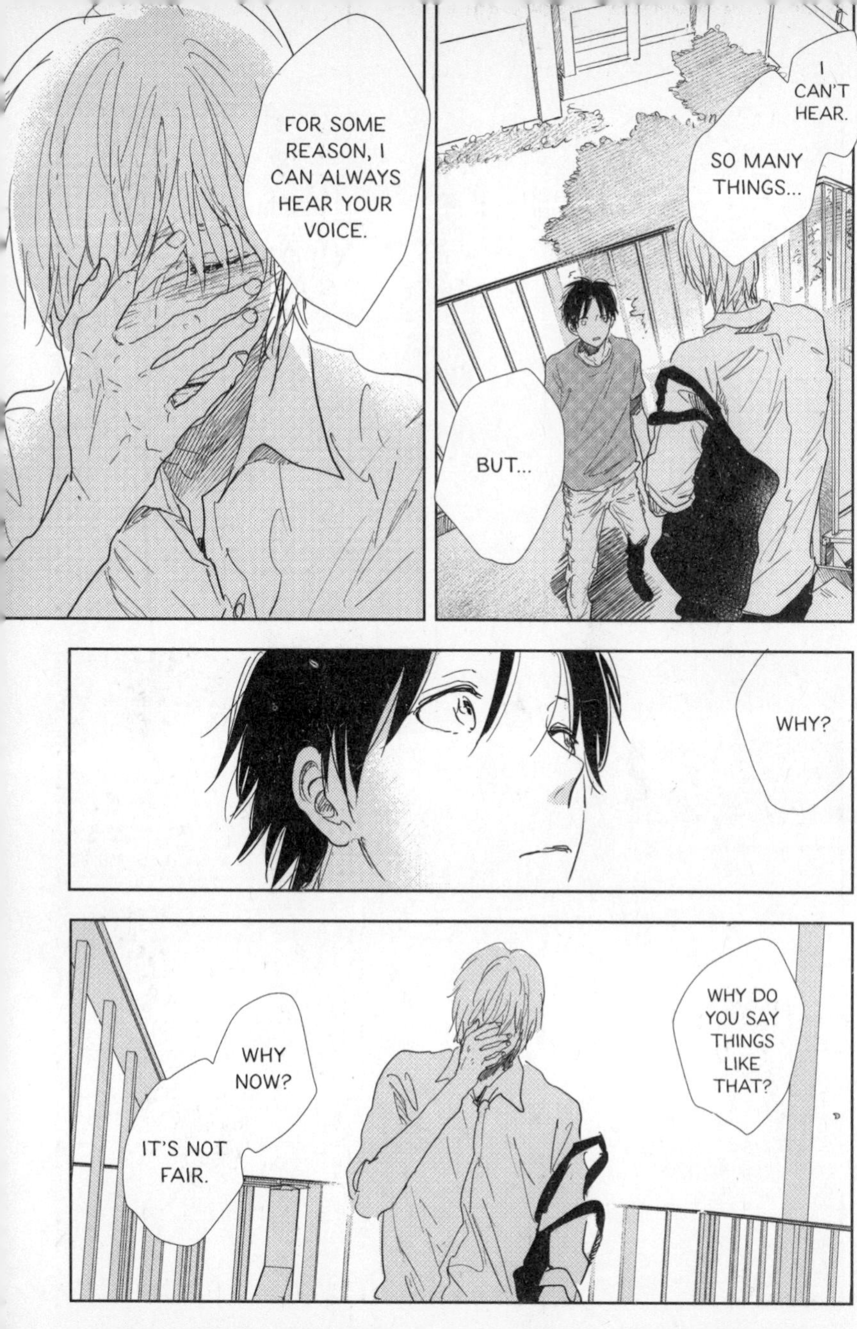
I CAN'T HEAR.
SO MANY THINGS...
BUT...
FOR SOME REASON, I CAN ALWAYS HEAR YOUR VOICE.
WHY?
WHY DO YOU SAY THINGS LIKE THAT?
WHY NOW?
IT'S NOT FAIR.

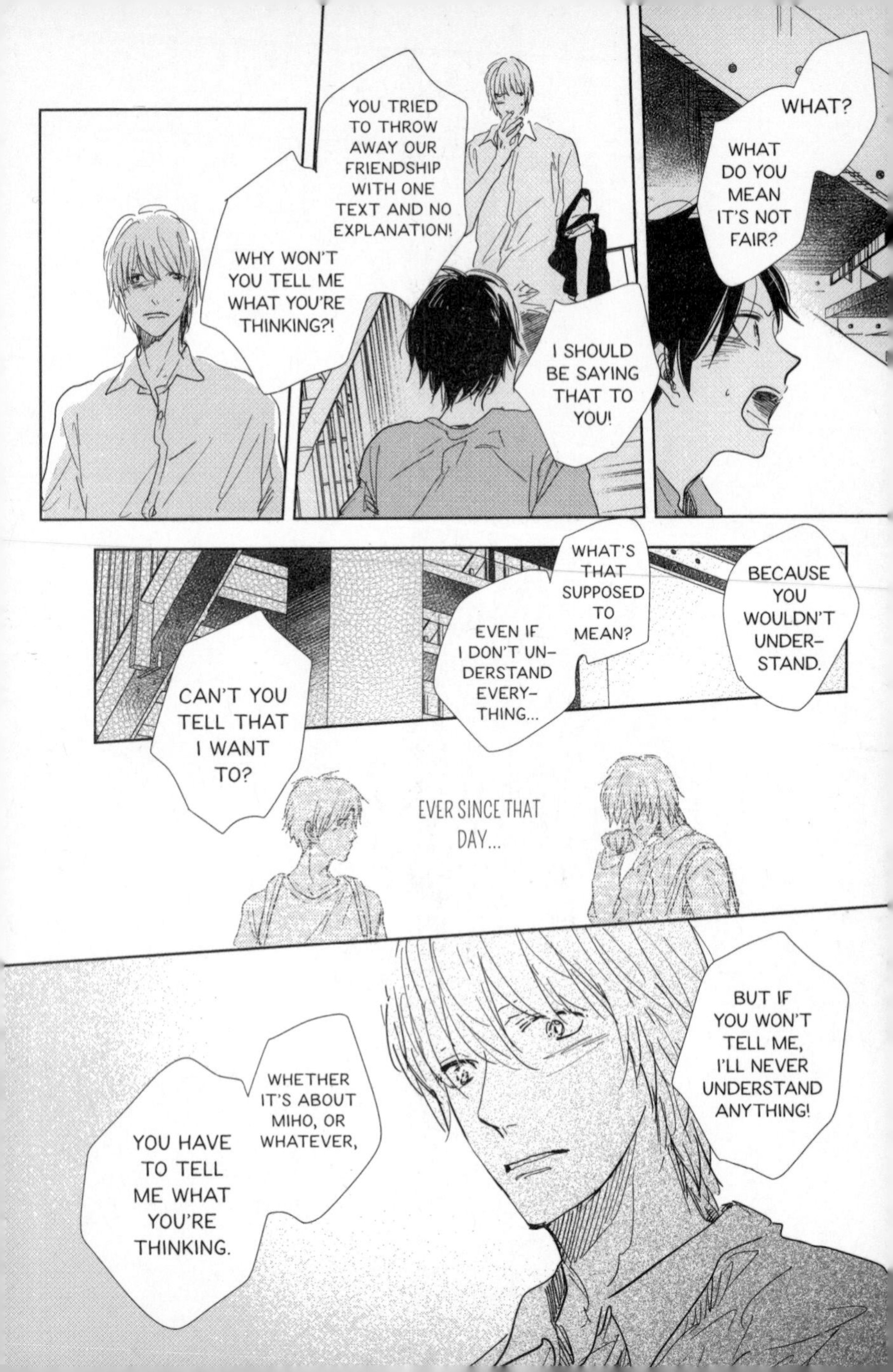
WHAT?
WHAT DO YOU MEAN IT'S NOT FAIR?
I SHOULD BE SAYING THAT TO YOU!
YOU TRIED TO THROW AWAY OUR FRIENDSHIP WITH ONE TEXT AND NO EXPLANATION!
WHY WON'T YOU TELL ME WHAT YOU'RE THINKING?!
BECAUSE YOU WOULDN'T UNDER-STAND.
WHAT'S THAT SUPPOSED TO MEAN?
EVEN IF I DON'T UN-DERSTAND EVERY-THING...
CAN'T YOU TELL THAT I WANT TO?
EVER SINCE THAT DAY...
BUT IF YOU WON'T TELL ME, I'LL NEVER UNDERSTAND ANYTHING!
WHETHER IT'S ABOUT MIHO, OR WHATEVER,
YOU HAVE TO TELL ME WHAT YOU'RE THINKING.

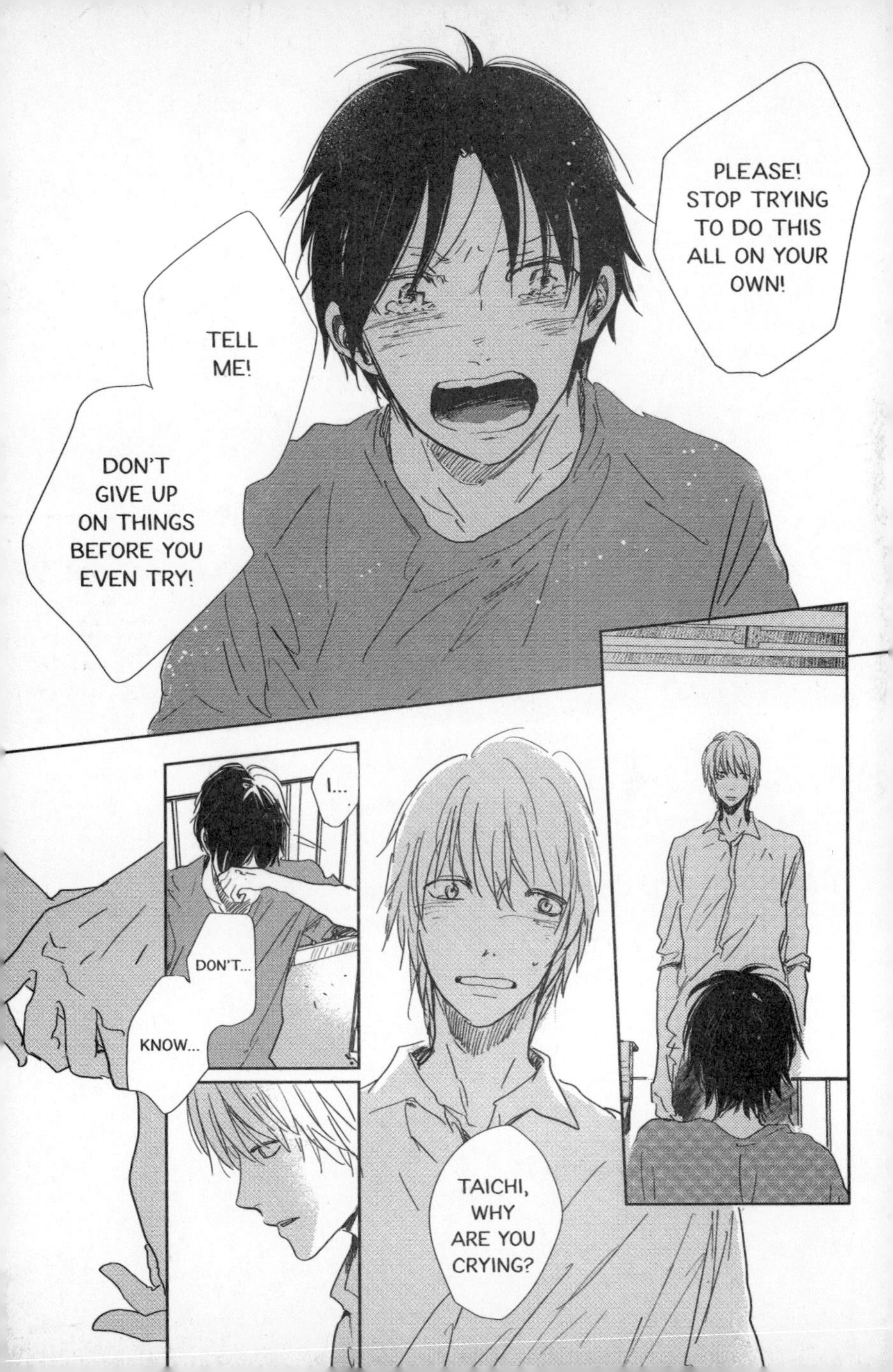
PLEASE! STOP TRYING TO DO THIS ALL ON YOUR OWN!
TELL ME!
DON'T GIVE UP ON THINGS BEFORE YOU EVEN TRY!
TAICHI, WHY ARE YOU CRYING?
I...
DON'T...
KNOW...

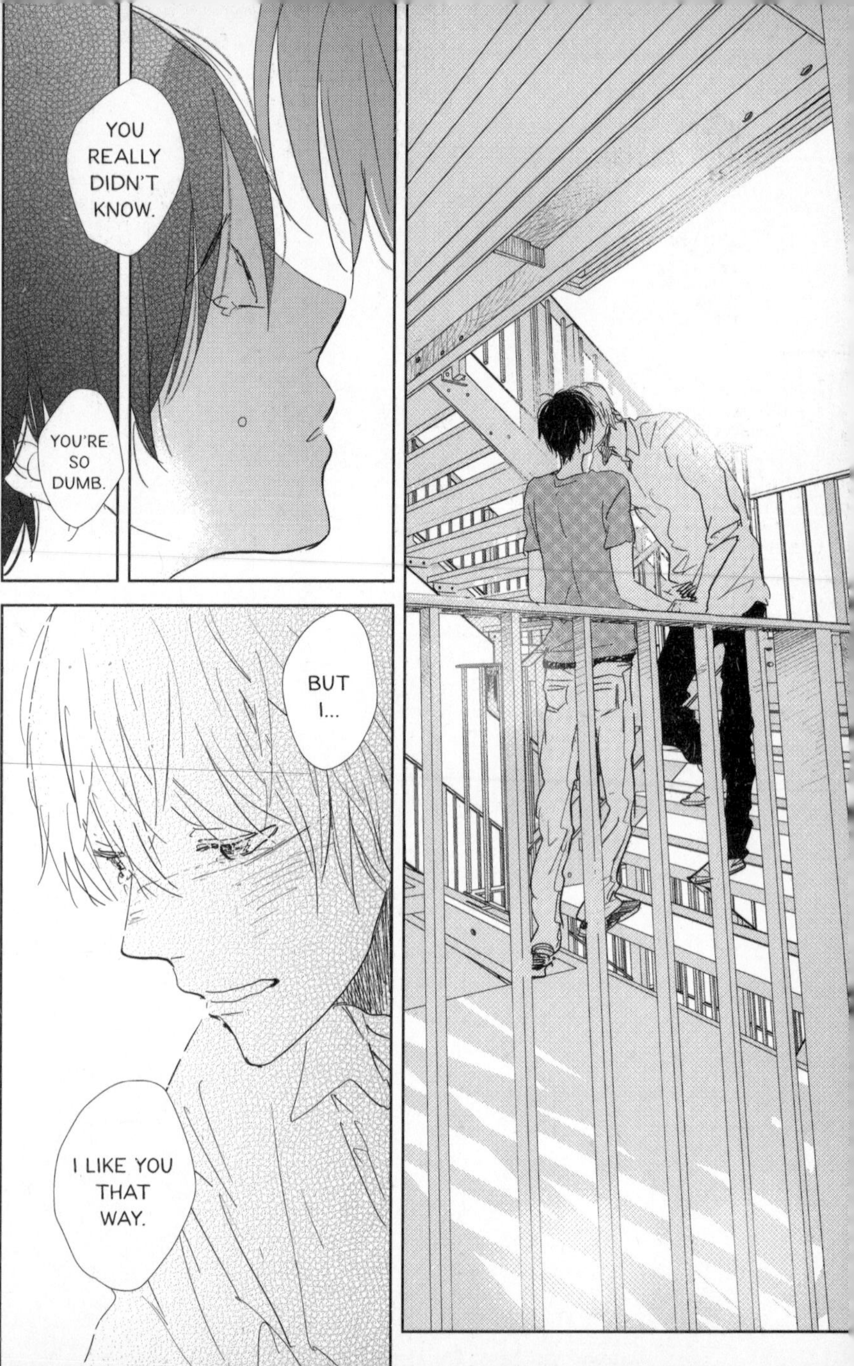
YOU REALLY DIDN'T KNOW.
YOU'RE SO DUMB.
BUT I...
I LIKE YOU THAT WAY.

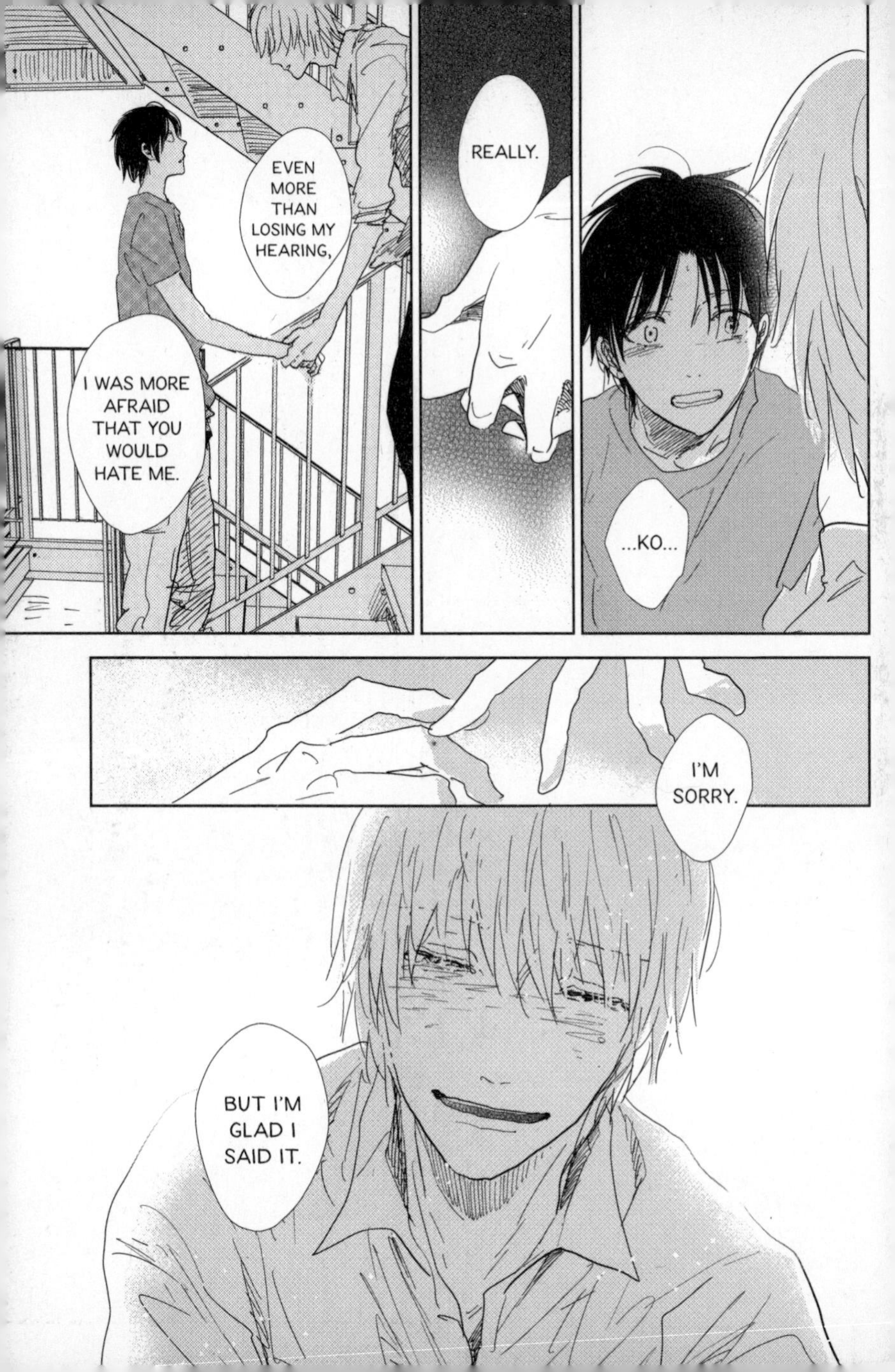
...KO...
REALLY.
EVEN MORE THAN LOSING MY HEARING,
I WAS MORE AFRAID THAT YOU WOULD HATE ME.
I'M SORRY.
BUT I'M GLAD I SAID IT.

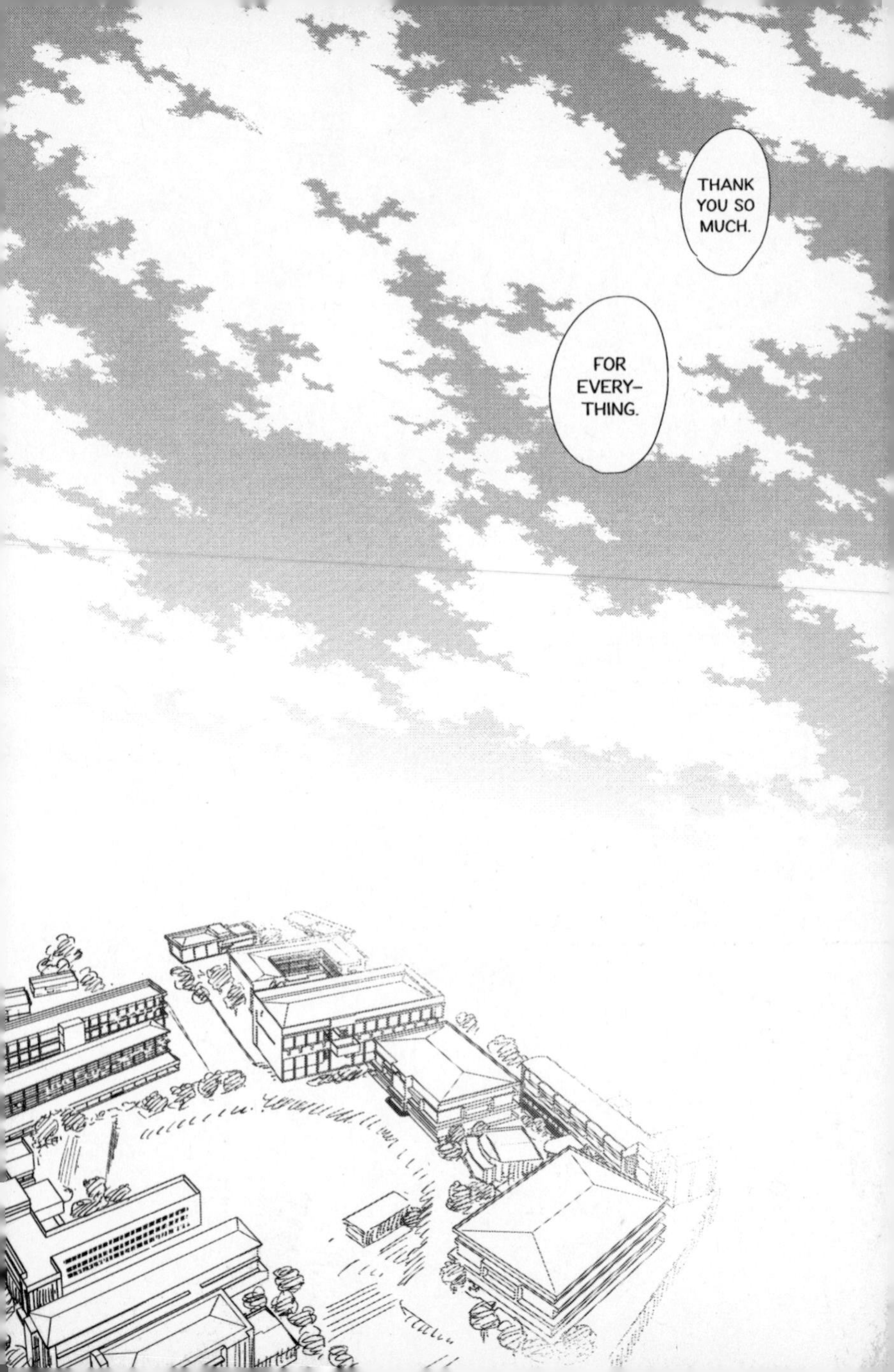
THANK YOU SO MUCH.
FOR EVERY-THING.

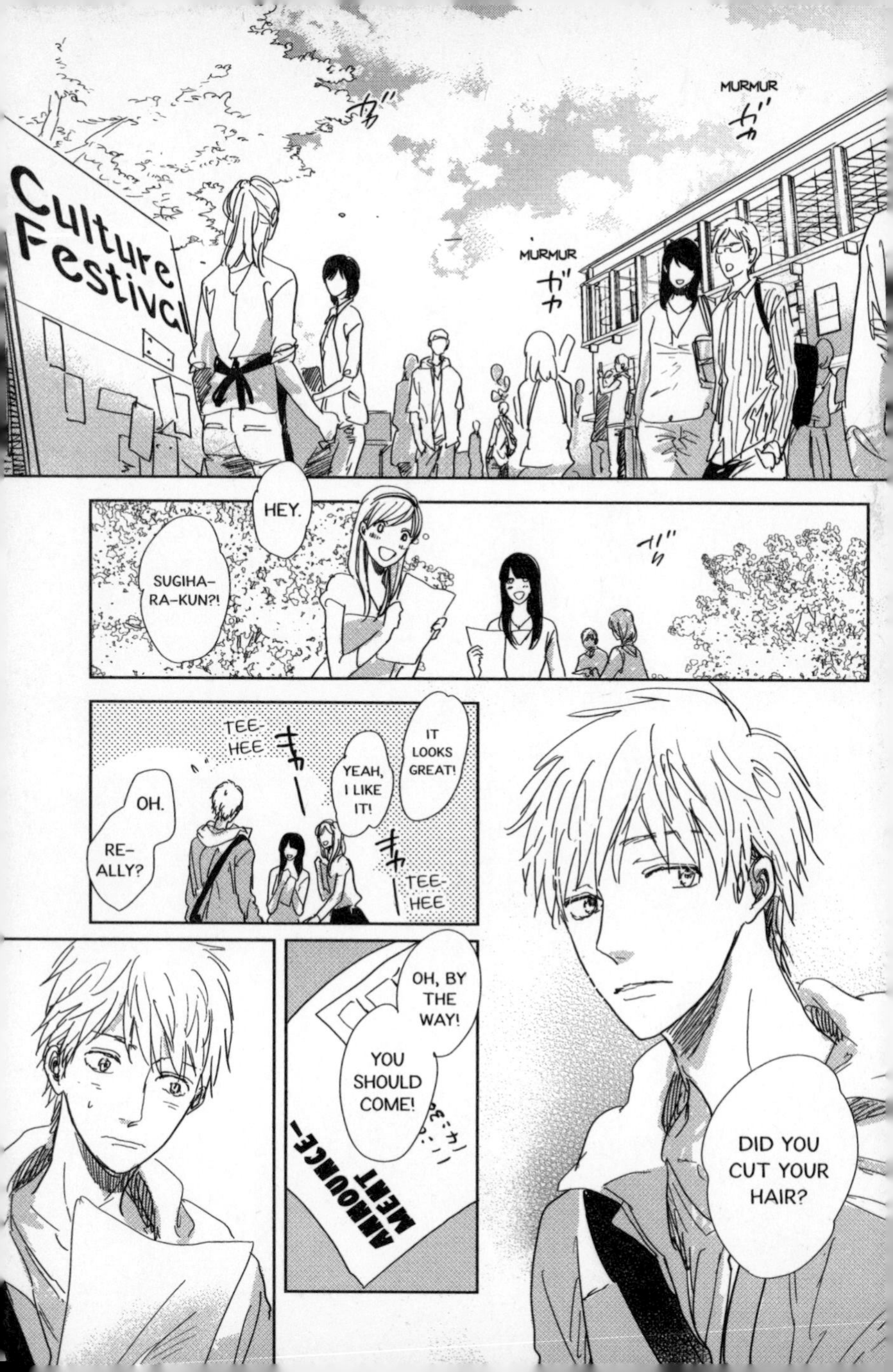
MURMUR
ガヤ
MURMUR
ガヤ
Culture Festival
HEY.
SUGIHARA-KUN?!
DID YOU CUT YOUR HAIR?
IT LOOKS GREAT!
YEAH, I LIKE IT!
TEE-HEE
TEE-HEE
OH.
RE-ALLY?
OH, BY THE WAY!
YOU SHOULD COME!
ANNOUNCE-MENT

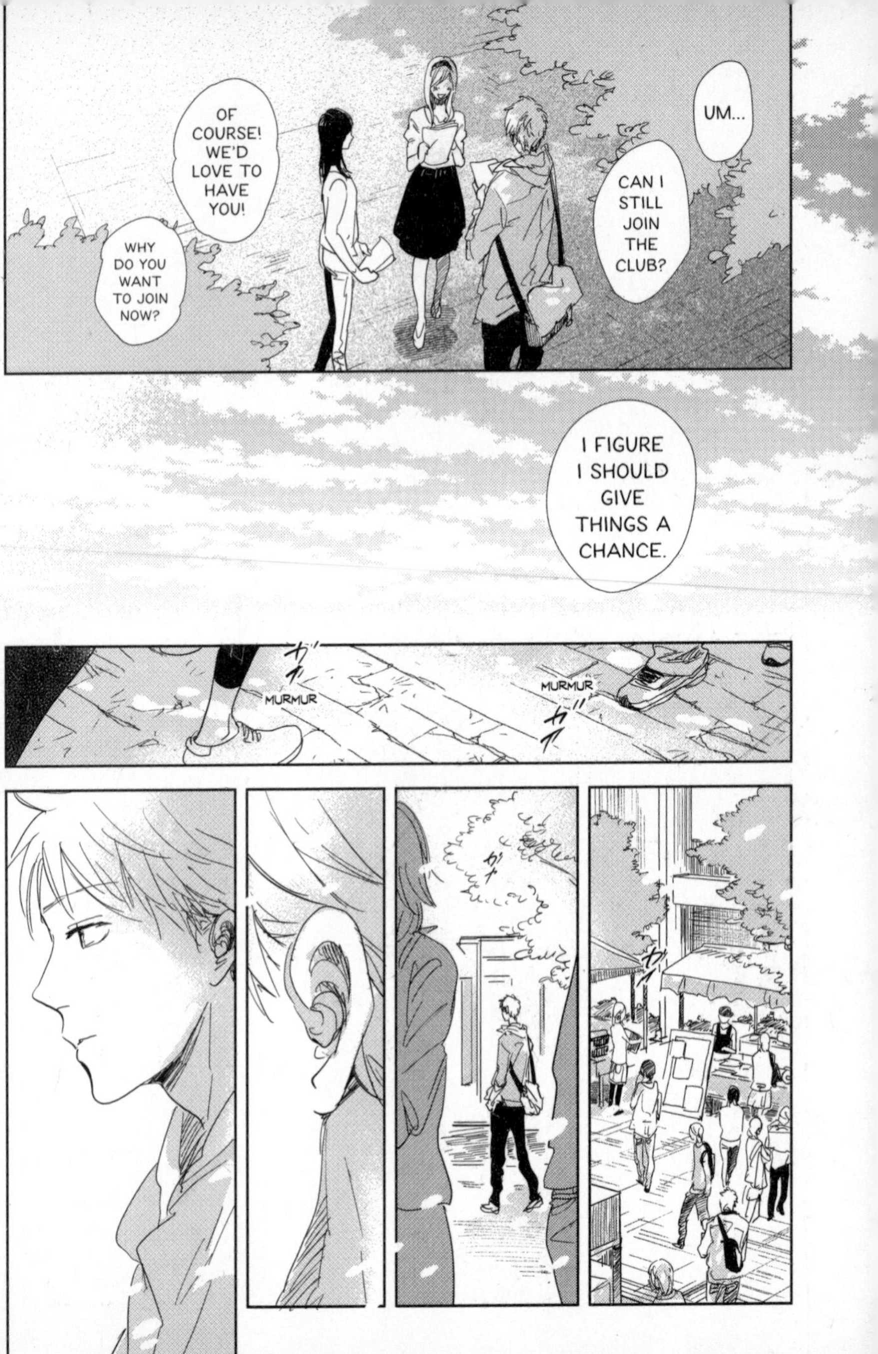
UM...
CAN I STILL JOIN THE CLUB?
OF COURSE! WE'D LOVE TO HAVE YOU!
WHY DO YOU WANT TO JOIN NOW?
I FIGURE I SHOULD GIVE THINGS A CHANCE.
MURMUR
MURMUR

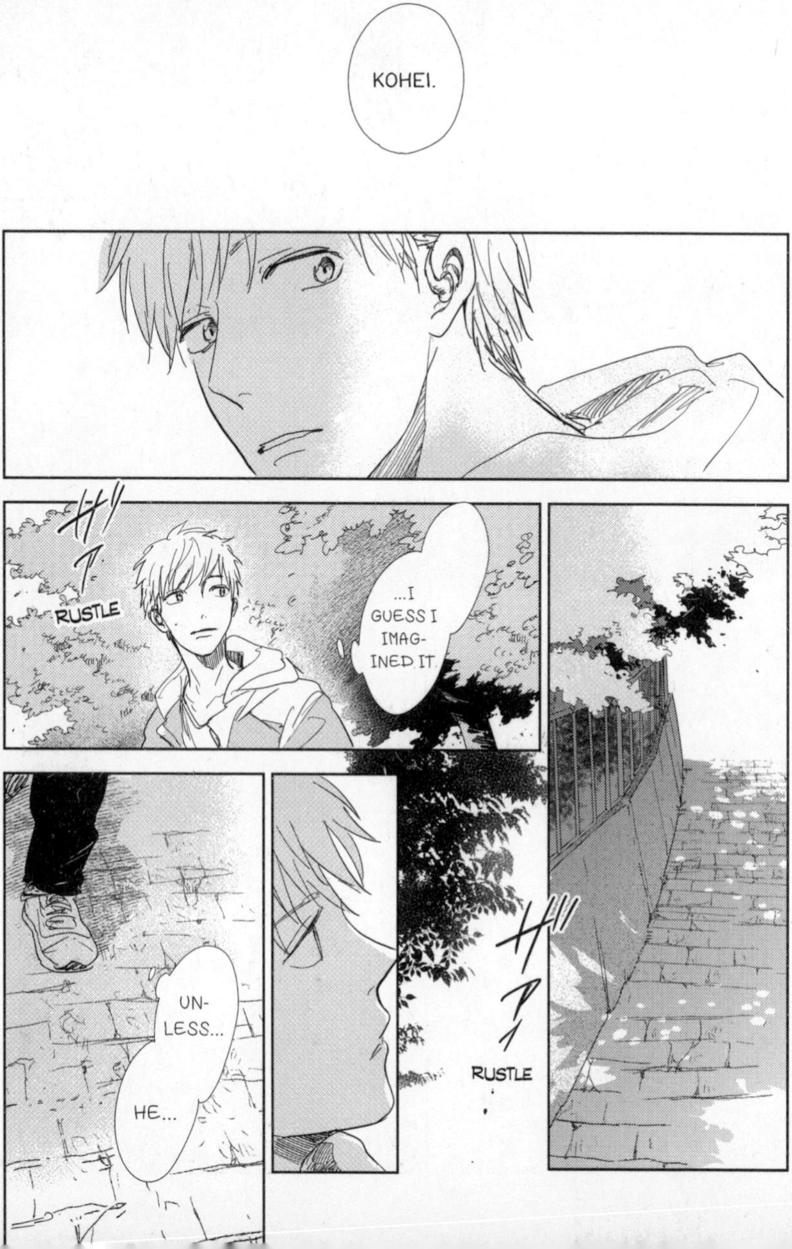
KOHEI.
RUSTLE
...I GUESS I IMAGINED IT.
RUSTLE
UN-LESS...
HE...

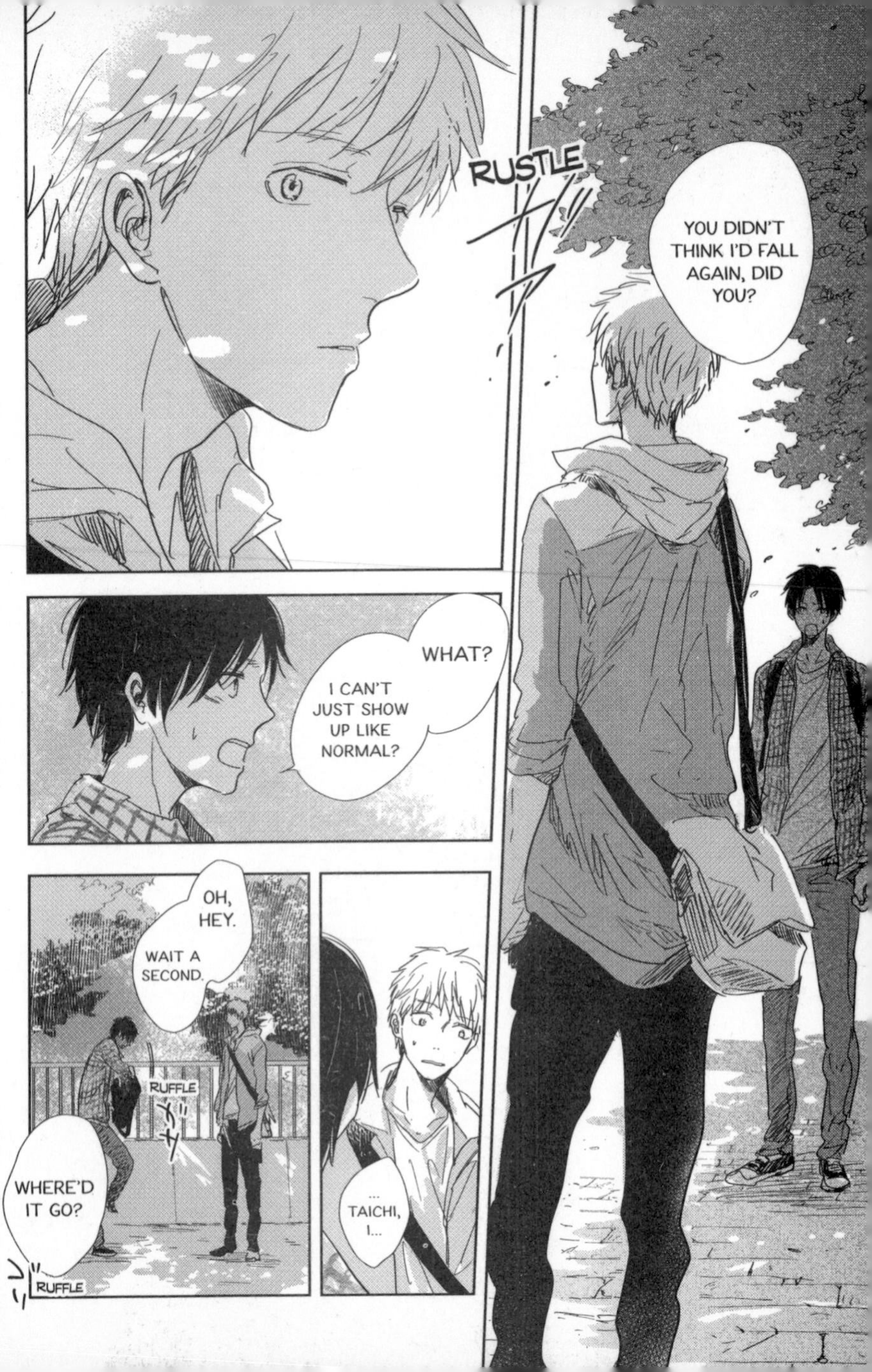

YOU DIDN'T THINK I'D FALL AGAIN, DID YOU?
RUSTLE
WHAT?
I CAN'T JUST SHOW UP LIKE NORMAL?
... TAICHI, I...
OH, HEY.
WAIT A SECOND.
RUFFLE
WHERE'D IT GO?
RUFFLE

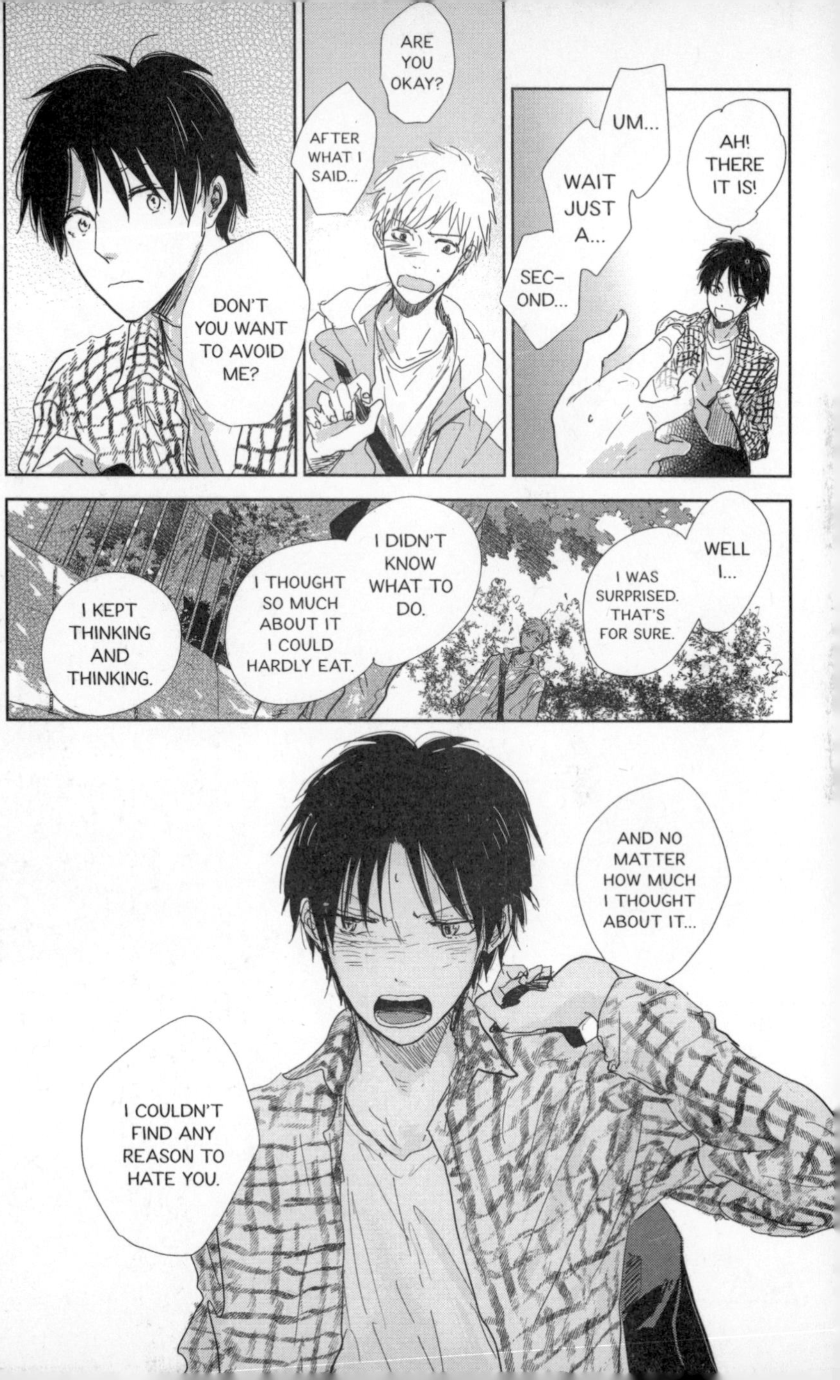
AH! THERE IT IS!
UM...
WAIT JUST A...
SEC-OND...
ARE YOU OKAY?
AFTER WHAT I SAID...
DON'T YOU WANT TO AVOID ME?
WELL I...
I WAS SURPRISED. THAT'S FOR SURE.
I DIDN'T KNOW WHAT TO DO.
I THOUGHT SO MUCH ABOUT IT I COULD HARDLY EAT.
I KEPT THINKING AND THINKING.
AND NO MATTER HOW MUCH I THOUGHT ABOUT IT...
I COULDN'T FIND ANY REASON TO HATE YOU.

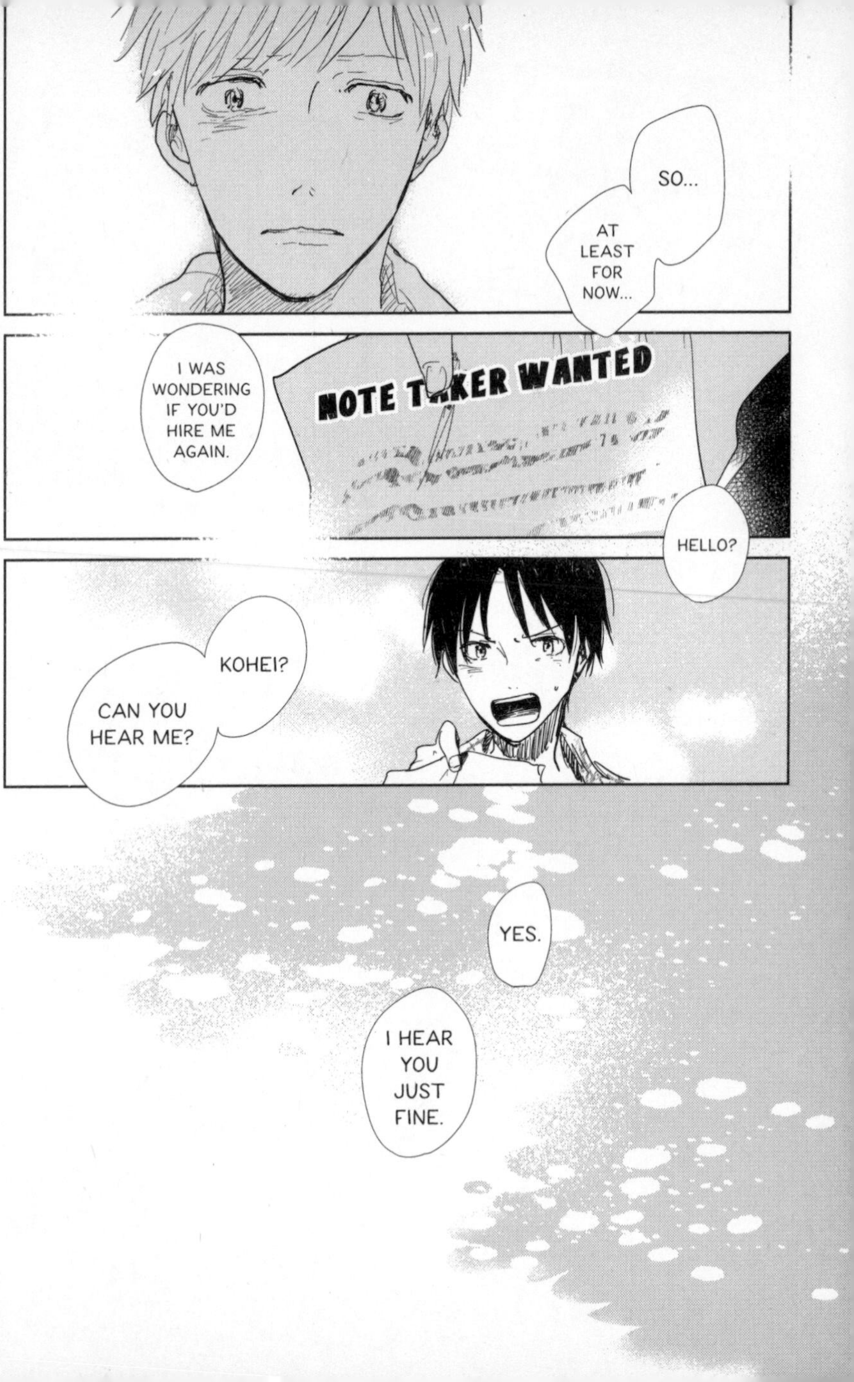
SO...
AT LEAST FOR NOW...
NOTE TAKER WANTED
I WAS WONDERING IF YOU'D HIRE ME AGAIN.
HELLO?
KOHEI?
CAN YOU HEAR ME?
YES.
I HEAR YOU JUST FINE.

i hear
the
sunspot

i hear the sunspot

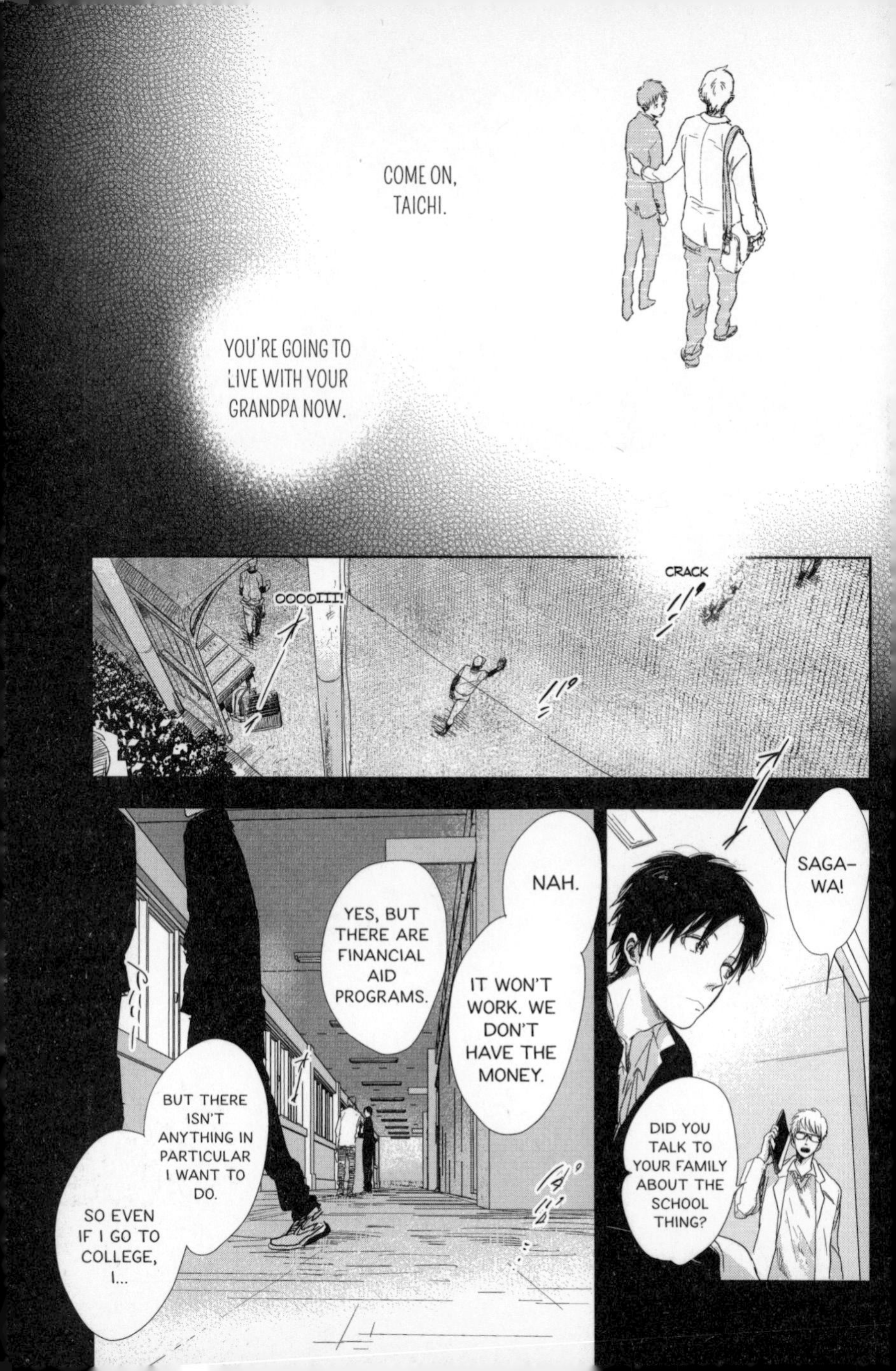
COME ON, TAICHI.
YOU'RE GOING TO LIVE WITH YOUR GRANDPA NOW.
CRACK
OOOOIII!
SAGA-WA!
DID YOU TALK TO YOUR FAMILY ABOUT THE SCHOOL THING?
NAH.
IT WON'T WORK. WE DON'T HAVE THE MONEY.
YES, BUT THERE ARE FINANCIAL AID PROGRAMS.
BUT THERE ISN'T ANYTHING IN PARTICULAR I WANT TO DO.
SO EVEN IF I GO TO COLLEGE, I...

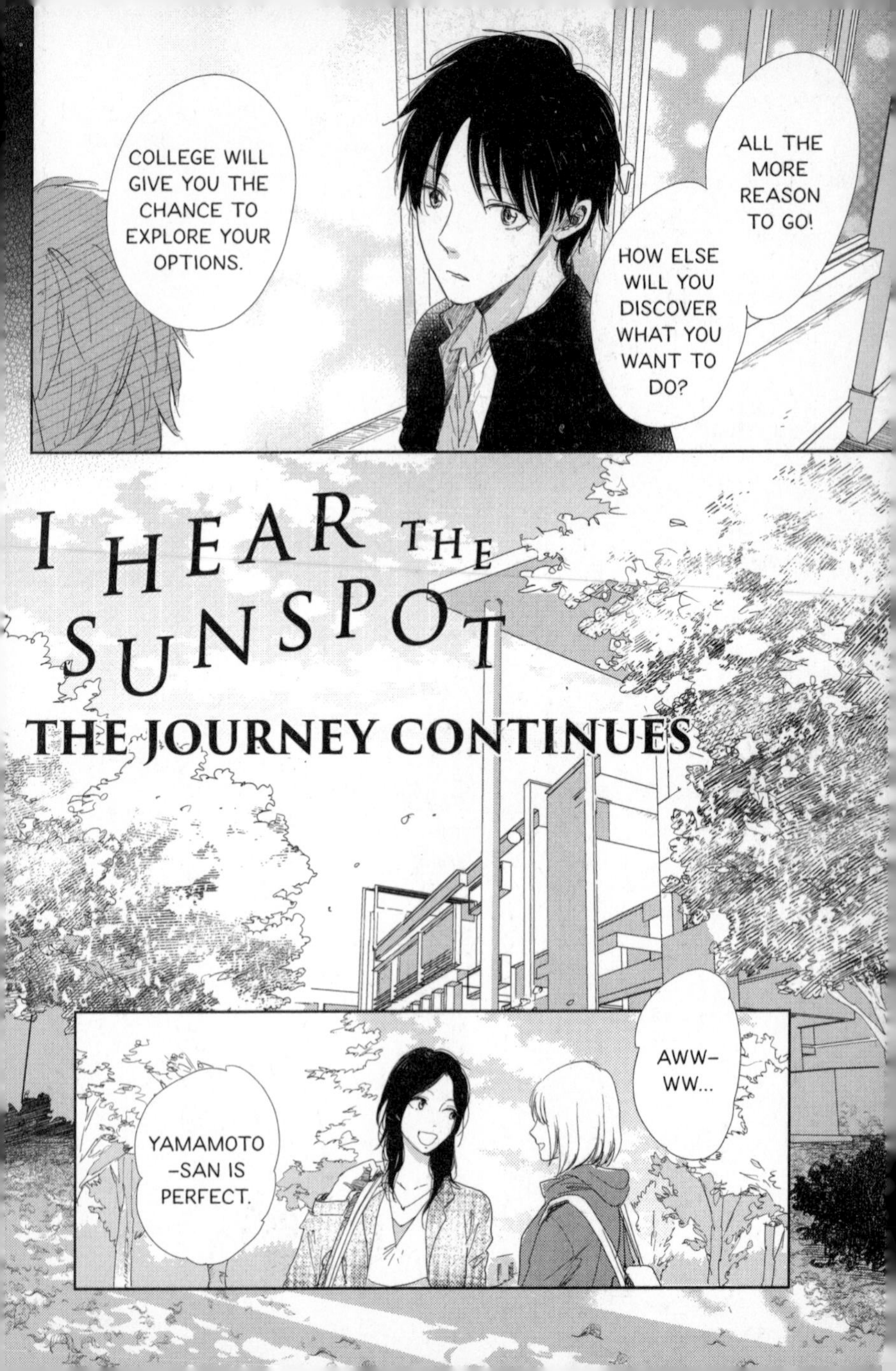
ALL THE MORE REASON TO GO!
HOW ELSE WILL YOU DISCOVER WHAT YOU WANT TO DO?
COLLEGE WILL GIVE YOU THE CHANCE TO EXPLORE YOUR OPTIONS.
I HEAR THE SUNSPOT
THE JOURNEY CONTINUES
AWW-WW...
YAMAMOTO-SAN IS PERFECT.

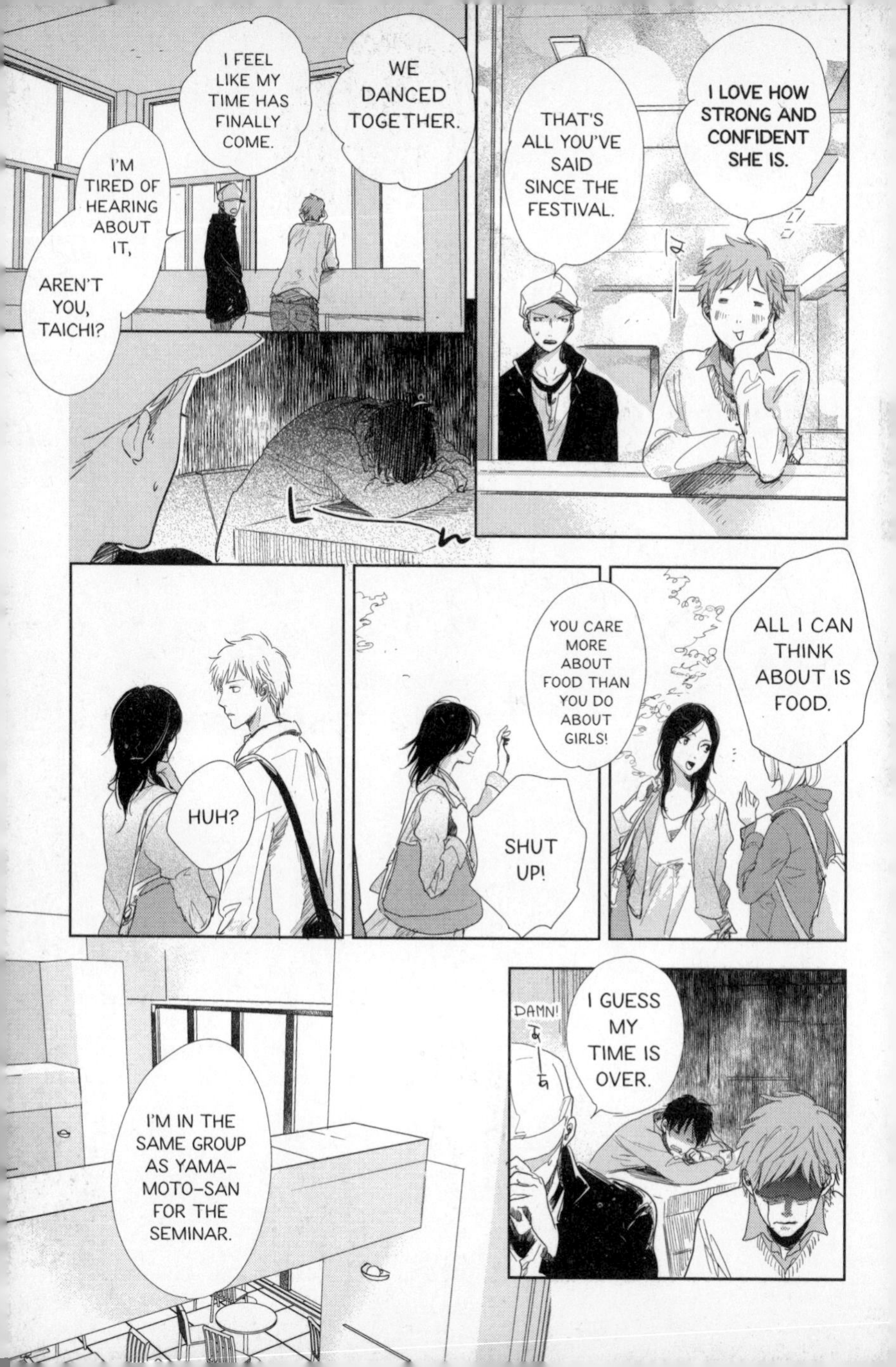
I LOVE HOW STRONG AND CONFIDENT SHE IS.
THAT'S ALL YOU'VE SAID SINCE THE FESTIVAL.
WE DANCED TOGETHER.
I FEEL LIKE MY TIME HAS FINALLY COME.
I'M TIRED OF HEARING ABOUT IT,
AREN'T YOU, TAICHI?
ALL I CAN THINK ABOUT IS FOOD.
YOU CARE MORE ABOUT FOOD THAN YOU DO ABOUT GIRLS!
SHUT UP!
HUH?
I GUESS MY TIME IS OVER.
DAMN!
I'M IN THE SAME GROUP AS YAMA-MOTO-SAN FOR THE SEMINAR.

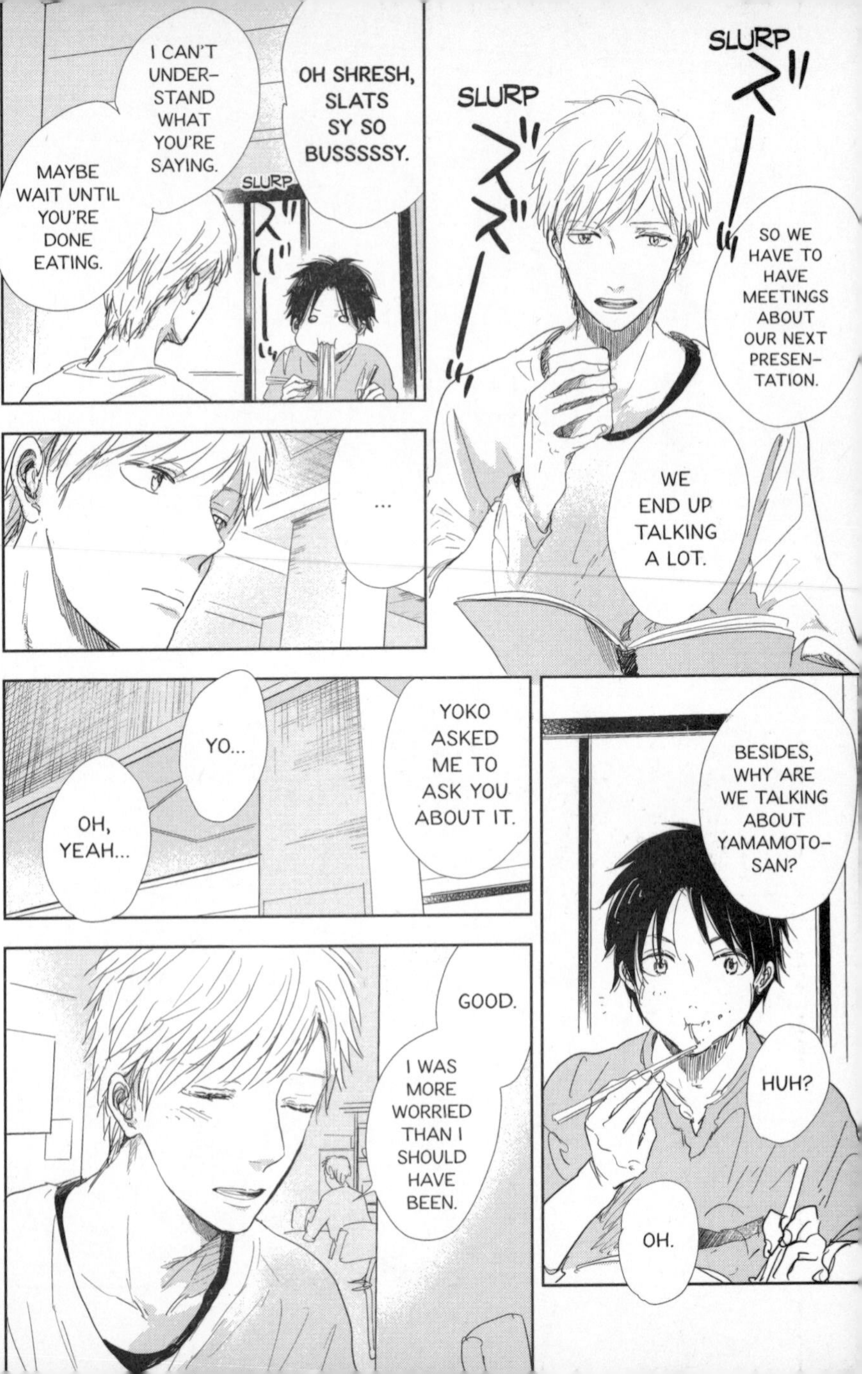
SLURP
SLURP
SO WE HAVE TO HAVE MEETINGS ABOUT OUR NEXT PRESENTATION.
WE END UP TALKING A LOT.
OH SHRESH, SLATS SY SO BUSSSSSY.
SLURP
I CAN'T UNDER-STAND WHAT YOU'RE SAYING.
MAYBE WAIT UNTIL YOU'RE DONE EATING.
...
BESIDES, WHY ARE WE TALKING ABOUT YAMAMOTO-SAN?
HUH?
OH.
YOKO ASKED ME TO ASK YOU ABOUT IT.
YO...
OH, YEAH...
GOOD.
I WAS MORE WORRIED THAN I SHOULD HAVE BEEN.

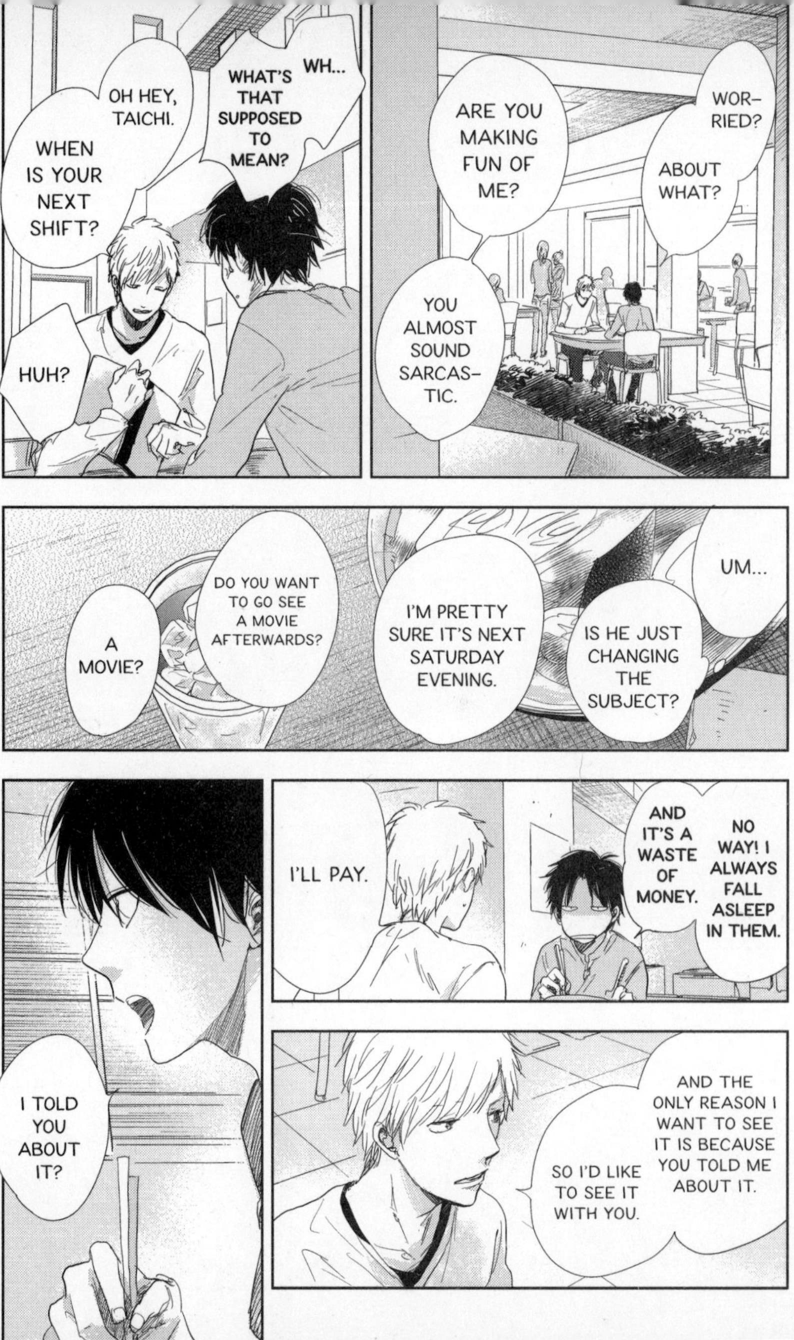
WOR–RIED?
ABOUT WHAT?
ARE YOU MAKING FUN OF ME?
YOU ALMOST SOUND SARCAS–TIC.
WH...
WHAT'S THAT SUPPOSED TO MEAN?
OH HEY, TAICHI.
WHEN IS YOUR NEXT SHIFT?
HUH?
UM...
IS HE JUST CHANGING THE SUBJECT?
I'M PRETTY SURE IT'S NEXT SATURDAY EVENING.
DO YOU WANT TO GO SEE A MOVIE AFTERWARDS?
A MOVIE?
NO WAY! I ALWAYS FALL ASLEEP IN THEM.
AND IT'S A WASTE OF MONEY.
I'LL PAY.
AND THE ONLY REASON I WANT TO SEE IT IS BECAUSE YOU TOLD ME ABOUT IT.
SO I'D LIKE TO SEE IT WITH YOU.
I TOLD YOU ABOUT IT?

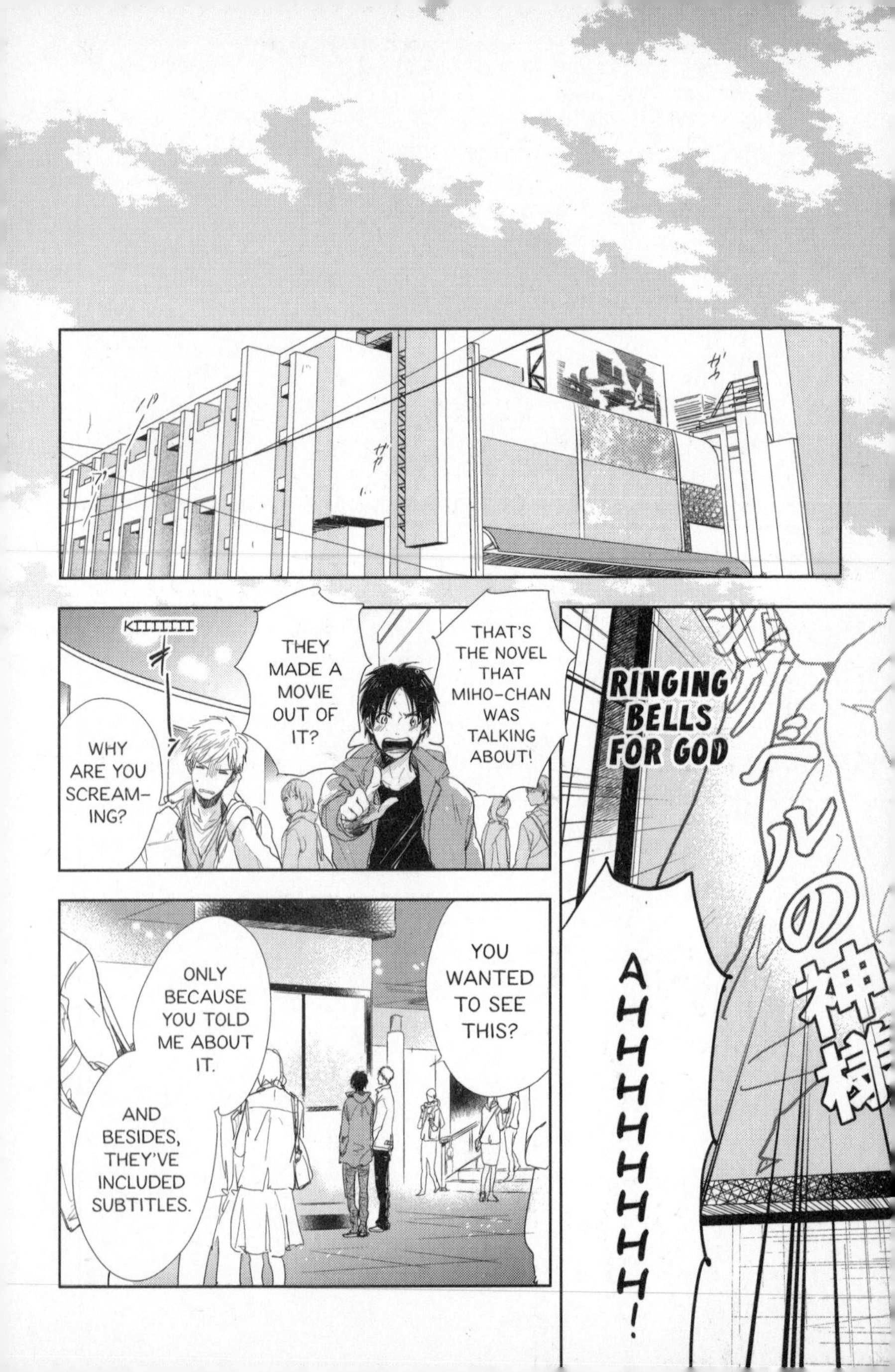
RINGING BELLS FOR GOD
の神様
AHHHHHHHHHH!
THAT'S THE NOVEL THAT MIHO-CHAN WAS TALKING ABOUT!
THEY MADE A MOVIE OUT OF IT?
KIIIIIII
WHY ARE YOU SCREAMING?
YOU WANTED TO SEE THIS?
ONLY BECAUSE YOU TOLD ME ABOUT IT.
AND BESIDES, THEY'VE INCLUDED SUBTITLES.

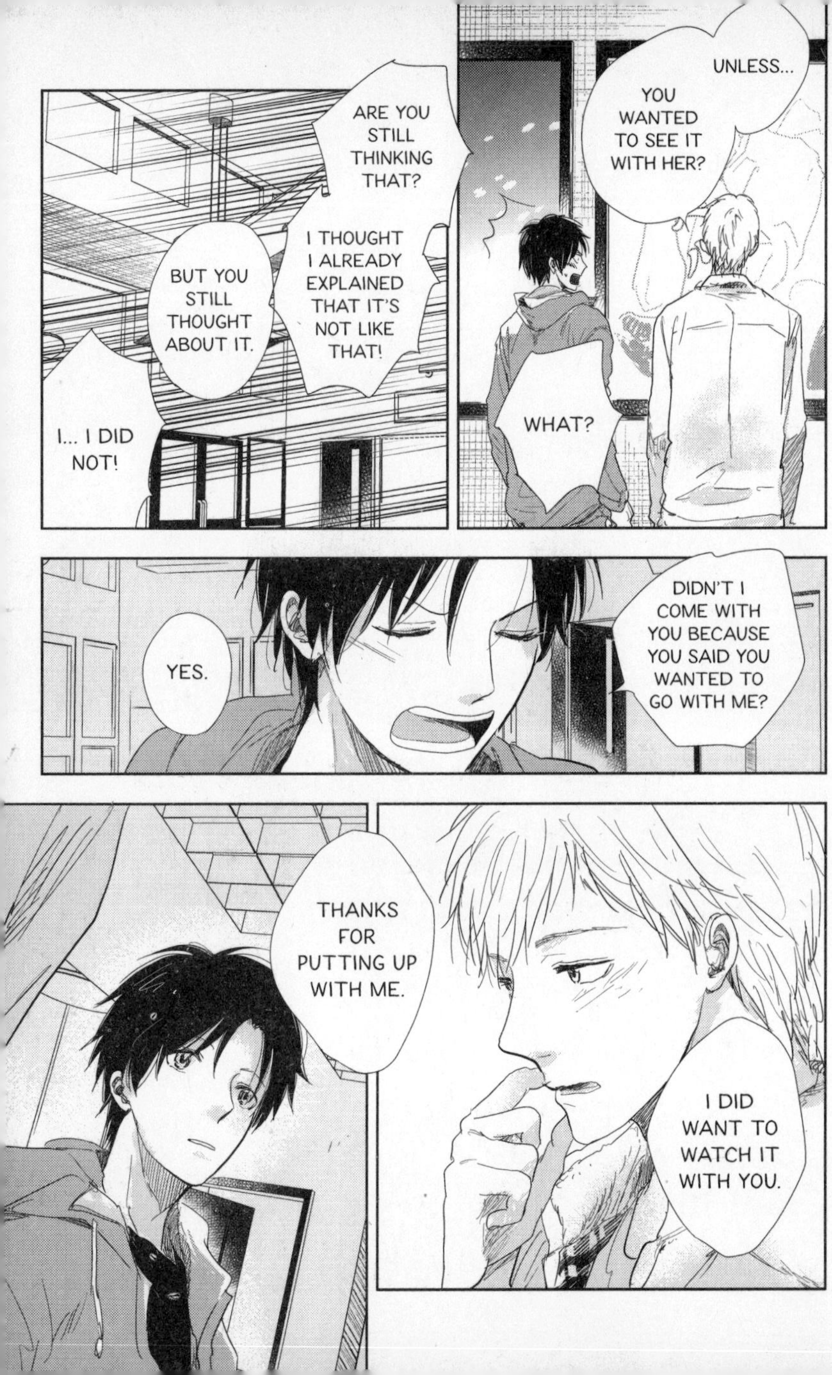
UNLESS...
YOU WANTED TO SEE IT WITH HER?
WHAT?
ARE YOU STILL THINKING THAT?
I THOUGHT I ALREADY EXPLAINED THAT IT'S NOT LIKE THAT!
BUT YOU STILL THOUGHT ABOUT IT.
I... I DID NOT!
DIDN'T I COME WITH YOU BECAUSE YOU SAID YOU WANTED TO GO WITH ME?
YES.
THANKS FOR PUTTING UP WITH ME.
I DID WANT TO WATCH IT WITH YOU.

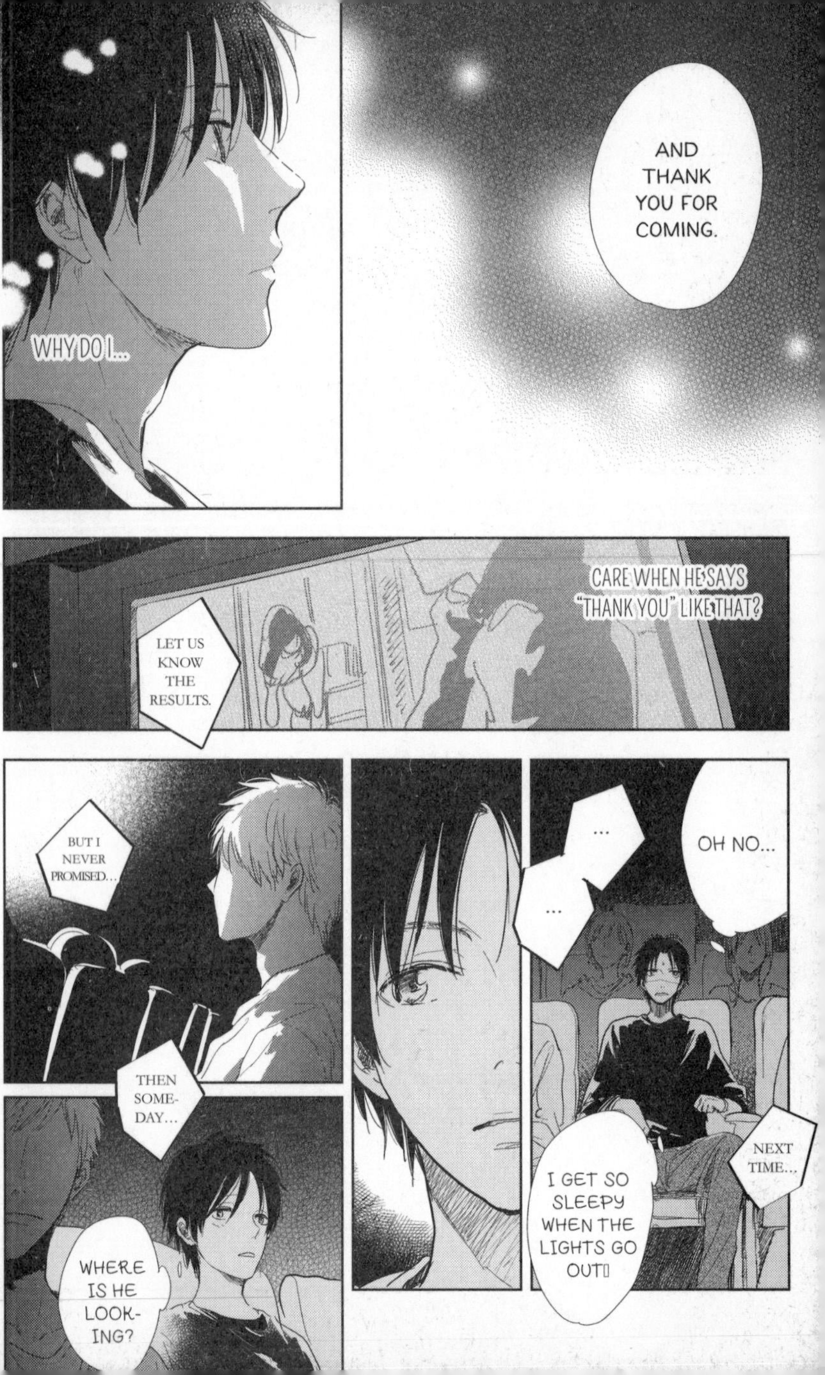
AND THANK YOU FOR COMING.
WHY DO I...
CARE WHEN HE SAYS "THANK YOU" LIKE THAT?
LET US KNOW THE RESULTS.
OH NO...
...
...
NEXT TIME...
I GET SO SLEEPY WHEN THE LIGHTS GO OUT
BUT I NEVER PROMISED...
THEN SOME-DAY...
WHERE IS HE LOOK-ING?

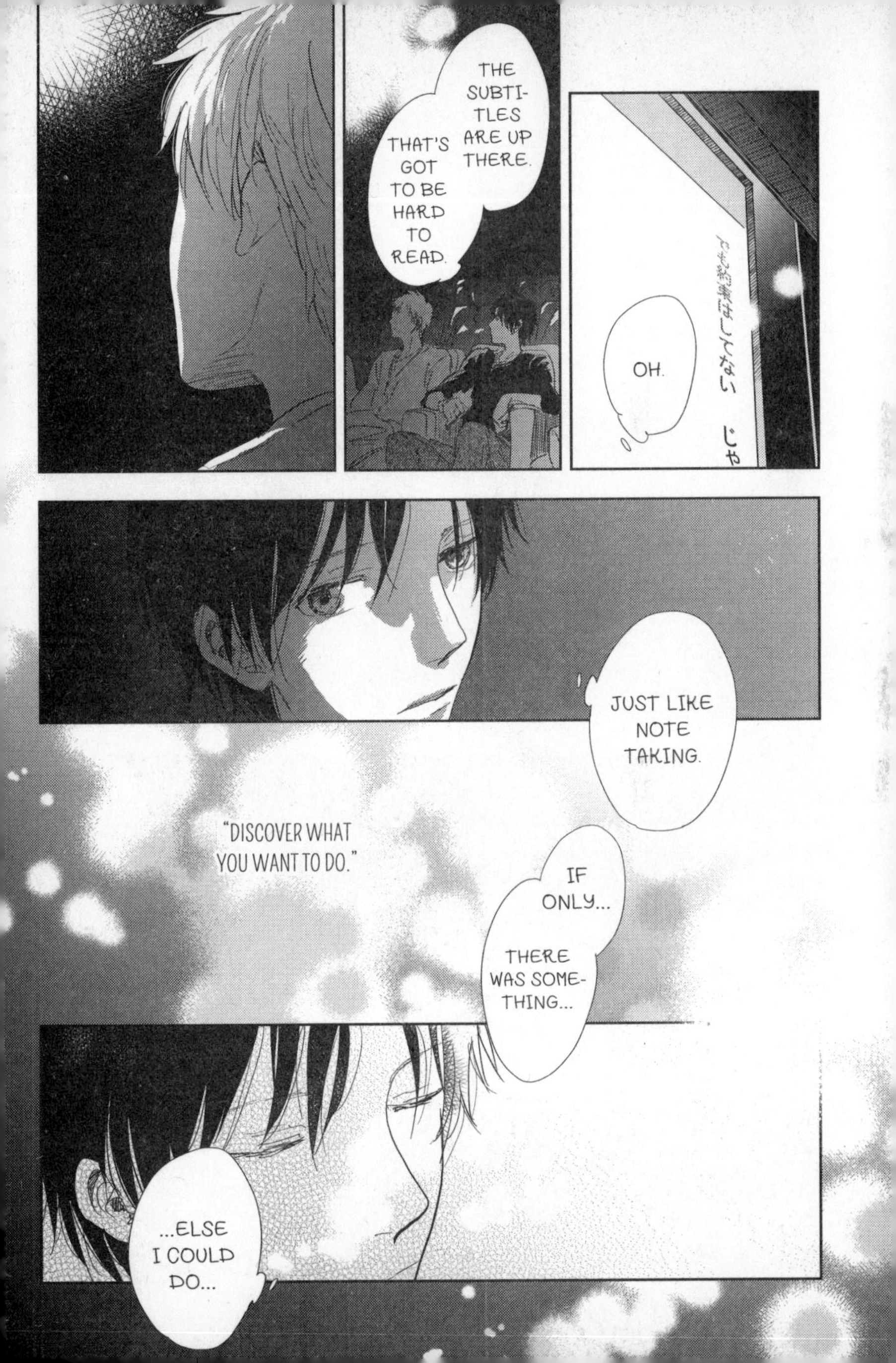
じゃ
はしてない
OH.
THE SUBTITLES ARE UP THERE.
THAT'S GOT TO BE HARD TO READ.
JUST LIKE NOTE TAKING.
"DISCOVER WHAT YOU WANT TO DO."
IF ONLY...
THERE WAS SOMETHING...
...ELSE I COULD DO...

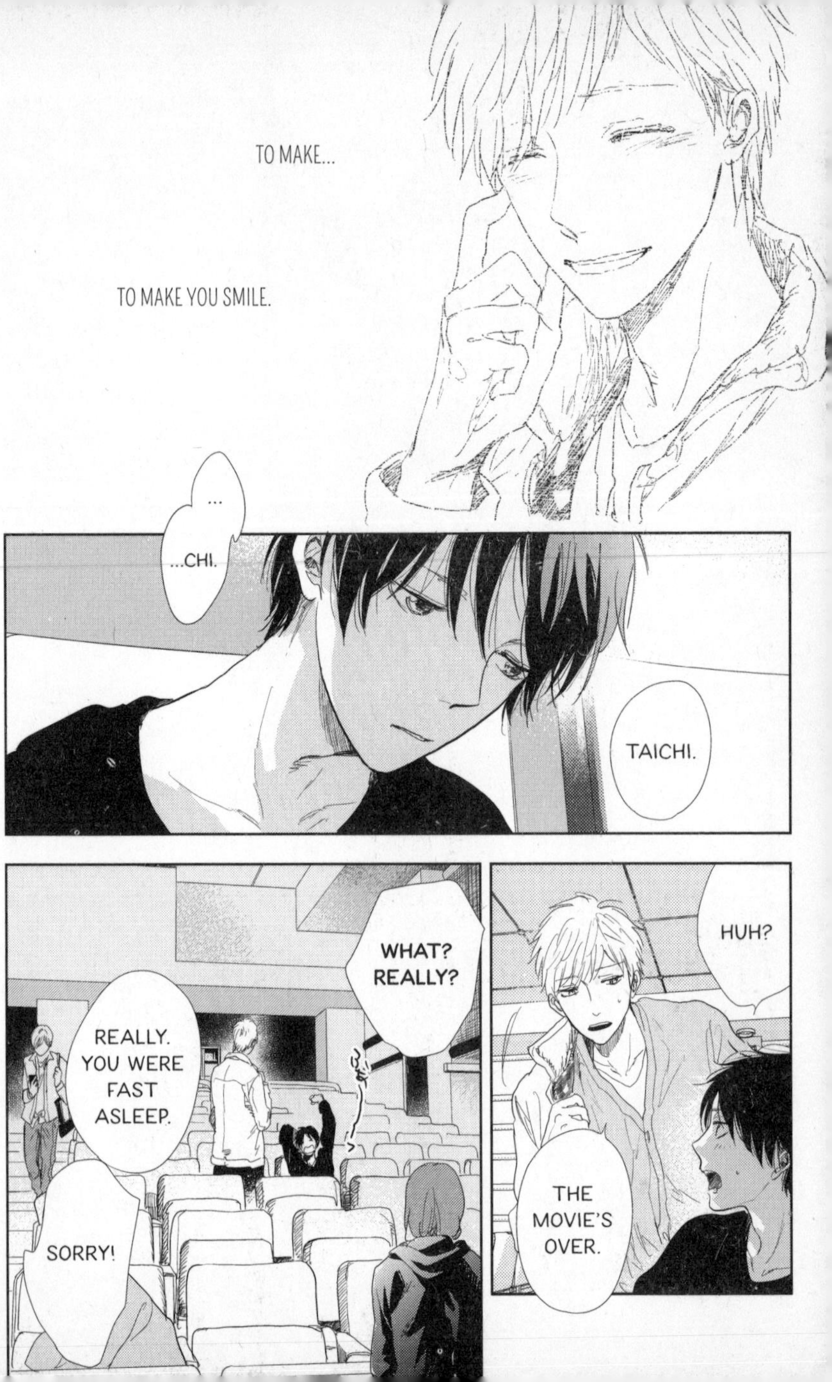
TO MAKE...
TO MAKE YOU SMILE.
...
...CHI.
TAICHI.
HUH?
THE MOVIE'S OVER.
WHAT? REALLY?
REALLY. YOU WERE FAST ASLEEP.
SORRY!

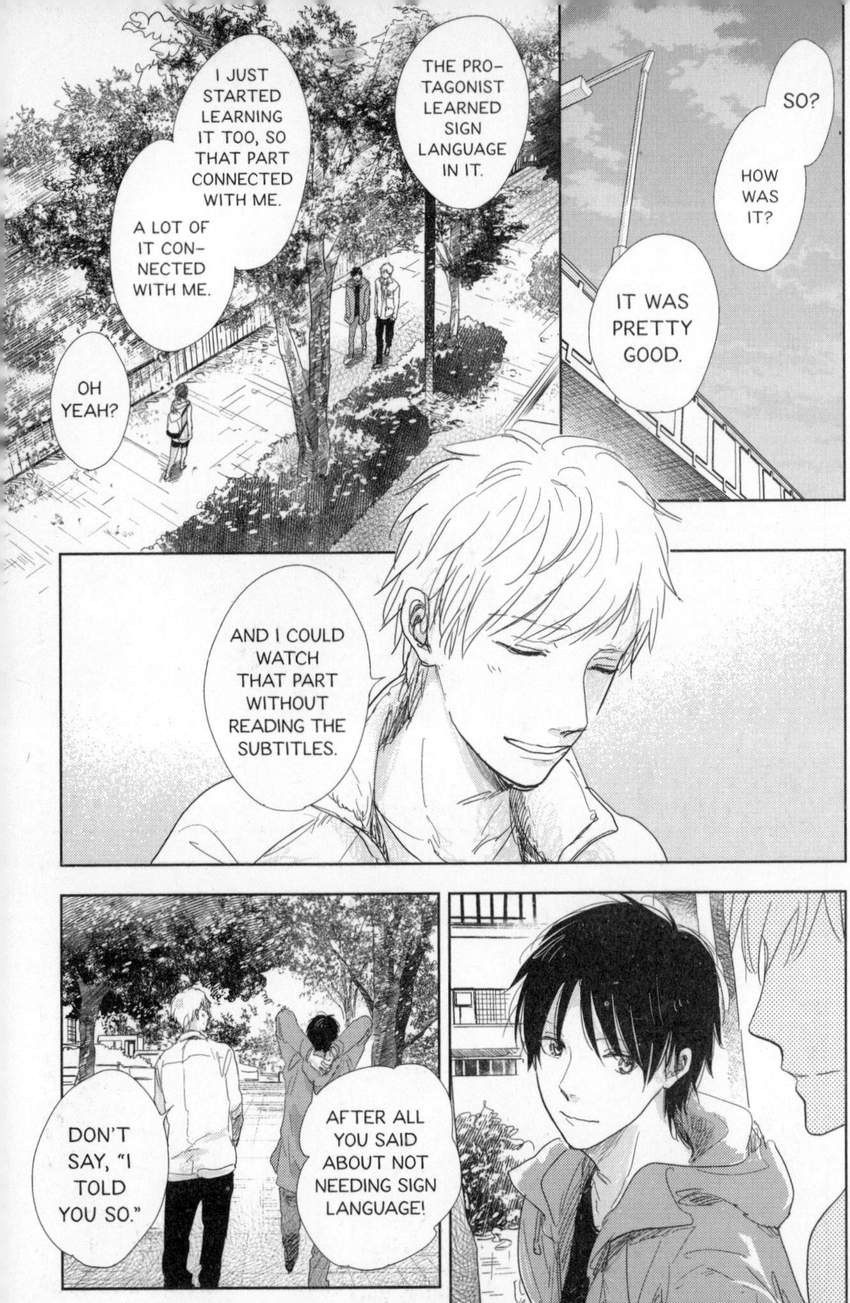
SO?
HOW WAS IT?
IT WAS PRETTY GOOD.
THE PRO-TAGONIST LEARNED SIGN LANGUAGE IN IT.
I JUST STARTED LEARNING IT TOO, SO THAT PART CONNECTED WITH ME.
A LOT OF IT CON-NECTED WITH ME.
OH YEAH?
AND I COULD WATCH THAT PART WITHOUT READING THE SUBTITLES.
AFTER ALL YOU SAID ABOUT NOT NEEDING SIGN LANGUAGE!
DON'T SAY, "I TOLD YOU SO."

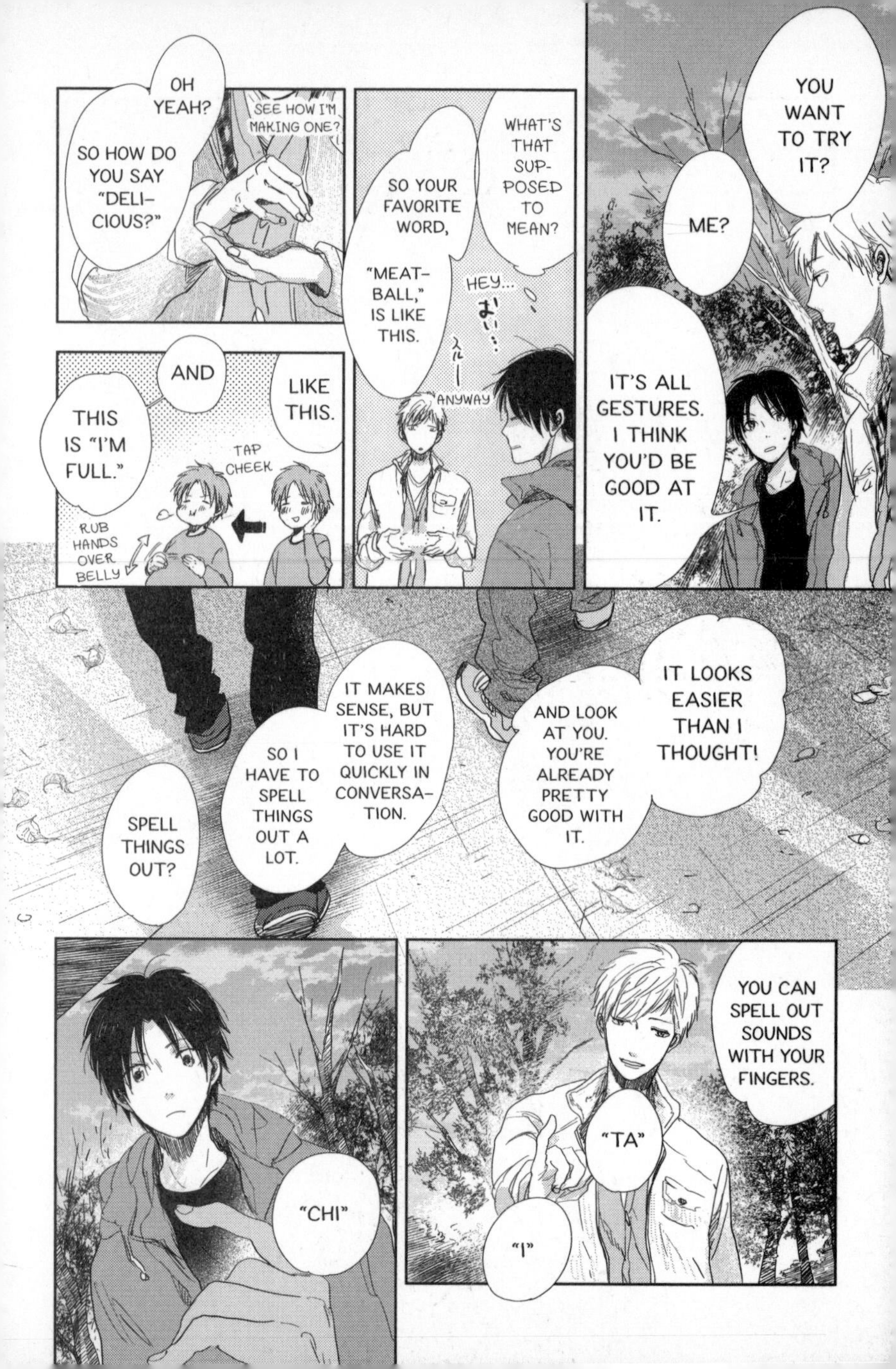
YOU WANT TO TRY IT?
ME?
IT'S ALL GESTURES. I THINK YOU'D BE GOOD AT IT.
WHAT'S THAT SUP-POSED TO MEAN?
SO YOUR FAVORITE WORD,
"MEAT-BALL," IS LIKE THIS.
HEY...
おい..
スルー
ANYWAY
OH YEAH?
SEE HOW I'M MAKING ONE?
SO HOW DO YOU SAY "DELI-CIOUS?"
LIKE THIS.
AND
THIS IS "I'M FULL."
TAP CHEEK
RUB HANDS OVER BELLY
IT LOOKS EASIER THAN I THOUGHT!
AND LOOK AT YOU. YOU'RE ALREADY PRETTY GOOD WITH IT.
IT MAKES SENSE, BUT IT'S HARD TO USE IT QUICKLY IN CONVERSA-TION.
SO I HAVE TO SPELL THINGS OUT A LOT.
SPELL THINGS OUT?
YOU CAN SPELL OUT SOUNDS WITH YOUR FINGERS.
"TA"
"I"
"CHI"

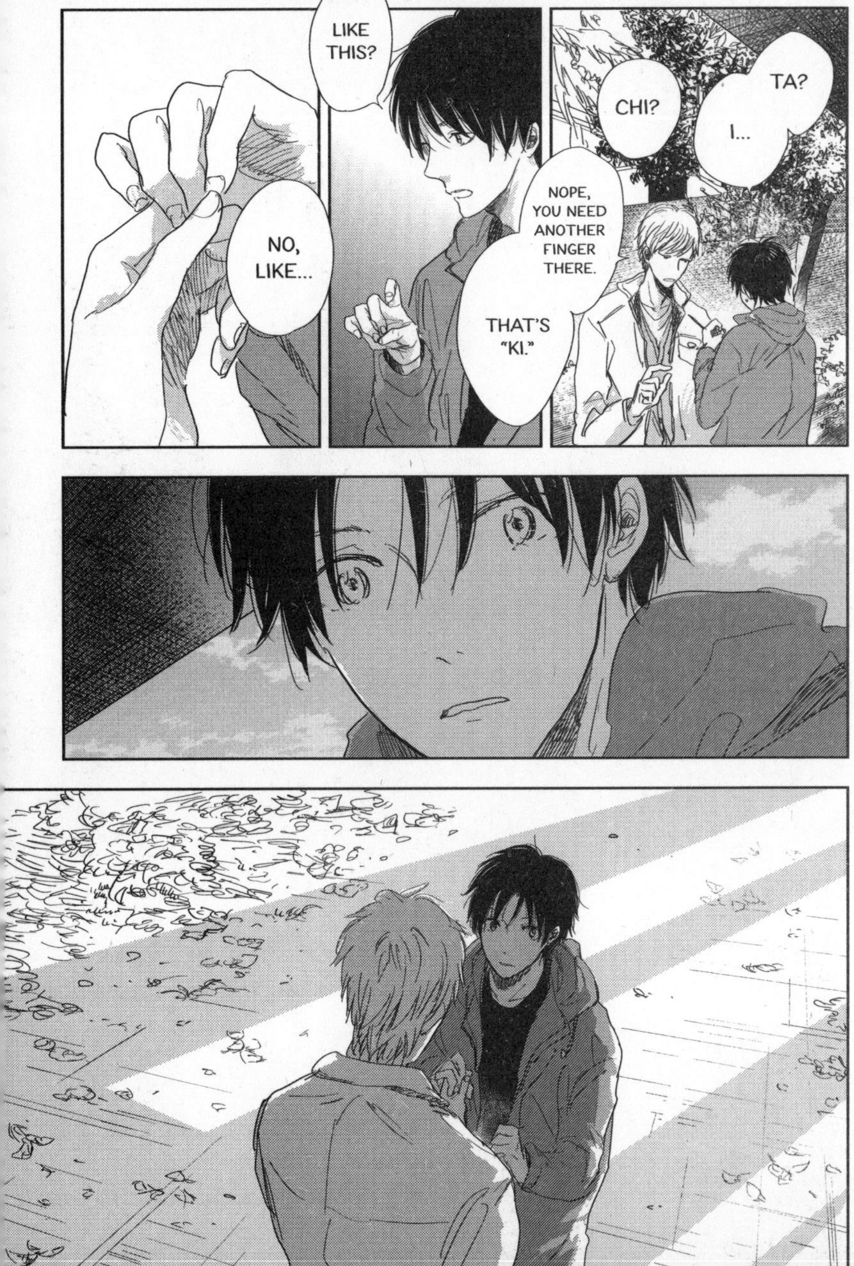
TA?
I...
CHI?
NOPE, YOU NEED ANOTHER FINGER THERE.
THAT'S "KI."
LIKE THIS?
NO, LIKE...

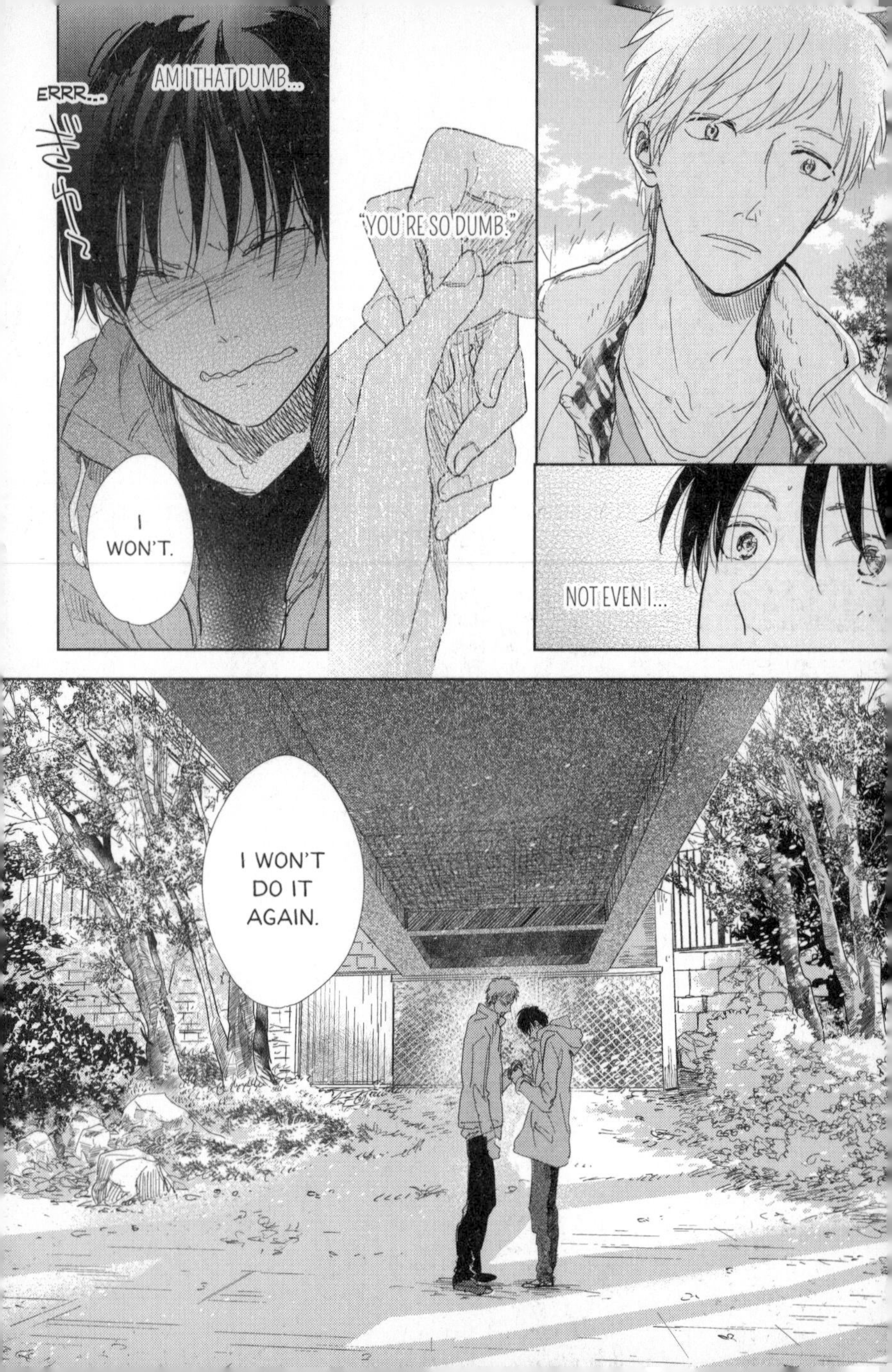
NOT EVEN I...
"YOU'RE SO DUMB."
AM I THAT DUMB...
ERRR...
I WON'T.
I WON'T DO IT AGAIN.

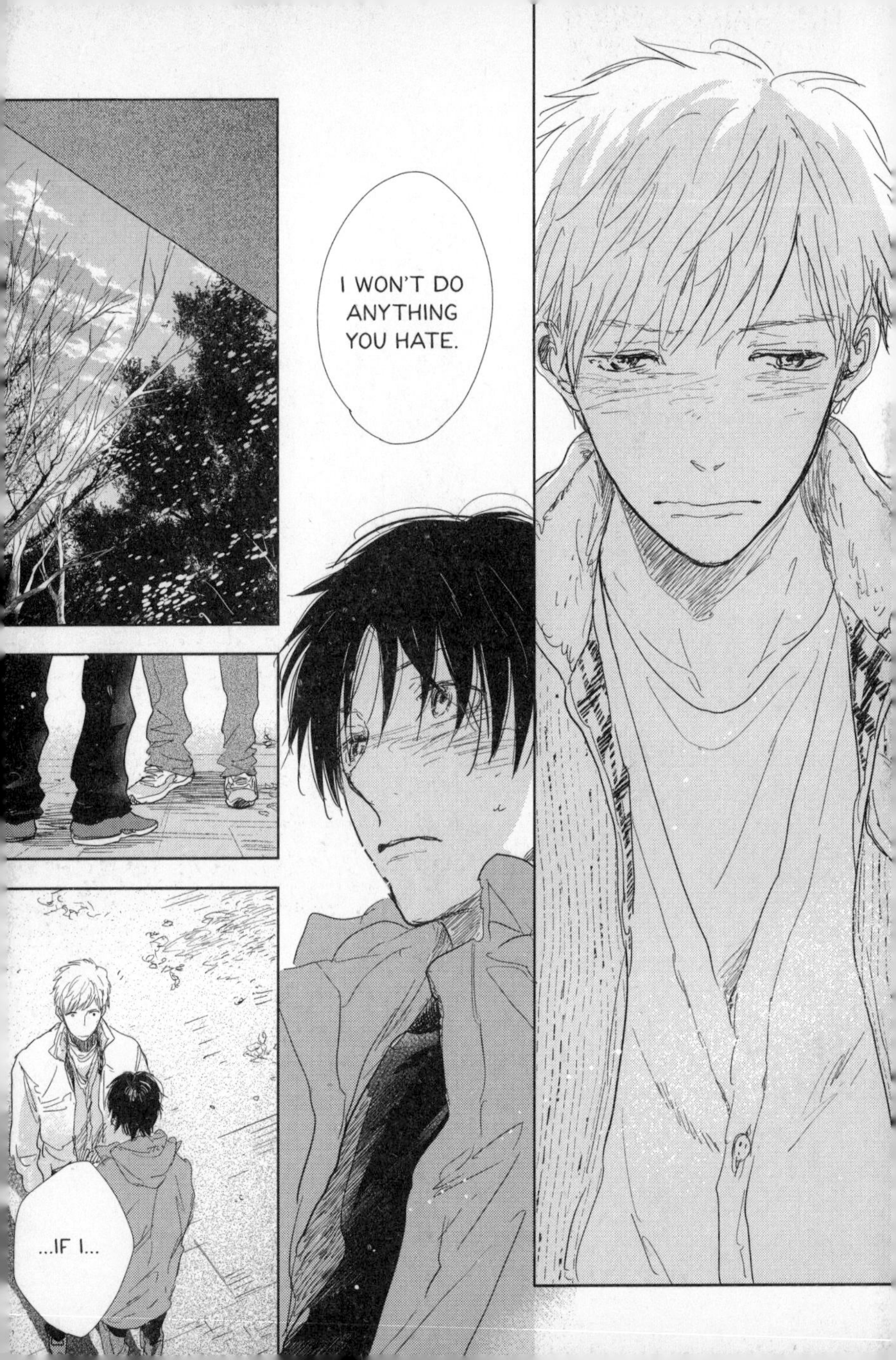
I WON'T DO ANYTHING YOU HATE.
...IF I...

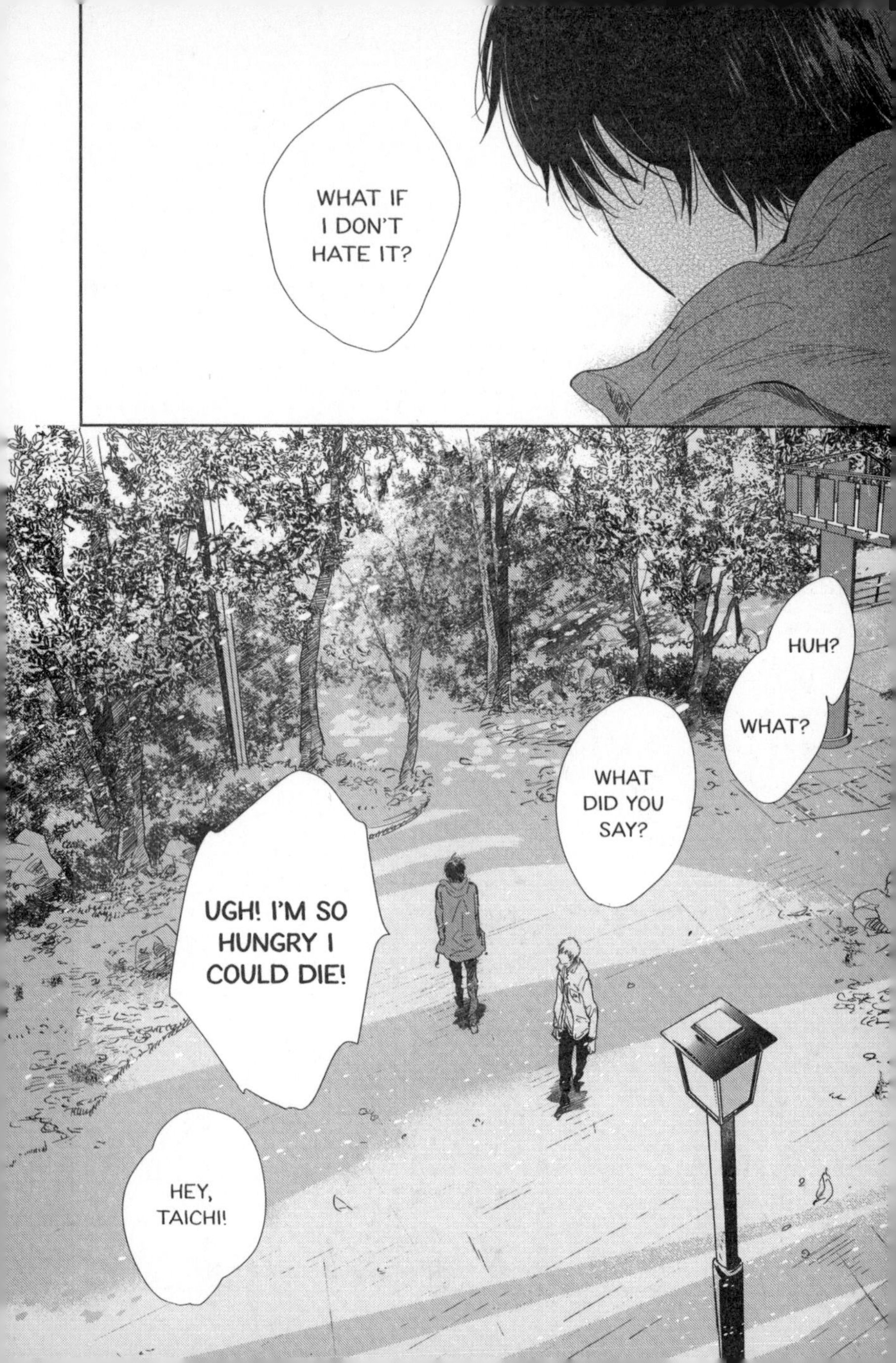
WHAT IF I DON'T HATE IT?
HUH?
WHAT?
WHAT DID YOU SAY?
UGH! I'M SO HUNGRY I COULD DIE!
HEY, TAICHI!

SOMETHING LIKE AN AFTERWORD:

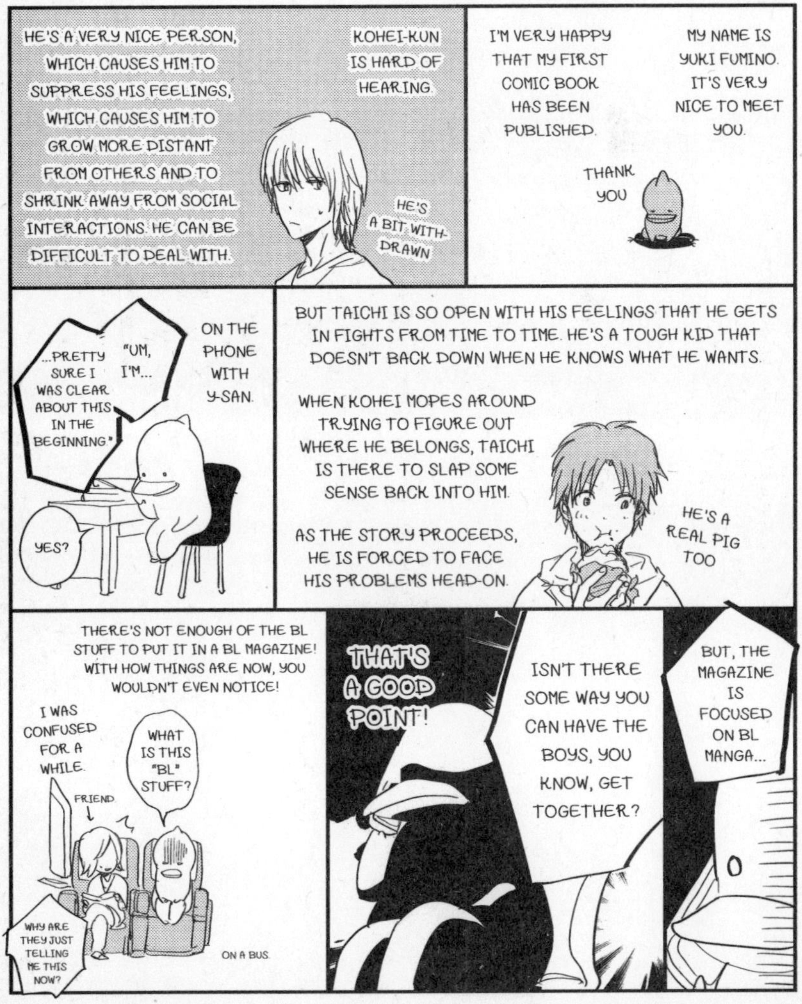

MY NAME IS YUKI FUMINO. IT'S VERY NICE TO MEET YOU.
I'M VERY HAPPY THAT MY FIRST COMIC BOOK HAS BEEN PUBLISHED.
THANK YOU
KOHEI-KUN IS HARD OF HEARING.
HE'S A VERY NICE PERSON, WHICH CAUSES HIM TO SUPPRESS HIS FEELINGS, WHICH CAUSES HIM TO GROW MORE DISTANT FROM OTHERS AND TO SHRINK AWAY FROM SOCIAL INTERACTIONS. HE CAN BE DIFFICULT TO DEAL WITH.
HE'S A BIT WITH-DRAWN
BUT TAICHI IS SO OPEN WITH HIS FEELINGS THAT HE GETS IN FIGHTS FROM TIME TO TIME. HE'S A TOUGH KID THAT DOESN'T BACK DOWN WHEN HE KNOWS WHAT HE WANTS.
WHEN KOHEI MOPES AROUND TRYING TO FIGURE OUT WHERE HE BELONGS, TAICHI IS THERE TO SLAP SOME SENSE BACK INTO HIM.
AS THE STORY PROCEEDS, HE IS FORCED TO FACE HIS PROBLEMS HEAD-ON.
HE'S A REAL PIG TOO
ON THE PHONE WITH Y-SAN.
"UM, I'M...
...PRETTY SURE I WAS CLEAR ABOUT THIS IN THE BEGINNING."
YES?
BUT, THE MAGAZINE IS FOCUSED ON BL MANGA...
ISN'T THERE SOME WAY YOU CAN HAVE THE BOYS, YOU KNOW, GET TOGETHER?
THAT'S A GOOD POINT!
THERE'S NOT ENOUGH OF THE BL STUFF TO PUT IT IN A BL MAGAZINE! WITH HOW THINGS ARE NOW, YOU WOULDN'T EVEN NOTICE!
WHAT IS THIS "BL" STUFF?
I WAS CONFUSED FOR A WHILE.
FRIEND
ON A BUS.
WHY ARE THEY JUST TELLING ME THIS NOW?

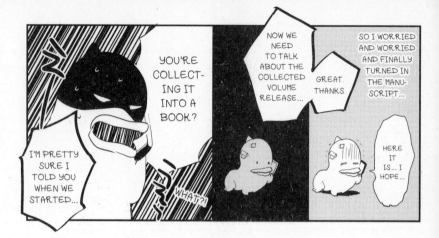

SO I WORRIED AND WORRIED AND FINALLY TURNED IN THE MANU-SCRIPT...
HERE IT IS... I HOPE...
NOW WE NEED TO TALK ABOUT THE COLLECTED VOLUME RELEASE...
GREAT. THANKS.
YOU'RE COLLECT-ING IT INTO A BOOK?
WHAT?!
I'M PRETTY SURE I TOLD YOU WHEN WE STARTED...

SO THE WHOLE PRODUCTION WAS A BIT SLOPPY, BUT I WAS LUCKY ENOUGH TO HAVE MY WORK COLLECTED IN THIS VOLUME.

TO THOSE OF YOU WHO JUST PICKED THIS BOOK UP.
TO THOSE OF YOU WHO HAVE BEEN READING FROM THE START.

TO MY MANAGER Y-SAN, TO THE DESIGNER THAT MADE THIS BEAUTIFUL COVER...

I WANT TO THANK YOU ALL FROM THE BOTTOM OF MY HEART.

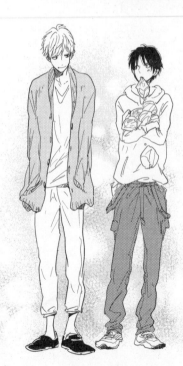

AND I HOPE WE WILL MEET AGAIN SOON.

--FUMINO

I Hear the Sunspot
(original Japanese title: Hidamari Ga Kikoeru)

Copyright © 2014 Yuki Fumino
English translation rights arranged with France Shoin
through Japan UNI Agency, Inc., Tokyo

ISBN: 978-1-944937-30-0

Written and illustrated by Yuki Fumino
English Edition Published by One Peace Books 2017

Printed in Canada

3 4 5 6 7 8 9 10

One Peace Books
43-32 22nd Street STE 204 Long Island City New York 11101
www.onepeacebooks.com